What Is Special About Special Education?

What Is Special About Special Education?

Examining the Role of Evidence-Based Practices

Bryan G. Cook
and
Barbara R. Schirmer
Editors

pro-ed

PRO-ED, Inc.
8700 Shoal Creek Blvd.
Austin, TX 78757-6897
800/897-3202
www.proedinc.com

Portions of this text have been adapted from material that previously appeared in *The Journal of Special Education,* © PRO-ED, Inc.

PRO-ED, Inc.

Library of Congress Cataloging-in-Publication Data

What is special about special education : examining the role of evidence based practices / Bryan G. Cook and Barbara R. Schirmer, editors.
p. cm.
"This text has been adapted from material that previously appeared in The Journal of Special Education."
Includes bibliographical references.
ISBN 1-4164-0183-0
1. Special education. 2. Children with disabilities—Education. I. Cook, Bryan G. II. Schirmer, Barbara R. III. Journal of special education (Austin, Tex.)
LC3965.W45 2005
371.9--dc22

2005020496

Printed in the United States of America

1 2 3 4 5 6 7 8 9 10 06 05 04 03 02

To Ben (the rastus) and Barb (dear friend and second mom)

Table of Contents

PART III

Recommendations for Making Special Education More Special

PART IV

Conclusion

Preface and Acknowledgments

Bryan G. Cook and **Barbara R. Schirmer**

As colleagues at Kent State University in the late 1990s, the two of us had many conversations about the public perception and future of special education. We were struck by the growing number of disdainful accounts of contemporary special education and found our own perspectives to be quite at odds with what we were reading and hearing. As individuals with experience as special education teachers, teacher educators, and researchers, we believed that the field has had a primarily positive impact and served an important role in providing an appropriate education for millions of students with disabilities. Although we clearly saw the need for improvements in many areas, we did not see the special education system as fundamentally flawed. How then, we wondered, could our views and experiences be so discrepant with those of critics calling for the field to be fundamentally changed or even dismantled?

We concluded that, at its essence, special education should satisfy three criteria to be considered efficacious and truly special: (a) A range of teaching practices that have been shown to work for students with disabilities must have been developed; (b) those effective practices must have been implemented, and implemented with fidelity; and (c) the effective practices must be in some way be unique to special education; that is, they could not be used as well or as frequently in the absence of special education. If these premises were sound, we believed that special education could be considered truly special and our experiences and viewpoint—that special education has a positive impact and should fundamentally be maintained—had credibility. With that in mind, we set out to examine whether special education was, indeed, fulfilling its purpose. We immediately recognized that the vast array of services and populations encompassed within contemporary special education necessitated the involvement of others—scholars with expertise and knowledge in specific, critical areas in special education.

We invited leading scholars to examine the question of whether special education is truly special. The result was a special issue of *The Journal of Special Education* in the fall of 2003. The restrictions of journal length limited the number of topics we could cover, and subsequently we looked for a venue that could offer greater breadth of coverage. Thus, this book was conceived. We asked the JSE authors to update their work if appropriate and invited other scholars well known for their research to submit chapters on new topics, such as English language learners with disabilities, deaf students, teacher education in special education, and three areas related to making special education more special and effective (i.e., understanding the relation of research design to the type of evidence, synthesizing research findings to identify evidence-based practices, and supporting teachers in adopting evidence-based practices).

We recognize that this is by no means an exhaustive or definitive commentary on the topic. Indeed, we realize that these chapters may raise more questions than they answer. We do hope that this work represents one piece of an ongoing analysis that can be used to support meritorious aspects of special education, highlight areas in need of improvement, and make recommendations for addressing problematic aspects.

It is our goal that the chapters in this book will facilitate readers' contributions toward making special education more special and effective for students with disabilities—by implementing research-based practices for students with disabilities, disseminating information about evidence-based practices, conducting high-quality research on practices in special education, synthesizing and evaluating research evidence regarding the effectiveness of instructional practices, or providing new perspectives and recommendations on improving the cycle of research-to-practice. We are in debt to our chapter authors. Melody, Tim, Jim, Stan, Naomi, Sam, Mark, Sharon, Sylvia, Paula, Sharon, Diane, Karena, Janette, Margarita, Paul, Anne, Mary, John, Paige, Patricia, Russell, and Jeanne, thank you for your hard work, your careful scholarship, and your collegiality. We also want to recognize and thank Ralph Ferretti and Skip MacArthur—coeditors of *The Journal of Special Education*—for their assistance and enthusiasm regarding the first part of the project. We want to express a special thanks to Judy Voress, editor at PRO-ED. She encouraged us to develop this book, gave us lots of flexibility in conceptualizing the project, and offered supportive comments even when we were less than punctual in submitting the manuscript.

We are most appreciative to our respective families. Thanks to Lysandra, Zoe, and Ben Cook; and Jack Schirmer, Alison and Jeffrey Lockman, and Todd and Christine Schirmer.

Chapter 1

Special Education for Students With Learning Disabilities:

What Makes It So Special?

Sharon Vaughn and **Sylvia Linan-Thompson**

The question that guides this chapter is, "How is special education for students with learning disabilities special?" We considered approaching this question by reviewing the studies of instruction and services for students with learning disabilities (LD) and reporting on the effectiveness of those practices in providing a differentiated and appropriate education for students with LD. At least with respect to the education that students with LD receive within general education, existing reviews reveal that undifferentiated instruction not specifically designed to meet the instructional needs of the student with learning disabilities prevails (for reviews, see Baker & Zigmond, 1995; McIntosh, Vaughn, Schumm, Haager, & Lee, 1993; Zigmond & Baker, 1995; Zigmond et al., 1995). This chapter addresses aspects of special education that are associated with improved outcomes for students with LD (see the Appendix for a summary of these instructional practices).

This chapter first briefly reviews the literature about how special education was initially conceptualized for students with LD and how instructional models for effective instruction for students with LD have shifted from underlying process approaches to an emphasis on instructional effectiveness based on students' learning in core academic areas. We then describe those instructional practices associated with improved outcomes for students with LD. Last, we describe a three-tiered model for providing response to intervention.

Background on Special Education for Students With LD

For many students with disabilities, the initial goal of special education was to ensure that they were provided an opportunity to attend school and profit from education. Students with moderate and severe disabilities had frequently been excluded from public schools; P.L. 94-142 (the Education for All Handicapped Children Act of 1975, reauthorized as the Individuals with Disabilities Education Act of 1990, amended 1997), mandated that all individuals would receive a free and appropriate public education. It was not until 1977 that students with LD were guaranteed special education services. For students with LD, most of whom were already provided education within the general education system, their special needs would now be identified and they would be provided with a special education.

Initially, defining and providing a special education for students with LD was a challenge for educators. Little was known about what an effective educational program for students with LD should look like. As a result, the special education of students with LD has traveled a somewhat rocky road of false starts, misconceptions, and misinformed ideas. Recently, research syntheses have provided considerable guidance for research-based practices for teaching students with LD (Kavale & Forness, 2000; Swanson, Hoskyn, & Lee, 1999; Vaughn, Gersten, & Chard, 2000).

Diagnosing and Remediating Underlying Process Disabilities: The Hallmark of Early Instruction for Students With LD

Early thinking about educational interventions for students with LD was based on models of neurological disorders in which identification and treatment of learning problems were linked to the underlying processes that interfered with effective learning for students with LD. Although it may be accurate that many students with LD have underlying neurological or information processing disorders, we have been singularly unsuccessful at reliably identifying these difficulties and designing specific treatments to remediate them (see, for a review, Lyon, 1985; Mann, 1979).

It is simply not possible to examine early work on assessing and treating students with LD without reviewing the work of Samuel Kirk. As early as 1962, Kirk presented the notion of intraindividual differences to describe what was special about educating students with LD. He later described it as a concept that

> directs attention not to the comparison of one child with another but to differences of ability within a single child. In other words, the concept of intraindividual differences leads logically to psychometric tests that could measure a number of specific and discrete areas of psycho-educational development. Its principal use is to diagnose a child's psycholinguistic abilities so that remediation can follow. (Kirk & Kirk, 1971, pp. 11–12)

Kirk's statement summarizes the foundation of early intervention work in LD. He hypothesized that the psychoeducational strengths and weaknesses that contributed to students' learning could be identified and an educational treatment plan that capitalized on students' strengths and remediated their weaknesses could be defined. With this course charted, many assessment and remediation practices in LD were devised and implemented. Johnson and Myklebust (1967) also contributed significantly to early understanding of the treatment of students with LD. They identified procedures for conducting an intensive diagnostic study and then an individualized plan that was based on a language deficit model.

Measures such as the *Illinois Test of Psycholinguistic Ability* (ITPA; Kirk, McCarthy, & Kirk, 1968) were designed to determine students' strengths and weaknesses and to prescribe corresponding treatment. The ITPA, which early on was frequently used to diagnose processing problems, consists of three dimensions: (a) channels of communication, which include the modes of expression for receiving and expressing information; (b) psycholinguistic processes, which relate to the acquisition of language; and (c) levels of organization, which refers to communication habits involving more complex mediated learning (representational level) and less voluntary learning (automatic level). Subtests from the ITPA allowed diagnosticians to generate student profiles that corresponded with each of these three dimensions of the test. Specific tasks, activities, and instructional programs were specified for instructing students in the processes that corresponded with their performance on the tasks (Kirk & Kirk, 1971). A hallmark of this theory of remediation is that students with general low academic ability resulting from such factors as lack of educational opportunity would benefit from high-quality general education practices, whereas students with a specific learning disability/identified processing difficulties would require practices that are "unique, uncommon, of unusual quality, and [that], in particular, supplement the organization and instructional procedures used with the majority of children" (Kirk & Elkins, 1975, p. 637).

The concern with the process-to-treatment approach has been that underlying learning deficits and processes were not reliably identified and the corresponding treatment was not specific to the learning problems. Although the efficacy of psycholinguistic training has been much debated, in fact, treatments were not powerful enough to make discernible differences in academic learning—the most important outcome (Hammill &

Larsen, 1974, 1978; Kavale, 1981; Larsen, Parker, & Hammill, 1982; Lund, Foster, & McCall-Perez, 1978). The emphasis on underlying mechanisms related to learning yielded undue focus on remediating process deficits and too little focus on instructing students in their target areas of need (e.g., reading, math). Thus, the model of process deficit identification and remediation as a means to resolving LD went unsupported (Chall, 2000; Kavale, 1980; Kavale & Forness, 2000; Kavale & Mattson, 1983; Silver, 2001). However, despite lack of support for process identification and treatment models, they persist.

The primary challenge of this model is that we did not have, nor do we presently have, adequate knowledge about the neurological underpinnings of learning and learning disability. Furthermore, we lack the measurement precision needed to identify specific process disorders in learning (Keogh, 1994a; Lyon, 1994). Also, we have not been able to successfully match the subtype of a learning problem with appropriate treatments. For example, we do not know if a visual processing deficit corresponds to categorically different remediation techniques than do other reading deficits. However, past failures in identifying and remediating processing problems do not necessarily forecast future failures. Future research may yield better scientific understanding of these principles, and a return to this model may appropriately serve individuals with LD. Thus, theoretically sound and empirically driven work that attempts to better inform these issues could provide a valuable contribution to identifying and treating learning disabilities.

Modality-Matched and Multisensory Approaches

Modality refers to sight, hearing, touch, or movement. The learning modality approach to instruction is based on the assumptions that (a) learners have preferred modalities for learning and (b) if teaching is redesigned to rely more directly on this preferred modality, then students will learn more readily and rapidly. Thus, for teachers of students with LD, the rationale is to identify each student's preferred modality and to match teaching to this modality preference. An extension of modality-matched instruction is learning styles, in which the teacher identifies types of tasks that fit the students' learning orientation and provides instruction that allows students to use the preferred types of tasks. However, there is little empirical support for the use of modality-matched instruction or learning styles as a means to enhance outcomes for students with LD (Arter & Jenkins, 1979; Kavale & Forness, 1987; Kavale, Hirshoren, & Forness, 1998; Larrivee, 1981).

Multisensory instruction refers to designing instruction that uses all pathways to the brain simultaneously—including visual, auditory, and kinesthetic-tactile (McIntyre & Pickering, 1995). From the early work of Fernald (1943), Gillingham and Stillman (1936), and Orton (1937), a multisensory approach to teaching students with learning/reading disabilities has been advocated. "All of the usable linkages between vision, audition, and kinesthesis should be established during remediation of reading difficulties" (Orton, 1937, p. 17). Despite positive outcomes for individual cases (Fernald & Keller, 1921; Strauss & Lehtinen, 1947), there is no compelling evidence to suggest that a multisensory approach to instruction is necessary for students with learning or reading disabilities. Thus, practices that have historically been associated with special education—psycholinguistic training, modality-matched instruction, and multisensory teaching—have not consistently been associated with positive effects on learning outcomes for students with LD.

Academic Instruction for Students With LD

Several instructional approaches have yielded significant outcomes for students with LD. Research-based practices that are effective for the special education of students with LD are well specified, are explicit, are carefully designed, and relate closely to the area of instructional need (e.g., reading, spelling, math). Torgesen (1996) noted that special education for students with LD is more explicit, intensive, and supportive than general education.

D. Fuchs (1996) argued that two important attributes of effective special education for students with LD are individualization and validation. Curriculum-based measures (Deno, 1985) and other progress-monitoring tools (Good & Kaminski, 1996) are critical for ensuring that intervention is responsive to the needs of individual students (D. Fuchs, 1996). Validation can be tested in several ways, but perhaps the most powerful way is through experimental studies that are conducted over time and yield converging evidence (Stanovich, 2000; Vaughn & Dammann, 2001). Teachers can use validated approaches, monitor student progress, and then make adjustments to ensure individualization. As teachers monitor progress, they should closely observe instructional features, such as pacing, group size, and amount of time; instructional materials; and the instructional approach itself.

Effective instructional approaches for students with LD and their effect sizes have been reported in several sources (L. S. Fuchs, Fuchs, Hamlett, & Ferguson, 1992; Gersten, Schiller, & Vaughn, 2000; Gersten & Vaughn, 2001; Kavale & Forness, 2000; Stecker & Fuchs, 2000; Swanson et al., 1999; Vaughn et al., 2000) and are summarized briefly in the Appendix.

In summary, professionals interested in providing the most effective special education for students with LD initially used psycholinguistic and underlying process models to identify LD and to attempt to develop cures. Within the last 15 to 20 years considerably more emphasis has been placed on devising effective interventions that are linked closely with the academic needs of students. Academic intervention has had considerable overall effects on instructional outcomes for students with LD; however, some students have not successfully responded to treatments that have been effective for students with related problems (O'Connor, 2000; Torgesen, 2000).

Instructional Practices Associated With Improved Outcomes for Students With LD

In addition to research on effective instructional practices for students with LD, a knowledge base on how best to deliver these instructional services in ways that meet the needs of diverse students is accumulating. One early intervention/prevention approach is to layer reading instruction in tiers, or levels, that begin with effective practices implemented classwide and then provide successive levels of support to students as needed (Dickson & Bursuck, 1999; O'Connor, 2000) by including ongoing screening and progress monitoring as part of the classwide intervention.

For example, O'Connor (2000) aimed to reduce reading failure in kindergartners by providing instruction across four levels that varied in length (number of minutes per session), intensity (number of times per week and group size), and duration (number of weeks). O'Connor's project provided instruction to these students for 2 years (kindergarten through first grade); at the end of first grade, reading failure among the at-risk children had declined. Nevertheless, the proportion of children referred for special education services did not decrease; O' Connor attributed this to the limited resources available within the schools, which precluded provision of the most intense level of intervention needed by the minimal-gains children. Dickson and Bursuck (1999) also provided a three-tiered system that varied along the dimensions studied by O'Connor. They found high effect sizes primarily for students at risk for reading failure who were placed in small-group intensive interventions. Dickson and Bursuck also lamented the lack of time and resources available to continue to support change in teachers' instruction. These findings support the contention that researchers need to continue to explore ways to reach this subgroup of readers within the scope of existing resources in the schools.

Small-Group Instruction

One variable in these prevention/early intervention models for struggling readers is the teacher–student ratio (or student group size) during instruction. Lower teacher–student ratios increase teacher–student interactions, individualization of instruction, student on-task behavior, and teacher monitoring and feedback (Elbaum, Vaughn, Hughes, & Moody, 2000; Thurlow, Ysseldyke, Wotruba, & Algozzine, 1993). For reading instruction, group size is particularly relevant for several reasons: (a) Smaller group sizes are associated with improved outcomes (Lou et al., 1996; Swanson, Carson, & Saches-Lee, 1996); (b) the range of reading abilities represented in general education classrooms may be from three to five grade levels, and smaller groups reduce variability of instructional needs of students (Elbaum, Vaughn, Hughes, & Moody, 1999); (c) group size impacts the amount and quality of oral language among English language learners (Gersten & Jimenez, 1998); and (d) reading instruction for students at risk for reading disabilities can be tailored to students' individual needs only if students are taught in small groups (Gelzheiser, Meyers, Slesinski, Douglas, & Lewis, 1994; Gunning, 1998; Rashotte, MacPhee, & Torgesen, 2001).

The optimal group size for young students who are struggling to learn to read has not been definitively established (Thurlow et al., 1993). From a meta-analysis of grouping practices and reading outcomes for students with disabilities, Elbaum et al. (1999) reported that effect sizes for students receiving instruction in alternative grouping formats were considerably higher than those for students receiving whole-class instruction. Although there was no evidence of the superiority of one group size over another, there was evidence supporting both small groups and student pairs. Similarly, other analyses with general education students have indicated that small-group or one-on-one instruction is associated with higher achievement gains than whole-class grouping (Kulik & Kulik, 1987; Lou et al., 1996; Slavin, 1987). A study targeting both monolingual English speakers and English language learners compared the efficacy of supplemental reading instruction in group sizes of one teacher with one student (1:1), with three students (1:3), and with 10 students (1:10) during supplemental reading instruction; the content and intensity of instruction were held constant (Vaughn, Linan-Thompson, Kouzekanani, et al., 2003). Results of this study indicated that students in the 1:1 and 1:3 conditions made similar gains in phoneme segmentation, fluency, and comprehension that were maintained at a 4-month follow-up and that were greater than gains for students in the 1:10 group.

Accelerating Intensity Through One-on-One Instruction

For many students, whole-class or large-group instruction may not provide the directed, intensive, specific instruction they require. Even small-group instruction may not be enough; one-on-one instruction may be required. Several studies offer support for the effectiveness of one-on-one instruction, particularly with students who have been identified as at risk or as having reading or learning disabilities (Bloom, 1984; Elbaum et al., 2000; Juel, 1991; Wasik & Slavin, 1993). A recent meta-analysis found that supplemental 1:1 reading interventions for students at risk for reading failure resulted in reading outcomes for participating students that exceeded outcomes of controls by an average of .41 *SD*—a modest, but for these readers, quite notable, amount. Interventions in which the tutoring was provided by trained volunteers or college students were highly effective (Elbaum et al., 2000). Two recent studies of intensive 1:1 interventions for students at risk for reading disabilities have yielded impressive results. Vellutino et al. (1996) provided up to two semesters of tutoring in letter identification, phoneme awareness, and word-reading skills in 20-minute daily sessions for struggling first-grade readers. This 1:1 tutoring helped the majority of students become average readers. Torgesen et al. (2001) were also able to demonstrate significant improvements in decoding skills of students with significant reading disabilities following 80 hours of instruction in phonological decoding strategies. The instruction was provided one-to-one, in two 50-minute sessions per day. Results indicated that decoding accuracy reached national averages but speed of decoding did not. These studies suggest that critical features of reading instruction, when combined with 1:1 tutoring in sessions of sufficient intensity, can make an impact on the acquisition of literacy skills by students with reading disabilities.

Duration of Intervention

Another variable that may impact the effectiveness of an intervention is the duration of the intervention, or intensity. Duration can refer to the length of intervention and may be a preset number of sessions, or it may be determined by mastery of preset criteria at specific intervals. Providing the intervention for more than one session each day can also enhance intensity. Torgesen and colleagues (2001) provided two sessions per day (50 minutes each session) of intensive one-on-one instruction to students with severe reading problems. The students made significant gains, and most students maintained these gains for 2 years. Furthermore, 19 of 49 students were able to return to general education and were no longer identified as in need of special education. To determine the length of intervention needed by second-grade students struggling with reading, Vaughn, Linan-Thompson, and Hickman-Davis (2003) provided 54 second-grade students who were struggling with reading with small-group instruction for 10, 20, or 30 weeks. Students continued to receive supplemental instruction until the preestablished grade-level criteria were met. Of the 45 students available at all assessment points, 24% ($n = 11$) failed to reach the criteria after 30 weeks of intervention, whereas 22% ($n = 10$) met exit criteria after 10 weeks of intervention, 33% ($n = 15$) after 20 weeks, and 20% ($n = 9$) after 30 weeks. Thus, group size and intensity of intervention are variables that can be manipulated to influence intervention effectiveness for students with LD.

Model for Primary, Secondary, and Tertiary Interventions

We propose that to make special education special for students with LD, the instruction coordinated between general and special education should be streamlined by implementing an intervention model that capitalizes on existing research in instruction, instructional grouping, and duration. We adopt a view explicated by Keogh (1994b; Keogh, Wilcoxen, & Bernheimer, 1986) that prevention and intervention are "inextricably linked." Keogh (1994b, p. 64) stated, "The same procedures or services may serve preventive or treatment purposes relative to the context in which they are delivered or when they are implemented." Instruction at each level (primary, secondary, and tertiary) is more intense and explicit, and the instructional group size is reduced to optimize learning opportunities for students. Throughout the three levels, progress monitoring is used to determine whether or not students are responding to instruction. With this model, both mastery of content and growth rate are monitored and used to make instructional and placement decisions. Although this model focuses on supplemental instruction, it was influenced by the work on alternative models for identifying students with disabilities developed by L. S. Fuchs and Fuchs (1998) and implemented by Speece and Case (2001). We will first describe each level of intervention and then describe how a student moves through the levels.

The first level, primary instruction, takes place in the general education classroom and consists of the grade-level curriculum. Providing general education teachers intensive and ongoing professional development on effective instructional practices such as flexible grouping, scaffolding, and formative feedback is essential to ensure that all students have access to the curriculum. A significant part of the professional development is training on the use of progress monitoring to inform instruction and as a means for identifying students who are not benefiting significantly from classroom instruction and who require supplemental instruction.

The second level of instruction, secondary intervention, may take place in the setting designated as appropriate (within the classroom or outside the classroom as a pull-out program). This more intensive and explicit instructional program, coordinated with the primary instruction, can be provided by the teacher or by other school personnel and would parallel classroom instruction. To provide ample opportunities for students to enter and exit secondary intervention, we describe it as having two opportunities to participate in the second level of intervention—each lasting approximately 10 weeks (50 sessions) each. This instruction provides students who meet criteria the opportunity to exit intensive instruction after just 10 weeks; those students who do not meet criteria have the opportunity to continue with instruction as needed. Instruction that focuses on students' needs as determined by progress monitoring is provided daily in homogeneous small groups. Sessions are between 20 and 40 minutes long, depending on the grade level, need, group size, and resources available.

The third level of instruction, tertiary intervention, may be special education. A student who has failed to respond to enhanced classroom instruction and secondary instruction would have considerable data for the educator to consider when determining if he or she should be referred for special education. At this level, students would receive sustained intensive instruction provided by appropriate personnel.

Movement between the levels is fluid and is based on progress monitoring and mastery of benchmarks. At the beginning of the year, students lacking basic skills in a particular area (e.g., reading, writing, or math) at the time of the first assessment are assigned to a secondary intervention group for supplemental instruction. At the end of the first 10 weeks, students are assessed, and those who have mastered the benchmarks according to preset criteria no longer receive supplemental secondary intervention. Those students who do not reach the benchmarks after receiving secondary intervention may be provided additional secondary intervention, referred for special services, and/or given a tertiary intervention. Again, students who meet the exit criteria no longer receive the supplemental instruction. Those students who do not meet exit criteria after receiving secondary intervention may then be provided more intensive intervention or referred for special education. Students in tertiary intervention continue to be assessed regularly along with their classmates. Students who receive tertiary intervention are provided the most intensive and specific intervention; their progress is monitored weekly, and instruction is adjusted as needed.

This framework provides a systematic procedure for providing supplemental instruction based on progress-monitoring data to students who require various levels of support to benefit from classroom instruction. There are several advantages to using this type of model. First, both students that require additional instruction from time to time and students who require long-term instructional support can be served. All the students in the class are assessed throughout the year to ensure they are making adequate gains, so students who fall behind later in the year or students who fall behind again after exiting secondary intervention can receive additional support. This procedure provides a means for accessing supplemental instruction by students who often do not require special education but are consistently and continuously falling behind.

Furthermore, special education students benefit from the use of a dynamic and fluid approach centered on progress monitoring. First, students are provided multiple opportunities to reach grade-level benchmarks while receiving supplemental instruction before they are eligible for special education. Then, once they are eligible for special education, the level of support that they receive is based on how well they benefit from instruction, as measured by their performance on progress-monitoring measures and their response to instruction. This also provides a means for students' performance to meet established criteria for exit from special education.

Finally, this model can be implemented at both the elementary and secondary levels since it depends on responding to student needs. At the secondary level, special education teachers can provide secondary and tertiary intervention to students in their areas of need.

Conclusion

Historically, we have approached special education for students with LD by attempting to identify their processing deficits and then matching treatment practices to their processing needs—often referred to as remediation of the deficit. Although we may eventually have adequate information about learning processes and instruction to implement the process deficit and remediation model, recent research suggests that currently the most productive model for improving outcomes for students with disabilities is one in which students' instructional gaps are clearly identified, their progress relative to these gaps monitored, and explicit and intensive intervention provided to ensure progress.

So, what should be special about special education for students with LD? In most cases, it will not be the content. We want students with disabilities to have access to the same curriculum, including higher order processing skills and problem solving, as their nondisabled peers. What should be special is the delivery of instruction, since their needs are rarely met through general education instruction alone. We know that students benefit from explicit and systematic instruction that is closely related to their area of instructional need. But how much additional instruction do students need, and in what format? We know less about the effects of variables such as group size, duration, and intensity, although recent research in this area is promising. As we begin to gather evidence of how these variables interact, we may have to think not only about how we deliver instruction and who delivers instruction to students at risk for and with LD, but also about the extent to which schools will be able to implement and sustain a new way of doing special education.

AUTHORS' NOTE

We would like to thank Alison Gould Boardman and Diane Haager for their valuable review of this chapter.

REFERENCES

Arter, J. A., & Jenkins, J. R. (1979). Differential diagnosis-prescriptive teaching: A critical appraisal. *Review of Educational Research, 49,* 517–555.

Baker, J. M., & Zigmond, N. (1995). The meaning and practice of inclusion for students with learning disabilities: Themes and implications from the five cases. *The Journal of Special Education, 29,* 163–180.

Bloom, B. S. (1984). The 2 sigma problem: The search for methods of group instruction as effective as one-to-one tutoring. *Educational Researcher, 13,* 4–16.

Chall, J. S. (2000). *The academic achievement challenge: What really works in the classroom?* New York: Guilford Press.

Deno, L. S. (1985). Curriculum-based measurement: The emerging alternative. *Exceptional Children, 52,* 219–232.

Dickson, S. V., & Bursuck, W. D. (1999). Implementing a model for preventing reading failure: A report from the field. *Learning Disabilities Research & Practice, 14,* 191–202.

Education for All Handicapped Children Act of 1975, 20 U.S.C. § 1400 *et seq.* (1975).

Elbaum, B. E., Vaughn, S., Hughes, M. T., & Moody, S. W. (1999). Grouping practices and reading outcomes for students with disabilities. *Exceptional Children, 65,* 399–415.

Elbaum, B. E., Vaughn, S., Hughes, M. T., & Moody, S. W. (2000). How effective are one-to-one tutoring programs in reading for elementary students at risk for reading failure? *Journal of Educational Psychology, 92,* 605–619.

Fernald, G. M. (1943). *Remedial techniques in basic school subjects.* New York: McGraw-Hill.

Fernald, G. M., & Keller, H. (1921). The effect of kinesthetic factors on the development of word recognition in the case of non readers. *Journal of Educational Research, 4,* 355–377.

Fuchs, D. (1996). Educational intervention and students with learning disabilities. *Learning Disabilities: A Multidisciplinary Journal, 7*(2), 63–67.

Fuchs, L. S., & Fuchs, D. (1998). Treatment validity: A unifying concept for reconceptualizing the identification of learning disabilities. *Learning Disabilities Research & Practice, 13,* 204–219.

Fuchs, L. S., Fuchs, D., Hamlett, C. L., & Ferguson, C. (1992). Effects of expert system consultation within curriculum-based measurement, using a reading maze task. *Exceptional Children, 58,* 436–450.

Gelzheiser, L. M., Meyers, J., Slesinski, C., Douglas, C., & Lewis, L. (1994). *Patterns of accommodations provided to students with disabilities in integrated classrooms.* (ERIC Document Reproduction Service No. ED 395 401)

Gersten, R. M., & Jiménez, R. T. (1998). *Promoting learning for culturally and linguistically diverse students: Classroom applications from contemporary research.* (ERIC Document Reproduction Service No. ED 415 715)

Gersten, R., Schiller, E. P., & Vaughn, S. (2000). *Contemporary special education research: Syntheses of the knowledge base on critical instructional issues.* Mahwah, NJ: Erlbaum.

Gersten, R., & Vaughn, S. (2001). Instructional interventions for students with learning disabilities. *The Elementary School Journal, 101,* 247–377.

Gillingham, A., & Stillman, B. W. (1936). *Remedial work for reading, spelling, and penmanship.* New York: Sachett & Wilhelms.

Good, R. H., & Kaminski, R. A. (1996). Assessment for instructional decisions: Toward a proactive/prevention model of decision-making for early literacy skills. *School Psychology Quarterly, 11,* 326–336.

Gunning, T. G. (1998). *Assessing and correcting reading and writing.* Boston: Allyn & Bacon.

Hammill, D. D., & Larsen, S. C. (1974). The effectiveness of psycholinguistic training. *Exceptional Children, 41,* 5–14.

Hammill, D. D., & Larsen, S. C. (1978). The effectiveness of psycholinguistic training: A reaffirmation of position. *Exceptional Children, 44,* 402–414.

Individuals with Disabilities Education Act of 1990, 20 U.S.C. § 1400 *et seq.* (1990) (Amended 1997).

Johnson, D., & Myklebust, H. R. (1967). *Learning disabilities: Educational principles and practices.* New York: Grune & Stratton.

Juel, C. (1991). Cross-age tutoring between student-athletes and at-risk children. *The Reading Teacher, 45,* 178–186.

Kavale, K. A. (1980). Auditory-visual integration and its relationship to reading achievement: A meta-analysis. *Perceptual and Motor Skill, 51,* 947–955.

Kavale, K. A. (1981). Functions of the *Illinois Test of Psycholinguistic Abilities* (ITPA): Are they trainable? *Exceptional Children, 47,* 496–510.

Kavale, K. A., & Forness, S. R. (1987). Substance over style: Assessing the efficacy of modality testing and teaching. *Exceptional Children, 54,* 228–239.

Kavale, K. A., & Forness, S. R. (2000). Policy decisions in special education: The role of meta-analysis. In R. Gersten, E. P. Schiller, & S. Vaughn (Eds.), *Contemporary special education research* (pp. 281–326). Mahwah, NJ: Erlbaum.

Kavale, K. A., Hirshoren, A., & Forness, S. R. (1998). Meta-analytic validation of the Dunn and Dunn model of learning-style preferences: A critique of what was Dunn. *Learning Disabilities Research & Practice, 13,* 75–80.

Kavale, K. A., & Mattson, D. (1983). "One jumped off the balance beam": Meta-analysis of perceptual-motor training. *Journal of Learning Disabilities, 16,* 165–173.

Keogh, B. K. (1994a). A matrix of decision points in the measurement of learning disabilities. In G. R. Lyon (Ed.), *Frames of reference for the assessment of learning disabilities* (pp. 15–26). Baltimore: Brookes.

Keogh, B. K. (1994b). What the special education agenda should look like in the year 2000. *Learning Disabilities Research & Practice, 9,* 62–69.

Keogh, B. K., Wilcoxen, A. G., & Bernheimer, L. (1986). Prevention services for at risk children: Evidence for policy and practice. In D. C. Farran & J. D. McKinney (Eds.), *Risk in intellectual and psychological development* (pp. 287– 316). New York: Academic Press.

Kirk, S. A., & Elkins, J. (1975). Characteristics of children enrolled in the Child Service Demonstration Centers. *Journal of Learning Disabilities, 8,* 31–38.

Kirk, S. A., & Kirk, W. D. (1971). *Psycholinguistic learning disabilities: Diagnosis and remediation.* Urbana: University of Illinois.

Kirk, S. A., McCarthy, J. J., & Kirk, W. D. (1968). *Examiner's manual: Illinois Test of Psycholinguistic Abilities.* Urbana: University of Illinois.

Kulik, J. A., & Kulik, C. C. (1987). Effects of ability grouping on student achievement. *Equity and Excellence, 23*(1-2), 22–30.

Larrivee, B. (1981). Modality preference as a model for differentiating beginning reading instruction: A review of the issues. *Learning Disability Quarterly, 4,* 180–188.

Larsen, S. C., Parker, R. M., & Hammill, D. D. (1982). Effectiveness of psycholinguistic training: A response to Kavale. *Exceptional Children, 49,* 60–66.

Lou, Y., Abrami, P. C., Spence, J. C., Poulsen, C., Chambers, B., & d'Apollonia, S. (1996). Within-class grouping: A meta-analysis. *Review of Educational Research, 66,* 423–458.

Lund, K. A., Foster, G. E., & McCall-Perez, F. C. (1978). The effectiveness of psycholinguistic training: A reevaluation. *Exceptional Children, 44,* 310–319.

Lyon, G. R. (1985). Identification and remediation of learning disability subtypes: Preliminary findings. *Learning Disabilities Research & Practice, 1,* 21–35.

Lyon, G. R. (1994). Critical issues in the measurement of learning disabilities. In G. R. Lyon (Ed.), *Frames of reference for the assessment of learning disabilities* (pp. 3–13). Baltimore: Brookes.

Mann, L. (1979). *On the trail of process.* New York: Grune & Stratton.

McIntosh, R., Vaughn, S., Schumm, J., Haager, D., & Lee, O. (1993). Observations of students with learning disabilities in general education classrooms. *Exceptional Children, 60,* 249–261.

McIntyre, C. W., & Pickering, J. S. (1995). *Clinical studies of multisensory structured language education for students with dyslexia and related disorders.* Salem, OR: IMSLEC.

O'Connor, R. (2000). Increasing the intensity of intervention in kindergarten and first grade. *Learning Disabilities Research & Practice, 15,* 43–54.

Orton, S. T. (1937). *Reading, writing and speech problems in children.* New York: Norton.

Rashotte, C. A., MacPhee, K., & Torgesen, J. K. (2001). The effectiveness of a group reading instruction program with poor readers in multiple grades. *Learning Disability Quarterly, 24,* 119–134.

Silver, L. B. (2001). Controversial therapies. *Perspectives, 27*(3), 5–8.

Slavin, R. E. (1987). Ability grouping and student achievement in elementary schools: A best-evidence synthesis. *Review of Educational Research, 57,* 293–336.

Speece, D. L., & Case, L. P. (2001). Classification in context: An alternative approach to identifying early reading disability. *Journal of Educational Psychology, 93,* 735–749.

Stanovich, K. E. (2000). *Progress in understanding reading.* New York: Guilford.

Stecker, P. M., & Fuchs, L. S. (2000). Effecting superior achievement using curriculum-based measurement: The importance of individual progress monitoring. *Learning Disabilities Research & Practice, 15,* 128–134.

Strauss, A. A., & Lehtinen, L. E. (1947). *Psychopathology and education of the brain-injured child.* New York: Grune & Stratton.

Swanson, H. L., Carson, C., & Saches-Lee, C. M. (1996). A selective synthesis of intervention research for students with learning disabilities. *School Psychology Review, 25,* 370–391.

Swanson, H. L., Hoskyn, M., & Lee, C. (1999). *Interventions for students with learning disabilities.* New York: Guilford.

Thurlow, M. L., Ysseldyke, J. E., Wotruba, J. W., & Algozzine, B. (1993). Instruction in special education classrooms under varying student-teacher ratios. *The Elementary School Journal, 93,* 305–320.

Torgesen, J. K. (1996). Thoughts about intervention research in learning disabilities. *Learning Disabilities: A Multidisciplinary Journal, 7*(2), 55–58.

Torgesen, J. K. (2000). Individual differences in response to early interventions in reading: The lingering problem of treatment resisters. *Learning Disabilities Research & Practice, 15,* 55–64.

Torgesen, J. K., Alexander, A. W., Wagner, R. K., Rashotte, C. A., Voeller, K. K. S., & Conway, T. (2001). Intensive remedial instruction for children with severe reading disabilities: Immediate and long-term outcomes from two instructional approaches. *Journal of Learning Disabilities, 34,* 33–58.

Vaughn, S., & Dammann, J. E. (2001). Science and sanity in special education. *Behavior Disorder, 27*(1), 21–29.

Vaughn, S., Gersten, R., & Chard, D. J. (2000). The underlying message in LD intervention research: Findings from research syntheses. *Exceptional Children, 67,* 99–114.

Vaughn, S., Linan-Thompson, S., & Hickman-Davis, P. (2003). Response to instruction as a means of identifying students with reading/learning disabilities. *Exceptional Children, 69,* 391–409.

Vaughn, S., Linan-Thompson, S., Kouzekanani, K., Bryant, D. P., Dickson, S., & Blozis, S. A. (2003). Reading instruction grouping for students with reading difficulties. *Remedial and Special Education, 24,* 301–315.

Vellutino, F., Scanlon, D. M., Sipay, E., Small, S., Pratt, A., Chen, R., & Denckla, M. (1996). Cognitive profiles of difficult-to-remediate and readily remediated poor readers: Early intervention as a vehicle for distinguishing between cognitive and experiential deficits as basic causes of specific reading disability. *Journal of Educational Psychology, 88,* 601–638.

Wasik, B. A., & Slavin, R. E. (1993). Preventing early reading failure with one-to-one tutoring: A review of five programs. *Reading Research Quarterly, 28,* 178–200.

Zigmond, N., & Baker, J. M. (1995). Concluding comments: Current and future practices in inclusive schooling. *The Journal of Special Education, 29,* 245–250.

Zigmond, N., Jenkins, J., Fuchs, L. S., Deno, S., Fuchs, D., Baker, J. N., et al. (1995, March). Special education in restructured schools: Findings from three multi-year studies. *Phi Delta Kappan, 76,* 531– 540.

Appendix: How Do Interventions That Are Effective for Students With LD Impact Students Without LD?

Adapted from Vaughn, Gersten, and Chard (2000)

Instructional practices implemented to benefit students with LD also support the learning of average- to high-achieving students.

Effective instructional practices for students with LD have value when implemented in general and special education settings for a range of student learners.

Which Instructional Features Are the Most Effective for Students With LD?

- Provide direct and explicit instruction.
- Sequence and make visible the elements students need to know to learn skills and strategies.
- Break down tasks into component parts and fade prompts or cues.
- Control task difficulty (e.g., sequence examples and problems to maintain high levels of success and match task difficulty with student abilities and emerging skills).
- Provide formative feedback (by teachers and/or peers) to guide and correct.
- Higher order processing skills and problem solving can facilitate the integration of knowledge and skills as students address increasingly complex problems and projects, especially in math and science.
- Model and teach strategies for generating questions and thinking aloud while reading, writing, or working on a scientific or mathematical problem (e.g., self-questioning or meta-cognitive strategies).
- Provide students with opportunities to work with other students to construct projects and solve problems.
- Teach the lower level skills that students need to think about to resolve higher order problems.
- Learn when, where, and how to apply strategies to assist students in developing plans of action to guide their learning.
- Teach learning strategies (e.g., study skills).
- Assist students in identifying specific contexts in which to use each strategy.
- Teach students to ask themselves questions when they read.
- Use small groups for reading instruction to facilitate engagement and progress in learning to read.
- Use small, interactive groups and pairs.
- Implement individual instruction (one adult with one student) whenever feasible.
- Monitor progress of specific academic skills.

- Monitor students' progress in the critical elements of reading (e.g., phonemic awareness, fluency, alphabetic principle) and math.
- Collect and use ongoing progress-monitoring data to guide instruction, particularly in target areas where students have special needs.
- Implement activities that allow students to identify and manipulate orally the individual sounds in words.
- Provide instruction in reading regular and irregular words fluently.
- Provide ample opportunities for students to practice reading for fluency.
- Pair students for activities that focus on fluency.
- Teach explicitly the critical steps in the writing process (e.g., model how to use these steps by writing several samples; support student learning by using "think sheets," prompt cards, or a mnemonic).
- Allow students to use "text structure" or conventions characteristic of a specific writing genre (e.g., persuasive, narrative, or comparison/contrast) as a guide during writing activities.
- Provide both teacher and peer feedback.
- Provide instruction in spelling and handwriting—include speed of writing.
- Encourage interactive dialogue between teacher and student and between students.
- Provide ongoing and systematic feedback (teachers and/or peers) to assist students with LD in repairing misunderstandings, revising their writing, or understanding text.
- Foster the development of a positive self-concept in students with LD at the elementary level by providing high-quality academic interventions.

Chapter 2

What Is Special About Special Education for Students With Emotional or Behavioral Disorders?

Timothy J. Landrum, Melody Tankersley, and **James M. Kauffman**

Describing what is special about special education for students with emotional or behavioral disorders (EBD) presents a uniquely difficult challenge, given that students with EBD probably experience less school success than any other subgroup of students with or without disabilities. It has been well documented that students with disabilities experience poorer outcomes than their nondisabled peers (e.g., Blackorby & Wagner, 1996), but for students with EBD in particular, the outlook for school and later life success historically has been quite bleak. Students with EBD generally earn lower grades, fail more courses, are retained in grade more often, pass minimum competency tests at lower rates, and have more difficulty adjusting to adult life than students with other disabilities (e.g., Frank, Sitlington, & Carson, 1995; Koyangi & Gaines, 1993). Perhaps one of the greatest obstacles to improving their outcomes may be school attendance; it has been estimated that 43% to 56% of students with EBD drop out of school, a rate almost twice that for all students with disabilities (Marder, 1992).

This relatively negative assessment of the current state of affairs for students with EBD demands some qualification, and in fact should not be taken as evidence of an inability to intervene effectively. For example, students with EBD typically are identified not at an early age, when their problems are most amenable to treatment (e.g., Walker et al., 1996), but much later in their development, when problems are predictably severe and intractable. Moreover, only a fraction of those who probably need intervention for their emotional or behavioral disorders are actually identified and served (e.g., Kauffman, 2005; U.S. Department of Health and Human Services, 2001). Most likely, then, those served are students with the most severe problems and intense needs. Simple logic suggests that failure to identify early, and limiting of the population to include only those with the most extreme and protracted problems, do not portend success (Kauffman, 1999; Walker, Colvin, & Ramsey, 1995). Thus, it is not surprising that concerns about the effectiveness of special education are particularly serious with regard to students with EBD.

Despite the challenges associated with education and treatment of students with EBD, credible research supports a number of promising interventions (see Dunlap & Childs, 1996; Shinn, Walker, & Stoner, 2002). In this chapter we address three questions with regard to the literature on effective practices for students with EBD. First, which research-based practices offer the most promise for working effectively with students with EBD? We frame the answer to this question around the idea that students with EBD present instructional and management problems quite different from those of most students without disabilities. Second, are these effective practices implemented with regularity and fidelity in schools and classrooms? Third, are these practices unique to the field of special education, or do they simply reflect sound educational practice? In other words, is special education for students with EBD special?

Effective Practice in Emotional or Behavior Disorders

Although there may be risk in treating the population of students with EBD as a homogenous group, it proves useful to structure a discussion of effective practice with some generalizations about the behavior and performance of students identified with EBD. First, students with EBD by definition tend to display disproportionately high rates of inappropriate behavior and conversely low rates of positive behavior compared to students without behavior problems (e.g., Walker, Hops, & Greenwood, 1993; Walker, Shinn, O'Neill, & Ramsey, 1987). Second, they tend to experience academic difficulties that are at least related, if not causally linked, to their behavioral excesses and deficits (e.g., Dishion, Patterson, Stoolmiller, & Skinner, 1991; Kupersmidt & Coie, 1990; Lipsey & Derzon, 1998; Lloyd, Hallahan, Kauffman, & Keller, 1998). Finally, students with EBD typically have social difficulty in relating to both peers and adults (Walker, 1995; Walker et al., 1995). In each of these three contexts—inappropriate behavior, academic learning problems, and ineffectual interpersonal relationships—we consider the extent to which the field has developed a set of effective practices. In Table 1, we have listed for each of these contexts some potential target areas for intervention and examples of specific practices that have empirical support. It should be noted that these lists are not exhaustive, but are representative of potential targets and effective practices that address what we believe are the areas of greatest need for most children and adolescents with EBD. Following is a brief overview of the interventions listed in Table 1.

Interventions for Inappropriate Behavior

Although the challenges that students with EBD present can seem complex and insurmountable, one could argue that these difficulties can be explained as a combination of behavioral excesses (too much negative behavior) and deficits (not

TABLE 1. Promising Interventions for Students with Emotional and Behavioral Disorders (EBD)

Characteristics of students with EBD	Potential targets of intervention	Examples of effective practices
Inappropriate behavior	Excesses • Aggression • Disruptive classroom behavior Deficits • Social withdrawal • Noncompliance	• Reinforcement (positive, differential, negative) • Precision requests • Behavioral momentum • Time-out • Response cost • Group-oriented contingencies (e.g., the Good Behavior Game) • Continuous monitoring of student performance (e.g., single-subject research evaluation methods)
Academic learning problems	• Achievement • Attention to task • Academic responding • Reciprocal Peer Tutoring	• Direct instruction • Self-monitoring • Class Wide Peer Tutoring • Continuous monitoring of student performance (e.g., curriculum-based measurement, single-subject research evaluation methods)
Unsatisfactory interpersonal relationships	• Social skills • Language skills	• Direct instruction of individually targeted behaviors • Modification of antecedents and consequences • Opportunity to practice in natural settings

enough appropriate behavior). We do not mean to reduce the constellation of problems experienced by most students with EBD to a simple matter of contingencies; however, credible evidence suggests that successful interventions for these students must be built upon a behavioral foundation (e.g., Walker et al., 1995; Walker, Forness, et al., 1998). The basic concept underlying behavioral procedures is a simple one: (a) Environmental cues, or antecedents, set the occasion for behavior; (b) behavior occurs; and (c) a consequence ensues—that is, a new stimulus is added or a stimulus already present is avoided or withdrawn (see Alberto & Troutman, 2003). This behavioral equation allows two points for intervention—prior to the behavioral occurrence (i.e., antecedent) and after the behavior occurs (i.e., consequence).

Although a vast literature supports the application of behavioral procedures in education (e.g., Kauffman, Mostert, Trent, & Pullen, in press; Shinn et al., 2002; Walker et al., 1995), it is perplexing that some question the value of such interventions (e.g., Kohn, 1993), while others disagree over fundamental aspects of behavioral concepts (see Biederman, Davey, Ryder, & Franchi, 1994; Ward, 1995). In our view, behavioral procedures are woefully misunderstood (see Maag, 2001; Walker, Forness, et al., 1998), and, as we discuss in a later section, they are frequently implemented incorrectly or insufficiently, leading to the erroneous conclusion that behavioral procedures do not work. We take the overwhelming empirical evidence that has accrued over the past 30 years as good reason for educators working with students with EBD to focus considerable attention toward altering antecedents and consequences in the environment to increase the likelihood that appropriate behavior will occur and reduce the likelihood that inappropriate behavior will occur.

Altering Antecedents. Among the most challenging and far-reaching behaviors frequently demonstrated by students with EBD is noncompliance (Patterson, Reid, & Dishion, 1992; Walker, 1995). Noncompliance in school situations refers to refusal of or lack of appropriate response to the directive of an adult who has made a request of the student (Walker & Walker, 1991). The likelihood of a student complying with a directive may be enhanced by the way the directive is delivered—an antecedent to compliance. Two methods of framing directives have been shown to increase the probability of students' complying: precision requests (e.g., Montgomery & Ayllon, 1993; Neville & Jenson, 1984; Rhode, Jensen, & Reavis, 1993) and behavioral momentum, also called interspersal training and pretask requesting (e.g., Mace et al., 1988; Munk & Repp, 1994; Singer, Singer, & Horner, 1987).

Precision requests involve delivering directives in a format that is predictable for students (uses discriminative stimuli), provides opportunity for the child to comply (wait time), and incorporates consequences (reinforcement for compliance and punishment for noncompliance). Initially developed by Forehand and McMahon (1981), the command format has been modified (Neville & Jenson, 1984; Rhode et al., 1993) to involve an initial request for compliance that is delivered with the word please (or some synonym), such as, "Please sit in your seat." During a 5- to 10-second wait interval, if the student complies, he or she is reinforced. If the student does not comply, the teacher provides a second request with the prompting phrase "you need to" preceding the instruction, such as "You need to sit in your seat." If during a 5- to 10-second wait interval the student complies, he or she is reinforced. If after the wait interval the student has not complied, the teacher institutes a reductive technique. Musser, Bray, Kehle, and Jenson (2001) used the precision request program as a standardized procedure for giving directions to reduce disruptive classroom behavior in three students with EBD. The results showed that, on average, students' disruptive behaviors decreased from baseline levels of 37% of intervals observed to intervention and follow-up levels of 10%.

Behavioral momentum is another method for delivering directives that increases compliance. Behavioral momentum involves the teacher delivering a set of high-probability directives (those that the student is most likely to engage in or comply with) before delivering a low-probability directive (the request that the student is most likely to refuse). Researchers (e.g., Ardoin, Martens, & Wolfe, 1999; Belfiore, Lee, Scheeler, & Klein, 2002) have found that compliance to less preferred requests was enhanced when those less preferred (low probability of compliance) requests were preceded by student compliance to a sequence of highly preferred (high probability of compliance) requests or actions. For example, Belfiore and colleagues identified the preferred and nonpreferred academic tasks of two students with EBD. When nonpreferred tasks were preceded by three brief highly preferred academic tasks, students' latency of nonpreferred task completion was reduced and their rate of task completion was increased.

Altering Consequences. Consequences occur after the production of a behavior and have the effect of either increasing or decreasing the future rate or probability of the behavior. Reinforcement is the consequence if the future rate of the behavior increases, and punishment is the consequence if the future rate of the behavior decreases. One of the most obvious examples of altering consequences in classrooms involves an easy-to-implement application of reinforcement. Specifically, the effect of positive teacher attention, or praise, on the social and academic behavior of students with behavioral problems is well established. Even 2 decades ago, Strain, Lambert, Kerr, Stagg, and Lenkner (1983) suggested that "literally hundreds of classroom based studies have shown that teachers' delivery of social reinforcement can result in improved academic performance . . . rule-following and good school deportment . . . cognitive and linguistic performance . . . and increased social responsiveness" (p. 243). Descriptions of praise and its effective use are abundant in the special education literature (e.g., Alberto & Troutman, 2003; Axelrod, 1983). By definition, praise must first be contingent (i.e., delivered when and only when a targeted appropriate behavior is displayed); to be effective, it should also be immediate, specific, and descriptive so that the student understands exactly what behavior is being acknowledged (Sutherland, Copeland, & Wehby, 2001); and finally, it should result in an increase in the occurrence of the behavior targeted. Indeed, for any consequence to be a reinforcer, there must be an increase in the future rate of the behavior.

Hall, Lund, and Jackson (1968) provided an example of this with elementary-age pupils who showed high rates of disruptive behavior and a failure to work. Teacher attention provided contingently upon the occurrence of appropriate study behavior resulted in dramatic increases in these children's rates of appropriate study behavior. Madsen, Becker, and Thomas (1968) similarly found that praise for appropriate behavior contributed to substantial reductions in the inappropriate classroom behavior of four students characterized by a high rate of problem behavior in two elementary classrooms. In their praise intervention, Madsen et al. asked teachers to focus on "catching the child being good" (p. 145) by making a positive comment about the child's appropriate behavior. These researchers assessed change by measuring the number of intervals in which disruptive behavior occurred. Inappropriate behavior occurred on average during 47% of intervals during baseline, but was reduced to 21% during the first phase involving praise, and, following a return to baseline, to 15% during a second phase including teacher praise.

Punishments, by definition, are consequences that reduce the occurrence of behavior. There are four general classes of punishment: those that rely on (a) reinforcement strategies (e.g., differential reinforcement of other behavior, differential reinforcement of incompatible behavior), (b) extinction (terminating reinforcement), (c) removal of desirable stimuli (e.g., response cost), and (d) presentation of aversive stimuli (Alberto & Troutman, 2003). Although each class of punishment utilizes different techniques, all claim the same effect of reducing behavior.

Differential reinforcement of other behavior (DRO) and differential reinforcement of incompatible behavior (DRI) are variations on the idea that reducing an aberrant behavior may be accomplished by reinforcing (i.e., increasing) a behavior that is inconsistent with the negative behavior targeted for reduction. Conyers et al. (2004) evaluated the effects of a DRO procedure on the disruptive behavior of a class of 25 preschool children who were described as exhibiting a "high level of disruptive behaviors" (p. 411). The DRO procedure in this study consisted of the teacher awarding a token at the end of specified intervals to all children who had not exhibited any disruptive behavior during that interval. Conyers et al. observed a reduction in disruptive behavior from 64% of intervals during baseline to an average of 27% of intervals during the final six sessions of the DRO condition.

Extinction, often referred to as "planned ignoring," involves the cessation or withholding of a reinforcer. Obviously, extinction is most useful when the contingency that has been maintaining a negative or undesirable behavior can be identified and then altered. A frequent target for extinction is disruptive behavior that may be maintained by teacher attention. For example, in the Hall et al. (1968) study described earlier to demonstrate the effective use of praise, teachers were also taught to ignore students' nonstudy behavior. Indeed, extinction is typically applied in this fashion as a complement to other reinforcement contingencies (Alberto & Troutman, 2005). As Axelrod (1983) noted, "What was important was providing the attention for appropriate behavior, rather than for inappropriate behavior" (p. 7).

Given the obvious focus on negative behavior and behavior reduction, punishment as a whole has been the source of some controversy (see Repp & Singh, 1990). However, this controversy is primarily aimed at one class of punishment—the presentation of aversive stimuli—given that the potential for misuse of aversives is great. Because of the typically well-developed nature of behavioral problems (Patterson et al., 1992), no single technique will be sufficient to make behavioral progress for most students with EBD. Therefore, the use of punishment techniques to reduce inappropriate behaviors is often necessary in conjunction with the use of reinforcement techniques to teach or increase appropriate behavior. Evidence suggests that two punishment techniques in particular, timeout from positive reinforcement (e.g., Salend & Gordon, 1987) and response cost (e.g., Proctor & Morgan, 1991), are among the easiest to implement and most effective strategies available to the classroom teacher for reducing inappropriate behaviors of students (e.g., Walker, 1995; Witt & Elliott, 1982).

Timeout from positive reinforcement involves the student losing the opportunity to be reinforced for a specified amount of time when inappropriate behavior occurs (Axelrod, 1983). Alberto and Troutman (2003) have provided an excellent overview of the various forms of timeout, including (a) nonseclusionary timeout, which typically means that the student remains in the classroom or original setting, but loses the opportunity to earn reinforcement; (b) exclusionary timeout, in which the student is generally removed from the classroom or activity; and (c) seclusionary timeout, in which the student might be isolated for brief period of time in a timeout room. While each of these forms of timeout can be effective, the potential for misuse is great, especially with the more restrictive forms involving exclusion or seclusion. Thus, the least restrictive form, nonseclusionary timeout, is generally preferred by teachers. A popular and effective variation of nonseclusionary timeout was first reported by Foxx and Shapiro (1978), who used a timeout ribbon procedure. Students in this study wore a ribbon as long as they were behaving appropriately; the ribbon indicated that the student was free to engage in the activity at hand and would earn attention or other reinforcers from the teacher. Students who misbehaved lost their ribbons for a brief period of time, during which they would not earn any reinforcement or attention from the teacher. Results showed that students' misbehavior dropped from 42% of the time during baseline to 6% during the timeout ribbon procedure.

Response cost involves the removal of a privilege or an earned reinforcer when inappropriate behavior occurs (Axelrod, 1983). Applications of response cost are particularly straightforward in cases where students earn points or tokens for appropriate behavior, assignment completion, and so on, as part of an overall management plan. The addition of a response cost element to such a system simply means that if students engage in specific misbehavior, they lose a certain number of points or tokens. In the Conyers et al. (2004) study described earlier, the DRO procedure was compared to a response cost intervention in an alternating treatments design. In the response cost intervention, 15 tokens were placed beside each student's name on a board, and students were told that if they exhibited any predefined disruptive behavior during a particular interval, they would lose one token. Tokens could later be exchanged for candy. Results showed that the rate of disruptive behavior fell from 64% during baseline to only 5% during the initial response cost phase. A return to baseline conditions resulted in disruptive behavior increasing to 52%, followed by a second phase of response cost where disruptive behavior occurred less than 10% of the time, even as intervals were increased from 1 to as many as 12 minutes.

Consequences, whether reinforcement or punishment, can be delivered individually or to groups of students to alter the occurrence of behavior. Group-oriented contingencies are those in which consequences for the entire group are based on the performance of one or more individuals within the group (e.g., Kauffman, Mostert, et al., in press). The Good Behavior Game (GBG), for example, has repeatedly been shown to decrease disruptive and aggressive behaviors in the classroom (e.g., Darveaux, 1984; Dolan et al., 1993; Harris & Sherman, 1973). Originally introduced by Barrish, Saunders, and Wolf (1969), the GBG relies on the presentation of group contingencies in the context of team competition that enlists peer influence for supporting positive behavior. Using the GBG, the classroom is divided into two teams that compete for rewards or privileges delivered for low levels of rule infraction (see Tankersley, 1995, for an overview). Rules, such as remaining in seat and working quietly, are defined, and each infraction is assigned a demerit by making a tally mark on the board for the team of the rule breaker. If one or both teams receive fewer than the predetermined number of demerits (most research sets the criterion at four to five demerits), the team earns the reward. The GBG is one of the most widely studied classwide interventions, and results have consistently shown that while engaged in playing the GBG, students display fewer episodes of disruptiveness such as out-of-seat behavior and talking out (e.g., Darveaux, 1984; Dolan et al., 1993; Fishbein & Wasik, 1981; Harris & Sherman, 1973; Ialongo, Poduska, Werthamer, & Kellam, 2001; Kellam, Rebok, Ialongo, & Mayer, 1994; Medland & Stachnik, 1972).

Interventions for Academic Learning Problems

Examining the academic problems of students with EBD demands that we attend to both the achievement problems that typify this population and the behavioral characteristics that probably further inhibit their school performance (see Kauffman, 2005). Although academic-related behaviors such as attention to task, academic engagement, and academic responding are critical for making students available for learning, improvements in these behaviors may be short-lived if students do not simultaneously receive appropriate instruction for their skill deficits (see, e.g., Broughton & Lahey, 1978). Consequently, interventions must target not only effective instruction designed to enhance achievement (e.g., direct instruction), but also learning strategies that enhance students' ability to attend, retain information, and apply knowledge in appropriate contexts.

Among instructional strategies, direct instruction has perhaps the richest empirical history in enhancing the academic achievement of struggling learners. But as Walker et al. (1995) argued, there is a paucity of research focusing specifically on academic interventions for students with the serious behavior problems typical of EBD. Nonetheless, we agree with their assessment that "direct instruction has a number of features that are particularly suitable for meeting these challenging needs" (p. 101). One of the key advantages of direct instruction for low-achieving students is its emphasis on academic engagement. Research has shown that academic achievement is significantly related to academic engagement rates, or the proportion of instructional time during which students are engaged in learning, as demonstrated by behaviors such as attending to task, working on assignments, and participating in class activities (e.g., Greenwood, 1991; Greenwood, Delquadri, & Hall, 1984)—critical areas of behavior in which students with EBD often have problems (e.g., Walker et al., 1995). Thus the key features of direct instruction—including the structure, sequencing, and pacing of instruction, as well as the provision of frequent corrective feedback and opportunities for practice of newly acquired skills—provide unique opportunities for advancing the academic success of students with EBD. ClassWide Peer Tutoring (CWPT; see Delquadri, Greenwood, Whorton, Carta, & Hall, 1986) and Reciprocal Peer Tutoring (RPT; e.g., Fantuzzo, King, & Heller, 1992; Pigott, Fantuzzo, & Clement, 1986) have also been shown to increase students' academic engagement and responding rates. Both techniques use a peer-supervising (rather than actual peer tutoring) format and are based on the reinforcement principles of group-oriented contingencies. CWPT involves students in a gamelike format for responding in which their peer partners determine the accuracy of their responses. Tutors monitor their partners' work and provide encouragement and motivation—by assigning points for correct responses—as they complete their work. Points earned by partners are added to a team total. Teams that meet criteria or receive the most points can earn daily or weekly rewards. Among the many studies that have been conducted on this intervention, CWPT has been shown to be very effective in teaching spelling to third and fourth graders (Delquadri, Greenwood, Streton, & Hall, 1983; Maheady & Harper, 1987; Mallette, Harper, Maheady, & Dempsy, 1991); in teaching reading, math, and spelling to students identified as at risk for school failure (Greenwood et al., 1984; Greenwood et al., 1987); and in teaching social studies to junior high school students (Maheady, Harper, & Sacca, 1988). Consistently, the results have shown increases in students' academic learning and achievement after CWPT has been implemented.

Reciprocal Peer Tutoring uses peers to supervise academic responding, as does CWPT, allowing all students in the classroom to be engaged while the teacher can monitor and support individual students. Also like CWPT, RPT provides tutors with correct answers for the tasks so that errors are immediately corrected. However, RPT, which has been used primarily in the context of mathematics instruction, incorporates self-monitoring procedures (see following paragraph) as well as subgroup contingencies, with groups of students selecting and working to obtain their own group rewards (e.g., Fantuzzo et al., 1992; Pigott et al., 1986). Because CWPT and RPT provide a format for peers to supervise academic responding, students can engage in direct practice of specific academic skills with opportunity for immediate error correction or reinforcement.

Attention to task is another academic-related skill that students with EBD often lack (Kauffman, 2005). At minimum, attention is the critical first step in engaging students academically so that they can best profit from instruction. Self-monitoring is one strategy that has been effective for increasing students' attention to task. The term *self-monitoring* (other terms include *self-recording* or *self-management*) refers to a set of interventions that involve teaching students systematic procedures for observing, evaluating, and recording their own behavior during specific times (e.g., during independent seatwork). A rich literature base has accrued in this area (see reviews by Lloyd, Forness, & Kavale, 1998; Lloyd, Landrum, & Hallahan, 1991) documenting the effectiveness of self-management procedures. Generally, the procedures are easy to implement, and positive results have been observed both in students' rates of on-task behavior and academic productivity (Lloyd, Bateman, Landrum, & Hallahan, 1989). The basic components of self-monitoring include a cue of some type (e.g., a tone or timer) to prompt students to engage in the self-monitoring routine, which typically involves a self-question, such as "Was I paying attention?" Students then record their answers on a prepared recording sheet. Training students to use self-monitoring is generally accomplished in brief sessions over 1 day or 2 days, and students may then use the procedures during specific sessions at different times throughout the day. By their nature, self-monitoring interventions are most suited to helping students who have difficulty staying on task and completing assignments during classwork or seatwork. Lloyd and Landrum (1990) and Lloyd et al. (1991) have provided an extensive overview of self-monitoring research and a description of intervention components.

Another important feature of effective intervention for students with EBD involves the continuous monitoring of student performance (e.g., Peacock Hill Working Group, 1991). This ongoing monitoring is as important for behavioral interventions as for academic instruction. In the context of academic instruction, curriculum-based measurement (CBM) involves measuring students' performance on brief, standardized assessments developed directly from the curriculum in which students are working; this ongoing measurement in turn provides the teacher with information on which to base further instruction (Deno, 1985, this volume). Similarly, behavioral intervention effectiveness is also enhanced when interventions are designed (e.g., functional assessment), modified, and evaluated (i.e., comparisons are made between baseline and intervention levels of behavior) using ongoing repeated measurement of the target behaviors (see, e.g., Kazdin, 1982).

Interventions for Interpersonal Relationships

By definition, students with EBD experience difficulty in their interpersonal relationships with peers and adults, and thus social skills intervention is a standard component of virtually all programming for these students. The effectiveness of social skills intervention, nevertheless, is routinely called into question. For example, meta-analytic summaries of the intervention literature (e.g., Forness, Kavale, Blum, & Lloyd, 1997; Lloyd, Forness, & Kavale, 1998) have not shown promising effect sizes for social skills interventions. These results may stem from the generic nature of most interventions (e.g., packaged curricula delivered to an entire class or even an entire school).

As an alternative to such interventions, Gresham (2002) has argued that social skills interventions for students with EBD must be based on carefully and individually targeted behaviors that serve to (a) promote skill acquisition, (b) enhance skill performance, (c) remove competing problem behaviors, and/or (d) facilitate generalization. Moreover, Walker and his colleagues have recommended (a) teaching social skills as one would teach any academic subject, relying on the same effective instructional procedures (e.g., direct instruction), and (b) accompanying social skills instruction with planned response opportunities, consistent feedback on performance, and the use of contingencies, particularly in natural settings as newly acquired skills are applied (see Walker, Schwarz, Nippold, Irvin, & Noell, 1994). Such recommendations are not specific to one intervention per se; rather, they are research-based practices that have been shown to be effective across a variety of academic areas and behavioral skills and for a variety of student populations.

Another consideration in relation to social skills is students' ability to use language effectively. Research has shown that a large percentage of students with EBD have language disorders (Benner, Nelson, & Epstein, 2002; Rogers-Adkinson & Griffith, 1999), particularly in the area of pragmatic language skills—those skills associated with the use of language and nonverbal communication in social situations. Indeed, Benner et al. noted that nearly three out of four children identified with EBD also have significant language difficulties, while over half of students with diagnosed language delays also were identified with EBD. Because the field is just beginning to study the relationship between language and behavior problems (Rogers-Adkinson & Griffith, 1999), specific effective practices for students with EBD have not been well established. However, techniques based on known effective practices, such as varying antecedents (e.g., directives) and providing opportunities for students to work together (e.g., ClassWide Peer Tutoring), allow students to practice teacher-to-student and student-to-student communication in the natural environment of the classroom (Audet & Tankersley, 1999).

Implementing What We Know: Is Research Translated Into Practice?

Despite the growing list of research-based approaches available for intervening with the behavioral, learning, and social problems characteristic of students with EBD, the research-to-practice dilemmas that plague all of special education are equally problematic here. Research has shown that many of the effective practices at our disposal are not routinely implemented (e.g., Meadows, Neel, Scott, & Parker, 1994; Shores et al., 1993). As Kauffman (1996) asserted, there may even be an inverse relationship between implementation of an instructional practice and its research support. Perhaps the most glaring examples in the case of students with EBD are in the areas of contingent teacher attention and early intervention or prevention. In the former, a number of observational studies have shown that teachers infrequently use positive attention in their classrooms. In an early study of teacher responses to behavior, Strain et al. (1983) found that teacher attention followed compliance only about 10% of the time, and, furthermore, that 82% of the children in their study who were rated low in social adjustment never received positive consequences for compliance. In classrooms specifically for students with EBD, Shores et al. (1993) found teacher praise rates as low as one per hour. Similar results from other studies forced Wehby,

Symons, Canale, and Go (1998) to conclude that "teacher praise . . . is almost nonexistent in classrooms for children with E/BD" (p. 51).

That teachers do not always use effective interventions has become a frequent topic in the educational literature as scholars debate the research-to-practice gap that most agree afflicts education (Carnine, 1997; Landrum & Tankersley, 1999). That evidence-based practices must become the standard in schools seems irrefutable; but a further concern in using such practices has to do with intervention integrity. As Malouf and Schiller (1995) have lamented, "When research does find its way into practice, it is often misapplied" (p. 419). Intervention integrity, also known as treatment fidelity or intervention adherence (Moncher & Prinz, 1991), is compromised when teachers fail to implement a strategy completely or implement a strategy imprecisely or inadequately. Indeed, research has shown that the extent to which interventions are implemented as designed is directly associated with the degree of behavior change (e.g., Allinder & Oats, 1997; Gansle & McMahon, 1997; Greenwood, Terry, Arreaga-Mayer, & Finney, 1992; Gresham, Gansle, Noell, Cohen, & Rosenblum, 1993).

Many factors are related to intervention integrity. Telzrow and Beebe (2002) and Gresham (1989) concluded that interventions most acceptable to teachers, and accordingly most likely to be implemented with integrity, are (a) easy to implement, (b) not time-intensive, (c) positive, (d) perceived to be effective by the teacher, and (e) compatible with the context in which the intervention will be employed (e.g., resources available, teacher experiences, treatment philosophy, instructional environment). Unfortunately, many interventions that have proven effective for addressing the behavioral and academic needs of students with EBD do not meet these criteria (Telzrow & Beebe, 2002) and therefore are not likely to be implemented with integrity, if implemented at all.

In addition to choosing interventions that are empirically supported and implementing them with integrity, interventions must also be implemented early in the cycle of behavioral problems. Indeed, compelling evidence suggests that the development of behavioral disorders can be ameliorated dramatically if intervention is provided early and intensively (see Shinn et al., 2002). Longitudinal studies have shown that students who are identified with behavioral disorders have recognizable problem behavior even before entering first grade, and that these problem behaviors are stable through 3- and 6-year follow-ups (Achenbach, Howell, McConaughy, & Stranger, 1995; McConaughy, Stranger, & Achenbach, 1992). Moreover, research has shown that preventive efforts can break this cycle (see Shinn et al., 2002). Nonetheless, as a field, we remain reluctant to intervene early. In fact, Kauffman (1999) has enumerated a number of ways that professionals, in essence, "prevent prevention" of EBD, including resisting labeling for fear of stigmatization, refusing to invest resources in prevention programs, and denying the deviance of children's behavior for reasons that may be associated with age (development) or diversity.

As schools and educators face greater and more frequent behavioral challenges (Walker, Forness, et al., 1998; Walker, Kavanagh, et al., 1998), questions remain about the capacity of both general and special education teachers to deal with the most difficult students they encounter. Unfortunately, it appears that many, if not most, teachers are inadequately trained to intervene and effectively manage the more serious behavioral and instructional challenges that students with EBD are likely to present (see Kauffman & Wong, 1991). For example, there is evidence that when teaching students with EBD in general education classes, many teachers do not modify their instructional or management techniques (Meadows et al., 1994). Moreover, even teachers of students with EBD may lack sufficient training in empirically sound practices (Bullock, Ellis, & Wilson, 1994).

Is Education for Students With EBD Special?

Whether effective teachers of students with EBD are uniquely trained specialists who bring to bear distinctive skills unlike those associated with teaching nondisabled students or students with other disabilities remains unclear. Kauffman and

Wong (1991) commented on this phenomenon a decade ago, concluding that there may indeed be a set of specialized skills that teachers must exercise to be effective with students with the most severe behavior disorders. Kauffman et al. (2002) described the successful application of such specialized skills in a separate class for students with EBD, suggesting that the keys to success may lie at least partially in the contextual variables that can characterize a separate class. As they noted, the structure, intensity, precision, and relentlessness with which teachers deliver, monitor, and adapt instruction are surely beyond that which would be possible in a general education classroom.

In our judgment, the procedures outlined in Table 1 are probably appropriate for any learner. That is, they are based on principles of learning that should be effective for anyone learning a new skill or generalizing a behavior. However, it should also be clear that many of these interventions would not be necessary for typically developing learners. Many of these strategies require a significant investment of teacher time, effort, and skill to ensure intervention integrity. Thus we would argue that although the procedures we espouse for students with EBD are generally effective teaching practices, there is probably no reason to suggest that all teachers learn these skills and use them with all students (see Kauffman & Hallahan, 2005; Kauffman & Landrum, in press). However, we do believe that any teacher specializing in the education of students with EBD should be knowledgeable about and competent in implementing at minimum the procedures we have suggested here—and implementing them with a very high degree of precision, which is a defining element of what makes special education special (Kauffman, 2002; Kauffman & Hallahan, 2005).

In determining whether interventions for students with EBD are effective, it is important to understand that we are probably not going to cure the emotional or behavioral problems that students with EBD present, given that (a) by the time they are identified for special education services they typically have a lengthy history of difficult behavior (Duncan, Forness, & Hartsough, 1995) and are well along the typical trajectory for academic and social failure, and (b) EBD seems to be a life-course-persistent state—even when preventive efforts are applied. Recognizing that these students probably will need support throughout their school careers (see, e.g., Wolf, Braukmann, & Ramp, 1987) is an uncomfortable but necessary step in ensuring that their education remains special.

At best, perhaps, we will be able to alleviate some of the symptoms and reduce the frequency and intensity of the problems associated with EBD by using effective techniques to address inappropriate behavior, enhance learning, and influence social interactions. But, this is special. These are not techniques that students with EBD are likely to be exposed to outside of special education (Kauffman et al., 2002), yet they are the techniques that afford the strongest potential to influence learning and behavior positively. Of course, special education for students with EBD could be much more special (i.e., effective) if effective practices were (a) implemented frequently throughout their school careers with integrity and (b) implemented early, before their behavior has become so entrenched and intractable. Only when we start identifying children early for services and implementing proactive, effective, preventive strategies with persistent regularity and integrity throughout their educational experiences will we see just how special special education for children with EBD can be.

Conclusion

Although it might be argued that specific research with participants identified with EBD is needed to verify the effectiveness of any intervention before it can be recommended as best practice for students with EBD, we counter that many of the interventions currently available have in fact been validated with students displaying the types of learning, behavioral, and social problems that are typical of students with EBD. While recognizing the need to expand our understanding of what works for students with EBD, we also believe that greater resources must be brought to bear on the problems associated with implementing what is already known to be effective. Such efforts must be made at the earliest possible age, and procedures must be implemented with integrity and precision. Finally, these efforts must be sustained over time—in many cases, over school careers or even the life spans of individuals with EBD.

The final question posed in this chapter asks: Is special education for students with EBD special? It certainly is. And it can become even more special if we take full advantage of the currently available technology of behavioral and instructional intervention. Indeed, we think it has the potential to become extraordinary.

REFERENCES

Achenbach, T. M., Howell, C. T., McConaughy, S. H., & Stranger, C. (1995). Six-year predictors of problems in a national sample: 1. Cross-informant syndromes. *Journal of the American Academy of Child and Adolescent Psychiatry, 34,* 336–347.

Alberto, P. A., & Troutman, A. C. (2003). *Applied behavior analysis for teachers* (6th ed.). Upper Saddle River, NJ: Merrill.

Allinder, R. M., & Oats, R. G. (1997). Effects of acceptability on teachers' implementation of curriculum-based measurement and student achievement in mathematics computation. *Remedial and Special Education, 18,* 113–120.

Ardoin, S. P., Martens, B. K., & Wolfe, L. A. (1999). Using high-probability instruction sequences with fading to increase student compliance during transition. *Journal of Applied Behavior Analysis, 32,* 339–351.

Audet, L. R., & Tankersley, M. (1999). Implications of communication and behavioral disorders for classroom management: Collaborative intervention techniques. In D. Rogers-Adkinson & P. Griffith (Eds.), *Communication disorders and children with psychiatric and behavioral disorders* (pp. 403–440). San Diego: Singular.

Axelrod, S. (1983). *Behavior modification for the classroom teacher* (2nd ed.). New York: McGraw-Hill.

Barrish, H. H., Saunders, M., & Wolf, M. M. (1969). Good Behavior Game: Effects of individual contingencies for group consequences on disruptive behavior in a classroom. *Journal of Applied Behavior Analysis, 2,* 119–124.

Belfiore, P. J., Lee, D. L., Scheeler, M. C., & Klein, D. (2002). Implications of behavioral momentum and academic achievement for students with behavior disorders: Theory, application, and practices. *Psychology in the Schools, 39,* 171-179.

Benner, G. J., Nelson, J. R., & Epstein, M. H. (2002). Language skills of children with EBD: A literature review. *Journal of Emotional and Behavioral Disorders, 10,* 43–56.

Biederman, G. B., Davey, V. A., Ryder, C., & Franchi, D. (1994). The negative effects of positive reinforcement in teaching children with developmental delay. *Exceptional Children, 60,* 458–465.

Blackorby, J., & Wagner, M. (1996). Longitudinal post school outcomes of youth with disabilities: Findings from the national longitudinal transition study. *Exceptional Children, 62,* 399–414.

Broughton, S. F., & Lahey, B. B. (1978). Direct and collateral effects of positive reinforcement, response cost, and mixed contingencies for academic performance. *Journal of School Psychology, 16,* 126–136.

Bullock, L. M, Ellis, L. L., & Wilson, M. J. (1994). Knowledge/skills needed by teachers who work with students with severe emotional/behavior disorders: A revisitation. *Behavioral Disorders,* 19, 108–125.

Carnine, D. (1997). Bridging the research-to-practice gap. *Exceptional Children, 63,* 513–521.

Conyers, C., Miltenberger, R., Maki, A., Barenz, R., Jurgens, M., Sailer, A., Haugen, M., & Kopp, B. (2004). A comparison of response cost and differential reinforcement of other behavior to reduce disruptive behavior in a preschool classroom. *Journal of Applied Behavior Analysis, 37,* 411–415.

Darveaux, D. X. (1984). The Good Behavior Game plus merit: Controlling disruptive behavior and improving student motivation. *School Psychology Review, 13,* 510-514.

Delquadri, J. C., Greenwood, C. R., Whorton, D., Carta, J. J., & Hall, R. V. (1986). Classwide peer tutoring. *Exceptional Children, 52,* 535–542.

Deno, S. L. (1985). Curriculum-based measurement: The emerging alternative. *Exceptional Children, 52,* 219–232.

Delquadri, J. C., Greenwood, C. R., Stretton, K., & Hall, R. V. (1983). The peer tutoring spelling game: A classroom procedure for increasing opportunity to respond and spelling performance. *Education and Treatment of Children, 6,* 225–239.

Dishion, T. J., Patterson, G. R., Stoolmiller, M., & Skinner, M. L. (1991). Family, school, and behavioral antecedents to early adolescent involvement with antisocial peers. *Developmental Psychology, 27,* 172–180.

Dolan, L. J., Kellam, S. G., Brown, C. H., Werthamer-Larsson, L., Rebok, G. W., Mayer, L. S., Laudolff, J., Turkkan, J. S., Ford, C., & Wheeler, L. (1993). The short-term impact of two classroom-based preventive interventions on aggressive and shy behaviors and poor achievement. *Journal of Applied Developmental Psychology, 14,* 317–345.

Duncan, B. B., Forness, S. R., & Hartsough, C. (1995). Students identified as seriously emotionally disturbed in day treatment: Cognitive, psychiatric, and special education characteristics. *Behavioral Disorders, 20,* 238–252.

Dunlap, G., & Childs, K. E. (1996). Intervention research in EBD: An analysis of studies from 1980–1993. *Behavioral Disorders, 21,* 125–136.

Fantuzzo, J. W., King, J. A., & Heller, L. R. (1992). Effects of reciprocal peer tutoring on mathematics and school adjustment: A component analysis. *Journal of Educational Psychology, 84,* 331–339.

Fishbein, J. E., & Wasik, B. H. (1981). Effect of the Good Behavior Game on disruptive library behavior. *Journal of Applied Behavior Analysis, 14,* 89–93.

Forehand, R., & McMahon, R. J. (1981). *Helping the noncompliant child: A clinician's guide to parent training.* New York: Guilford.

Forness, S. R., Kavale, K., Blum, S., & Lloyd J. W. (1997). Mega-analysis of meta-analyses: What works in special education and related services. *Teaching Exceptional Children, 29,* 4–9.

Foxx, R. M., & Shapiro, S. T. (1978). The timeout ribbon: A nonexclusionary timeout procedure. *Journal of Applied Behavior Analysis, 11,* 125–136.

Frank, A. R., Sitlington, P. L., & Carson, R. R. (1995). Young adults with behavioral disorders: A comparison with peers with mild disabilities. *Journal of Emotional and Behavioral Disorders, 3,* 156–164.

Gansle, K. A., & McMahon, C. M. (1997). Component integrity of teacher intervention management behavior using a student self-monitoring treatment: An experimental analysis. *Journal of Behavioral Education, 7,* 405–419.

Greenwood, C. R. (1991). Longitudinal analysis of time, engagement, and achievement in at-risk versus non-risk students. *Exceptional Children, 57,* 521–535.

Greenwood, C. R., Delquadri, J. C., & Hall, R. V. (1984). Opportunity to respond and student academic performance. In W. L. Heward, T. E. Heron, D. S. Hill, & J. Trap-Porter (Eds.), *Focus on behavior analysis in education* (pp. 58–88). Columbus, OH: Merrill.

Greenwood, C. R., Dinwiddie, G., Bailey, V., Carta, J. J., Dorsey, D., Kohler, F. W., Nelson, C., Rotholz, D., & Schulte, D. (1987). Field replication of classwide peer tutoring. *Journal of Applied Behavior Analysis, 20,* 151–160.

Greenwood, C. R., Terry, B., Arreaga-Mayer, C., & Finney, R. (1992). The classwide peer tutoring program: Implementation factors moderating students' achievement. *Journal of Applied Behavior Analysis, 25,* 101–116.

Gresham, F. M. (1989). Assessment of treatment integrity in school consultation and prereferral intervention. *School Psychology Review, 18,* 37–50.

Gresham, F. M. (2002). Teaching social skills to high-risk children and youth: Preventive and remedial strategies. In M. R. Shinn, H. H. Walker, & G. Stoner (Eds.), *Interventions for academic and behavior problems II: Preventive and remedial approaches* (pp. 403–432). Bethesda, MD: National Association of School Psychologists.

Gresham, F. M., Gansle, K. A., Noell, G. H., Cohen, S., & Rosenblum, S. (1993). Treatment integrity of school-based intervention studies: 1980–1990. *School Psychology Review, 22,* 254–272.

Hall, R. V., Lund, D., & Jackson, D. (1968). Effects of teacher attention on study behavior. *Journal of Applied Behavior Analysis, 1,* 1–12.

Harris, V. W., & Sherman, J. A. (1973). Use and analysis of the "Good Behavior Game" to reduce disruptive classroom behavior. *Journal of Applied Behavior Analysis, 6,* 405–417.

Ialongo, N., Poduska, J., Werthamer, L., & Kellam, S. (2001). The distal impact of two first-grade preventive interventions on conduct problems and disorder in early adolescence. *Journal of Emotional and Behavioral Disorders, 9,* 146-160.

Kauffman, J. M. (1996). Research to practice issues. *Behavioral Disorders, 22,* 55-60.

Kauffman, J. M. (1999). How we prevent the prevention of emotional and behavioral disorders. *Exceptional Children, 65,* 448–468.

Kauffman, J. M. (2005). *Characteristics of emotional and behavioral disorders of children and youth* (7th ed.). Upper Saddle River, NJ: Merrill/Prentice Hall.

Kauffman, J. M. (2002). *Education deform: Bright people sometimes say stupid things about education.* Lanham, MD: Scarecrow Education.

Kauffman, J. M., Bantz, J., & McCullough, J. (2002). Separate and better: A special public school class for students with emotional and behavioral disorders. *Exceptionality, 10,* 149–170.

Kauffman, J. M., & Hallahan, D. P. (2005). *Special education: What it is and why we need it.* Boston: Allyn & Bacon.

Kauffman, J. M., & Landrum, T. J. (in press). Educational service interventions and reforms. In J. W. Jacobson & J. A. Mulick (Eds.), *Handbook of intellectual and developmental disabilities.* New York: Kluwer.

Kauffman, J. M., Mostert, M. P., Trent, S. C., & Pullen, P. L. (in press). *Managing classroom behavior: A reflective case-based approach* (4th ed.). Boston: Allyn & Bacon.

Kauffman, J. M., & Wong, K. L. H. (1991). Effective teachers of students with behavioral disorders: Are generic teaching skills enough? *Behavioral Disorders, 16,* 225–237.

Kazdin, A. E. (1982). *Single-case research designs: Methods for clinical and applied settings.* New York: Oxford University Press.

Kellam, S. G., Rebok, G. W., Ialongo, N., & Mayer, L. S. (1994). The course and malleability of aggressive behavior from early first grade into middle school: Results of a developmental epidemiologically-based preventive trial. *Journal of Child Psychology & Psychiatry & Allied Disciplines, 35,* 259–281.

Kohn, A. (1993). *Punished by rewards.* New York: Houghton Mifflin.

Koyangi, C., & Gaines, S. (1993). *All systems failure: An examination of the results of neglecting the needs of children with serious emotional disturbance.* Washington, DC: National Mental Health Association.

Kupersmidt, J. B., & Coie, J. D. (1990). Preadolescent peer status, aggression, and school adjustment as predictors of externalizing problems in adolescence. *Child Development, 61,* 1350–1362.

Landrum, T. J., & Tankersley, M. (1999). Emotional and behavioral disorders in the new millennium: The future is now. *Behavioral Disorders, 24,* 319–330.

Lipsey, M. W., & Derzon, J. H. (1998). Predictors of violent or serious delinquency in adolescence and early adulthood: A synthesis of longitudinal research. In R. Loeber & D. P. Farrington (Eds.), *Serious and violent juvenile offenders: Risk factors and successful interventions* (pp. 86–105). Thousand Oaks, CA: Sage.

Lloyd, J. W., Bateman, D. F., Landrum, T. J., & Hallahan, D. P. (1989). Self-recording of attention versus productivity. *Journal of Applied Behavior Analysis, 22*, 315–323.

Lloyd, J. W., Forness, S. R., & Kavale, K. A. (1998). Some methods are more effective. *Intervention in School and Clinic, 33*, 195–200.

Lloyd, J. W., Hallahan, D. P., Kauffman, J. M., & Keller, C. E. (1998). Academic problems. In T. R. Kratochwill & R. J. Morris (Eds.), *The practice of child therapy* (3rd ed., pp. 167–198). Boston: Allyn & Bacon.

Lloyd, J. W., & Landrum, T. J. (1990). Self-recording of attending to task: Treatment components and generalization of effects. In T. E. Scruggs & B. Y. L. Wong (Eds.), *Intervention research in learning disabilities* (pp. 235–262). New York: Springer-Verlag.

Lloyd, J. W., Landrum, T. J., & Hallahan, D. P. (1991). Self-monitoring applications for classroom interventions. In G. Stoner, M. R. Shinn, & H. M. Walker (Eds.), *Interventions for achievement and behavior problems in regular class settings* (pp. 201–213). Stratford, CT: National Association of School Psychologists.

Maag, J. W. (2001) Rewarded by punishment: Reflections on the disuse of positive reinforcement in schools. *Exceptional Children, 67*, 173–186.

Mace, F. C., Hock, M. L., Lalli, J. S., West, B. J., Belfiore, P., Pinter, E., & Brown, D. F. (1988). Behavioral momentum in the treatment of noncompliance. *Journal of Applied Behavior Analysis, 21*, 123–141.

Madsen, C. H., Becker, W. C., & Thomas, D. R. (1968). Rules, praise, and ignoring: Elements of elementary classroom control. *Journal of Applied Behavior Analysis, 1*, 139-150.

Maheady, L., & Harper, G. (1987). A class-wide peer tutoring program to improve spelling test performance of low-income, third- and fourth-grade students. *Education and Treatment of Children, 10*, 120–133.

Maheady, L., Harper, G. R., & Sacca, K. (1988). Classwide peer tutoring system in a secondary resource room program for the mildly handicapped. *Journal of Research and Development in Education, 21*(3), 76-83.

Mallette, B., Harper, G. F., Maheady, L., & Dempsy, M. (1991). Retention of spelling words acquired using a peer-mediated instructional procedure. *Education and Training in Mental Retardation, 26*, 156–164.

Malouf, D. B., & Schiller, E. P. (1995). Practice and research in special education. *Exceptional Children, 61*, 414–424.

Marder, C. (1992). Education after secondary school. In M. Wagner, R. D'Amico, C. Marder, L. Newman, & J. Blackorby (Eds.), *What happens next? Trends in post-school outcomes of youth with disabilities. The second comprehensive report from the National Longitudinal Transition Study of Special Education Students* (pp. 3-1–3-39). Menlo Park, CA: SRI International.

McConaughy, S. H., Stranger, C., & Achenbach, T. M. (1992). Three-year course of behavioral/emotional problems in a national sample of 4- to 16-year-olds: I. Agreement among informants. *Journal of the American Academy of Child and Adolescent Psychiatry, 31*, 932–940.

Meadows, N. B., Neel, R. S., Scott, C. M., & Parker, G. (1994). Academic performance, social competence, and mainstream accommodations: A look at mainstreamed and nonmainstreamed students with serious behavioral disorders. *Behavioral Disorders, 19*, 170–180.

Medland, M. B., & Stachnik, T. J. (1972). Good-Behavior Game: A replication and systematic analysis. *Journal of Applied Behavior Analysis, 5*, 45-51.

Moncher, F. J., & Prinz, R. J. (1991). Treatment fidelity in outcome studies. *Clinical Psychology Review, 11*, 247–266.

Montgomery, R. W., & Ayllon, T. (1993). The effects of "do," "don't," and "wait" requests training on compliance behavior and stimulus generalizations. *Journal of Behavior Therapy and Experimental Psychiatry, 24*, 171–180.

Munk, D. D., & Repp, A. C. (1994). The relationship between instructional variables and problem behavior: A review. *Exceptional Children, 60*, 390–401.

Musser, E. H., Bray, M. A., Kehle, T. J., & Jenson, W. R. (2001). Reducing disruptive behaviors in students with serious emotional disturbance. *School Psychology Review, 30*, 294–304.

Neville, M. H., & Jenson, W. R. (1984). Precision command and the "sure I will" program: A quick and efficient compliance training sequence. *Child and Family Behavior Therapy, 6*, 61–65.

Patterson, G. R., Reid, J. B., & Dishion, T. J. (1992). *Antisocial boys: Vol. 4. A social international approach.* Eugene, OR: Castalia.

Peacock Hill Working Group (Kauffman, J. M., Lloyd, J. W., Cook, L., Cullinan, D., Epstein, M. H., Forness, S. R., Hallahan, D. P., Nelson, C. M., Polsgrove, L., Sabornie, E. J., Strain, P. S., & Walker, H. M.). (1991). Problems and promises in special education and related services for children and youth with emotional or behavioral disorders. *Behavioral Disorders, 16*, 299–313.

Pigott, H. E., Fantuzzo, J. W., & Clement, P. W. (1986). The effects of reciprocal peer tutoring and group contingencies on the academic performance of elementary school children. *Journal of Applied Behavior Analysis, 19*, 93–98.

Proctor, M. A., & Morgan, D. (1991). Effectiveness of a response cost raffle procedure on the disruptive classroom behavior of adolescents with behavior problems. *School Psychology Review, 20*, 97–109.

Repp, A., & Singh, N. (1990). *Perspectives on the use of nonaversive and aversive interventions for persons with developmental disabilities.* Sycamore, IL: Sycamore.

Rhode, G., Jensen, W. R., & Reavis, H. K. (1993). *The tough kid book: Practical classroom management strategies.* Longmont, CO: Sopris West.

Rogers-Adkinson, D., & Griffith, P. (Eds.) (1999). *Communication disorders and children with psychiatric and behavioral disorders.* San Diego: Singular.

Salend, S. J., & Gordon, B. D. (1987). A group-oriented time-out ribbon procedure. *Behavioral Disorders, 12*, 131–137.

Shinn, M. R., Walker, H. M., & Stoner, G. (Eds.). (2002). *Interventions for academic and behavior problems II: Preventive and remedial approaches.* Bethesda, MD: National Association of School Psychologists.

Shores, R. E., Jack, S. L., Gunter, P. L., Ellis, D. N., DeBriere, T. J., & Wehby, J. H. (1993). Classroom interactions of children with behavior disorders. *Journal of Emotional and Behavioral Disorders, 1,* 27–39.

Singer, G. H., Singer, J., & Horner, R. H. (1987). Using pretask requests to increase the probability of compliance for students with severe disabilities. *Journal of the Association for Persons with Severe Handicaps, 12,* 287–291.

Strain, P. S., Lambert, D. L., Kerr, M. M., Stagg, V., & Lenkner, D. A. (1983). Naturalistic assessment of children's compliance to teachers' requests and consequences for compliance. *Journal of Applied Behavior Analysis, 16,* 243–249.

Sutherland, K. S., Copeland, S., & Wehby, J. H. (2001). Catch them while you can: Monitoring and increasing the use of effective praise. *Beyond Behavior, 11,* 46–49.

Tankersley, M. (1995). A group-oriented contingency management program: A review of the research on the Good Behavior Game and implications for teachers. *Preventing School Failure, 40,* 19–24.

Telzrow, C. F., & Beebe, J. J. (2002). Best practices in facilitating intervention adherence and integrity. In A. Thomas & J. Grimes (Eds.), *Best practices in school psychology, Vol. 2* (pp. 503–516). Bethesda, MD: National Association of School Psychologists.

U.S. Department of Health and Human Services. (2001). *Report of the Surgeon General's Conference on Children's Mental Health: A national action agenda.* Washington, DC: Author.

Walker, H. M. (1995). *The acting-out child: Coping with classroom disruption* (2nd ed.). Longmont, CO: Sopris West.

Walker, H. M., Colvin, G., & Ramsey, E. (1995). *Antisocial behavior in school: Strategies and best practices.* Pacific Grove, CA: Brooks/Cole.

Walker, H. M., Forness, S. R., Kauffman, J. M., Epstein, M. H., Gresham, F. M., Nelson, C. M., & Strain, P. S. (1998). Macro-social validation: Referencing outcomes in behavioral disorders to societal issues and problems. *Behavioral Disorders, 24,* 7–18.

Walker, H. M., Hops, H., & Greenwood, C. R. (1993). *RECESS: A program for reducing negative-aggressive behavior.* Seattle, WA: Educational Achievement Systems.

Walker, H. M., Horner, R. H., Sugai, G., Bullis, M., Sprague, J. R., Bricker, D., & Kaufman, M. J. (1996). Integrated approaches to preventing antisocial behavior patterns among school-age children and youth. *Journal of Emotional and Behavioral Disorders, 4,* 194–209.

Walker, H. M., Kavanagh, K., Stiller, B., Golly, A., Severson, H. H., & Feil, E. G. (1998). First Step to Success: An early intervention approach for preventing school antisocial behavior. *Journal of Emotional and Behavioral Disorders, 6,* 66–80.

Walker, H. M., Schwarz, I. E., Nippold, M., Irvin, L. K., & Noell, J. (1994). Social skills in school-age children and youth: Issues and best practices in assessment and intervention. *Topics in Language Disorders: Pragmatics and Social Skills in School Age Children and Adolescents, 14*(3), 70–82.

Walker, H. M., Shinn, M. R., O'Neill, R. E., & Ramsey, E. (1987). A longitudinal assessment of the development of antisocial behavior in boys: Rationale, methodology and first year results. *Remedial and Special Education, 8*(4), 7–16, 27.

Walker, H. M., & Walker, J. E. (1991). *Coping with noncompliance in the classroom: A positive approach for teachers.* Austin, TX: PRO-ED.

Ward, P. C. (1995). A response to "The Negative Effects of Positive Reinforcement in Teaching Children with Developmental Delays." *Exceptional Children, 61,* 489–492.

Wehby, J. H., Symons, F. J., Canale, J. A., & Go, F. J. (1998). Teaching practices in classrooms for students with emotional and behavioral disorders: Discrepancies between recommendations and observations. *Behavioral Disorders, 24,* 51–56.

Witt, J. C., & Elliott, S. N. (1982). The response cost lottery: A time efficient and effective classroom intervention. *Journal of School Psychology, 20,* 155–161.

Wolf, M. M., Braukmann, C. J., & Ramp, K. A. (1987). Serious delinquent behavior as part of a significantly handicapping condition: Cures and supportive environments. *Journal of Applied Behavior Analysis, 20,* 347–359.

Chapter 3

What Is Special About Special Education for Students With Severe Disabilities?

Diane M. Browder and **Karena Cooper-Duffy**

The literature reflects several approaches to defining the unique educational needs of students with severe disabilities. One method is to define professional consensus through national surveys (Kleinert & Kearns, 1999; Meyer, Eichinger, & Park-Lee, 1987). For example, in defining criteria for Kentucky's alternate assessment, Kleinert and Kearns asked respondents to rate the importance of several performance indicators. Some of the highest rated indicators were integrated environments, functionality, age appropriateness, choice making, and the use of multiple settings for instruction. A second option is to use the research summaries typical of major texts on educating this population (e.g., Cipani & Spooner, 1994; Ryndak & Alper, 1996; Snell & Brown, 2000; Westling & Fox, 2000). For example, Snell and Brown have described the importance of the supportive school practices of inclusion; collaborative teams; integrated therapy; systematic, activity-based instruction; data-based decision making; and positive behavior support. A third alternative is to consider legal mandates, such as the IDEA Amendments of 1997 (Shriner, 2000), and litigation, such as that for the extended school year (Etscheidt, 2002). A fourth approach is to consider the literature that highlights the perspectives of families (Erwin & Soodak, 1995) or students with disabilities themselves (Ruef & Turnbull, 2002).

All of these alternatives provide important guidance on what is special about the education of students with severe disabilities. This chapter offers a "snapshot" of best practice against the backdrop of current educational reform reflected in the No Child Left Behind Act of 2001 (NCLB, 2002). NCLB has numerous provisions with implications for special education; two will be considered here: (a) the requirement to assess students in reading, math, and then later, science, and (b) the expectation for adequate yearly progress (AYP). The IDEA Amendments of 1997 (IDEA 1997) require that all students participate in state- and districtwide assessments, and NCLB requires annual performance assessments in reading and math in Grades 3 through 8. Both IDEA 1997 and NCLB allow alternate assessments with accommodations for students who cannot participate in state- or districtwide assessments. States have developed specific alternate assessment procedures (Thompson & Thurlow, 2001) that include reading and math categories (Browder, Ahlgrim-Dezell, et al., 2005). Although research is now emerging on states' alternate assessment practices, many questions remain about how best to measure the progress of students with severe disabilities on the basis of state academic standards (Browder, Spooner, et al., in press).

The Council for Exceptional Children has noted that one of the most significant ways NCLB will affect policy is through the requirement for AYP. NCLB states that within 12 years, schools must demonstrate that students in Grades 3 through 8 are making AYP toward 100% proficiency in reading and math. Schools are able to use alternate achievement standards to count up to 1% of students with significant cognitive disabilities as proficient in computing AYP (U.S. Department of Education, 2003). Alternate assessment based on alternate achievement standards must be aligned with a state's academic content standards, promote access to the general curriculum, and reflect professional judgment of the highest achievement standards possible (200.1(d)) (U.S. Department of Education, 2003). Besides its strong emphasis on assessment outcomes, NCLB also includes more than 100 references to "scientifically based research." The law requires that federal grantees use their funds on evidence-based strategies, putting educational research in an unprecedented spotlight (Feuer, Towne, & Shavelson, 2002).

To highlight what is special about educating students with severe disabilities in the current era, we will consider (a) changing curricular priorities and (b) identifying evidence-based instructional practices to meet these priorities.

Changing Curricular Priorities and Research on Skill Acquisition

In the late 1970s, experts like Lou Brown (Brown et al., 1979) revolutionized the field by challenging professionals to use the "criterion of ultimate functioning" to select skills for instruction for students with severe disabilities. Teaching teams began to consider whether skills were "functional" (i.e., usable in daily life) and "age appropriate" (i.e., typical of same-age peers who are nondisabled) before including them on the Individualized Education Program (IEP). Nearly all curricular models that followed (Browder, 1987; Falvey, 1989; Ford et al., 1989; Giangreco, Cloninger, & Iverson, 1998; Neel & Billingsley, 1989; Wilcox & Bellamy, 1987) shared two common characteristics: (a) the identification of life domains for curriculum planning (e.g., community, vocational, home, recreation) and (b) some type of prioritization process to select skills for a student on the basis of preferences and functional use. Research on skill acquisition has also reflected this focus on functional skills. In a comprehensive review, Snell (1997) identified 123 studies that demonstrated successful acquisition of functional skills by students with intellectual disabilities. Nearly half of the participants in these studies had severe mental retardation (45%). Demonstrations of functional skill acquisition included all major life domains—vocational, leisure, home, community, and embedded skills (such as communication, choice making, functional academics, and motor skills).

Despite this large volume of research, careful inspection reveals that few studies have included participants with combinations of severe cognitive, motor, and sensory disabilities who may need ongoing support in their daily routines. For students with multiple disabilities, the educational goal may be partial participation in routines through learning specific responses that increase choice and personal control in daily routines (Ferguson & Baumgart, 1991). Some research supports this partial participation approach. For example, Snell, Lewis, and Houghton (1989) reported that students with limited motor skills (e.g., students with quadriplegia) learned to open their mouths to signal readiness for help to have their teeth brushed. Kennedy and Haring (1993) taught students with significant disabilities to make choices in social interactions.

Taken together, these studies on teaching functional life skills and partial participation provide a strong research foundation for teaching students skills to participate in their daily routines. One might conclude from this research that what is special about education for students with severe disabilities is the need for a functional life-skills curriculum distinct from general education. However, researchers have also focused in the last 2 decades on addressing inclusion in general education settings for students with severe disabilities. In fact, the curricular area with the greatest growth in research with this population from 1976 to 1995 was social inclusion (Nietupski, Hamre-Nietupski, Curtin, & Shrikanth, 1997). During this era, access to the general curriculum for students with severe disabilities involved providing social inclusion in typical classrooms while addressing functional skills. In a study that illustrated this approach, Hunt, Staub, Alwell, and Goetz (1994) demonstrated that students with significant cognitive disabilities could acquire basic communication and motor skills in the context of a general education geometry lesson as a cooperative learning group.

With the NCLB requirement to assess all students in reading, math, and science, the need for students not only to have access to general education but also to make progress in the general curriculum became clearer. Prior to NCLB some states had begun to design alternate assessments with strong links to academic content (Browder, Flowers, et al., 2004). Experts had also advocated that access to the general curriculum required general curriculum planning with decisions about adapting and adding content versus relying on a separate curriculum (Wehmeyer, Agran, & Lattin, 2001).

Most research on academics for this population has not focused on the general curriculum but instead has targeted functional reading and math. Functional reading includes sight word instruction with real-life applications; functional math focuses on such practical skills as using money and telling time (Browder, 2001). In a research review, Browder and Grasso (1999) identified 43 studies on teaching money skills; 10 of these included individuals with severe mental retardation. In these studies, the math expectations were minimal; students learned either to use money without counting it or to count to less than 20. Browder and Xin (1998) located 48 studies on teaching sight words, several of which included participants with severe mental retardation or autism. Only a few focused on acquiring sight words in general education. In one such study (Schoen & Ogden, 1995), the general education teacher taught sight words to a small group of students with and without disabilities. In another study (Wolery, Werts, Snyder, & Caldwell, 1994), peer tutors effectively provided sight word instruction. Besides having few examples in general education contexts, most functional reading research lacks measures of comprehension (Browder & Xin, 1998).

When Brown et al. (1979) challenged the field to focus on age-appropriate, functional skills for students with severe disabilities, the current wealth of research on teaching students to participate more fully in communities, jobs, recreational settings, and their homes did not yet exist. In accepting this challenge, both practitioners and researchers began to create the evidence that students could learn these skills so that 20 years later, more than 100 studies illustrate the skills this population can acquire (Snell, 1997). The pursuit of this evidence continues with the need for more demonstrations with students with the most significant disabilities. The new challenge for researchers and practitioners is to find ways to create access to the general curriculum. As noted by Wehmeyer et al. (2001), this access does not exclude making decisions to augment the academic content of the grade level with additional instruction planned through the IEP process (e.g., functional skills, social inclusion). Nor does general curriculum access mean expecting the student with severe disabilities to master all of the grade-level content to show AYP. States can apply alternate achievement standards that are aligned with the grade-level academic content standards (U.S. Department of Education, 2003.) In practice, this means deciding how a student with severe disabilities who is 10 will show AYP in fifth-grade reading, math, and science; and then the next year, show progress in sixth grade. There are at least three new concepts to be considered in this changing curricular context.

First is the idea that all students have the opportunity to learn academic content. Current research provides minimal guidance for setting expectations because, traditionally, this population has received minimal academic instruction. For example, qualitative research including content analyses of textbooks (Katims, 2000) and ethnographic studies of children's school experiences (Kliewer, 1998) reveals a consistent lack of focus on reading. In our own earlier writing, we sometimes proposed bypassing academic instruction for some students (Browder & Snell, 2000). One criterion for academic exclusion was that the student had substantial life-skill learning needs. In contrast, no research exists to indicate that mastery of certain life skills is a prerequisite to academic learning. It is possible that some students who have had difficulty learning functional skills because of the motor responses involved may be able to learn academic tasks using assistive technology.

What is also new is the need to address the sequential nature of general curriculum. Functional curriculum planning usually involves a catalog approach instead of a sequential approach. There is no specific sequence such as learning to wash hands before learning to cross the street. In contrast, general curriculum is sequential, with different skills achieved in third grade compared with eighth grade. For the first time, educators must consider different grade-level expectations for students with significant cognitive disabilities in setting alternate achievement standards.

A third concept to consider is that of partial participation (Ferguson & Baumgart, 1991). From the research on functional skills, it is clear that students who do not master all skills for their age level can learn meaningful subsets of these skills (Kennedy & Haring, 1993; Snell et al., 1989). For example, some high school students can drive to the mall, make a purchase, and talk with friends. A student with severe disabilities might get a ride to the mall, indicate choice for a purchase to a friend who helps with the transaction, and use a communication device to interact with peers. For grade-level achievement standards, proficiency would be full mastery of the third-grade content. An alternate achievement standard, such as partial participation, defines proficiency as some meaningful, less complex performance of this grade-level content. Third graders may be expected to read a passage and select a title that represents the main idea. The student with severe disabilities may hear the story read and select a picture that represents the main idea. Others may be able to read a modified version of the story that uses a simpler reading level and picture symbols.

To summarize, the current context for curricula for students with severe disabilities is one of reform created by the goal of access to the general curriculum and the requirements of NCLB. What is special for the education of students with severe disabilities is not the choice of a separate, functional curriculum. Instead, students with severe disabilities need instruction in the academic content of the general curriculum for their grade level. What is unique is the decision-making process used to determine how to access, adapt, and augment this general curriculum. This decision making will identify ways for students to meet alternate achievement standards that are linked to the academic content and may also target functional skills and social opportunities.

Instructional Strategies to Promote AYP

Alternate achievement standards should reflect professional judgment of the highest achievement possible as well as alignment with the states' academic content standards (U.S. Department of Education, 2003). Numerous studies demonstrate that students with significant cognitive disabilities can acquire new skills (e.g., Nietupski et al., 1997; Snell, 1997). In many of these studies, students learned to perform the skill without prompting and did so in less than a year. Although studies do not yet exist with this population on achievement of the broad array of academic content typically reflected in state standards, the extant research suggests that it is feasible to set expectations for new learning within the time frame of a school year. In beginning to apply this expectation for annual progress, it is important to identify the evidence about the types of instructional strategies that are associated with skill acquisition.

One of the keys to successful yearly progress is team planning. Research has shown that the use of teams can be an effective means to involve general educators in developing positive behavior supports (Ellingston, Miltenberger, Stricker, Galensky, & Garlinghouse, 2000) and to eliminate barriers to inclusive practices (Salisbury, Evans, & Palombaro, 1997). A person-centered team approach can also promote parental involvement (Miner & Bates, 1997). Achievement of state standards, including alternate standards, may similarly be enhanced through involvement of the IEP team. General educators bring to the team their knowledge of both the standards and the curricular resources. Parents offer insight into how to build on the student's ability and provide appropriate supports as the team considers ways to document achievement. Special educators have experience in developing individualized instructional strategies to promote learning. These strategies include (a) defining assessment, (b) promoting yearly progress, (c) enhancing generalization, and (d) incorporating the use of assistive technology as needed. Each of these specialized strategies will now be described in more detail.

Defining Assessment

One of the most difficult challenges in documenting progress on state standards is defining assessment. In most research on skill acquisition with this population, the assessment is direct observation of the student performing the target skill. This assessment may focus on a single, discrete response, such as choice making (e.g., Kennedy

& Haring, 1993); a set of discrete responses, such as sight words (e.g., Collins, Branson, & Hall, 1995); or a chained response, such as the task analysis to do laundry (e.g., McDonnell & McFarland, 1988). This skill may also be a generalized response that has utility across more than one context, such as requesting (e.g., Chadsey-Rusch & Halle, 1992) or street crossing (e.g., Horner, Jones, & Williams, 1985). Some researchers have focused on a "pivotal response" that will enable the student to make a broader range of responses. For example, Hughes, Hugo, and Blatt (1996) taught students to problem solve in the context of daily living skills. Koegel, Koegel, Shoshan, and McNerney (1999) demonstrated through long-term outcome data that teaching the pivotal response of self-initiation had an important influence on a variety of postintervention outcomes (e.g., school performance and friendships).

Most resources on assessment for students with severe disabilities recommend these same types of direct observations to monitor IEP progress (Browder, 2001; Brown & Snell, 2000). While some states use similar performance assessments in their alternate assessments, many rely on portfolios of student achievement. Portfolio assessment has been proposed as an alternative way to capture student progress (Siegel-Causey & Allinder, 1998), but few studies using this approach exist. The studies that are available come from the emerging literature on alternate assessment and include some support for the technical quality of this approach (Browder, Karvonen, Davis, Fallin, & Courtade-Little, 2005; Kleinert, Kearns, & Kennedy, 1997). Given the strong foundation of research using direct assessment of performance, teachers may want to consider this approach in planning how to obtain portfolio entries. For example, to illustrate a student's achievement in identifying the main idea of a story, the assessment might focus on discrete responses (e.g., correct picture chosen to illustrate the story), generalized responses (e.g., work samples from a variety of stories; with unprompted correct selections by the later selections), or task-analytic assessment (data sheet showing steps performed on computer in scanning and selecting text and pictures in text that support main idea). For ongoing IEP progress monitoring, the team might target selection of a correct picture to answer "what" and "who" questions, a pivotal response usable across academic contexts.

Promoting Yearly Progress

The teaching team also needs to develop strategies to promote achievement of the state standards (or alternate standards) within the school year to show AYP. In a review of instructional research with students with severe disabilities, Ault, Wolery, Doyle, and Gast (1989) identified several effective prompting systems including time delay, least intrusive prompts, and graduated guidance. In time delay, the instructor gives immediate assistance for errorless responding and then delays this prompt by a few seconds over teaching trials. In least intrusive prompts, the instructor uses graduated assistance (e.g., from verbal direction to a model to physical guidance) until the student makes the target response. Graduated guidance involves giving progressive physical assistance as needed. Several other authors have also provided comprehensive reviews that support the effectiveness of these methods (Demchak, 1990; Schoen, 1986). Research additionally shows that effective interventions are characterized by defined feedback, which includes descriptive praise for a correct response and instructive error correction (Werts, Wolery, Holcombe, & Gast, 1995). For example, if a student reads the word *milk* correctly, the teacher may say, "Good, 'milk,'" or may expand this to include additional feedback, "Good, 'milk' is found in the dairy section of the store." If read incorrectly, the teacher may say, "No, the word is 'milk'" or add further instruction by saying, "No, the word is 'milk.' M-I-L-K, 'milk.' Now you say it."

Although these studies offer clear guidance on defining and teaching target skills, they are less clear on how to do so in general education settings. As Snell (1997) has noted, most intervention research has occurred in self-contained special education classrooms or schools, although some studies have been conducted in community settings. Surveys show that most experts recommend the use of systematic instruction in inclusive school contexts (Jackson, Ryndak, & Billingsley, 2000), but these strategies may not currently be endorsed by general educators in these contexts (Billingsley & Kelley, 1994). McDonnell (1998) has noted that general educators may rely on curriculum-focused strategies rather than individual student-focused strategies because of the need to cover content with a large group of students.

In the 1990s, limited evidence emerged providing models for embedding individual student-focused strategies in general education settings. One option is to train peer tutors. In both Collins et al. (1995) and Wolery et al. (1994), peers who were nondisabled learned to use systematic prompting methods that resulted in the students with disabilities mastering new skills. A second option is to embed this instruction in the context of a cooperative learning group. In Hunt et al. (1994), students with significant cognitive disabilities learned basic skills like reaching and grasping in the context of a general education group activity. A third alternative is to use observational learning. For example, in Werts, Caldwell, and Wolery (1996), students learned daily routines by watching their peers perform these tasks. General education teachers may also be able to make slight modifications in their style of group instruction to promote learning. Collins, Hall, Branson, and Holden (1999) found that students with moderate cognitive disabilities were able to learn factual statements that the general education teacher presented repeatedly throughout a group lecture.

Students may also learn to use self-instructional strategies, such as following picture cues (Wehmeyer, Agran, & Hughes, 1998). In a study by Krantz, MacDuff, and McClannahan (1993), students with autism learned to participate in family routines by following picture activity schedules. Students may also learn to follow audiotaped cues to perform each step of a daily routine (Grossi, 1998). Whether using pictures or audio cues, the student learns to refer to the prompt and then perform the activity without assistance. Recently, Agran, Blanchard, and Wehmeyer (2000) demonstrated a self-determined model of learning in which students learned to identify a problem, potential solutions to a problem, barriers to solving the problem, and consequences of their solution. For example, the teacher may begin by having the student consider the question, "What do I want to learn?"

Enhancing Generalization

To demonstrate achievement of state standards, students may have to demonstrate generalization as well as acquisition of skills. One empirically supported method to promote generalization for students with severe disabilities is general case instruction, in which the teacher selects a set of examples that sample the variations students will encounter in their daily routines (Horner, McDonnell, & Bellamy, 1986). After training across settings (e.g., following directions), the teacher assesses performance in untrained contexts (e.g., novel streets) to determine if generalization has occurred. Research has also shown that classroom simulations of a community activity, such as using an automated teller, can be effective when paired with some opportunities for community practice (Browder & Bambara, 2000). To demonstrate generalization of academic responses, teachers may use a variety of teaching materials. For example, to link to a state reading standard on gaining information from text, students may use a new sight word to locate information in a newspaper headline, textbook caption, and a teacher handout.

Incorporating the Use of Assistive Technology

To make AYP, students may also benefit from the use of augmentative and alternative communication (AAC; Blischak, Loncke, & Waller, 1997; Mirenda, 1990). Kozleski (1991) used time delay to teach individuals with severe cognitive and physical impairments to match objects with pictures on a communication board and then to use these pictures to make requests. Similarly, Dyches (1998) used a system of least intrusive prompting to teach four elementary schoolchildren with autism and severe cognitive disabilities to use communication switches. Researchers have also taught students to use unaided AAC systems, such as sign language. McNaughton and Light (1993) taught a young woman with severe cognitive disabilities to use manual signs in naturally occurring contexts throughout her day; Venn et al. (1993) taught three children with autism and severe disabilities to sign during snack time.

Research has also shown that the introduction of AAC can decrease problem behavior through what is called functional communication training (Carr & Durand, 1985; Durand & Carr, 1991). Researchers have taught students to request attention by signing "help" (Horner & Day, 1991) or pressing a button that yields a statement such as "I need help" (Horner, Sprague, O'Brien, & Heathfield, 1990), and to request an object (Durand & Kishi, 1987) or a break (Bird, Dores, Moniz, & Robinson, 1989) with sign language. AAC has further been shown to improve interactions between students with severe disabilities and their peers when peers receive instruction in eliciting conversational turn taking (Hunt, Alwell & Goetz, 1991; Hunt, Alwell, Goetz, & Sailor, 1990). This use of AAC may also help students participate in inclusive classrooms (Mirenda & Calculator, 1993). While research supports using AAC with students who have severe intellectual disabilities to improve communication and replace problem behavior, additional work is needed to foster understanding about how AAC can help students access the general curriculum.

Use of Evidence-Based Practices

Research on skill acquisition offers many examples of effective practices, but an important concern is whether practitioners actually implement these practices. Ayres, Meyer, Erevelles, and Park-Lee (1994) surveyed special education teachers in five states within regions known for their efforts to develop quality educational programs for students with severe disabilities. Teachers' self-reports revealed that the presence of best practice indicators (e.g., inclusion, data-based instruction, home–school communication) was related to both teacher skill and implementation difficulty. Teachers described time constraints and weak administrative support as two major obstacles in implementing research-based practices. For example, teachers found it difficult to give students the individualized instruction they needed.

Surveys of general educators also have found mixed levels of implementation of evidence-based practices. Agran and Alper (2000) surveyed general education teachers to identify the instructional strategies they used with students with disabilities in their classes. The general education teachers reported using a few evidence-based procedures, such as providing students with increasing or decreasing assistance as needed, but they used few targeted strategies, such as time delay and picture cues.

Teachers appear to find it challenging to create access to the general curriculum. In a survey by Agran, Alper, and Wehmeyer (2002), special education teachers ranked grooming, social skills, communication, choice making, and problem solving as more important than academic skills in creating access to the general curriculum for their students with severe disabilities. Although their students were involved in general education classes, the teachers did not necessarily consider access to the general curriculum appropriate for them and did not think their students should be held accountable to the same standards as their peers. It is not clear whether these findings reflect the recent emphasis on access to the general curriculum. Williams, Fox, Thousand, and Fox (1990) found that teachers were more favorable about inclusive practices if they had experience with them. Thus, it seems plausible that teachers may change their perspective on teaching academic content standards as they gain experience with this practice and as states create alternate achievement standards that teachers can use as benchmarks for their students' progress.

Building on Evidence-Based Practices

The limited research on academic content instruction for this population creates a challenge for practitioners seeking examples from the literature. The current era is one of curricular reform, with educators challenged to create ways to teach and assess all students on state academic content standards at each grade level. Wehmeyer et al. (2001) has recommended using team decision making for curriculum planning to access the general curriculum. Prior research on the benefits of educational teams for this population supports this approach (e.g., Ellingston et al., 2000; Salisbury et al., 1997). The requirement to address standards in reading, math, and science does not preclude a continued focus on functional skills.

Future IEPs for students with severe disabilities will probably contain a blend of academic and functional objectives. What is different is that the IEP team begins with the assumption that every student should receive instruction on the academic content for his or her grade level.

Some research also indicates that students with severe disabilities can learn academic skills, such as the generalization of picture categories (Hupp, 1986) and sight word reading (Gast, Doyle, Wolery, Ault, & Farmer, 1991). Students with severe disabilities can benefit from whole-group instruction or cooperative learning activities within a typical class, but they may also need individualized instruction with systematic prompting and fading to meet expectations for yearly progress. Moreover, students may need opportunities to practice skills across a variety of settings. An augmentative communication system and other assistive technology may also be needed to provide students a means to expand their use of symbolic communication related to academic content.

Conclusion

This chapter provides a snapshot of special education for students with severe disabilities in the early 21st century by focusing on two requirements of NCLB. What should not be special is reliance on a separate functional curriculum; students with severe disabilities need access to the general curriculum. To show AYP in reading, math, science, and other state standards, students need instruction in grade-level academic content. What may be special are the achievement levels targeted (e.g., alternate achievement standards for the grade level), the supports used to access the curriculum (e.g., assistive technology, systematic instruction), and the methods used to document achievement (e.g., alternate assessments). What may also be special are the additional goals targeted through the IEP process that go beyond the state's academic content standards (e.g., functional goals; social inclusion).

REFERENCES

Agran, M., & Alper, S. (2000). Curriculum and instruction in general education: Implications for service delivery and personnel preparation. *Journal of the Association for Persons with Severe Handicaps, 25,* 167–174.

Agran, M., Alper, S., & Wehmeyer, M. (2002). Access to the general curriculum for students with significant cognitive disabilities: What it means to teachers. *Education and Training in Mental Retardation and Developmental Disabilities, 37,* 123–133.

Agran, M., Blanchard, C., & Wehmeyer, M. L. (2000). Promoting transition goals and self-determination through student self- directed learning: The self-determined learning model of instruction. *Education and Training in Mental Retardation and Developmental Disabilities, 35,* 351–364.

Ault, M. J., Wolery, M., Doyle, P. M., & Gast, D. L. (1989). Review of comparative studies in the instruction of students with moderate and severe handicaps. *Exceptional Children, 55,* 346–356.

Ayres, B. J., Meyer, L. H., Erevelles, N., & Park-Lee. S. (1994). Easy for you to say: Teacher perspectives on implementing most promising practices. *Journal of the Association for Persons with Severe Handicaps, 19,* 84–93.

Billingsley, F., & Kelley, B. (1994). An examination of the acceptability of instructional practices for students with severe disabilities in general education settings. *Journal of the Association for Persons with Severe Handicaps, 19,* 75–83.

Bird, F., Dores, P., Moniz, D., & Robinson, J. (1989). Reducing severe aggressive and self-injurious behaviors with functional communication training: Direct, collateral and generalized results. *American Journal on Mental Retardation, 94,* 37–48.

Blischak, D., Loncke, F., & Waller, A. (1997). Intervention for persons with developmental disabilities. In L. Lloyd, D. Fuller, & H. Arvidson (Eds.), *Augmentative and alternative communication: A handbook of principles and practices* (pp. 299–388). Boston: Allyn & Bacon.

Browder, D. (1987). *Assessment of individuals with severe handicaps.* Baltimore: Brookes.

Browder, D. (2001). *Curriculum and assessment for students with moderate and severe disabilities.* New York: Guilford.

Browder, D. M., Ahlgrim-Dezell, L. A., Flowers, C., Karvonen, M., Spooner, F., & Algozzine, R. (2005). How states implement alternate assessment for students with disabilities and recommendations for national policy. *Journal of Disability and Policy Studies, 15,* 209–220.

Browder, D. M., & Bambara, L. M. (2000). Home and community. In M. E. Snell & F. Brown (Eds.), *Instruction of students with severe disabilities* (5th ed., pp. 543–582). Upper Saddle River, NJ: Merrill/Prentice Hall.

Browder, D., Flowers, C., Ahlgrim-Delzell, L., Karvonen, M., Spooner, F., & Algozzine, R. (2004). The alignment of alternate assessment content with academic and functional curricula. *The Journal of Special Education, 37,* 211–223.

Browder, D. M., & Grasso, E. (1999). Teaching money skills to individuals with mental retardation: A literature review with practical applications. *Remedial and Special Education, 20,* 297–308.

Browder, D. M., Karvonen, M., Davis, S., Fallin, K., &

Courtade-Little, C. (2005). The impact of teacher training on state alternate assessment scores. *Exceptional Children, 71,* 267–282.

Browder, D. M., & Snell, M. E. (2000). Functional academics. In M. E. Snell & F. Brown (Eds.), *Instruction of students with severe disabilities* (5th ed, pp. 453–492). Upper Saddle River, NJ: Merrill/Prentice Hall.

Browder, D. M., Spooner, F., Algozzine, R., Ahlgrim-Dezell, L. A., Flowers, C., & Karvonen, M. (in press). *What we know and need to know about alternate assessment.*

Browder, D. M., & Xin, Y. (1998). A review and meta-analysis of sight word instruction with students with disabilities. *The Journal of Special Education, 32,* 130–153.

Brown, F., & Snell, M. E. (2000). Measurement, evaluation, and analysis. In M. E. Snell & F. Brown (Eds.), *Instruction of students with severe disabilities* (5th ed., pp. 173–206). Upper Saddle River, NJ: Merrill/Prentice Hall.

Brown, L., Branston, M. B., Hamre-Nietupski, S., Pumpian, I., Certo, N., & Gruenewald, L. (1979). A strategy for developing chronological age-appropriate and functional curricular content for severely handicapped adolescents and young adults. *The Journal of Special Education, 13,* 81–90.

Carr, E., & Durand, V. (1985). Reducing behavior problems through functional communication training. *Journal of Applied Behavior Analysis, 18,* 111–126.

Chadsey-Rusch, J., & Halle, J. (1992). The application of general case instruction to the requesting repertoires of learners with severe disabilities. *Journal of the Association for Persons with Severe Handicaps, 17,* 121–132.

Cipani, E. C., & Spooner, F. (1994). *Curricular and instructional approaches for persons with severe disabilities.* Boston: Allyn & Bacon.

Collins, B. C., Branson, T. A., & Hall, M. (1995). Teaching generalized reading of cooking product labels to adolescents with mental disabilities through the use of key words taught by peer tutors. *Education and Training in Mental Retardation and Developmental Disabilities, 30,* 65–75.

Collins, B. C., Hall, M., Branson, T. A., & Holder, M. (1999). Acquisition of related and unrelated factual information delivered by a teacher in an inclusive setting. *Journal of Behavioral Education, 9,* 223–238.

Demchak, M. A. (1990). Response prompting and fading methods: A review. *American Journal on Mental Retardation, 94,* 603–615.

Durand, V., & Carr, E. (1991). Functional communication training to reduce challenging behavior: Maintenance and application to new settings. *Journal of Applied Behavior Analysis, 24,* 251–264.

Durand, V., & Kishi, G. (1987). Reducing severe behavior problems among persons with dual sensory impairments: An evaluation of a technical assistance model. *Journal of the Association for Persons with Severe Handicaps, 12,* 2–10.

Dyches, T. (1998). Effects of switch training on the communication of children with autism and severe disabilities. *Focus on Autism and Other Developmental Disabilities, 13,* 151–163.

Ellingston, S. A., Miltenberger, R. G., Stricker, J., Galensky, T. L., & Garlinghouse, M. (2000). Functional assessment and intervention for challenging behaviors in the classroom by general classroom teachers. *Journal of Positive Behavioral Interventions, 2,* 85–97.

Erwin, E. J., & Soodak, L. C. (1995). I never knew I could stand up to the system: Families' perspectives on pursuing inclusive education. *Journal of the Association for Persons with Severe Handicaps, 12,* 87–95.

Etscheidt, S. (2002). Extended school year services: A review of eligibility criteria and program appropriateness. *Research and Practice for Persons with Severe Disabilities, 27,* 188–203.

Falvey, M. (1989). *Community-based curriculum: Instructional strategies for students with severe handicaps.* Baltimore: Brookes.

Ferguson, D. L., & Baumgart, D. (1991). Partial participation revisited. *Journal of the Association for Persons with Severe Handicaps, 16,* 218–227.

Feuer, M. J., Towne, L., & Shavelson, R. J. (2002). Scientific culture and educational research. *Educational Researcher, 31*(8), 4–14.

Ford, A., Schnorr, R., Meyer, L., Davern, L., Black, J., & Dempsey, P. (1989). *The Syracuse community-referenced curriculum guide for students with moderate and severe disabilities.* Baltimore: Brookes.

Gast, D. L., Doyle, P. M., Wolery, M., & Ault, M. J., & Farmer, J. A. (1991). Assessing the acquisition of incidental information by secondary-age students with mental retardation: Comparison of response prompting strategies. *American Journal on Mental Retardation, 96,* 63–80.

Giangreco, M. F., Cloninger, C. J., & Iverson, V. S. (1998). *Choosing options and accommodations for children* (2nd ed.). Baltimore: Brookes.

Grossi, T.A. (1998). Using a self-operated auditory prompting system to improve the work performance of two employees with severe disabilities. *Journal of the Association for Persons with Severe Handicaps, 23,* 149–154.

Horner, R. H., & Day, H. (1991). The effects of response efficiency on functionally equivalent competing behaviors. *Journal of Applied Behavior Analysis, 24,* 719–732.

Horner, R. H., Jones, D. N., & Williams, J. A. (1985). A functional approach to teaching generalized street crossing. *Journal of the Association for Persons with Severe Handicaps, 10,* 71–78.

Horner, R. H., McDonnell, J. J., & Bellamy, G. T. (1986). Teaching generalized skills: General case instruction in simulation and community settings. In R. H. Horner, L. H. Meyer, & H. D. Fredericks (Eds.), *Education of learners with severe handicaps: Exemplary service strategies* (pp. 289–314). Baltimore: Brookes.

Horner, R., Sprague, J., O'Brien, M., & Heathfield, L. (1990). The role of response efficiency in the reduction of problem behavior through functional equivalence training: A case study. *Journal of the Association for Persons with Severe Handicaps, 15,* 91–97.

Hughes, C., Hugo, K., & Blatt, J. (1996). Self-instructional intervention for teaching generalized problem-solving within a functional task sequence. *American Journal on Mental Retardation, 100,* 565–579.

Hunt, P., Alwell, M., & Goetz, L. (1991). Interacting with peers through conversation turntaking with a communication book adaptation. *Augmentative and Alternative Communication, 7,* 117–126.

Hunt, P., Alwell, M., Goetz, L., & Sailor, W. (1990). Generalized effects of conversation skill training. *Journal of the Association for Persons with Severe Handicaps, 15,* 250–260.

Hunt, P., Staub, D., Alwell, M., & Goetz, L. (1994). Achievement by all students within the context of cooperating groups. *Journal of the Association for Persons with Severe Handicaps, 19,* 290–301.

Hupp, S. C. (1986). Effects of stimulus mode on the acquisition, transfer, and generalization of categories by severely mentally retarded children and adolescents. *American Journal on Mental Deficiency, 90,* 579–587.

Individuals with Disabilities Education Act of 1990, 20 U.S.C. § 1400 *et seq.* (1990) (Amended 1997).

Jackson, L., Ryndak, D. L., & Billingsley, F. (2000). Useful practices in inclusive education: A preliminary view of what experts in moderate to severe disabilities are saying. *Journal of the Association for Persons with Severe Handicaps, 25,* 129–141.

Katims, D. S. (2000). Literacy instruction for people with mental retardation: Historical highlights and contemporary analysis. *Education and Training in Mental Retardation and Developmental Disabilities, 35,* 3–15.

Kennedy, C. H., & Haring, T. G. (1993). Teaching choice making during social interactions to students with profound multiple disabilities. *Journal of Applied Behavior Analysis, 26,* 63–76.

Kleinert, H. L., & Kearns, J. F. (1999). A validation study of the performance indicators and learner outcomes of Kentucky's alternate assessment for students with significant disabilities. *Journal of the Association for Persons with Severe Handicaps, 24,* 100–110.

Kleinert, H. L., Kearns, J. F., & Kennedy, S. (1997). Accountability for all students: Kentucky's alternate portfolio assessment for students with moderate and severe cognitive disabilities. *Journal of the Association for Persons with Severe Handicaps, 22,* 88–101.

Kliewer, C. (1998). Citizenship in the literature community: An ethnography of children with Down Syndrome and the written word. *Exceptional Children, 64,* 167–180.

Koegel, L., Koegel, R. L., Shoshan, Y., & McNerney, E. (1999). Pivotal response intervention II: Preliminary long-term outcome data. *Journal of the Association for Persons with Severe Handicaps, 24,* 186–198.

Kozleski, E. (1991). Expectant delay procedure for teaching requests. *Augmentative and Alternative Communication, 7,* 11–19.

Krantz, P. L., MacDuff, M. T., & McClannahan, L. E. (1993). Programming participation in family activities for children with autism. Parents' use of photographic activity schedules. *Journal of Applied Behavior Analysis, 26,* 137–138.

McDonnell, J. (1998). Instruction for students with severe disabilities in general education settings. *Education and Training in Mental Retardation, 33,* 199–215.

McDonnell, J. J., & McFarland, S. (1988). A comparison of forward and concurrent chaining strategies in teaching laundromat skills to students with severe handicaps. *Research and Intervention in Developmental Disabilities, 9,* 177–194.

McNaughton, D., & Light, J. (1993). Teaching facilitators to support the communication skills of an adult with severe cognitive disabilities: A case study. *Augmentative and Alternative Communication, 5,* 35–41.

Meyer, L., Eichinger, J., & Park-Lee, S. (1987). A validation of program quality indicators in educational services for students with severe disabilities. *Journal of the Association for Persons with Severe Handicaps, 12,* 251–263.

Miner, C., & Bates, P. (1997). The effect of person centered planning activities on the IEP/transition planning process. *Education and Training in Mental Retardation and Developmental Disabilities, 32,* 105–112.

Mirenda, P. (1990). Augmentative and alternative communication techniques. In J. Downing (Ed.), *Teaching communication skills to students with severe disabilities* (pp. 119–138). Baltimore: Brookes.

Mirenda, P., & Calculator, S. (1993). Enhancing curricula design. *Clinics in Communication Disorders, 3,* 43–58.

Neel, R. S., & Billingsley, F. F. (1989). *IMPACT: A functional curriculum handbook for students with moderate to severe disabilities.* Baltimore: Brookes.

Nietupski, J., Hamre-Nietupski, S., Curtin, S., & Shrikanth, K. (1997). A review of curricular research in severe disabilities from 1976–1995 in six selected journals. *The Journal of Special Education, 31,* 36–55.

The No Child Left Behind Act of 2001, 20 U.S.C. 70 § 6301 *et seq.* (2002).

Ruef, M. B., & Turnbull, A. P. (2002). The perspectives of individuals with cognitive disabilities and/or autism on their lives and their problem behavior. *Research and Practice for Persons with Severe Disabilities, 27,* 125– 140.

Ryndak, D. L., & Alper, S. (Eds.). (1996). *Curriculum content for students with moderate and severe disabilities in inclusive settings.* Boston: Allyn & Bacon.

Salisbury, C. L., Evans, I. M., & Palombaro, M. M. (1997). Collaborative problem solving to promote the inclusion of young children with significant disabilities in primary grades. *Exceptional Children, 63,* 195–209.

Schoen, S. F. (1986). Assistance procedures to facilitate the transfer of stimulus control: Review and analysis. *Education and Training of the Mentally Retarded, 21,* 62–74.

Schoen, S. F., & Ogden, S. (1995). Impact of time delay, observational learning, and attentional cueing upon word recognition during integrated small group instruction. *Journal of Autism and Developmental Disorders, 25,* 503–519.

Shriner, J. G. (2000). Legal perspectives on school outcomes assessment for students with disabilities. *The Journal of Special Education, 33,* 232–239.

Siegel-Causey, E., & Allinder, R. M. (1998). Using alternate assessment for students with severe disabilities: Alignment with best practices. *Education and Training in Mental Retardation and Developmental Disabilities, 33,* 168–178.

Snell, M. E. (1997). Teaching children and young adults with mental retardation in school programs: Current research. *Behavior Change, 14,* 1–33.

Snell, M. E., & Brown, F. (2000). *Instruction of students with severe disabilities* (5th ed.). Upper Saddle River, NJ: Merrill/Prentice Hall.

Snell, M. E., Lewis, A. P., & Houghton, A. (1989). Acquisition and maintenance of toothbrushing skills by students with cerebral palsy and mental retardation. *Journal of the Association for Persons with Severe Handicaps, 14,* 216–226.

Thompson, S., & Thurlow, M. (2001). *2001 state special education outcomes: A report on state activities at the beginning of a new decade.* Minneapolis: University of Minnesota, National Center on Educational Outcomes.

U.S. Department of Education. (2003, December 9). Title I—Improving the Academic Achievement of the Disadvantaged; Final Rule, 68 *Fed. Reg.* 236.

Venn, M., Wolery, M., Fleming, L., DeCesare, L., Morris, A., & Cuffs, M. (1993). Effects of teaching preschooler peers to use mand-model procedure during snack activities. *American Journal of Speech Language Pathology, 3,* 38–46.

Wehmeyer, M. L., Agran, M., & Hughes, C. (1998). *Teaching self-determination to students with disabilities: Basic skills for successful transition.* Baltimore: Brookes.

Wehmeyer, M. L., Agran, M., & Lattin, D. (2001). Achieving access to the general curriculum for students with mental retardation: A curriculum decision-making model. *Education and Training in Mental Retardation and Developmental Disabilities, 36,* 327–342.

Werts, M. G., Caldwell, N. K., & Wolery, M. (1996). Peer modeling of response chains: Observational learning by students with disabilities. *Journal of Applied Behavior Analysis, 29,* 53–66.

Werts, M. G., Wolery, M., Holcombe, A., & Gast, D. L. (1995). Instructive feedback: Review of parameters and effects. *Journal of Behavioral Education, 5,* 55–75.

Westling, D. L., & Fox, L. (2000). *Teaching students with severe disabilities.* Upper Saddle River, NJ: Merrill/Prentice Hall.

Wilcox, B., & Bellamy, G. T. (1987). *The activities catalog: An alternative curriculum for youth and adults with severe disabilities.* Baltimore: Brookes.

Williams, W., Fox, T. S., Thousand, J., & Fox, W. (1990). Level of acceptance and implementation of best practices in the education of students with severe handicaps in Vermont. *Education and Training in Mental Retardation, 25,* 120–131.

Wolery, M., Werts, M. G., Snyder, E. D., & Caldwell, N. K. (1994). Efficacy of constant time delay implemented by peer tutors in general education classrooms. *Journal of Behavioral Education, 4,* 415–436.

Chapter 4

What Is Special About Special Education for English Language Learners?

Janette K. Klingner and **Margarita Bianco**

What is special about special education for English language learners? In this chapter we provide an overview of bilingual/ESL (English as a Second Language) special education. Born in 1973, the field of bilingual/ESL special education is more than just a combination of the separate fields of mainstream special education, bilingual education, and ESL education (Baca & Cervantes, 1998). It is its own entity, with its own research base, and includes specialized teacher education and professional development programs, curricula, assessment procedures, and instructional practices (Baca & De Valenzuela, 1994). We describe effective practices that have been developed in bilingual/ESL special education or with English language learners with learning disabilities (LD). When applicable, to some extent we also discuss lessons learned from research with English language learners who may be struggling but do not necessarily have disabilities. We finish the chapter by addressing the question, "Does the use of these practices necessitate special education?"

Background

Who are English language learners with disabilities? At present, *English language learner* is the preferred term to describe students with less than full proficiency in English, and includes students with adequate conversational skills who have not yet developed full cognitive academic language proficiency (Gersten & Baker, 2000). We know that students with disabilities are a very heterogeneous group. This is also quite true for English language learners, who vary in language proficiency, socioeconomic status, previous schooling experiences, nationality, immigration status, and generation in the United States, among other factors (August & Hakuta, 1997).

The percentage of English language learners attending schools in the United States is growing rapidly. In 2003, the U.S. Department of Education reported that there were more than 3.5 million English language learners in U.S. schools. According to the 2000 census, the percentage of the school-age population speaking a home language different from English was 42.6% in California and 32.4% in Texas. This percentage was over 20% in Arizona, Florida, Nevada, New Jersey, New Mexico, New York, and Rhode Island, and in 12 other states the percentage surpassed 10% (U.S. Census Bureau, 2003). If current trends continue, by the year 2030, about 40% of the school population across the United States will speak English as a second language (U.S. Department of Education, 2003). The population of English language learners is no longer confined to certain geographic areas, but has spread to the extent that now virtually all of the nation's school districts include at least some students who speak a language other than English at home (Zehler et al., 2003). The majority of English language learners, or about 77%, speak Spanish as their first language. Also, it is notable that Hispanics are the fastest growing ethnic group in U.S. schools, and have passed African Americans as the largest minority group in the United States (U.S. Census Bureau, 2001). Yet services for English language learners with disabilities appear to be inadequate. In a recent survey of school districts across the nation, Zehler and colleagues (2003) found that 75% of districts serving English language learners with disabilities do not provide programs designed especially for these students, and the majority of English language learners with disabilities receive special education services in segregated contexts. Compared to English language learners without disabilities, English language learners with disabilities are more likely to receive fewer language support services and to be instructed in English only. Zehler and colleagues also found that the instructional programs provided to English language learners with disabilities are not as aligned with state content and performance standards as are programs for other students.

There is still much we do not know about English language learners placed in special education programs. The limited data we do have suggest that most English language learners in special education struggle with reading. They are most often identified as having LD (56%); the second most common category is speech and language impairments (24%; U.S. Department of Education, 2003). Yet we know little about other characteristics of these students; only a few researchers have studied subpopulations of English language learners in special education. Artiles and colleagues (Artiles, Rueda, Salazar, & Higareda, 2002; Artiles, Trent, & Palmer, 2004) conducted research on English language learners in Southern California. They disaggregated data by language proficiency and other factors in examining placement patterns across special educational programs, grade levels, and language programs (straight English immersion, modified English immersion, or bilingual) in 11 urban districts during the 1998–99 school year (see Note). They found that English language learners in English immersion classrooms were more likely to be placed in special education than students in modified English immersion or bilingual programs. Notably, English language learners who tested as limited in their native language *and* English showed the highest rates of special education placement. Artiles et al. concluded that we need to know more about the specific characteristics of English language learners, particularly students who test as limited in multiple languages.

Ruiz (1995) conducted an in-depth study of 10 children in a self-contained bilingual special education classroom in a California elementary school. Her purpose was to develop profiles of the English language learners placed in special education. She found three types of students, ranging from those with severe language learning disabilities to those who seemed not to have disabilities at all, and emphasized the importance of the instructional context in revealing the range of students' communicative and academic competencies. Some students appeared to be very competent in some settings but not in others. This research has important implications for those making eligibility decisions and points to the need to observe students across settings and in varied contexts.

Compounding these issues is the phenomenon that English language learners tend to be disproportionately represented in special education programs (experiencing both under- and over-identification, depending on the district; Artiles & Trent, 2000). We know that students struggle in school for a variety of reasons, only some of which are related to intrinsic deficits or disabilities. Some students underachieve because of inadequate instruction or a lack of opportunity to learn (Harry & Klingner, 2005). Additional factors that can affect learning include a mismatch between home and school cultures, challenges attributable to the second language acquisition process, socioeconomic and related variables, and experiences with discrimination. Collier and Hoover (1987) noted that some behaviors that appear to indicate a learning disability may be normal for the child's cultural background or a by-product of the acculturation process. Also, because the characteristics of students acquiring a new language in many ways parallel those of students with language and learning disabilities, it can be very difficult to determine who actually has a disability (Ortiz, 1997; Ortiz et al., 1985; Ortiz, García, Wheeler, & Maldonado-Colon, 1986). Second-language acquisition is a complicated process, influenced by many factors, including but not limited to the sociocultural environment, language proficiency in the first language, students' and others' attitudes toward the native language and English, personality attributes, and perceived status (August & Hakuta, 1997).

It is important for school personnel to identify the multiple possible sources of a student's difficulties so that they can provide appropriate prereferral interventions, identify additional sources of support, and justify a possible referral to special education (Barrera, 1995; S. B. Garcia & Ortiz, 1988; Harry & Klingner, 2005; Klingner & Artiles, 2003). Once a student has been referred for a formal special education evaluation, the challenges continue (Wagner, Francis, & Morris, 2005). Historically, the majority of English language learners have been assessed inappropriately due to the misapplication of tests used to identify an IQ–achievement discrepancy (Jiménez, Siegel, & Lopez, 2003), misunderstandings about students' language abilities (Oller, 1991), and cultural differences (Ortiz & Maldonado-Colon, 1986; Salend, Garrick Duhaney, & Montgomery, 2002). Three different studies of psychologists' assessment practices found that English language learners were almost always tested only in English, regardless of their dominant language, and that interpretations of test results failed to take into account issues of language difference or the amount of English instruction students had received (Barrera Metz, 1988; Maldonado-Colon, 1986; Ochoa, Powell, & Robles-Piña, 1996; Ochoa, Rivera, & Powell, 1997). For example, in their sample of 859 school psychologists from eight states who indicated they had prior experience conducting bilingual psychoeducational assessments, Ochoa et al. (1996) found that only 6% reported asking for the students' home language and 1% attempted to determine if a discrepancy between achievement and ability occurred in both English and the student's home language.

The research base in bilingual/ESL special education regarding instructional practices is limited (Artiles et al., 2004; Gersten & Baker, 2000). In general, research in the field of bilingual/ESL special education has focused more on referral, identification, and assessment issues than on validating instructional practices. Gersten and Baker lamented the lack of quality and quantity in instructional intervention studies involving English language learners with disabilities. Many best practices are based on research with English language learners *without* disabilities (Müller & Markowitz, 2004).

Special education researchers typically have omitted culturally and linguistically diverse students from their samples, or have not adequately described variables related to diversity. Artiles, Trent, and Kuan (1997) conducted a review of 22 years of empirical research published in special education journals and noted a substantial disregard for diversity issues. They described the proportion of articles that addressed issues of diversity as alarmingly low. Ortiz (1997) cautioned that language dominance and proficiency are important research variables that are too often avoided, and that this practice limits the application of such studies, especially for teachers who have culturally and linguistically diverse students in their classes. Bos and Fletcher (1997) and Keogh, Gallimore, and Weisner (1997) emphasized the importance of researchers' including sufficient information about the language proficiency, ethnicity, and other characteristics of participants in their reports. When English language learners are included in the samples of intervention studies, data should be disaggregated to show how treatment(s) may have differentially affected students with varying levels of English proficiency and other characteristics.

Instruction for English Language Learners with Disabilities

The best programs for English language learners with disabilities incorporate supportive, culturally responsive learning environments and validated instructional practices (Ortiz, 1997, 2001). Optimal programs include native language instruction and a focus on English language development in addition to validated practices in literacy and the content areas. It is this heightened focus on *language* that makes bilingual/ESL special education "special" in comparison with generic special education. In this section of the chapter, we first list key principles of instruction grounded in research with culturally and linguistically diverse populations with special needs. We then describe culturally responsive learning environments and validated instructional practices.

Instructional Principles

We draw from various reviews of the literature in summarizing what experts have recommended as best practice for English language learners with disabilities (Gersten & Baker, 2000; Müller & Markowitz, 2004; Ortiz, 2001). Gersten and Baker's review is unique in that they used a qualitative multivocal method in which they conducted interviews with professional educators and researchers around the country in addition to synthesizing the extant literature. They found that effective instruction for English language learners with disabilities

- incorporates the native language in strategic ways (Cardelle-Elawar, 1990; Jiménez & Gersten, 1999; Klingner & Vaughn, 1996; Lopez-Reyna, 1996; Miniccuci et al., 1995; Tikunoff et al., 1991);
- helps students access and connect with their prior knowledge and build new knowledge (Brophy, 1992; Leinhardt, 1992; Saunders, O'Brien, Lennon, & McLean, 1998);
- assists students in applying concepts to the tasks at hand as well as to their own lives (Burke, Hagan, & Grossen, 1998);
- incorporates features of students' home cultures in the curriculum (Au & Kawakami, 1994; Ortiz & Wilkinson, 1991);
- provides multiple and varied opportunities for students to review previously learned concepts (Cummins, 1984; Ortiz & Wilkinson, 1991; Willig, Swedo, & Ortiz, 1987);
- builds and uses vocabulary as a "curricular anchor" (Gersten & Baker, 2000; Saunders et al., 1998);
- preteaches critical vocabulary (Rousseau, Tam, & Ramnarain, 1993);
- uses visuals to reinforce concepts and vocabulary (E. Reyes & Bos, 1998; Rousseau et al., 1993);
- focuses on higher order thinking and active problem solving (Gersten & Baker, 2000; Willig et al., 1987);
- emphasizes collaborative learning activities, including cooperative learning and peer tutoring (Gersten & Baker, 2000; Klingner & Vaughn, 1996, 2000; Muñiz-Swicegood, 1994);
- provides students with frequent opportunities to use language for both conversational and academic purposes (McGroarty, 1989; Willig et al., 1987);
- includes formal and informal opportunities for students to practice throughout the day (Cardelle-Elawar, 1990; Gersten & Baker, 2000);
- promotes active engagement and uses time effectively (Padrón & Waxman, 1999);
- moderates cognitive and language demands (August & Hakuta, 1997; Gersten & Baker, 2000); and
- provides focused, explicit feedback that is adapted to the learner's level (Cardelle-Elawar, 1990; Henderson & Landesman, 1995).

Gersten and Baker (2000) also identified practices that can hinder students' development, such as (a) insufficient attention to language development, (b) insufficient attention to cultural variables, and (c) insufficient attention to students' background knowledge.

Supportive, Culturally Responsive Learning Environments

The cultural and social contexts within which instruction takes place are of critical importance (Alvermann, 2005; Au, 1995; S. B. Garcia, Wilkinson, & Ortiz, 1995; Lucas, Henz, & Donato, 1990; Moore, 1996). School climates that foster academic success are caring communities that reflect the philosophy that all students can learn and that educators are responsible for helping them learn (Cummins, 1989). Positive school environments are characterized by (a) strong administrative leadership, (b) high expectations for student achievement, (c) challenging and appropriate curricula and instruction, (d) a safe and orderly environment, and (e) ongoing, systematic evaluation of student progress (Ortiz, 2001). "Most learning problems can be prevented if students are in positive school and classroom contexts that accommodate individual differences" (Ortiz, 2001, p. 1).

Contexts for learning should be grounded in the belief that culturally and linguistically diverse students can excel in academic endeavors if (a) their culture, language, heritage, and experiences are valued and used to facilitate their learning and development; (b) they are provided access to high-quality teachers, programs, curricula, and resources; and (c) they are taught with validated instructional practices (Nieto, 2002). Planning should begin with the assumption that every learner "brings a valid language and culture to the instructional context" (M. Reyes, 1992, p. 427). In presenting recommendations from the Hispanic Dropout Project, Lockwood and Secada (1999) underscored "the importance of respect and its place in schooling as a basic, fundamental condition without which Hispanic students will find it difficult to achieve academic success" (p. 4). One way to do this is by tapping into and building on students' cultural funds of knowledge (Moll, 1990, 1992; Moll & González, 1994). Tapping into such cultural funds of knowledge does more than help students activate schema; it is a way of validating their ways of thinking, acting, and being.

It is essential for teachers and other school personnel to establish connections within local communities and to build collaborative relationships with families (G. E. Garcia, 1991). As Jiménez (2001) has emphasized, it is important for teachers to get to know their students individually and make an effort to learn more about their families and communities. Parents of English language learners should be considered valued partners in the education of their children (Cummins, 1994). When educators become involved with culturally and linguistically diverse families, they are more likely to develop understanding and appreciation for the social, linguistic, and cultural contexts in which children are being raised (Ortiz, 1997, 2001).

Much can be learned from observational studies of effective schools and classrooms. Several themes cut across this work. Berman et al. (1995) studied eight schools, Grades 4 through 8, nominated for providing outstanding learning opportunities for English language learners and all students Classroom-level attributes included (a) effective language development strategies and (b) curricula and instructional strategies that engaged students in meaningful, in-depth learning. Lucas (1996) studied six exemplary high schools and found the following attributes: (a) The students' native language and culture were valued; (b) teachers had high expectations for student success; (c) parent involvement was high; (d) school personnel were committed to empowerment through education; and (e) students benefited from a challenging, academic curriculum (access to quality academics) while learning English.

Findings from the few observational studies conducted in bilingual special education classrooms have focused on the value of providing a nurturing, supportive environment as a backdrop for instruction (Lopez-Reyna, 1996; Ruiz, 1989, 1995). Teachers in these classrooms stressed meaning making through active engagement in authentic learning activities. Both Lopez-Reyna and Ruiz noted that student performance varied depending on the learning context. They emphasized the importance of looking for the upper range of English language learners' academic, linguistic, and social skills.

Validated Instructional Practices

In this section of the chapter we describe instructional practices for English language learners with disabilities. We focus on reading. First we provide an overview of methods for teaching students who struggle with decoding and other aspects of early literacy. Then we discuss comprehension strategies.

Interventions for Struggling Readers. Recently, there has been an upsurge in research focused on examining the efficacy of reading interventions for English language learners with reading difficulties (De La Colina, Parker, Hasbrouck, & Lara-Alecio, 2001; Denton, Anthony, Parker & Hasbrouck, 2004, Escamilla, Loera, Ruiz, & Rodriguez, 1998; Linan-Thompson, Vaughn, Hickman-Davis, & Kouzekanani, 2003; Linan-Thompson, Vaughn, Prater, & Cirino, in press; Nag-Arulmani, Reddy, & Buckley, 2003; Vaughn, Mathes, Linan-Thompson, & Francis, 2005). These studies all focused on English language learners who showed signs of struggling and who received supplemental intensive instruction. In some of these studies, students were instructed in their native language, while in others they received instruction in English only. We discuss a few of these studies here; others we describe later in the chapter.

Reading Recovery/*Descubriendo la Lectura*. *Descubriendo la Lectura* is a Spanish version of Reading Recovery (Clay, 1985). Both provide short-term interventions of one-to-one tutoring for low-achieving first graders. Students receive daily half-hour lessons for 12 to 20 weeks. As soon as students can read as well as their classmates who have been making adequate progress, lessons are discontinued. Escamilla et al. (1998) found that outcomes for *Descubriendo la Lectura* students were comparable to outcomes for Reading Recovery students. About 8 of 10 students who received the full series of lessons were able to read and write with the average range of performance of their class. The few students who were still having difficulty were referred for further evaluation. However, in a similar study, Neal and Kelly (1999) found that one fourth of the English language learners who participated in Reading Recovery or *Descubriendo la Lectura* did not complete the program due to insufficient progress. This was the group of students with the lowest skills prior to intervention. These findings suggest that Reading Recovery may not be an appropriate intervention for students who are the most at risk for reading difficulties: Students are dropped from the program if they do not respond. It may be these students who would be most likely to qualify for special education, particularly in a response to intervention (RTI) model.

Read Naturally. De La Colina et al. (2001) studied Read Naturally, which is an intensive reading intervention that combines repeated reading of connected text, vocabulary and comprehension instruction, and progress monitoring, using Spanish materials. They found that Read Naturally led to measurable improvements in fluency and, to a lesser extent, comprehension with first- and second-grade English language learners considered low achieving and at risk. Students who were highly engaged improved the most. Denton et al. (2004) also investigated the effectiveness of Read Naturally, though in English. Their participants included second- through fifth-grade English language learners identified by their teachers as having difficulty learning to read. Denton et al. found no statistically significant differences and only minimal effect sizes favoring Read Naturally over a control condition on word identification, word attack, and passage comprehension measures.

Read Well. Denton et al. (2004) also investigated the effectiveness of Read Well, a program that combines systematic, explicit phonics instruction with practice in decodable text and contextualized vocabulary and comprehension instruction. The second- through fifth-grade struggling English language learners in their study were tutored in English reading three times a week in 40-minute periods for 10 weeks. In comparison with matched students who did not receive this extra intervention, the Read Well students showed significantly more growth in word identification, but not in word attack (nonword reading) or comprehension. The authors speculated that students' lack of growth in comprehension could have been due to insufficient emphasis on helping students acquire English vocabulary. In Read Well, vocabulary instruction is informal rather than systematic.

Phonological Awareness. Nag-Arulmani et al. (2003) sought to determine if students who were struggling with reading in a nondominant language would respond better to a phonological intervention versus one that addressed oral proficiency. Participants included 118 third-grade English language learners (90 with reading difficulties in English as an additional language, and 28 without reading difficulties), randomly assigned to the phonological intervention, the language exposure intervention, or a control group. The group of students who received explicit phonological instruction showed significantly better gains in reading than the language proficiency and control groups. The intervention was most effective for the children who began the study with the lowest levels of single-word reading, phonological awareness, and decoding skills.

Validated Approaches for Enhancing Reading Comprehension

Though not numerous, a handful of studies have tested the effectiveness of approaches for improving the reading comprehension of English language learners with disabilities. This work has been conducted on graphic organizers, reciprocal teaching, collaborative strategic reading, and classwide peer tutoring.

Graphic Organizers. Bos and Anders (1992) assigned 42 elementary bilingual students with LD to one of four groups: semantic mapping, semantic feature analysis, semantic/syntactic feature analysis, or definition instruction (the control condition). Semantic mapping involves diagramming related concepts from a reading passage or oral lesson. Semantic feature analysis requires categorizing important concepts from a reading passage by summarizing distinct ways in which related concepts are similar and different. Semantic/syntactic feature analysis entails predicting the relationships among concepts and the answers for cloze-type sentences using a relationship matrix as a guide. Over a 2-week period, students participated in group instruction for three practice sessions and three treatment sessions. Effect sizes for the three treatment groups compared with the definition instruction group were high ($ES = .81$). These findings suggest that graphic organizers can be useful for helping English language learners with disabilities learn key concepts and vocabulary. Similarly, Bos, Allen, and Scanlon (1989) and Gallego, Durán, and Scanlon (1990) achieved positive results using graphic organizers to enhance comprehension. Semantic mapping has also been recommended as a strategy for improving the content area learning of English language learners (Echevarria & Graves, 1998; O'Malley & Chamot, 1990; M. Reyes & Molner, 1991), though there is no efficacy research.

Modified Reciprocal Teaching. Klingner and Vaughn (1996) investigated the effectiveness of an adapted version of reciprocal teaching (Palincsar & Brown, 1984) for improving the content area reading comprehension of 26 middle school English language learners with LD. Traditional reciprocal teaching takes place in the form of a dialogue between teachers and students as they read segments of text and rotate through four strategies: summarizing, question generating, clarifying, and predicting. The teacher and students take turns assuming the role of teacher in leading this dialogue. Klingner and Vaughn (1996) added a strategy to help students activate their prior knowledge. Students in their study participated in 15 days of teacher-facilitated strategy instruction while reading grade-level expository passages. They were then randomly divided into two groups; one group was assigned to a cross-age tutoring condition and the other to a cooperative learning condition. Students in the first group tutored younger English language learners with LD in the comprehension strategies, and students in the other group continued applying the strategies while working in small peer-led groups.

Students in both groups showed substantial progress in reading comprehension over the entire course of the study. A key finding was that a greater range of students benefited from strategy instruction than had been predicted—students who began the study with comprehension levels substantially higher than their decoding levels as well as students who were adequate decoders but initially lower in comprehension benefited. Students with very low initial decoding skills (below a third-grade level) were least likely to show improvement. Students with beginning to intermediate levels of English and Spanish proficiency showed less growth on outcome measures than those students with higher oral proficiency, with one exception. Results suggested that collaborative comprehension strategy instruction benefits English language learners with LD.

Collaborative Strategic Reading. Klingner, Vaughn, and Schumm (1998) further adapted reciprocal teaching, refining the comprehension strategies and adding components of cooperative learning (e.g., Johnson & Johnson, 1989) to create collaborative strategic reading (CSR). CSR was designed to promote content learning, language acquisition, and reading comprehension in diverse classrooms that include English language learners with LD (Klingner, Vaughn, Dimino, Schumm, & Bryant, 2001). CSR includes before-reading ("preview"), during-reading ("click and clunk" and "get the gist"), and after-reading ("wrap-up") comprehension strategies. Initially, the teacher teaches the strategies to the whole class. When students preview, they think about what they already know about the topic and predict what they think they will learn. While reading, they monitor their comprehension (i.e., identify "clicks" and "clunks") and take steps to improve understanding when comprehension breaks down. They also find the main idea of each section of text. Whey students wrap up, they generate questions about the important ideas in the passage they have read and review what was learned. Once students have learned to apply the strategies on their own, the teacher divides them into small groups of four or five students. Each student in a group performs a different role (e.g., leader, clunk expert, gist expert, announcer, encourager). Students record their ideas in CSR learning logs and complete various follow-up activities (e.g., semantic maps and games to reinforce vocabulary).

Klingner et al. (1998) found that students in fourth-grade heterogeneous, diverse classrooms who learned CSR from researchers outperformed their peers in control classrooms on comprehension measures. Klingner, Vaughn, Argüelles, Hughes, and Ahwee (2004) achieved similar findings in a study of 10 fourth-grade classrooms in which five classroom teachers taught CSR. Klingner and Vaughn (2000) investigated the frequency and means by which bilingual fifth-grade students helped each other and their classmates who were English language learners while using CSR, and found that students assisted one another in understanding word meanings, getting the main idea, asking and answering questions, and relating what they were learning to previous knowledge. Students' scores on English vocabulary tests increased significantly from pre- to posttesting. These studies have important implications not only for the value of comprehension strategy instruction, but also in that they support the effectiveness of cooperative learning.

Classwide Peer Tutoring. Arreaga-Mayer and her colleagues (Arreaga-Mayer, 1998a, 1998b; Arreaga-Mayer & Greenwood, 1986) have developed, implemented, and evaluated the effectiveness of classwide peer tutoring (CWPT) in reading and spelling with culturally and linguistically diverse students. Students coteach each other and provide support and feedback. CWPT provides specific, well-organized task structures to ensure that students acquire critical knowledge in reading and spelling. CWPT also includes mechanisms for individual accountability to ensure that all students profit from the tutoring. The teacher's role is to select appropriate materials and monitor student progress.

While CWPT is an effective strategy for students with disabilities as well as typical students, it was originally developed for culturally and linguistically diverse students (Greenwood, Arreaga-Mayer, Utley, Gavin, & Terry, 2001). For English language learners, CWPT provides active opportunities to converse in English, retrieve knowledge and skills in their native language (Arreaga-Mayer, 1998a), and, if necessary, continue practice based on immediate feedback from their tutors. Arreaga-Mayer (1998b) contended that CWPT is consistent with Gersten and Jiménez' (1998) eight constructs for effective instruction for English language learners: challenge, involvement, success, scaffolding/cognitive strategies, collaborative/cooperative learning, feedback, techniques for second language acquisition, and respect for cultural diversity. CWPT was designed to increase students' opportunity to respond (Delquadri, Whorton, Carta, & Hall, 1986, 1986; Greenwood et al., 1989), a critical feature for English language learners (Gersten & Baker, 2000). This opportunity to respond has been defined as "environmental factors (e.g., time allocated for instruction, curriculum, tasks presented to students, and teacher behaviors) and the amount of active student responding (e.g., reading aloud, writing, and talking academic)" (Delquadri et al., 1986, p. 536). CWPT increases students' opportunity to respond by assigning them to tutor–tutee dyads. In each dyad, students have a chance to be both the tutee and the tutor in the same session. Thus, all students are actively engaged in teaching and learning the day's skills or content.

Future Directions—Response to Intervention and "Tiered" Models

In the 2004 reauthorization of IDEA, states may choose to discontinue the use of the IQ–achievement discrepancy and eliminate the requirement for IQ tests as part of the special education identification process. States have the option of using response to intervention (RTI) criteria as part of the identification process. This change has dramatic implications for English language learners suspected of having learning disabilities.

An initial step in addressing the disproportionate numbers of English language learners being referred for special education involves reducing the bias in the referral and identification process (Donovan & Cross, 2002) and preventing academic failure by providing support and quality instruction *before* a student fails. "Tiered models" associated with response to intervention (RTI) hold promise for addressing these concerns for culturally and linguistically diverse students. Using RTI as a system to provide early screening, ongoing monitoring, and intensive support for English language learners has potential to significantly reduce disproportionate representation by diminishing inappropriate referrals that result from teacher or assessment bias (Vaughn & Fuchs, 2003).

Response to intervention models have recently received considerable attention, particularly as an alternative to the IQ–discrepancy model for identifying students with LD (Speece, Case, & Molloy, 2003; Vaughn & Fuchs, 2003). Although RTI models may be implemented in various ways, including differences in the number of levels of support, the general framework of the model remains the same. Generally, the first tier is considered quality instruction and ongoing progress monitoring within the general education classroom. The second tier is characterized by providing intensive support for students who did not meet expected benchmarks (i.e., who did not make adequate progress in the core program). When students do not adequately respond to the second tier of intervention, they either qualify for special education or for special education evaluation (Fuchs, Mock, Morgan, & Young, 2003).

Although there is limited research on using RTI for English language learners, recent investigations have produced promising results and initial support for the use of this model with at-risk English language learners (Haager, 2004; Linan-Thompson et al., 2003; Linan-Thompson et al., in press; Vaughn, Linan-Thompson, & Hickman, 2003; Vaughn et al., 2005). A critical consideration in determining the value of RTI as a means for providing early intervention and appropriate identification of English language learners is determining what interventions are associated with improved outcomes for this population (Vaughn et al., 2005). Vaughn and colleagues (2005) have discussed the promising results of implementing focused reading interventions coupled with language development activities while incorporating ESL best practices (e.g., repetitive language, modeling information, facial expressions and gestures in teaching vocabulary, explicit instruction in English language usage).

Haager (2004) described implementing an RTI model with English language learners in several urban schools in California. The project focused on providing basic reading intervention and monitor reading progress. Teachers conducted ongoing assessments of student performance using *Dynamic Indicators of Basic Early Literacy Skills* (DIBELS). In addition to the core reading program, students in Tier 2 benefited from additional small-group instruction focusing on core beginning reading skills while teachers incorporated English language development instruction. Haager reported anecdotally that referral rates for special education were significantly reduced across grades and schools. Equally important, a number of first- and second-grade students were identified for special education assistance, which is earlier than with discrepancy-formula-based models.

The success of the RTI process for English language learners is largely dependent on several factors. First, a critical aspect of preventing academic failure involves creating a learning environment that nurtures academic success and views students' cultural and linguistic diversity as a rich resource (Baca, 2002; Nieto, 2004; Ortiz, 1997, 2002). Teachers need a variety of research-based instructional approaches specifically designed for at-risk non–native English speakers (McCardle, Mele-McCarthy, Cutting, Leos, & D'Emilio, 2005). Teachers need to know if their interventions are effective and how to adjust instruction for students who do not respond to the first, second, or third tier of intervention (McCardle, Mele-McCarthy, & Leos, 2005). There is a large body of knowledge on effective research-based strategies for monolingual English speakers, and although it might seem advisable to use these strategies with English language learners, it is important to recognize that it may be more appropriate to use different approaches (McCardle, Mele-McCarthy, & Leos, 2005). Fortunately, recent research is building this knowledge base (August, Carlo, Dressler, & Snow, 2005; Haager, 2004; Klingner & Vaughn, 1996; Linan-Thompson et al., 2003; Linan-Thompson et al., in press; Vaughn et al., 2003; Vaughn et al., 2005). Continued research on the use of RTI with English language learners is necessary, particularly because the model seems to hold promise in addressing the over- and underrepresentation of English language learners in special education. Implicit in its success, however, is that each level of support must be culturally and linguistically responsive (Ortiz, 2002) and provide effective, research-based interventions with ongoing, culturally sensitive progress monitoring.

A Proposed RTI Model for English Language Learners

We suggest the following four-tiered RTI model for English language learners. We draw from the literature in recommending this model, but do so in a way that combines what has been learned about effective practice from qualitative studies as well as from quantitative and mixed-methods studies. We also draw heavily from the work of Alba Ortiz and Shernaz Garcia on prereferral interventions. The model we propose has yet to be researched with all of the components we suggest.

Tier 1

The first tier should consist of quality instruction with ongoing progress monitoring within the general education classroom (Vaughn & Fuchs, 2003). The quality of instruction is largely dependent on several teacher-related factors in addition to curricular factors. For English language learners these factors include the teacher's knowledge of bilingual education and ESL teaching methods, as well as the fidelity with which teachers implement these methods and instructional strategies. It is also important that teachers understand the language acquisition process and the principles of culturally responsive pedagogy. According to Ortiz (2002), fewer English language learners would need to be referred for special education if schools effectively responded to their language and learning needs.

In order for Tier 1 to be effective in preventing academic failure and providing English language learners with opportunities to learn, general education teachers need to be provided with professional development on research-based instructional strategies for this population. Professional development focused on preparing classroom teachers to use these instructional strategies would improve the quality of instruction for English language learners and increase opportunities to learn. Teachers should be familiar with instructional strategies linked to academic growth for their population of students as well as assessment procedures that can be used to monitor progress, particularly in language and literacy development (Ortiz, 2001). They also need to have an in-depth understanding of (a) the students they serve and their unique language and learning needs, (b) the relationship of native language proficiency to the development of English, and (c) the social and cultural contexts that affect learning. Thus, professional development should include four critical components:

1. information about how to implement validated instructional practices for English language learners
2. information about how to monitor progress and assess the learning of English language learners
3. information about the language acquisition process
4. information and experiences designed to help participants develop the attributes of culturally responsive teachers

This last component might be considered controversial, given that it has not been a component in experimental and quasi-experimental research studies. Yet many researchers and scholars have described the kinds of dispositions and practices of culturally responsive teachers. Culturally responsive teachers specifically acknowledge the need for students to find relevant connections among themselves, the subject matter, and the tasks they are asked to perform (Montgomery, 2001; Salend et al., 2002). These teachers help their students bridge borders between their home and school cultures, recognize and understand differences in the social milieus, and build on the knowledge and skills that their students bring with them to school learning. In doing so, these teachers demonstrate their care, respect, and commitment to each student's learning abilities, desires, and potentialities (Gay, 2000). Culturally responsive teachers validate and affirm the individual worth of each student (Ladson-Billings, 1994). Nieto (1999) has emphasized that culturally responsive teachers are experts in instruction and management and are able to simultaneously challenge and support their students. Culturally responsive teachers feel a strong sense of responsibility for all students, including students referred for or already placed in special education (G. E. Garcia, 1991; Villegas & Lucas, 2002).

Tier 2

When English language learners have not reached expected benchmarks or have not made adequate progress in a culturally and linguistically responsive classroom, the second tier of intervention is needed. In this tier, a level of intensive support is provided that supplements the core curriculum and is determined based on student needs (as identified by ongoing progress monitoring). The intervention may take place in the general education classroom or in the form of a pull-out program.

For many English language learners, Tier 2 may be an intensive supplemental reading program such as those described by Linan-Thompson et al. (2003), Linan-Thompson et al. (in press), Haager (2004), and Vaughn et al. (2005). Tier 2 may also involve one-on-one tutoring or participating in one or more services provided by Title 1 funds (Ortiz, 2002). The type of program and the amount of time a student spends in the program may vary from school to school; however, the central focus of Tier 2 is providing English language learners with supplemental instruction to prevent academic failure. For those students who adequately respond to the intervention, a process should be in place to maintain and monitor academic gains. For English language learners who do not adequately respond to intensive supplemental instruction, Tier 2 becomes the gatekeeper for possible referral to special education and helps address the challenging question of when English language learners should be referred for a special education evaluation.

Tier 3

We suggest that this phase of a multitiered model should start with a referral to a school-level support team such as a Teacher Assistance Team (TAT) to collaborate and design an effective intervention plan (Chalfant & Pysh, 1989; Chalfant, Pysh, & Moultrie, 1979). According to Ortiz (2002), when teachers request the assistance of a TAT, they are essentially requesting assistance for themselves; they are not referring the student to the team. This difference distinguishes the process from that of prereferral intervention and allows the classroom teacher to maintain ownership of the student's challenges and progress (Garcia & Ortiz, 2004; Ortiz, 2002). This phase in the model can begin while the student is receiving supplemental instruction and thus might overlap with Tier 2.

For struggling English language learners, it is essential for TAT members to consider issues related to second-language acquisition. In addition to general education teachers serving on the TAT, it is suggested that a bilingual or ESL specialist also participate to some degree. The ESL specialist can share valuable insight and understanding of second-language acquisition issues and how they relate to the academic performance of English language learners (Roache, Shore, Gouleta, & de Obaldia Butkevich, 2003) or model effective instructional strategies for the classroom teachers (S. B. Garcia & Ortiz, 1988, 2004). Researchers have recommended that teams have a wide range of meaningful strategies available to them and develop specific instructional objectives based on student performance data (S. B. Garcia & Ortiz, 1988, 2004; Harry & Klingner, 2005). The ESL specialist could offer suggestions for a variety of instructional strategies, help develop specific instructional objectives that include attention to language acquisition, and offer guidance with culturally sensitive ongoing assessment.

Special education personnel may also play a key role on a TAT. The special educator is equipped with knowledge of effective strategies for students with learning differences and/or behavioral challenges. Similar to the ESL specialist on the TAT, special educators can offer suggestions or model techniques for incorporating effective instructional practices. For example, general education teachers may need guidance with sequencing skills (e.g., breaking down the task, providing step-by-step prompts), controlling task difficulty, or learning how to incorporate cognitive and metacognitive strategy instruction.

Fortunately, resources are available to help direct and evaluate schools' special education referral procedures for English language learners. S. B. Garcia and Ortiz (1988) developed a flowchart to guide practitioners through the decision-making process. The flowchart and accompanying list of questions help school personnel evaluate whether students have been provided with meaningful, appropriate prereferral strategies and adequate opportunities to learn. Further, questions are raised to help practitioners evaluate a student's difficulties across time and settings. More recently, a self-assessment guide was developed by the National Association for Bilingual Education (National Association for Bilingual Education & ILIAD Project, 2002) to help school administrators assess their school's referral process for English language learners. The guide describes the provisions for English language learners detailed in IDEA 1997 and suggests how these should be operationalized in schools. Several areas are evaluated, including (a) data collection procedures, (b) communication with English language learners and their parents, (c) parental involvement, (d) TATs, (e) evaluation procedures, and (f) professional development programs.

Tier 4

This tier would be special education. Instruction at this level is tailored to the individual needs of the student, and is intensive and ongoing. Unlike the interventions provided in the second or third tiers, this assistance is not limited to a set number of days but rather is fluid, flexible, and long term, based on students' needs. The principles and practices described in this chapter then apply.

Conclusion

For special education to be truly "special" for English language learners, the school community must collaborate and attend to the various needs, strengths, and challenges these students bring to their classrooms. Special education teachers must work side by side with ESL specialists and general education teachers to ensure that suggested interventions and ongoing assessments are aligned with the student's English language proficiency. In order for struggling English language learners to make significant academic gains, their linguistic needs must be addressed in *all* aspects of their individualized programs. Further, special educators, general education teachers, and ESL specialists must develop an understanding of the complex interaction that occurs between language, culture, *and* disability (Chamberlin, 2005) and systematically address these aspects in culturally responsive instructional planning (Cloud, 2002).

Does the use of these practices necessitate special education? We believe that the answer to this question is a resounding "yes." As we have discussed throughout this chapter, bilingual/ESL special education teachers require a special knowledge base (Baca & Cervantes, 1998). To address the complexities of effectively identifying, assessing, and instructing English language learners suspected of having a disability requires personnel who fully understand all relevant issues. To accomplish this goal, schools must have personnel who have received specialized training, a strong prereferral process, and support services and programs outside of special education (Baca & Cervantes, 1998; S. B. Garcia & Malkin, 1993; S. B. Garcia & Ortiz, 1988).

With the reauthorization of IDEA and the possible transition to RTI models, it is clear that there will be new roles for special education teachers. On the one hand, bilingual/ESL special education teachers may have fewer students identified as having disabilities on their caseloads (if, as we would hope, more students are helped through early interventions and general education support, and fewer students are placed in special education), but on the other hand, their participation in other aspects of instruction will probably change. Time spent consulting and collaborating with general education teachers and ESL teachers is likely to increase. More than ever, a special education teacher will need to be a "Jack (or Jane) of all trades," knowledgeable not only about special education, bilingual education, and English for speakers of other languages, but also about the intersection of all three.

NOTE

In English immersion programs, students receive instruction primarily in English with their first language used sparingly and for clarification purposes only. In modified English immersion programs, instruction is provided primarily in English, with some first language support to help clarify concepts. Bilingual education includes core instruction in the first language as well as English language development. All programs have English proficiency as their principal goal.

REFERENCES

Alvermann, D. (2005). Exemplary literacy instruction in Grades 7–12: What counts and who's counting? In J. Flood & P. Anders (Eds.), *Literacy development of students in urban schools: Research and policy* (p. 187–201). Newark, DE: International Reading Association.

Arreaga-Mayer, C. (1998a). Increasing active student responding and improving academic performance through classwide peer tutoring. *Intervention in School and Clinic, 34*, 89–94.

Arreaga-Mayer, C. (1998b). Language-sensitive peer-mediated instruction for culturally and linguistically diverse learners in the intermediate elementary grades. In R. M. Gersten & R. T. Jiménez (Eds.), *Promoting learning for culturally and linguistically diverse students* (pp. 73–90). Belmont, CA: Wadsworth.

Arreaga-Mayer, C., & Greenwood, C. R. (1986). Environmental variables affecting the school achievement of culturally and linguistically different learners: An instructional perspective. *Journal of the National Association of Bilingual Education, 10*(2), 113–135.

Artiles, A. J., Rueda, R., Salazar, J., & Higareda, I. (2002). Factors associated with English-language learner representation in special education: Evidence from urban school districts in California. In D. J. Losen & G. Orfield (Eds.), *Racial inequity in special education* (pp. 117–136). Cambridge, MA: Harvard University Press.

Artiles, A. J., & Trent, S. C. (2000). Representation of culturally/linguistically diverse students. In C. R. Reynolds & E. Fletcher-Jantzen (Eds.), *Encyclopedia of special education* (Vol. 1, 2nd ed., pp. 513–517). New York: Wiley.

Artiles, A. J., Trent, S. C., & Kuan, L. A. (1997). Learning disabilities research on ethnic minority students: An analysis of 22 years of studies published in selected referred journals. *Learning Disabilities Research and Practice, 12*, 82–91.

Artiles, A. J., Trent, S. C., & Palmer, J. D. (2004). Culturally diverse students in special education: Legacies and prospects. In J. A. Banks & C. M. Banks (Eds.), *Handbook of research on multicultural education* (2nd ed., pp. 716–735). San Francisco: Jossey-Bass.

Au, K. (1995). Multicultural perspectives on literacy research. *Journal of Reading Behavior, 27*, 85–100.

Au, K., & Kawakami, A. (1994). Cultural congruence in instruction. In E. Hollins, J. King, & W. Hayman (Eds.), *Teaching diverse populations* (pp. 5–23). Albany: State University of New York.

August, D., Carlo, M., Dressler, C., & Snow, C. (2005). The critical role of vocabulary development for English language learners. *Learning Disabilities Research and Practice, 20*, 50–57.

August, D., & Hakuta, K. (1997). *Improving schooling for language minority children: A research agenda.* Washington, DC: National Academy Press.

Baca, L. M. (2002). Educating English language learners with special education needs: Trends and future directions. In A. J. Artiles & A. A. Ortiz (Eds.), *English language learners with special education needs: Identification, placement, and instruction* (pp. 191–202). Washington, DC: Center for Applied Linguistics.

Baca, L. M., & Cervantes, H. T. (Eds.). (1998). *The bilingual special education interface.* Upper Saddle River, NJ: Merrill/Prentice Hall.

Baca, L. M., & De Valenzuela, J. S. (1994, Fall). Reconstructing the bilingual special education interface. *NCBE Program Information Guide Series, 20.* Retrieved August 2, 2001, from http://www.ncela.gwu.edu/ncbepubs/pigs/pig20.htm.

Barrera, I. (1995, Summer). To refer or not to refer: Untangling the web of diversity, deficit, and disability. *New York State Association for Bilingual Education Journal, 10*, 54–66. Retrieved February 18, 2005, from http://www.ncela.gwu.edu/miscpubs/nysabe/vol10/nysabe107.htm.

Barrera Metz, I. (1988). The relative importance of language and culture in making assessment decisions about Hispanic students referred to special education. *Journal for the National Association for Bilingual Education, 12*, 191–218.

Berman, P., McLaughlin, B., McLeod, B., Minicocci, C., Nelson, B., & Woodworth, K. (1995). *School reform and student diversity, Volume II: Case studies of exemplary practices for LEP students.* Santa Cruz, CA: National Center for Research on Cultural Diversity and Second Language Learning. (ERIC Document Reproduction Service No. 397 548)

Bos, C. S., Allen, A. A., & Scanlon, D. J. (1989). Vocabulary instruction and reading comprehension with bilingual learning disabled students. In S. McCormick & J. Zutell (Eds.), *Cognitive and social perspectives for literacy research and instruction: Thirty-eighth yearbook of the National Reading Conference* (pp. 173–179). Chicago: National Reading Conference.

Bos, C. S., & Anders, P. L. (1992). Using interactive teaching and learning strategies to promote text comprehension and content learning for students with learning disabilities. *International Journal of Disability, Development and Education, 39*, 225-238.

Bos, C. S., & Fletcher, T. V. (1997). Sociocultural considerations in learning disabilities inclusion research: Knowledge gaps and future directions. *Learning Disabilities Research & Practice, 12*, 92–99.

Brophy, M. (1992). Probing the subtleties of subject-matter teaching. *Educational Leadership, 49*(7), 4–8.

Burke, M., Hagan, S., & Grossen, B. (1998). What curricular design and strategies accommodate diverse learners? *Teaching Exceptional Children, 31*(1), 34–48.

Cardelle-Elawar, M. (1990). Effects of feedback tailored to bilingual students' mathematics needs on verbal problem solving. *The Elementary School Journal, 91*, 165–175.

Chalfant, J., Pysh, M. (1989). Teacher Assistance Teams: Five descriptive studies on 96 teams. *Remedial and Special Education, 10*(6), 49–58.

Chalfant, J., Pysh, M., & Moultrie, R. (1979). Teacher Assistance Teams: A model for within-building problem solving. *Learning Disability Quarterly, 2*, 85–96.

Chamberlin, S.P. (2005). Recognizing and responding to cultural difference in education of culturally and linguistically diverse learners. *Intervention in School and Clinic, 40*, 195–211.

Clay, M. M. (1985). *The early detection of reading difficulties.* Portsmouth, NH: Heinemann.

Cloud, N. (2002). Culturally and linguistically responsive instructional planning. In A. J. Artiles & A. A. Ortiz (Eds.), *English language learners with special education needs: Identification, placement, and instruction* (pp. 107–132). Washington, DC: Center for Applied Linguistics.

Collier, C., & Hoover, J. J. (1987). Sociocultural considerations when referring minority children for learning disabilities. *Learning Disabilities Focus, 3*(1), 39–45.

Cummins, J. (1984). *Bilingualism and special education: Issues in assessment and pedagogy.* San Diego: College Hill.

Cummins, J. (1989). A theoretical framework for bilingual special education. *Exceptional Children, 56*, 111–119.

Cummins, J. (1994). Knowledge, power, and identity in teaching English as a second language. In F. Genesee (Ed.), *Educating second language children: The whole child, the whole curriculum, the whole community* (pp. 103–125). Cambridge, England: Cambridge University Press.

De La Colina, M. G., Parker, R. I., Hasbrouck, J. E., & Lara-Alecio, R. (2001). Intensive intervention in reading fluency for at-risk beginning Spanish readers. *Bilingual Research Journal, 25*, 503–538.

Delquadri, J. C., Greenwood, C. R., Whorton, D., Carta, J. J., & Hall, R. V. (1986). Classwide Peer Tutoring. *Exceptional Children, 52*, 535–542.

Denton, C. A., Anthony, J. L., Parker, R., & Hasbrouck, J. (2004). Effects of two tutoring programs on the English reading development of Spanish-English bilingual students. *The Elementary School Journal, 104*, 289–305.

Donovan, S., & Cross, C. (2002). *Minority students in special and gifted education.* Washington, DC: National Academy Press.

Echevarria, J., & Graves, A. (1998). *Sheltered content instruction: Teaching English-language learners with diverse abilities.* Boston: Allyn & Bacon.

Escamilla, K., Loera, M., Ruiz, O., & Rodriguez, Y. (1998). An examination of sustaining effects in Descubriendo la Lectura programs. *Literacy Teaching and Learning: An International Journal of Early Reading and Writing, 3*(2), 59–81.

Fuchs, D., Mock, D., Morgan, P. L., & Young, C. L. (2003). Responsiveness -to-intervention: Definitions, evidence and implication for learning disability construct. *Learning Disabilities Research and Practice, 18*, 157–171.

Gallego, M. A., Durán, G. Z., & Scanlon, D. J. (1990). Interactive teaching and learning: Facilitating learning disabled students' progress from novice to expert. In J. Zutell & S. McCormick (Eds.), *Literacy theory and research: Analyses from multiple paradigms. Thirty-ninth yearbook of the National Reading Conference* (pp. 311–319). Chicago: National Reading Conference.

Garcia, G. E. (1991). Factors influencing the English reading test performance of Spanish speaking Hispanic children. *Reading Research Quarterly, 26*, 371–392.

Garcia, S. B., & Malkin, D. H. (1993). Towards defining programs and services for culturally and linguistically diverse learners in special education. *Teaching Exceptional Children, 26*(1), 52–58.

Garcia, S. B., & Ortiz, A. A. (1988, June). Preventing inappropriate referrals of language minority students to special education. *FOCUS/NCBE, 5*, 1–17.

Garcia, S. B., & Ortiz, A. A. (2004). *Preventing disproportionate representation: Culturally and linguistically responsive pre-referral interventions.* Denver: National Center for Culturally Responsive Education Systems (NCCRES).

Garcia, S. B., Wilkinson, C. Y., & Ortiz, A. A. (1995). Enhancing achievement for language minority student: Classroom, school, and family contexts. *Education and Urban Society, 27*, 441–462.

Gay, G. (2000). *Culturally responsive teaching: Theory, research, and practice.* New York: Teachers College Press.

Gersten, R., & Baker, S. (2000). What we know about effective instructional practices for English-language learners. *Exceptional Children, 66*, 454–470.

Gersten, R., & Jiménez, R. (1998). *Promoting learning for culturally and linguistically diverse students: Classroom applications from contemporary research.* Belmont, CA: Wadsworth.

Greenwood, C. R., Arreaga-Mayer, C., Utley, C. A., Gavin, K. M., & Terry, B. J. (2001). Class Wide Peer Tutoring Learning Management system: Applications with elementary-level English language learners. *Remedial and Special Education, 22*, 34–47.

Greenwood, C. R., Delquadri, J. C., & Hall, R. V. (1989). Longitudinal effects of Classwide Peer Tutoring. *Journal of Education Psychology, 81*, 371–383.

Haager, D. (2004, November). Promoting literacy development for English language learners learning in English: A case for explicit instruction. *Paper presented at the National Center for Culturally Responsive Educational*

Systems Research Conference on English Language Learners Struggling to Learn, Scottsdale, AZ.

Harry, B., & Klingner, J. K. (2005). *Crossing the border from normalcy to disability: Culturally and linguistically diverse students and the special education placement process.* New York: Teachers College Press.

Henderson, R. W., & Landesman, E. W. (1995). Effects of thematically integrated mathematics instruction on students of Mexican descent. *Journal of Educational Research, 88,* 290.

Individuals with Disabilities Education Improvement Act of 2004, 20 U.S.C. § 1400 *et seq.* (2004) (reauthorization of the Individuals with Disabilities Education Act of 1990).

Jiménez, R. T. (2001). "It's a difference that changes us": An alternative view of the language and literacy needs of Latina/o students. *The Reading Teacher, 54,* 736–742.

Jiménez, R. T., & Gersten, R. (1999). Lessons and dilemmas derived from the literary instruction of two Latina/o teachers. *American Education Research Journal, 36,* 265– 301.

Jiménez, J. E., Siegel, L. S., & Lopez, M. R. (2003). The relationship between IQ and reading disabilities in English-speaking Canadian and Spanish children. *Journal of Learning Disabilities, 36,* 15–23.

Johnson, D. W., & Johnson, R. T. (1989). Cooperative learning: What special educators need to know. *The Pointer, 33,* 5–10.

Keogh, B., Gallimore, R., & Weisner, T. (1997). A sociocultural perspective on learning and learning disabilities. *Learning Disabilities Research & Practice, 12,* 107–113.

Klingner, J., & Artiles, A. J. (2003). Bilingual special education: Contemporary challenges and prospective solutions. *Educational Leadership, 61*(2), 66–71.

Klingner, J. K., & Vaughn, S. (1996). Reciprocal teaching of reading comprehension strategies for students with learning disabilities who use English as a second language. *The Elementary School Journal, 93,* 275–293.

Klingner, J. K., & Vaughn, S. (2000). The helping behaviors of fifth-graders while using collaborative strategic reading (CSR) during ESL content classes. *TESOL Quarterly, 34,* 69–98.

Klingner, J. K., Vaughn, S., Argüelles, M. E., Hughes, M. T., & Ahwee, S. (2004). Collaborative strategic reading: "Real world" lessons from classroom teachers. *Remedial and Special Education, 25,* 291–302.

Klingner, J. K., Vaughn, S., Dimino, J., Schumm, J. S., & Bryant, D. P. (2001). *From clunk to click: Collaborative Strategic Reading.* Longmont, CO: Sopris West.

Klingner, J. K., Vaughn, S., & Schumm, J. S. (1998). Collaborative strategic reading during social studies in heterogeneous fourth-grade classrooms. *The Elementary School Journal, 99,* 3–21.

Ladson-Billings, G. (1994). *The dreamkeepers: Successful teachers of African American children.* San Francisco: Jossey-Bass.

Leinhardt, G. (1992). What research on learning tells us about teaching. *Educational Leadership, 49*(7), 200–225.

Linan-Thompson, S., Vaughn, S., Hickman-Davis, P., & Kouzekanani, K. (2003). Effectiveness of supplemental reading instruction for second-grade English language learners with reading difficulties. *The Elementary School Journal, 103,* 221–238.

Linan-Thompson, S., Vaughn, S., Prater, K., & Cirino, P. T. (in press). The response to intervention of English language learners at-risk for reading problems. *Journal of Learning Disabilities.*

Lockwood, A. T., & Secada, W. G. (1999, January). *Transforming education for Hispanic youth: Exemplary practices, programs, and schools.* Washington, DC: National Clearinghouse for Bilingual Education.

Lopez-Reyna, N. A. (1996). The importance of meaningful contexts in bilingual special education: Moving to whole language. *Learning Disabilities Research and Practice, 11,* 120–131.

Lucas, T. (1996). *Promoting secondary school transitions for immigrant adolescents.* (ERIC Document Reproduction Service No. 402 786)

Lucas T., Henz, R., & Donato, R. (1990). Promoting the success of Latino language minority students: An exploratory study of six high schools. *Harvard Educational Review, 60,* 315–340.

Maldonado-Colon, E. (1986). Assessment: Interpreting data of linguistically/culturally different students referred for disabilities or disorders. *Journal of Reading, Writing, and Learning Disabilities International, 2,* 73–83.

McCardle, P., Mele-McCarthy J., Cutting, L., Leos, K., & D'Emilio, T. (2005). Learning disabilities in English language learners: Identifying the issues. *Learning Disabilities Research & Practice, 20,* 1–5.

McCardle, P., Mele-McCarthy, J., & Leos, K. (2005). English language learners and learning disabilities: Research agenda and implications for practice. *Learning Disabilities Research & Practice, 20,* 68–78.

McGroarty, M. (1989). The benefits of cooperative learning arrangements in second language instruction. *Journal of the National Association for Bilingual Education, 13,* 127–143.

Miniccuci, C., Berman, P, McLaughlin, B., McLeod, B., Nelson, B., & Woodworth, K. (1995). School reform and student diversity. *Phi Delta Kappan, 77*(1), 77–80.

Moll, L. C. (Ed.). (1990). *Vygotsky and education: Instructional implications and applications of sociocultural psychology.* New York: Cambridge University Press.

Moll, L. C. (1992). Bilingual classroom studies and community analysis: Some recent trends. *Educational Researcher, 21*(2), 20–24.

Moll, L. C., & González, N. (1994). Critical issues: Lessons from research with language-minority children. *Journal of Reading Behavior, 26,* 439–456.

Montgomery, W. (2001). Literature discussion in the elementary school classroom: Developing cultural understanding. *Multicultural Education, 8,* 33–36.

Moore, D. W. (1996). Contexts for literacy in secondary schools. In D. J. Leu, C. K. Kinzer, & K. A. Hinchman (Eds.), *Literacies for the 21st century: Research and practice, forty-fifth yearbook of the National Reading Conference* (pp. 15–46). Chicago: National Reading Conference.

Müller, E., & Markowitz, J. (2004, March). *English language learners with disabilities.* Alexandria, VA: Project FORUM.

Muñiz-Swicegood, M. (1994). The effects of megacognitive reading strategy training on the reading performance and student reading analysis strategies of third grade bilingual students. *Bilingual Research Journal, 18,* 83–97.

Nag-Arulmani, S., Reddy, V., & Buckley, S. (2003). Targeting phonological representations can help in the early stages of reading in a non-dominant language. *Journal of Research in Reading, 26,* 49–68.

National Association for Bilingual Education (NABE) & ILIAD Project. (2002). *Determining appropriate referrals of English language learners to special education: A self-assessment guide for principals.* Washington, DC: National Association for Bilingual Education.

Neal, J. C., & Kelly, P. R. (1999). The success of Reading Recovery for English language learners and Descubriendo la Lectura for bilingual students in California. *Literacy Teaching and Learning, 2,* 81–108.

Nieto, S. (1999). *The light in their eyes.* New York: Teachers College Press.

Nieto, S. (2002). *Language, culture, and teaching: Critical perspectives for a new century.* Mahwah, NJ: Erlbaum.

Nieto, S. (2004). *Affirming diversity: The sociopolitical context of multicultural education.* Boston: Allyn & Bacon.

Ochoa, S. H., Powell, M. P., & Robles-Piña, R. (1996). School psychologists' assessment practices with bilingual and limited-English-proficient students. *Journal of Psychoeducational Assessment, 14,* 250–275.

Ochoa, S. H., Rivera, B. D., & Powell, M. P. (1997). Factors used to comply with the exclusionary clause with bilingual and limited-English-proficient pupils: Initial guidelines. *Learning Disabilities Research & Practice, 12,* 161–167.

Oller, J. W., Jr. (1991). Language testing research: Lessons applied to LEP students and programs. In *Proceedings of the first research symposium on limited English proficient students' issues: Focus on evaluation and measurement* (Vol. 2, pp. 42–123). Washington, DC: U.S. Department of Education, Office of Bilingual Education and Minority Language Affairs.

O'Malley, J. M., & Chamot, A. U. (1990). *Learning strategies in second language acquisition.* Cambridge, England: Cambridge University Press.

Ortiz, A. A. (1997). Learning disabilities occurring concomitantly with linguistic differences. *Journal of Learning Disabilities, 30,* 321–332.

Ortiz, A. A. (2001). *English language learners with special needs: Effective instructional strategies.* Washington, DC: ERIC Education Reports.

Ortiz, A. A. (2002). Prevention of school failure and early intervention for English language learners. In A. J. Artiles & A. A. Ortiz (Eds.), *English language learners with special education needs: Identification, placement, and instruction* (pp. 31–48). Washington, DC: Center for Applied Linguistics.

Ortiz, A. A., Garcia, S., Holtzman, W., Polyzoi, E., Snell, W., Wilkinson, C., & Willig, A. (1985). *Characteristics of limited English proficient Hispanic students in programs of the learning disabled: Implications for policy, practice and research.* Austin: University of Texas, Handicapped Minority Research Institute on Language Proficiency.

Ortiz, A. A., Garcia, S., Wheeler, D., & Maldonado-Colon, E. (1986). *Characteristics of limited English proficient students served in programs for the speech and language handicapped: Implications for policy, practice and research.* Austin: University of Texas, Handicapped Minority Research Institute on Language Proficiency.

Ortiz, A. A., & Maldonado-Colon, E. (1986). Recognizing learning disabilities in bilingual children: How to lessen inappropriate referrals of language minority students to special education. *Journal of Reading, Writing and Learning Disabilities International, 2,* 43–56.

Ortiz, A., & Wilkinson, C. (1991). Assessment and intervention model for the bilingual exceptional student (AIM for the BEST). *Teacher Education and Special Education, 14,* 35–42.

Padrón, Y. N., & Waxman, H. C. (1999). Classroom observations of the five standards of effective teaching in urban classrooms with English language learners. *Teaching and Change, 7,* 79–100.

Palincsar, A. S., & Brown, A. L. (1984). Reciprocal teaching of comprehension-fostering and comprehension-monitoring activities. *Cognition and Instruction, 1,* 117–175.

Reyes, E., & Bos, C. (1998). Interactive semantic mapping and charting: Enhancing content area learning for language minority students. In R. Gersten & R. Jiménez (Eds.), *Promoting learning for culturally and linguistically diverse students: Classroom applications from contemporary research* (pp. 133–152). Belmont, CA: Wadsworth.

Reyes, M. (1992). Challenging venerable assumptions: Literacy instruction for linguistically different students. *Harvard Educational Review, 62,* 427–446.

Reyes, M., & Molner, L. (1991). Instructional strategies for second-language learners in the content areas. *Journal of Reading, 35,* 96–103.

Roache, M., Shore, J., Gouleta, E., & de Obaldia Butkevich, E. (2003). An investigation of collaboration among school professionals serving culturally and linguistically diverse students with exceptionalities. *Bilingual Research Journal, 27*(1), 117–132.

Rousseau, M. K., Tam, B. K. Y., & Ramnarain, R. (1993). Increasing reading proficiency of language minority students with speech and language impairments. *Education and Treatment of Children, 16,* 254–271.

Ruiz, N. T. (1989). An optimal learning environment for Rosemary. *Exceptional Children, 56,* 130–144.

Ruiz, N. T. (1995). The social construction of ability and disability: II. Optimal and at-risk lessons in a bilingual special education classroom. *Journal of Learning Disabilities, 28,* 491–502.

Salend, S. J., Garrick Duhaney, L. M., & Montgomery, W. (2002). A comprehensive approach to identifying and addressing issues of disproportionate representation. *Remedial and Special Education, 23,* 289–299.

Saunders, W., O'Brien, G., Lennon, D., & McLean, J. (1998). Making the transition to English literacy successful: Effective strategies for studying literature with transition students. In R. Gersten & R. Jiménez (Eds.), *Effective strategies for teaching language minority students* (pp. 99–132). Belmont, CA: Wadsworth.

Speece, D. L., Case, L. P., & Molloy, D. E. (2003). Responsiveness to general education as the first gate to learning disabilities identification. *Learning Disabilities Research & Practice, 18*, 147–156.

Tikunoff, W. J., Ward, B. A., van Broekhuizen, L. D., Romero, M., Castaneda, L. V., Lucas, T., et al. (1991). *Final Report: A descriptive study of significant features of exemplary special alternative instructional programs*. Los Alamitos, CA: Southwest Regional Educational Laboratory.

U.S. Census Bureau. (2001, April 2). *U S. Census Bureau, Population Division*. Retrieved March 26, 2003 from http://www.census.gov/population/www/cen2000/phc-t1.html.

U.S. Census Bureau. (2003, February 25). *U.S. Census Bureau, Population Division*. Retrieved March 26, 2003 from http://www.census.gov/population/www/cen2000/phc-t20.html.

U.S. Department of Education. (2003, June). *Key indicators of Hispanic student achievement: National goals and benchmarks for the next decade*. Retrieved June 27, 2003, from http://www.ed.gov/pubs/hispanicindicators.

Vaughn, S., & Fuchs, L. S. (2003). Redefining learning disabilities as inadequate response to instruction: The promise and potential problems. *Learning Disabilities Research & Practice, 18*, 137–146.

Vaughn, S., Linan-Thompson, S., & Hickman, P. (2003). Response to instruction as a means of identifying students with reading/ learning disabilities. *Exceptional Children, 69*, 391–409.

Vaughn, S., Mathes, P. G., Linan-Thompson, S., & Francis, D. J. (2005). Teaching English language learners at risk for reading disabilities to read: Putting research to practice. *Learning Disabilities Research & Practice*, 20, 58–67.

Villegas, A. M., & Lucas, T. (2002). Preparing culturally responsive teachers: Rethinking the curriculum. *Journal of Teacher Education, 53*, 20–32.

Wagner, R. K., Francis, D. J., & Morris, R. D. (2005). Identifying English language learners with learning disabilities: Key challenges and possible approaches. *Learning Disabilities Research & Practice, 20*, 6–15.

Willig, A., Swedo, J., & Ortiz, A. (1987). *Characteristics of teaching strategies which result in high task engagement for exceptional limited English proficient students*. Austin: University of Texas at Austin, Handicapped Minority Research Institute on Language Proficiency.

Zehler, A., Fleischman, H., Hopstock, P., Stephenson, T., Pendzick, M., & Sapru, S. (2003). *Policy report: Summary of findings related to LEP and SPED-LEP students*. Report submitted by Development Associates, Inc., to U.S. Department of Education, Office of English Language Acquisition, Language Enhancement, and Academic Achievement of Limited English Proficient Students.

Chapter 5

What Is Special About Special Education for Students Who Are Deaf?

Barbara R. Schirmer

The question about what is special about special education for students who are deaf has been asked for centuries. One of the earliest documented records comes from the late 1500s, relating that Spanish Benedictine monk Pedro Ponce de León taught the deaf sons of lords and other wealthy and powerful individuals (Bender, 1970; Lang, 2003). From the 18th century to the present, the central issue has been the mode or language of communication used in instruction. The manualism–oralism debate endured from the 18th century through the mid-20th century; and the total communication–oralism, American Sign Language–oralism, American Sign Language–signed English debates have persisted from the 1960s to the present (see Note). There has been a persistent belief that an ideal communication mode exists; once it is identified, the puzzle of educating deaf and hard of hearing children would be solved.

Much of this research has been regarded with skepticism because studies often seem to have been carried out by individuals committed to a particular mode of communication. Indeed, until the *Journal of Deaf Studies and Deaf Education* was launched in 1995, the two main research journals in the field reflected the split between adherents of oralism and adherents of sign language. Studies showing the benefits of oralism have typically been published in *The Volta Review*, the research journal of the Alexander Graham Bell Association of the Deaf and Hard of Hearing, an organization that advocates oral education (e.g., Lane, 1976; McLaughlin, 1955), and studies showing the benefits of sign language have commonly been published in the *American Annals of the Deaf*, the journal of the Council of American Instructors of the Deaf (e.g., Stuckless & Birch, 1966; Vernon & Koh, 1970).

The outcome of this preoccupation with communication mode as the key to effective education of deaf students has been disappointing. Regardless of the latest trend in communication, the educational achievement of deaf students has remained relatively unchanged. Since the 1960s, studies assessing the academic achievement of deaf students have consistently found that they lag far behind their hearing peers (Allen, 1986; Gallaudet Research Institute, 2005b; Gentile & DiFrancesca, 1969; Trybus & Karchmer, 1977). Research has also shown very low reading achievement levels among this population, with the average deaf student gaining one third of a grade equivalent change each school year and the average reading level being fourth grade at high school graduation (Gallaudet Research Institute, 2005a; Holt, 1993; Wolk & Allen, 1984).

The lack of findings showing one communication mode to be superior to another does not mean that effective instructional practices with deaf students are completely elusive, however. The purpose of this chapter is to identify the body of research literature on effective instruction and address three questions about what is special about educating deaf students:

1. What are the empirically supported, effective practices for students who are deaf?
2. To what degree are these practices being used, and are they being implemented with fidelity?

3. Are these practices unique to deaf education settings, unique to deaf students, unique to the competencies of deaf education teachers, or could they be applied as effectively by general education teachers in inclusive settings?

The field of deaf education did not embrace people-first language ("person who is deaf") when it became common practice after the Education of the Handicapped Act was renamed the Individuals with Disabilities Education Act in the 1990 reauthorization. It is acceptable to, and even preferred by, many professionals and deaf individuals not to be restricted to people-first language. Thus, I use terms including *deaf student*, *deaf education*, *teacher of the deaf*, and *school for the deaf* in this chapter. Terms such as *person with hearing loss* or *person with hearing impairment* are not used because of the negative connotation implied by the notion that the individual has a deficiency or pathology. I use the term *deaf person* to refer to a broad range of individuals, from hard-of-hearing to profoundly deaf. And I use the term *Deaf* with an uppercase *D* to refer to deaf persons in the context of Deaf culture, which has its own linguistic and ethnic attributes.

What Are Effective Instructional Practices With Deaf Students?

Language is central to the lives of all individuals because it is the means for communicating, thinking, and learning. Learning language is the single greatest challenge for children who are deaf. Unlike other children, deaf children acquire language largely through their eyes; even for those who benefit from amplification or cochlear implant, auditory information is incomplete and often distorted. The educational issue for deaf children is not the degree of hearing ability but rather their ability to understand and communicate in a language that others share. Whether spoken, signed, or written, it is this shared language on which learning is based. Given the challenge of acquiring language, the primary focus of instruction for deaf students is developing a shared language and using this language through speech, sign language, reading, and writing.

Effective instructional practices for deaf students must, therefore, involve language learning. Indeed, language and literacy development form the core of what is special about deaf education. In this chapter, I review and analyze the efficacy of instructional practices for promoting language and literacy in deaf students. To a great extent, instructional practices have been borrowed from the wider field of education and other specialty areas, such as special education and bilingual education. One of the key issues in deaf education is the lack of research on the effectiveness of such practices with deaf and hard-of-hearing children.

Instructional Practices for Developing Language

During much of the 20th century, teaching methods designed for deaf children were based on the notion that deaf students needed to be made explicitly aware of the structure of the English language and drilled on these features through activities such as repeating the teacher's well-formed utterances and following model sentence patterns when writing (Caniglia, Cole, Howard, Krohn, & Rice, 1975; Fitzgerald, 1949; McAnally, Rose, & Quigley, 1998; Pugh, 1955). By the 1980s, it was recognized that labeling and drilling the deaf child on grammatical features had no significant or lasting influence on the child's internalization of the language itself, whether that language was English or American Sign Language (ASL), and alternative approaches were developed that were designed to create an environment replete with opportunities to interact with others using language for meaningful communication (Schirmer, 2000). These approaches were based on findings from the research on language acquisition with hearing children, which can be summarized as follows:

- The order of progression in knowledge of a first language varies little across children, regardless of the language (Brown, 1973; deVilliers & deVilliers, 1979; Gleason, 2004; Halliday, 1975; Lahey, 1988).
- Children need to have a considerable amount of experience in conversation with adults in order to learn language (Garton & Pratt, 1998; Wells, 1981).

- When conversing with young children, adults and even older children modify their language in ways that appear to be nurturing for language development. Characteristics include simplified and well-formed sentences, a slower pace with clear pauses between utterances, exaggerated stress and intonation, reference to concrete objects and actions in the child's environment, restricted vocabulary, many questions, and much redundancy (DePaulo & Bonvillian, 1978; Garton & Pratt, 1998; Grieser & Kuhl, 1988; Snow, 1986).
- Parents tend to exhibit sensitivity to their young children's well-formed and ill-formed utterances, respond to "mistakes" by rephrasing and expanding what the child has said, and disapprove only of the "truth value" of the child's utterance or the child's use of naughty words (Bohannon & Stanowicz, 1988; Brown & Hanlon, 1970; Farrar, 1992; Nelson, Welsh, Camarata, & Butkovski, 1995).

In response to these findings, deaf educators developed instructional approaches incorporating features of adult–child communication that promote language development in young, hearing, normally developing children, assuming that such practices would generalize to deaf language learners. It should be noted that few of these instructional practices have been empirically assessed to determine their effectiveness in enhancing the language development of deaf children.

Luetke-Stahlman (1993) advocated two categories of strategies—environmental and linguistic. Environmental strategies include setting up the physical environment so that the child has a need to use language, making sure that the child has opportunities to interact socially both verbally and nonverbally, and identifying moments in which the child is motivated to use language. Linguistic strategies include providing a language model that is somewhat more complex than the language the deaf child currently produces, asking questions that encourage the child to use targeted grammatical forms, expanding and recasting the child's utterances in conversation, engaging in self-talk so that the child can observe the adult using language, and adding new vocabulary and explanations when responding to the child. Although these strategies have been used successfully with hearing children, Luetke-Stahlman could find no studies using them with deaf children.

Several specific approaches for promoting language development are commonly endorsed in deaf education—instructional conversations, role playing, cooperative learning, peer tutoring, incidental teaching, thematic unit instruction, and bilingual/bicultural approaches (Easterbrooks & Baker, 2001; Schirmer, 2000; Stewart & Kluwin, 2001). In the following, I describe each of these instructional approaches and then discuss the research on efficacy with deaf students.

Instructional Conversations. In instructional conversations, the teacher uses conversational discourse during instruction rather than the question–answer routines that are more typical of classroom discourse. During question–answer routines, the teacher controls the dialogue, the child who is called on gives a brief answer, and the teacher's next question does not necessarily follow logically from the child's answer. The teacher controls the choice of topic, takes longer turns, monitors who takes turns and how long their turns are, and determines when the topic should be changed or terminated (Cazden, 2001; Nippold, 1998). In instructional conversations, the teacher focuses on concepts and academic content while simultaneously addressing the child's language needs through restating, clarifying, and extending what the child has expressed (Perez, 1996; Schirmer, 2000). These recastings of the child's language draw the child's attention to specific language features in ways similar to the conversational contexts of parent–child interaction that have been found to be the most conducive milieu for language development. The child who uses ASL engages in an instructional conversation in sign language with the teacher of the deaf or the sign language interpreter who is interpreting for the general education teacher.

Although the strategy of instructional conversations has been promoted for deaf children (Clarke, 1983; Clarke & Stewart, 1986; Kretschmer & Kretschmer, 1995; Weiss, 1986), only a few studies have examined its efficacy in that context. Prinz and Masin (1985) investigated the influence of adult recasting on deaf children's utterances. The participants were six children between the ages of 9 months and 6 years at the outset of the study, and their parents and teachers. Two children had deaf parents; the others had hearing parents. Parents and teachers were given training on how to recast the children's utterances into targeted syntactic structures that the children were not currently using in their language. After 5 months and at least 20 hours of intervention, Prinz and Masin found that the targeted structures appeared in the spontaneous communication of the children.

Wood and associates (D. J. Wood, Wood, Griffiths, Howarth, & Howarth, 1982; H. A. Wood & Wood, 1984) found that several conversational features worked in combination to encourage deaf children to be conversational partners with their teachers. Personal contributions, in the form of comments or statements, and phatics (phrases such as "Oh, that's interesting" and "I see," head nodding in response to the child's contribution, or repeating the child's comment) by the teacher resulted in greater conversational participation, elaborated answers, and greater asking of questions by the child. Asking questions, particularly stringing questions together, and requiring the child to repeat phrases resulted in little spontaneous conversational participation by the child. Wood and associates also found that simply asking teachers to become more responsive to the deaf children's responses produced better conversations—but not the lively or purposeful discussions the researchers had observed in other classrooms. They noted that the teachers often reverted to what the authors termed "repair" strategies in order to sort out what exactly the child was trying to express. I could find no research beyond the 1980s that examined the effectiveness of instructional conversations on improving or accelerating the language acquisition of deaf students.

A related approach, called "scaffolded conversations," was examined by Skarakis-Doyle and Murphy (1996). In a scaffolded conversation, the teacher is aware of the child's language goals and provides opportunities within the conversation to support the child's use of particular structures, meanings, and uses. The metaphor of the scaffold represents the temporary nature of the support structure that assists the child in using new grammatical forms and meanings. Skarakis-Doyle and Murphy used this approach with a 5-year-old deaf child and found that it facilitated her language acquisition.

Role Playing. In role playing, students recreate and act out a problem, event, or situation (Orlich, Harder, Callahan, Trevisan, & Brown, 2004; Rockler, 1988). In young children, imaginative play serves an important function in language development. Yawkey and Hrncir (1983) observed that role playing encourages the use of various forms of communication, development of social language, creative expression, and concentration in preschool children.

Stone (1988) developed an approach that incorporated conversational features into role playing. These conversational scenarios are carefully planned by the teacher to engage the deaf child in a realistic conversation that requires the child to use a specific conversational skill or language feature that the child has not yet mastered. The teacher sets up the role-playing situation by providing a description of the scenario to the child such as, "Let's pretend that your grandmother came for a visit last weekend. She took you to the zoo. On Monday, you come to school and tell your friend about it." The teacher takes the role of the friend and the child takes the role of him- or herself. According to Stone, several elements are essential to each scenario: (a) The situation and topic are familiar to the student; (b) the student understands the situation before beginning the role play; (c) the scenario involves a need to use the targeted conversational skill or language feature; (d) the teacher stays in role and does not tell the child what to say but rather allows the role-play situation and conversation to bring about a need to use the targeted skill; (e) if the child does not use the targeted skill or does not use it correctly, the teacher uses an intervention strategy; and (f) the conversation is carried to a logical conclusion. Stone recommended four possible intervention strategies; selection depends on how much difficulty the targeted skill is presenting to the child.

1. In teacher clarification, the teacher offers a statement that clarifies what the child has just expressed.

2. In requesting clarification, the teacher (a) makes a comment or looks at the child in a way that makes it obvious to the child that his or her utterance was not appropriate, (b) pauses, and (c) gives the child time to clarify the utterance.
3. In role switching, the teacher and student switch roles so that the teacher can demonstrate the targeted skill.
4. In prompting, the teacher steps out of the role play and points out to the child the place in the conversation where the child is making a mistake.

I could find no research on the effectiveness of role playing for enhancing the deaf child's language development.

Cooperative Learning and Peer Tutoring. Cooperative learning involves a set of teaching strategies that are designed to structure student-to-student interaction in the classroom in a way that fosters cooperation rather than competition or individualization. The aspect of cooperative learning that has been used to promote language development is the face-to-face interaction and social skills necessitated by cooperative learning activities (D. W. Johnson, Johnson, & Holubec, 1994; Schirmer, 2000). Peer tutoring is one child teaching another of approximately the same age and skill level (Greenwood, 1991). When used for drill and practice on functional academic skills such as spelling words and math facts, peer tutoring is effective in learning the information but not for developing language because of the nature of the communication between the peer tutors, which involves relatively brief comments (Delquadri, Greenwood, Whorton, Carta, & Hall, 1986). However, when used in learning activities that require lengthy student responses, peer tutoring appears to have the potential to encourage language development (Schirmer, 2000).

In spite of the promise of both approaches, I could find no research on either cooperative learning or peer tutoring as approaches for promoting language development in deaf children.

Incidental Teaching of Language. When the term *incidental* is used, it generally means that (a) two events occur concurrently, (b) one is major and one is minor, and (c) the minor event is fortuitous. When used in the context of teaching language, it means that the teacher uses every instructional event as an opportunity to develop a language skill (Schirmer, 2000; Staab, 1983; Warren & Kaiser, 1986). I found no research on face-to-face incidental teaching of language but one study was conducted on incidental teaching through Internet conversations.

Schirmer and Ingram (2003) conducted an investigation to determine if specific features of the written language of deaf students could be improved through teacher recasting during online discussion. Compared to e-mail or other asynchronous communications, online chats can provide a closer match to face-to-face conversation because the dialogue can take place in real time. When these conversations are used instructionally, the teacher can monitor them, incorporate conversational features that are particularly nurturing for language acquisition, and apply conversational strategies deliberatively in instructional contexts. Two experiments were carried out. Experiment 1 involved three pairs of high school students and Experiment 2 involved four pairs of middle school students. Each pair included one deaf student from a special school or class for deaf students and one hearing student from a public school. The students met daily online using classroom computers on which special software had been uploaded that allowed them to have a graphical discussion of an astronomy topic. The instructional intervention used by the online teacher, one of the investigators, was to recast the deaf students' written language using language structures that were not appearing consistently in their spontaneous writing. Only one of the three pairs completed Experiment 1; results indicated that the strategy was effective in promoting significant increases in the use of the targeted language structure. All pairs completed Experiment 2; results did not provide evidence for the effectiveness of the strategy in this experiment. The researchers concluded that recasting during online chats between peers may have potential as an effective intervention with deaf students at the high school age but not with younger deaf students. The strategy of incidental instruction may simply be ineffective unless paired with periods of direct instruction similar to the prompting intervention strategy in the conversational scenarios approach.

Thematic Unit Instruction. Thematic unit instruction is an approach in which each school subject focuses on the same topic for a unit of study and approaches the topic from the unique perspective of the discipline (Dillon, 1990; Jacobs, 1989). For deaf language learners, thematic unit instruction can promote vocabulary development because the common set of concepts that are explored in a thematic unit are expressed through a common set of vocabulary, and the learning of this vocabulary should become deeper as the nuances of meaning are examined and applied to a variety of contexts (Schirmer, 2000).

As with other approaches with a strong theoretical rationale, there appears to be no research on the relationship between thematic unit instruction and language development of deaf children.

Bilingual/Bicultural Approaches. Bilingual/bicultural approaches for teaching deaf students followed research in the 1970s demonstrating that ASL has a rule structure distinct from other languages, including English, and that it is as complex and rich as other languages (Klima & Bellugi, 1979; Stokoe, 1971). Bilingual/bicultural instruction is conducted in ASL, with the expectation that the students will use ASL for communication; English is taught through the written form only, with no or little use of spoken English. Bilingual/bicultural education was adapted from English as a Second Language (ESL) instruction designed for hearing students whose home language is different from the language used in school (Baker, 2001; Cummins, 1987; Romaine, 1995). These ESL approaches have not been easily adapted to language instruction with deaf children, who must learn a visual–gestural language without a written form (ASL) and a spoken language through its written form (English; Schirmer, 2000).

The interest in and advocacy for these approaches, typically referred to as "bi-bi," grew dramatically during the 1990s. Three attributes are considered integral: First, ASL is introduced as the child's first language and English is taught as a second language. Second, Deaf individuals play a major role in designing, implementing, and evaluating the educational program. Third, Deaf culture is part of the curriculum. Although many educational programs for deaf students incorporated bi-bi approaches during the 1990s, there has been a lack of research on their effectiveness. The rhetoric has been high, and the literature contains numerous articles and essays supporting bi-bi approaches. But the programs that have been implemented have not provided empirical data on effective and ineffective program features (e.g., Andrews, Ferguson, Roberts, & Hodges, 1997; Drasgow, 1998; J. Johnson, 1998; Neuroth-Gimbrone & Logiodice, 1992; Saunders, 1997; Strong, 1995).

Instructional Practices for Developing Reading

Instructional practices for developing reading in deaf children has followed a similar historical pattern to instructional practices for developing their language. Just as methods for teaching language were grounded in teaching the grammar of English, so it was research on the sentence structures that presented the most difficulty to deaf children that formed the basis for designing reading instruction. For example, *Reading Milestones* is a basal reading series that was developed specifically for deaf readers. Based on research conducted by Quigley and associates in the 1970s (e.g., Quigley, Power, & Steinkamp, 1977; Quigley, Wilbur, & Montanelli, 1974), it highlighted particular sentence structures as most problematic for deaf readers. The series controls the appearance of language structures so that structures considered to be easier are presented in the earliest materials, and as the child gains skill, stories with increasingly more complex sentence structures are presented (Quigley, McAnally, King, & Rose, 1991).

The general shift to whole-language approaches in the 1990s was paralleled in deaf education. Instruction based on whole language reflected constructivist theory, whereas earlier instruction, based on a skills approach, had reflected behaviorist theory. Whole language emphasized (a) the interrelationship between reading and writing, (b) the meaning of written language in contexts viewed as authentic because activities and materials involved reading complete texts and did not focus on skills instruction, (c) the belief that reading and writing were best acquired by providing children ample opportunity to engage in reading and to write for audiences that included individuals other than the teacher, (d) a focus on giving children choice about what they read and the topics on which they wrote, and (e) a view of the process of writing as more important than the correctness of the product (Goodman, 1989; Harste, 1989; Moorman, Blanton, & McLaughlin, 1994).

The swinging pendulum in reading education influenced preferred practices in deaf education. When code-based approaches to reading development were popular, teachers of the deaf focused on breaking the sentence code, although not the code at the word level through word recognition skills such as sight word learning and phonic analysis, as general education teachers did. When meaning-based approaches to reading development became popular, teachers of the deaf were encouraged to teach even more similarly to general education teachers; they were urged to focus on comprehension of what was referred to as authentic reading materials, distinguishing these materials from the contrived nature of basal reading materials that controlled for content and vocabulary (e.g., Livingston, 1997; Schleper, 1994). When the pendulum swung again in the late 1990s to incorporate what was believed to be the best aspects of code-based and meaning-based approaches, an approach sometimes referred to as balanced literacy, deaf education followed suit. Word recognition, and the deaf child's potential ability to use phonic analysis specifically to identify words in print, took on new importance (Schirmer & Williams, 2003). These parallel trends in reading practices have not been contemporaneous. Rather, practices in deaf education have trailed practices in reading education; when particular approaches are at peak interest in deaf education, the same approaches are waning in general education (Schirmer & Williams, 2003).

Currently, reading instruction for deaf children is typically structured around emergent reading, word recognition, fluency, and comprehension, each of which is discussed in the following sections. Again, there is a paucity of research on the effectiveness of these approaches in the teaching of deaf children, although some work has been done (Schirmer & McGough, 2005).

Emergent Reading. Two approaches to engaging young deaf children in literacy activities prior to formal instruction include interactive storybook reading and the use of sign print materials. In interactive storybook reading, the teacher reads a story aloud and engages the children in discussion. Andrews and Mason (1986a, 1986b) carried out a series of intervention studies with deaf kindergarten and first-grade children in which the teacher read the story using sign language; discussed the story; focused on target words from the story; and gave the children a copy of the story to read, retell, dramatize, and use for practicing fingerspelling and printing the target words. Children receiving the intervention outperformed the comparison group on story retelling and word recognition tasks. Several other studies showed that preschool deaf children demonstrate engagement and interest in storybook reading, although there appears to be no evidence beyond the Andrews and Mason studies that interactive storybook reading actually improves early reading performance (Gillespie & Twardosz, 1997; Rowe & Allen, 1995; Williams & McLean, 1997).

The results of two case studies of deaf preschoolers point to the potential effects of sign print (i.e., graphic representation of the sign, or sign language picture, above each English word) on word recognition. Maxwell (1984) carried out a longitudinal study of a deaf child interacting with her parents during interactive storybook readings. The child was age 2 at the outset and age 6 at the conclusion. Maxwell found that the child's attention to the sign print and matching of her own signs to the sign print were similar to how hearing children match speech to orthography. Rottenberg (2001), who examined the early reading development of a 4-year-old deaf child, found that the child relied heavily on the sign print initially but within a year relied increasingly on the printed text.

Word Recognition. Readers have essentially five strategies for recognizing words in print. Phonic analysis involves using the cues that letter–sound relationships offer. It is dependent on phonemic awareness, which is the child's ability to focus on and manipulate phonemes in spoken words. Analogy involves the use of the cues that similar known words offer. Structural analysis involves using the cues that morphemes offer. Context involves using the semantic and syntactic cues of known words in the sentence. Sight word recognition involves the ability of the reader to identify a word automatically.

I could find only one study in which the researchers examined the effects of teaching phonemic awareness to deaf readers. Schimmel, Edwards, and Prickett (1999) implemented a reading program with 48 elementary deaf students for 1 year. One of the five components of the program was phonemic awareness. No description of teaching strategies was provided. Although data indicated growth in phonemic awareness, the study did not indicate which aspects of intervention were responsible for the positive findings.

Several researchers have explored other codes unique to deaf readers for representing English phonemes, morphemes, and words. This small body of research indicates that some deaf students use fingerspelling when they read; they show increased word identification when they decode into fingerspelling; and better deaf readers may use visual codes, including a sign-based code (Hirsh-Pasek, 1987; Siedlecki, Votaw, Bonvillian, & Jordan, 1990; Transler, Leybaert, & Gombert, 1999). However, I could find no research assessing the effects of teaching deaf readers to use fingerspelling or sign language in decoding.

Of the other studies on word recognition with deaf readers, the focus has been exclusively on sight word development. In two studies, sight words were taught in the context of reading material. Koskinen, Wilson, and Jensema (1986) found that retention of sight vocabulary was greater in lessons using closed-captioned television than in traditional reading materials with deaf high school students. M. A. Johnson and Roberson (1988) engaged deaf kindergarten and first-grade students in a language experience instructional program in which the children dictated sentences to the teacher, the teacher wrote these in the form of a story, and the children used these stories as their reading material. The researchers reported that the kindergartners added 31 words and the first graders added 58 words to their reading vocabularies by the end of the 3-month program. The researchers provided no comparative data from the research literature to indicate if these results were significantly better than results with hearing or deaf children of comparable ages who did not receive the intervention.

Two studies addressed teaching sight words by matching the printed form to the signed form. In the Schimmel et al. (1999) reading program discussed earlier, one of the components was adapted Dolch word lists (i.e., words appearing with high frequency in typical reading material for children) linked to commonly used meanings with appropriate ASL signs. No information was provided regarding the techniques for teaching these as sight words. Descriptive data indicated gains on learning the Dolch words, although no statistical analysis was conducted to examine whether these gains were significant. Wauters, Knoors, Vervloed, and Aarnoutse (2001) investigated the effects of an instructional intervention designed to improve the word recognition of deaf elementary readers through pairing signs (in Sign Language of the Netherlands) with written words. Results showed that accuracy was significantly higher for words learned through speech accompanied by signs than for words learned only through speech.

Two studies involved the sight word learning of young deaf children. Suzuki and Notoya (1984) trained six mothers to teach their oral deaf children, who were between the ages of 1 and 3 at the outset of the study, to identify words matched with objects, pictures, or actions. After 45 months, the researchers found that the children's written vocabulary was significantly greater than their spoken vocabulary. Soderbergh (1985) conducted an investigation of an explicit approach for teaching sight vocabulary to deaf children between ages 3 and 6. One word was taught each day by matching the printed word with an object or action and the corresponding sign (in sign language). When the child had learned 50 common words, new words were embedded in simple sentences taken from a story, and one sentence was presented each day. As in Suzuki and Notoya, the children's written language appeared to positively influence spoken and sign language development.

Fluency. Fluency is the ability to read accurately, quickly, and with appropriate expression. The two most common types of fluency instruction are guided oral reading and independent silent reading (National Reading Panel, 2000). In guided oral reading approaches, students read passages orally with systematic and explicit guidance and feedback. In independent silent reading, students are encouraged to read extensively on their own or with minimal guidance and feedback. I could find no studies that examined guided oral reading and only one study that addressed independent oral reading as an approach for increasing fluency with deaf readers. Limbrick, McNaughton, and Clay (1992) calculated the quantity of time allocated in reading for 5- to 10-year-old deaf children and found a correlation between levels of engaged time and reading achievement.

Comprehension. The research literature on comprehension of deaf readers divides along two major categories: the readers' use of prior knowledge and their cognitive strategies.

Prior knowledge. The research on prior knowledge falls into four areas: knowledge of syntax, background knowledge of text topic, knowledge of text structure, and vocabulary knowledge.

1. *Knowledge of syntax:* The deaf reader has obvious difficulty with English syntax. Numerous studies have focused on the effects of syntactic difficulties on reading performance and ways to ameliorate these difficulties through syntactic manipulations of text material. Results have indicated that (a) efforts to control readability through manipulation of syntax and vocabulary may result in texts that are actually more difficult for deaf students to comprehend because of lack of text coherence, (b) syntactic complexity does not influence comprehension, (c) pictorial symbols improve comprehension, and (d) deaf readers are sensitive to text format (e.g., sentences divided into phrase units and inserted pictorial symbols; Diebold & Waldron, 1988; Gregory, 1987; Israelite & Helfrich, 1988; Negin, 1987).

2. *Background knowledge of text topic:* Studies with deaf readers support the conclusion that background knowledge directly influences reading comprehension (e.g., Garrison, Long, & Dowaliby, 1997), but intervention studies have shown mixed effects for approaches designed to build and activate students' prior knowledge of topics before reading. Findings indicate that (a) thematic organizers are not sufficient for activating or applying background knowledge; (b) summarizing an upcoming passage in ASL prior to reading improves comprehension; and (c) reading comprehension is more positively promoted by asking the students lengthy, multiple-part questions about an upcoming passage than asking brief questions before reading (Andrews, Winograd, & DeVille, 1994; Jackson, Paul, & Smith, 1997; Schirmer & Winter, 1993). This small body of empirical research is a promising indication that providing extensive information prior to reading is considerably more valuable than providing brief information.

3. *Knowledge of text structure:* The research on hearing children has shown that they expect text to have a predictable structure and demonstrate better comprehension and recall of text that adheres to predictable structures. Although it has been conjectured that deaf readers develop knowledge of text structure more slowly than hearing readers, the actual research evidence is inconclusive regarding the text structure knowledge of deaf readers (e.g., Griffith & Ripich, 1988; Schirmer 1993). In several intervention studies, approaches to teaching story structure to deaf readers that involved explicitly teaching story components, implicitly teaching these components through asking questions that highlight the components, and teacher mediation of children's story retellings all proved effective (Akamatsu, 1988; Cambra, 1994; Luetke-Stahlman, Griffiths, & Montgomery, 1998; Schirmer & Bond, 1990).

4. *Vocabulary knowledge:* Although the literature contains numerous theoretical and opinion articles on the importance of vocabulary on the reading comprehension of deaf readers, the three empirical studies with deaf participants provide limited evidence for the positive relationship between vocabulary knowledge and reading comprehension in deaf readers (e.g., Garrison et al., 1997; Kelly, 1996; LaSasso & Davey, 1987). Investigations of vocabulary interventions are also small in number. In the only intervention study I could find, deVilliers and Pomerantz (1992) examined the extent to which deaf students in middle and high school could learn vocabulary through written context that was lean (i.e., provided little information about meaning other than the word's

grammatical category), rich (i.e., provided a great deal of semantic information about the word), or explicit (i.e., provided a clear contrast or equivalence statement). Results showed that all of the students performed better with rich and explicit context. Findings also revealed that the better deaf readers were able to gain more from context than the poorer readers, independent of their language modes. The findings of this study suggest that the method of indirect instruction appears to hold promise. However, there is an inherent challenge in finding texts that consistently provide this kind of rich and explicit content.

Cognitive strategies. Cognitive strategies involve the ways that readers consciously monitor their comprehension and adapt their strategies to improve understanding (Schirmer & Williams, 2003). These include comprehension monitoring, question answering, question generating, mental imagery, and making inferences.

- Comprehension monitoring: Comprehension monitoring involves the readers' awareness and control over their own comprehension processes. It can be viewed as having four parts: knowing when you comprehend, knowing what you comprehend, knowing what you need to know in order to comprehend, and knowing how to invoke strategies to improve comprehension. Given the relatively weak comprehension-monitoring skills found in studies of deaf readers (Davey, 1987; Strassman, 1992), I expected to find intervention studies designed to improve their skills but found no empirical investigations designed specifically to improve comprehension monitoring.
- Question answering: Questions that teachers ask are designed to assess comprehension, extend comprehension, and provide models of self-questioning. For deaf readers, ability to answer questions is complicated by the relatively complex syntactic structure of question forms in English. Thus, question-answering difficulty can arise because of confusion caused by the form of the question as well as comprehension breakdowns. Two intervention studies were designed to improve comprehension through question answering. Dowaliby (1992) found that questions inserted immediately preceding a relevant page of text improved comprehension and questions inserted immediately following the page of text had no effect on comprehension with deaf college students. Schirmer and Woolsey (1997) studied the effects of teacher questions designed to encourage analysis, synthesis, and evaluation on the reading comprehension of deaf upper elementary children. Results showed a high correlation between ability to answer higher level thinking questions and inclusion of details, indicating that questions focusing on story details are not essential precursors to higher level thinking questions. However, the children had difficulty with seven reading tasks: understanding the intent of the question, locating pertinent information, considering consequential details, applying relevant and accurate background knowledge, relying appropriately on background knowledge, expressing self unambiguously, and providing a sufficient answer.
- Question generating: Related to question answering is question generating, which involves children posing and answering their own questions. In the one study I found on question generating with deaf readers, Livingston (1991) examined the strategy use of two deaf students enrolled in a basic reading course at a community college. Livingston found that the deaf students used self-questioning, as well as paraphrasing and integrating, in their written responses to reading a novel.
- Mental imagery: Mental imagery instruction involves asking readers to construct a visual or spatial represen-

tation of what they are reading. Given that sign language involves the visual and spatial modalities, mental imagery would appear to be a particularly cogent strategy for deaf readers. I found one study on teaching mental imagery to deaf students. Schirmer (1995) investigated the effectiveness of mental imagery as a reading comprehension strategy with deaf upper elementary students. Quantitative analysis showed no relationship between mental imagery and performance on comprehension measures; qualitative analysis revealed six qualities of thinking when the children engaged in mental imagery, including recollection, representation, analysis, inference, integration, and evaluation.

- Making inferences: Inferences are made by connecting background knowledge with information in the text being read. Good readers draw heavily on background knowledge to make inferences that are necessary for understanding the text (McKoon & Ratcliffe, 1992). I found one study on teaching inference-making skills to deaf readers. Walker, Munro, and Rickards (1998) found that upper elementary through high school deaf readers who were instructed in an inferential reading strategy showed greater gains in inferential and overall comprehension compared to students receiving conventional reading instruction.

Instructional Practices for Developing Writing

Traditional writing paradigms resulted in teaching strategies designed to provide instruction in skills and rules, practice in mastering techniques, and evaluation based on how error-free finished products were. The emphasis on teachers' comments, corrections, and grades on children's completed compositions led researchers to label this view of writing instruction as a writing-as-product approach (Hull, 1989). In the early 1970s, researchers began to ask new questions about writing. Instead of only asking questions about the teaching, evaluation, and development of writing skills, they started to ask questions about what individuals think about when they write. Findings from this body of research caused a shift in writing instruction, which was labeled writing-as-process (or process writing) approaches (Calkins, 1994; Emig, 1971; Graves, 1983). In product writing, stages of planning-writing-revising are seen as linear and discrete. In process writing, they are seen as dynamic and iterative.

Writing instruction with deaf students followed a similar pattern. Through the 1970s, instruction focused on producing grammatically correct sentences and appropriate vocabulary (Blackwell, Engen, Fischgrund, & Zarcadoolas, 1978; Caniglia et al., 1975; Heidinger, 1984), and research indicated that significant improvements in length and complexity of sentences written by deaf elementary children could be achieved with instruction that provided differential and immediate feedback on their writing of sentences (Heward & Eachus, 1979). However, instruction that focused exclusively on sentence-level grammar showed no lasting improvements in the writing of deaf students (Schirmer, 2000).

As writing process approaches took hold in general education, these approaches became popular in deaf education as well. Some of the literature involved descriptions of classroom writing programs believed to have a positive influence on the writing development of deaf students (Kluwin & Kelly, 1992; Luckner & Isaacson, 1990; Schleper, 1996). A few empirical investigations of instructional strategies were found to be positively related to improved writing, including instruction in the components of story structure and use of dialogue journals (Akamatsu, 1988; Cambra, 1994; Lieberth, 1991; Schirmer & Bond, 1990). In one study, researchers combined the benefits of product and process approaches by teaching deaf middle school students several key qualities of good writing and providing frequent feedback with a rubric that assessed their compositions along these dimensions of quality (Schirmer, Bailey, & Fitzgerald, 1999). Results showed improvement in traits related to topic, content, story development, and organization, but not text structure, voice/audience, word choice, sentence structures, and mechanics.

Summary of Effective Instructional Practices for Developing Language and Literacy

In returning to the question about what is special about educating deaf students—"What are the empirically supported, effective practices for students who are deaf?"—we know more about what is not effective than what is. We know that drill and practice on the grammatical features of language do not help deaf children become proficient in the language, whether that language is the spoken language of the hearing community or the sign language of the Deaf community. The evidence from research on the language acquisition of young hearing children suggests that approaches for teaching language should come as close as possible to simulating the environment in which children most effectively learn language. In this environment, the child engages in meaningful conversations with adults who modify their language in ways that support the child's emerging language abilities. Approaches that hold promise include instructional conversations, role playing, cooperative learning, peer tutoring, incidental teaching, thematic unit instruction, and bilingual/bicultural instruction.

We also know that among the approaches found to be effective for struggling readers, only a few have been investigated with deaf readers. On the one hand, we might assume that effective practices with struggling readers are generalizable to deaf readers. And this may be true for approaches for teaching literacy activities prior to formal instruction, fluency, and comprehension, specifically, approaches found to be effective with readers who struggle because of language-learning issues. However, the deaf child's challenges with letter–sound relationships raise questions about the applicability of many word recognition approaches, particularly for reading alphabetic languages such as English. From the research on deaf readers previously discussed, we know that preschool through high school deaf students can learn sight words, but no strategy, or set of strategies, has been shown to be most effective for teaching automatic word recognition. We do not know how many interactions with sight words are optimal at each age level, whether words are best taught in isolation or context, or which combination of word recognition skills enhances sight word retention. We have no research on teaching deaf students to use phonic analysis, analogy, structural analysis, or context for word recognition.

The research gives us no guidance on how best to teach fluency to deaf readers, although it is likely that the strategy of guided oral reading, which is effective with hearing readers, is applicable to deaf readers.

We know that prior knowledge of syntax, topic, text structure, and vocabulary are crucial for comprehension, but the only component for which we have empirically supported effective strategies with deaf readers is text structure. Similarly, we know that cognitive strategies employed before, during, and after reading are essential for comprehension, but the research on deaf readers is too limited to draw any conclusions about which strategies are most effective. Alternatively, the research with struggling readers has shown that explicit and systematic instruction is the key characteristic of effective comprehension instruction, regardless of strategy or technique. Consequently, it is not a great stretch from what we know about struggling readers to assume that explicitly and systematically teaching deaf students the prior knowledge they will need to interact with the author's structure and concepts, as well as the cognitive strategies for monitoring and improving understanding, will enhance comprehension.

We have little efficacy research on teaching writing to deaf readers, although explicit instruction in writing traits, such as story development and organization, appears to be a promising technique. Research with hearing students indicates that instruction should also involve providing much opportunity for students to write, share their writing, and receive timely and precise feedback.

As important as identifying evidence-based effective practices is, equally vital is the question of whether deaf education teachers use these practices to teach language and literacy to deaf students. Thus, this is the next question I address.

Do Deaf Education Teachers Use Effective Practices and Implement With Fidelity?

The question of whether deaf education teachers use evidence-based effective practices to teach language and literacy to deaf students is unanswered at this point; I could find no research examining this variable. The only investigations that came close to answering this question are the surveys of educational programs for deaf and hard of hearing students in the United States conducted by LaSasso (1987) in the mid-1980s and LaSasso and Mobley (1997) in the 1990s. Each school's program director or the individual most familiar with the reading program was asked to complete the survey. In both surveys, responses indicated that more than one third of deaf or hard of hearing students were estimated to be receiving special education services in the United States at the time. Survey questions were designed to elicit the following: (a) the extent to which basal reading series (in which relatively brief text selections are packaged in anthologies distinguished by progressive difficulty and detailed teaching instructions) and the language experience approach (in which children dictate ideas or experiences to the teacher, the teacher records their dictation into the form of an experience story, and the story becomes the children's reading material) were used, (b) the strengths and limitations of these two approaches, (c) the extent to which instructional programs had a whole-language orientation, (d) the extent and nature of print materials used, (e) the extent to which reading levels of the students and readabilities of the materials were calculated, (f) the extent of teachers' knowledge about teaching reading and professional development opportunities to upgrade knowledge and skills, and (g) factors influencing the development of reading programs. Following are the primary findings of the survey:

- The majority of programs used basal readers, although fewer in the mid-1990s (72%) compared to the mid-1980s (81%). The most popular basal reader in both surveys was *Reading Milestones*, the basal developed for deaf students that incorporates progressively more complex sentence structures. Programs using basals reported devoting more than 70% of instructional time to these materials with 5- to 12-year-old students. The two most frequent reasons cited for using basal readers was the requirement by state or school districts and the perceived belief that basals offered the best organizational framework for reading instruction.
- The majority of programs also used the language experience approach, with a greater number in the mid-1990s (81%) compared to the mid-1980s (75%). Most of these programs (91%) in the mid-1990s survey reported that the language experience approach fit into a whole-language framework (the question was not posed in the earlier survey). The two most frequent reasons cited for using the language experience approach were (a) the belief that it was the best approach and (b) the perceived absence of any appropriate basal or other method.
- The majority of programs in the mid-1990s survey (81%) reported that "whole language" characterized their reading program, but most of these (78%) also reported that the majority of their whole-language instruction was supplementary as opposed to primary (begging the question of why respondents would have characterized their reading programs as "whole language").
- The majority of programs in both surveys (84% and 83%, respectively, in the mid-1990s and mid-1980s) reported calculating students' reading levels. Of these, 82% in the mid-1980s and 64% in the mid-1990s listed one reason as knowing which level of printed materials to use with students, and 75% in the mid-1980s and 61% in the mid-1990s listed another reason as being a good way to measure growth in reading.

- A minority of programs (20% in the mid-1980s and 17% in the mid-1990s) reported using readability formulas to calculate the difficulty level of reading materials; 51% of the programs in the mid-1990s reported being unfamiliar with readability procedures (compared to 44% in the mid-1980s); and 40% in the mid-1990s considered teacher judgment to be superior to readability formulas (compared to 27% in the mid-1980s).
- Programs reported that the top influence on methods of reading instruction was research, followed closely by teachers' input. Of the programs using *Reading Milestones*, approximately 90% reported it was because the basal series was developed for deaf and hard of hearing students; 50% reported selecting it because their experience indicated it was effective.

I report so extensively on this particular set of surveys because first, it is the only such research I could find on instructional practices with deaf students, and second, it provides some evidence for a divide between research and practice in deaf education. At the time of the mid-1990s survey, whole language was in its heyday. Most programs reported that whole language characterized their reading program, but close to the same number reported relying predominantly on basal readers, which are viewed as antithetical to whole language. Between the 1980s and 1990s, although the percentage of programs assessing student reading levels remained unchanged, there was a steep decline in this assessment for the purpose of selecting reading materials and assessing student growth, two crucial activities for effective reading instruction. A low percentage of programs reported using any method for determining the difficulty level of reading materials other than teacher judgment, a relatively unreliable method for matching student reading level to text difficulty. And, most confounding, programs reported that the top influence on their choice of instructional approaches was research, yet most of these programs used *Reading Milestones*, an approach with no efficacy research.

I found no research literature on fidelity of implementation, but these same survey results point to the likelihood that deaf education teachers do not implement practices with fidelity. If programs can characterize their reading instruction as whole language, yet predominantly use a highly contrived basal reading series, the link between what research has discovered about effective practices and what the teacher actually does with these practices is tenuous at best.

Can Any Teacher in Any Setting Implement These Practices?

Deaf education has viewed itself as the most special of special education, so the notion that effective instructional practices can be implemented by teachers not trained to teach deaf children is anathema. Yet the research has not pointed to value added by having teachers of the deaf deliver instruction versus special education teachers or general education teachers. The inclusion movement opened the doors for the communication barrier to be reduced, if not fully eliminated, with sign language interpreters and real-time graphic display notetakers following deaf students into general education classrooms and resource rooms.

A more practical question might be, which teacher is more likely to implement empirically supported practices with deaf students? I am led to concur with the Zigmond's (this volume) point that effective interventions with special education students require a considerable investment of time and effort unsuited for classrooms of 25 and more students with a range of abilities and needs. Although the instructional practices discussed in this chapter may be effective with most or all students, these practices may be necessary only for the deaf students or others with similar language and literacy development issues.

Academic achievement levels of deaf students have been abysmally low for the history of deaf education, and there has been no perceivable improvement or decline with the changing demographics in placements from largely residential programs in the 1960s to predominantly local public school programs today. As settings have changed, the amount of time deaf students are taught directly by teachers of the deaf has lessened. Setting and teacher characteristics have had little influence on what appear to be virtually intractable challenges. It is unlikely that general education teachers would be able to offer the level of support needed by deaf students.

The problem in providing empirically supported, effective practices for students who are deaf is twofold. First, there is a paltry body of empirical research on teaching literacy to deaf students. Approaches for teaching language and literacy to children with learning issues similar to those of deaf students, such as second language learners and children with language disabilities, may be appropriate, but even these approaches should be replicated with deaf students to ensure applicability. The second issue is figuring out how to persuade teachers of the deaf to learn and use empirically validated practices.

NOTE

American Sign Language (ASL) is the language of Deaf individuals in the United States and Canada. It is a visual–gestural language with a grammatical rule structure that is distinct from that of English. As with most languages, ASL has regional and local dialects, although individuals using different dialects are able to communicate with one another. *Signed English* is a sign language system developed for use in educational settings that represents English in a visual–gestural modality; another term is *manually coded English*. *Pidgin Sign* refers to the use of signs from American Sign Language in English word order but without the grammatical complexity of either language; other terms include *Pidgin Sign Language* and *Pidgin Sign English*. *Total communication* refers to the method of communication employed in schools that involves the use of sign language (usually signed English or Pidgin Sign), fingerspelling, speech, speechreading, residual hearing, and amplification of sound; it is sometimes referred to as *simultaneous communication*. *Oralism* refers to the method of communication employed in schools that involves the use of speech, speechreading, residual hearing, stimulation of the auditory nerve fibers through a cochlear implant, and amplification of sound. *Manualism,* a term that went out of favor in the mid-20th century, refers to the use of sign language in instruction.

REFERENCES

Akamatsu, C. T. (1988). Summarizing stories: The role of instruction in text structure in learning to write. *American Annals of the Deaf, 133,* 294–302.

Allen, T. (1986). Patterns of academic achievement among hearing impaired students: 1974 and 1983. In A. N. Schildroth & M. A. Karchmer (Eds.), *Deaf children in America* (pp. 161–206). San Diego: Little, Brown.

Andrews, J. F., Ferguson, C., Roberts, S., & Hodges, P. (1997). What's up, Billy Jo? Deaf children and bilingual-bicultural instruction in east-central Texas. *American Annals of the Deaf, 142,* 16–25.

Andrews, J. F., Mason, J. (1986a). Childhood deafness and the acquisition of print concepts. In D. Yaden & S. Templeton (Eds.), *Metalinguistic awareness and beginning literacy: Conceptualizing what it means to read and write* (pp. 277–290). Portsmouth, NH: Heinemann.

Andrews, J. F., & Mason, J. (1986b). How do deaf children learn about prereading? *American Annals of the Deaf, 131,* 210–217.

Andrews, J. F., Winograd, P., & DeVille, G. (1994). Deaf children reading fables: Using ASL summaries to improve reading comprehension. *American Annals of the Deaf, 139,* 378–386.

Baker, C. (2001). *Foundations of bilingual education and bilingualism* (3rd ed.). Clevedon, England: Multilingual Matters.

Bender, R. E. (1970). *The conquest of deafness.* Cleveland: Case Western Reserve University.

Blackwell, P. M., Engen, E., Fischgrund, J. E., & Zarcadoolas, C. (1978). *Sentences and other systems: A language and learning curriculum for hearing-impaired children.* Washington, DC: Alexander Graham Bell Association for the Deaf.

Bohannon, J. N., & Stanowicz, L. (1988). The issue of negative evidence: Adult responses to children's language errors. *Developmental Psychology, 24,* 684–689.

Brown, R. (1973). *A first language: The early stages.* Cambridge, MA: Harvard University Press.

Brown, R., & Hanlon, C. (1970). Derivational complexity and order of acquisition in child speech. In J. R. Hayes (Ed.), *Cognition and the development of language* (pp. 11–53). New York: Wiley.

Calkins, L. M. (1994). *The art of teaching writing* (2nd ed.). Portsmouth, NH: Heinemann.

Cambra, C. (1994). An instructional program approach to improve hearing-impaired adolescents' narratives: A pilot study. *The Volta Review, 96,* 237–245.

Caniglia, J., Cole, N. J., Howard, W., Krohn, E., & Rice, M. (1975). *Apple tree.* Beaverton, OR: Dormac.

Cazden, C. B. (2001). *Classroom discourse: The language of teaching and learning* (2nd ed.). Portsmouth, NH: Heinemann.

Clarke, B. R. (1983). Competence in communication for hearing impaired children: A conversation, activity, experience approach. *B. C. Journal of Education, 7,* 15–17.

Clarke, B. R., & Stewart, D. A. (1986). Reflections on language programs for the hearing impaired. *The Journal of Special Education, 20,* 153–165.

Cummins, J. (1987). Bilingualism, language proficiency, and metalinguistic development. In P. Homel, M. Palil, & D. Aronson (Eds.), *Childhood bilingualism: Aspects of linguistic, cognitive, and social development* (pp. 57–73). Mahwah, NJ: Erlbaum.

Davey, B. (1987). Postpassage questions: Task and reader effects on comprehension and metacomprehension processes. *Journal of Reading Behavior, 19,* 261–283.

Delquadri, J., Greenwood, C. R., Whorton, D., Carta, J. J., & Hall, R. V. (1986). Classwide peer tutoring. *Exceptional Children, 52,* 535–542.

DePaulo, B. M., & Bonvillian, J. D. (1978). The effect on language development of the special characteristics of speech addressed to children. *Journal of Psycholinguistic Research, 7,* 189–211.

deVilliers, P. A., & Pomerantz, S. B. (1992). Hearing-impaired students learning new words from written context. *Applied Psycholinguistics, 13,* 409–431.

deVilliers, P. A., & deVilliers, J. G. (1979). *Early language.* Cambridge, MA: Harvard University Press.

Diebold, T. J., & Waldron, M. B. (1988). Designing instructional formats: The effects of verbal and pictorial components on hearing-impaired students' comprehension of science concepts. *American Annals of the Deaf, 133,* 30–35.

Dillon, D. (1990). Deaf readers. *Language Arts, 67,* 7–9.

Dowaliby, F. J. (1992). The effects of adjunct questions in prose for deaf and hearing students at different reading levels. *American Annals of the Deaf, 137,* 338–344.

Drasgow, E. (1998). American Sign Language as a pathway to linguistic competence. *Exceptional Children, 64,* 329–342.

Easterbrooks, S. R., & Baker, S. (2001). *Language learning in children who are deaf and hard of hearing: Multiple pathways.* Boston: Allyn & Bacon.

Emig, J. (1971). *The composing process of twelfth graders.* Urbana, IL: National Council of Teachers of English.

Farrar, J. (1992). Negative evidence and grammatical morpheme acquisition. *Developmental Psychology, 28,* 90–98.

Fitzgerald, E. (1949). *Straight language for the deaf.* Washington, DC: Volta Bureau.

Gallaudet Research Institute. (2005a). *Literacy and deaf students.* Retrieved May 3, 2005, from http://gri.gallaudet.edu/Literacy/index.html.

Gallaudet Research Institute. (2005b). *Stanford Achievement Test 10th edition norming.* Retrieved May 3, 2005, from http://gri.gallaudet.edu/~catraxle/sat10-faq.html.

Garrison, W., Long, G., & Dowaliby, F. (1997). Working memory capacity and comprehension processes in deaf readers. *Journal of Deaf Studies and Deaf Education, 2,* 78–94.

Garton, A, & Pratt, C. (1998). *Learning to be literate: The development of spoken and written language.* Oxford, England: Basil Blackwell.

Gentile, A., & DiFrancesca, S. (1969). *Academic achievement test performance of hearing-impaired students: Unites States, Spring, 1969.* (Series D, No. 1). Washington, DC: Gallaudet University, Center for Assessment and Demographic Studies.

Gillespie, C. W., & Twardosz, S. (1997). A group storybook-reading intervention with children at a residential school for the deaf. *American Annals of the Deaf, 141,* 320–332.

Gleason, J. B. (2004). *The development of language* (6th ed.). Boston: Allyn & Bacon.

Goodman, K. S. (1989). Whole-language research: Foundations and development. *The Elementary School Journal, 90,* 207–221.

Graves, D. H. (1983). *Writing: Teachers and children at work.* Portsmouth, NH: Heinemann.

Greenwood, C. R. (1991). Classwide peer tutoring: Longitudinal effects on the reading, language, and mathematics achievement of at-risk students. *Reading, Writing, and Learning Disabilities, 7,* 105–123.

Gregory, J. F. (1987). Oral word grouping and silent reading behaviors of deaf students. *B.C. Journal of Special Education, 11,* 149–158.

Grieser, D. L., & Kuhl, P. K. (1988). Maternal speech to infants in a tonal language: Support for universal prosodic features in motherese. *Developmental Psychology, 34,* 14–20.

Griffith, P. L., & Ripich, D. N. (1988). Story structure recall in hearing-impaired, learning-disabled, and nondisabled children. *American Annals of the Deaf, 133,* 43–50.

Halliday, M. A. K. (1975). *Learning how to mean: Explorations in the development of language.* New York: Elsevier-North Holland.

Harste, J. C. (1989). The future of whole language. *The Elementary School Journal, 90,* 243–249.

Heidinger, V. A. (1984). *Analyzing syntax and semantics: A self-instructional approach for teachers and clinicians.* Washington, DC: Gallaudet University Press.

Heward, W. L., & Eachus, H. T. (1979). Acquisition of adverbs and adjectives to sentences written by hearing impaired and aphasic children. *Journal of Applied Behavior Analysis, 12,* 391–400.

Hirsh-Pasek, K. (1987). The metalinguistics of fingerspelling: An alternate way to increase reading vocabulary in congenitally deaf readers. *Reading Research Quarterly, 22,* 455–474.

Holt, J. (1993). Stanford Achievement Test—8th edition: Reading comprehension sub-group results. *American Annals of the Deaf, 138,* 172–175.

Hull, G. A. (1989). Research on writing: Building a cognitive and social understanding of composing. In L. B. Resnick & L. E. Klopfer (Eds.), *Toward the thinking curriculum: Current cognitive research* (pp. 104–128). Alexandria, VA: Association for Supervision and Curriculum Development.

Israelite, N. K., & Helfrich, M. A. (1988). Improving text coherence in basal readers: Effects of revisions on the comprehension of hearing-impaired and normal-hearing readers. *The Volta Review, 90,* 261–276.

Jackson, D. W., Paul, P. V., & Smith, J. C. (1997). Prior knowledge and reading comprehension ability of deaf adolescents. *Journal of Deaf Studies and Deaf Education, 2,* 172–184.

Jacobs, H. H. (1989). *Interdisciplinary curriculum: Design and implementation.* Alexandria, VA: Association for Supervision and Curriculum Development.

Johnson, D. W., Johnson, R. T., & Holubec, E. J. (1994). *The new circles of learning: Cooperation in the classroom and school.* Alexandria, VA: Association for Supervision and Curriculum Development.

Johnson, J. (1998). New program builds bridges for hearing impaired. *American Language Review, 2*(2), 21–22.

Johnson, M. A., & Roberson, G. F. (1988). The language experience approach: Its use with young hearing-impaired students. *American Annals of the Deaf, 133,* 223–225.

Kelly, L. P. (1996). The interaction of syntactic competence and vocabulary during reading by deaf students. *Journal of Deaf Studies and Deaf Education, 1,* 75–90.

Klima, E., & Bellugi, U. (1979). *The signs of language.* Cambridge, MA: Harvard University.

Kluwin, T. N., & Kelly, A. B. (1992). Implementing a successful writing program in public schools for students who are deaf. *Exceptional Children, 59,* 41–53.

Koskinen, P. S., Wilson, R. M., & Jensema, C. J. (1986). Using closed-captioned television in the teaching of reading to deaf students. *American Annals of the Deaf, 131,* 43–46.

Kretschmer, R. r., & Kretschmer, L. W. (1995). Communication-based classrooms. *The Volta Review, 97*(5), 1–18.

Lahey, M. (1988). *Language disorders and language development.* Boston: Allyn & Bacon.

Lane, H. S. (1976). The profoundly deaf: Has oral education succeeded? *The Volta Review, 78,* 431–435.

Lang, H. G. (2003). Perspectives on the history of deaf education. In M. Marschark & P. E. Spencer (Eds.), *Oxford handbook of deaf studies, language, and education* (pp. 9–20). Oxford, England: Oxford University Press.

LaSasso, C. (1987). Survey of reading instruction for hearing-impaired students in the United States. *The Volta Review, 89,* 85–98.

LaSasso, C., & Davey, B. (1987). The relationship between lexical knowledge and reading comprehension for prelingually, profoundly hearing-impaired students. *The Volta Review, 89,* 211–220.

LaSasso, C. J., & Mobley, R. T. (1997). National survey of reading instruction for deaf or hard-of-hearing students in the U.S. *The Volta Review, 99,* 31–58.

Lieberth, A. K. (1991). Use of scaffolded dialogue journals to teach writing to deaf students. *Teaching English to Deaf and Second-Language Students, 9*(1), 10–13.

Limbrick, E. A., McNaughton, S., & Clay, M. M. (1992). Time engaged in reading: A critical factor in reading achievement. *American Annals of the Deaf, 137,* 309–314.

Livingston, S. (1991). Comprehension strategies of two deaf readers. *Sign Language Studies, 7,* 115–130.

Livingston, S. (1997). *Rethinking the education of deaf students: Theory and practice from a teacher's perspective.* Portsmouth, NH: Heinemann.

Luckner, J. L., & Isaacson, T. L. (1990). Teaching expressive writing to hearing-impaired students. *Journal of Childhood Communication Disorders, 13,* 135–152.

Luetke-Stahlman, B. (1993). Research-based language intervention strategies adapted for deaf and hard of hearing children. *American Annals of the Deaf, 138,* 404–410.

Luetke-Stahlman, B., Griffiths, C., & Montgomery, N. (1998). Development of text structure knowledge as assessed by spoken and signed retellings of a deaf second-grade student. *American Annals of the Deaf, 143,* 337–346.

Maxwell, M. (1984). A deaf child's natural development of literacy. *Sign Language Studies, 44,* 191–224.

McAnally, P. L., Rose, S., & Quigley, S. P. (1998). *Language learning practices with deaf children* (2nd ed.). Austin, TX: PRO-ED.

McKoon, G., & Ratcliffe, R. (1992). Inference during reading. *Psychological Review, 99,* 440–466.

McLaughlin, H. F. (1955). The advantage of the oral method. *The Volta Review, 57,* 209–210.

Moorman, G. B., Blanton, W. E., & McLaughlin, T. (1994). The rhetoric of whole language. *Reading Research Quarterly, 29,* 308–329.

National Reading Panel. (2000). *Report of the National Reading Panel. Teaching children to read: An evidence-based assessment of the scientific research literature on reading and its implications for reading instruction.* Washington, DC: U.S. Department of Health and Human Services.

Negin, G. A. (1987). The effects of syntactic segmentation on the reading comprehension of hearing impaired students. *Reading Psychology, 8,* 23–31.

Nelson, K. E., Welsh, J., Camarata, S., & Butkovski, N. (1995). Available input for language-impaired children and younger children of matched language levels. *First Language, 15,* 1–17.

Neuroth-Gimbrone, C., & Logiodice, C. M. (1992). A cooperative bilingual language program for deaf adolescents. *Sign Language Studies, 74,* 74–91.

Nippold, M. A. (1998). *Later language development: The school-age and adolescent years.* Austin, TX: PRO-ED.

Orlich, D. C., Harder, R. J., Callahan, R. C., Trevisan, M. S., & Brown, A. H. (2004). *Teaching strategies: A guide to better instruction* (7th ed.). Boston: Houghton Mifflin.

Perez, B. (1996). Instructional conversations as opportunities for English language acquisition for culturally and linguistically diverse students. *Language Arts, 73,* 173–181.

Prinz, P. M., & Masin, L. (1985). Lending a helping hand: Linguistic input and sign language acquisition in deaf children. *Applied Psycholinguistics, 6,* 357–370.

Pugh, B. L. (1955). *Steps in language development for the deaf.* Washington, DC: The Volta Bureau.

Quigley, S., McAnally, P., King, C., & Rose, S. (1991). *Reading milestones.* Austin, TX: PRO-ED.

Quigley, S., Power, D., & Steinkamp, M. (1977). The language structure of deaf children. *The Volta Review, 79,* 73–84.

Quigley, S., Wilbur, R., & Montanelli, D. (1974). Question formation in the language of deaf students. *Journal of Speech and Hearing Research, 17,* 699–713.

Rockler, M. J. (1988). *Innovative teaching strategies.* Scottsdale, AZ: Borsuch, Scarisbrick.

Romaine, S. (1995). *Bilingualism* (2nd ed.). Oxford, England: Basil Blackwell.

Rottenberg, C. (2001). A deaf child learns to read. *American Annals of the Deaf, 146,* 270–275.

Rowe, L., & Allen, B. (1995). Interactive storybook reading with young deaf children in school and home settings. In P. Dreyer (Ed.), *Towards multiple perspectives on literacy: Fifty-ninth Yearbook of the Claremont Reading Conference* (pp. 170–182). Claremont, CA: Claremont Reading Conference.

Saunders, J. (1997). Educating deaf and hearing children in a bilingual/bicultural environment. *CAEDHH, 23*(1), 61–68.

Schimmel, C. S., Edwards, S. G., & Prickett, H. T. (1999). Reading? . . . Pah! (I got it!): Innovative reading techniques for successful deaf readers. *American Annals of the Deaf, 144,* 298–308.

Schirmer, B. R. (1993). Constructing meaning from narrative text: Cognitive processes of deaf children. *American Annals of the Deaf, 138,* 397–403.

Schirmer, B. R. (1995). Mental imagery and the reading comprehension of deaf children. *Reading Research and Instruction, 34,* 177–188.

Schirmer, B. R. (2000). *Language and literacy development in children who are deaf* (2nd ed.). Boston: Allyn & Bacon.

Schirmer, B. R., Bailey, J., & Fitzgerald, S. M. (1999). Using a writing assessment rubric for writing development of children who are deaf. *Exceptional Children, 65,* 383–397.

Schirmer, B. R., & Bond, W. L. (1990). Enhancing the hearing impaired child's knowledge of story structure to improve comprehension of narrative text. *Reading Improvement, 27,* 242–254.

Schirmer, B. R., & Ingram, A. L. (2003). Using online chat to foster the written language development of students who are deaf. *Reading Online, 7*(1). Available at http://www.readingonline.org/articles/art_index.asp?HREF=/articles/schirmer/.

Schirmer, B. R., & McGough, S. M. (2005). Teaching reading to children who are deaf: Do the conclusions of the National Reading Panel apply? *Review of Educational Research, 75,* 83–117.

Schirmer, B. R., & Williams, C. (2003). Approaches to teaching reading. In M. Marschark & P. E. Spencer (Eds.), *Oxford handbook of deaf studies, language, and education* (pp. 110–122). Oxford, England: Oxford University Press.

Schirmer, B. R., & Winter, C. R. (1993). Use of cognitive schema by children who are deaf for comprehending narrative text. *Reading Improvement, 30,* 26–34.

Schirmer, B. R., & Woolsey, M. L. (1997). Effect of teacher questions on the reading comprehension of deaf children. *Journal of Deaf Studies and Deaf Education, 2,* 47–56.

Schleper, D. R. (1994). Whole language works . . . and I've got proof! *Perspectives in Education and Deafness, 12*(3), 12–16.

Schleper, D. R. (1996). Write that one down! Using anecdotal records to inform our teaching. *The Volta Review, 98,* 201–208.

Siedlecki, T., Votaw, M.C., Bonvillian, J. D., & Jordan, I. K. (1990). The effects of manual interference and reading level on deaf subjects' recall of word lists. *Applied Psycholinguistics, 11,* 185–199.

Skarakis-Doyle, E., & Murphy, L. (1996). Discourse-based language intervention: An efficacy study. *Journal of Children's Communication Development, 17*(2), 1–22.

Snow, C. E. (1986). Conversations with children. In P. Fletcher & M. Garman (Eds.), *Language acquisition: Studies in first language development* (pp. 69–89). Cambridge, England: Cambridge University Press.

Soderbergh, R. (1985). Early reading with deaf children. *Quarterly Review of Education, 15,* 77–85.

Staab, C. F. (1983). Language functions elicited by meaningful activities: A new dimension in language programs. *Language, Speech, and Hearing Services in Schools, 14,* 164–170.

Stewart, D. A., & Kluwin, T. N. (2001). *Teaching deaf and hard of hearing students: Content, strategies, and curriculum.* Boston: Allyn & Bacon.

Stokoe, W. (1971). *The study of sign language.* Silver Spring, MD: National Association of the Deaf.

Stone, P. (1988). *Blueprint for developing conversational competence: A planning/instruction model with detailed scenarios.* Washington, DC: Alexander Graham Bell Association for the Deaf.

Strassman, B. K. (1992). Deaf adolescents' metacognitive knowledge about school-related reading. *American Annals of the Deaf, 137,* 326–330.

Strong, M. (1995). A review of bilingual/bicultural programs for deaf children in North America. *American Annals of the Deaf, 140,* 84–94.

Stuckless, E. R., & Birch, J. W. (1966). The influence of early manual communication on linguistic development in deaf children. *American Annals of the Deaf, 111,* 452–460.

Suzuki, S., & Notoya, M. (1984). Teaching written language to deaf infants and preschoolers. *Topics in Early Childhood Special Education, 3*(4), 10–16.

Transler, C., Leybaert, J., & Gombert, J. (1999). Do deaf children use phonological syllables as reading units? *Journal of Deaf Studies and Deaf Education, 4,* 124–143.

Trybus, R., & Karchmer, M. (1977). School achievement scores of hearing impaired children: National data on achievement status and growth patterns. *American Annals of the Deaf, 122,* 62–69.

Vernon, M., & Koh, S.D. (1970). Early manual communication and deaf children's achievement. *American Annals of the Deaf, 116,* 569–574.

Walker, L., Munro, J., & Rickards, F. W. (1998). Teaching inferential reading strategies through pictures. *The Volta Review, 100,* 105–120.

Warren, S. F., & Kaiser, A. P. (1986). Incidental language teaching: A critical review. *Journal of Speech and Hearing Disorders, 51,* 291–299.

Wauters, L. N., Knoors, H. E. T., Vervloed, M. P. J., & Aarnoutse, C. A. J. (2001). Sign facilitation in word recognition. *The Journal of Special Education, 35,* 31–40.

Weiss, A. L. (1986). Classroom discourse and the hearing-impaired child. *Topics in Language Disorders, 6*(3), 60–70.

Wells, G. (1981). *Learning through interaction: The study of language development.* Cambridge, England: Cambridge University Press.

Williams, C., & McLean, M. (1997). Young deaf children's response to picture book reading in a preschool setting. *Research in the Teaching of English, 31,* 337–366.

Wolk, S., & Allen, T. E. (1984). A 5-year follow-up of reading comprehension achievement of hearing-impaired students in special education programs. *The Journal of Special Education, 18,* 161–176.

Wood, D. J., Wood, H. A., Griffiths, A. J., Howarth, S. P., & Howarth, C. I. (1982). The structure of conversations with 6- to 10-year-old deaf children. *Journal of Child Psychology, Psychiatry, and Allied Disciplines,23,* 295–308.

Wood, H. A., & Wood, D. J. (1984). An experimental evaluation of the effects of five styles of teacher conversation on the language of hearing-impaired children. *Journal of Child Psychology, Psychiatry, and Allied Disciplines, 25,* 45–62.

Yawkey, T. D., & Hrncir, E. J. (1983). Pretend play tools for oral language growth in the preschool. *The Journal of Creative Behavior, 16,* 265–271.

Chapter 6

A Unified Theory of Practice in Early Intervention/Early Childhood Special Education

Samuel L. Odom and **Mark Wolery**

In the United States, as in many other countries (Odom, Teferra, & Kaul, 2004), citizens have made a commitment to the care, welfare, development, and learning of infants and young children with identifiable disabilities, young children at clear risk of disability, and their families (Hanson, 2003). Societal values underlying this commitment are the recognition of the importance of providing support to those most in need, ensuring that such support is well planned, and basing practices on the available evidence of their effectiveness. Early intervention/early childhood special education (EI/ECSE), which has become a broad system of practices, is the institutional embodiment of these values. From this system of service, a "theory of practice" has emerged. In this chapter, we will discuss the evolution of EI/ECSE as a discipline, describe briefly the multiple theoretical orientations that serve as the foundation for EI/ECSE, propose that the multiple theories have led to a theory of practice in EI/ECSE, propose principles that reflect such a theory of practice, and identify practices associated with these principles that have a basis of evidence from the research literature.

What Is Special About EI/ECSE?

EI/ECSE occupies a unique niche in the field of education. Having historical roots in the fields of special education, early childhood education, and maternal and child health (Meisels & Shonkoff, 2000), and having blended its instructional methodology to become more compatible with current early childhood education (Sandall, McLean, Milagros, & Smith, 2000), effective practices in EI/ECSE draw from several bodies of professional literature and research. Its evolution from the practices of the late 1960s to the present has been fostered by the U.S. Department of Education's (Office of Special Education Programs) role in supporting innovation, research, systems change, and service provision (Gallagher, 2000); however, states are ultimately responsible for the implementation of services. In all states, early intervention programs for infants/toddlers and their families are available and monitored by a lead agency that the governor appoints, and state departments of education are responsible for services to preschool children. These two separate but related systems provide the service context for effective practice. EI/ECSE is different from early childhood education in its greater focus on family-centered services (especially at the EI level), individually planned educational programs, and specialized teaching approaches. It differs from school-age special education in its focus on early developmental skills that are precursors to current and later school success, and again, its emphasis on family-centered practices.

Conceptual/Theoretical Framework for EI/ECSE

Throughout its evolution, EI/ECSE has drawn from several different, and on the surface incompatible, theoretical perspectives. Current EI/ECSE practice is seated firmly in the traditional behaviorist theories of Skinner and Pavlov (Wolery, 2000), the cognitive–behavioral tradition of

Bandura (1976), and the neobehavioral blending of contextualism and behavior analysis (Odom & Loftin, 2005). Major contributions of this multifaceted perspective are practices having a strong empirical foundation, such as incidental teaching, functional assessment, positive behavior supports, and discrete trial instruction. Other contributions include attention to individualization and assessment practices for monitoring changes in children (McConnell, McEvoy, & Priest, 2002).

Constructivist theory also influences EI/ECSE practice. This theory has been shaped by the writings of Piaget and Vygtosky (Fosnot, 1996), the educational philosophy of Dewey (Greene, 1996), the more recent applied and theoretical work of Feuerstein and colleagues (Feuerstein, 1980; Klein, 2003), and the sociocultural research of Rogoff (2003) and Lave and Wenger (1991). Constructivist theory is the foundation for the guidelines of developmentally appropriate practices in early childhood education, as described by the National Association for the Education of Young Children (2005). Curricula for young children with and without disabilities have been based on a constructivist theoretical framework (e.g., Haywood, Brooks, & Burns, 1992). Major contributions of this perspective are an understanding of the content of children's development, an appreciation of the importance of children's self-initiated actions on and interactions with the environment, and recognition of the critical role adults play as mediators of children's learning.

Although some EI/ECSE professionals distance themselves from the early psychoanalytic work of Freud, Adler, and Jung, current developmental psychodynamic theory contributes to practice in EI/ECSE (Emde & Robinson, 2000). The difficulties in attachment formation have long been noted for some infants with disabilities and their caregivers (Emde & Brown, 1978; Fraiberg, 1975). The emphasis on building relationships with caregivers has guided practice in many infant programs (Bromwich, 1997); this emphasis is also a central feature in some programs for preschool-age children with disabilities (Greenspan & Wieder, 1999) and is of importance for all programs in EI/ECSE. In fact, infant mental health has become a major area of interest for EI/ECSE care providers (Hadadian, Tomlin, & Sherwood-Puzzello, 2005). The major contributions of this theory are the emphases on establishing and strengthening relationships with primary caregivers and on young children's social–emotional development.

Ecological theory also influences practice in EI/ECSE. Several useful ecological theories exist, but Bronfenbrenner's (1979) is the most prominent and influential. His ecological systems theory underlies our understanding of the many factors influencing EI/ECSE services (Odom, 2001), as well as how services are provided for families and children. Ecological psychology (e.g., Barker, 1968), in combination with applied behavior analysis (Morris & Midgley, 1990), serves as the foundation of ecobehavioral assessment, which has been used to identify influential elements of classrooms (Brown, Odom, Li, & Zercher, 1999; Odom, Favazza, Brown, & Horn, 2000). The major contributions of ecological theories are (a) its emphasis on factors within the immediate setting (e.g., home, classroom), (b) its recognition of the interrelating influences of different settings in which a child participates (e.g., communication between parents and teachers), and (c) its appreciation of the influences of the broader ecology (e.g., state policies, cultural values).

A Unified Theory of EI/ECSE Practice

EI/ECSE has moved from a set of practices based on single theoretical perspectives (e.g., constructivist, behaviorist) to a *theory of practice*, which others have called a *theory of change* (Brookes-Gunn, Berlin, & Fuligni, 2000; Weiss, 1995). This theory exists as a set of shared beliefs or *shared exemplars* (to use a concept proposed by Kuhn, 1970) among practitioners and scholars, with each having a body of research for its foundation. These shared beliefs, which constitute the tenets of the theory of practice, are listed in Table 1. Because this theory of practice draws from multiple psychological and educational theories, it can be described as a *unified* theory of early intervention practice. In the following sections, we describe each tenet of this theory and identify evidence-based practices exemplifying these tenets (see Note).

TABLE 1. A Unified Theory of Practice in EI/ECSE: Fundamental Tenants and Evidence-Based Practices

Families and homes are primary nurturing contexts

- Family-centered practices (Thompson et al., 1997)
- Social support and resource-based models (Dunst, 1999)
- Parent-implemented milieu teaching approaches (Kaiser & Hancock, 2003)
- Parent-education programs (Mahoney et al., 1999

Strengthening relationships is an essential feature of EI/ECSE

- Relationship-based programs (Mahoney & Perales, 2003)
- Parent–infant interaction programs (Girolametto, Verbey, & Tannock, 1994)
- Peer interaction programs (Odom et al, 1999)
- Professional collaboration programs (Lieber et al., 2001)

Children learn by acting on and observing their environment

- Contingently responsive environments (Landry et al., 2001)
- Participation in natural learning opportunities (Dunst et al., 2002)
- Participation in classrooms using recommended practices (Schwartz, Carta, & Grant, 1996)

Adults mediate children's experiences to promote learning and development

- Embedded learning opportunities (Woods et al., 2004)
- Incorporation of child choice (Reinhartsen et al., 2002)
- Routine structuring (Morrison et al., 2002)
- High-probability requests (Davis et al., 1994)
- Adult prompting and prompt-fading strategies (Wolery et al., 2002)

Participation in developmentally advanced settings is essential

- Learning opportunities in community and home contexts (Dunst et al, 2002)
- Participation in inclusive preschool play groups (Guralnick et al., 1996)
- Social integration interventions in inclusive settings (Hunt et al., 2004)

EI/ECSE practice is individually and dynamically goal-oriented

- Individualized assessment (Neisworth & Bagnato, 2000)
- Demands of environments is source of goal identification (Thurman & Widerstrom, 1990)
- Measures of individual growth for progress monitoring and decision-making about children's programs (Priest et al., 2001)
- Curriculum-based assessment (Bricker et al., 2003)

Program transition is enhanced by facilitating adults and experiences

- Assessment of the demands of the next setting and teaching of needed skills (Ager & Shapiro, 1995)
- Preparation of personnel and/or family for transition to next setting (Wyly et al., 1996)
- Interagency agreement to pave the way for transition (Rosenkoetter et al., 2001)

Broader ecological contexts influence families and EI/ECSE programs

- Family-centered planning (McWilliam et al., 1998)
- Resource mapping (Trivette et al, 1997)
- Culturally sensitive programs (Catlett et al., 2000)

Families and Homes Are Primary Nurturing Contexts

A fundamental supposition of EI/ECSE is that families and homes, except in cases where there is abuse, neglect, or severe privation, are primary nurturing environments for infants and young children with disabilities. The operating assumption is that children with disabilities who live with their families and participate in community life (i.e., the natural environment) are more likely to be similar to their siblings and age-mates without disabilities than if they lived in a facility with only others who have disabilities. This principle countered the practices of the first half of the 20th century, in which professionals advised parents was to place their young children with disabilities in residential facilities. One thing that is special about EI/ECSE is the support it provides to families, which in many cases allows their infant to remain a member of the family. This principle extends beyond homes and applies to activities in communities (Dunst, Bruder, Trivette, & Hambry, 2005) and the nature of resources and supports that families need to provide a nurturing environment (Diamond & Kontos, 2004).

Rearing a young child with disabilities, however, often presents challenges beyond those of rearing a child without disabilities. Families frequently report needing information about their child's disability, service options, available resources and supports, and other issues (Bailey, Blasco, & Simeonsson, 1992). The EI/ECSE field has long recognized the value of working with families, but that work has been refined by research and practice. Early programs focused on teaching parents to teach their children (Shearer & Shearer, 1972). Effective models exist for teaching parents to foster children's communication (Peterson, Carta, & Greenwood, 2005), as well as their social (Mahoney & Perales, 2003), literacy (Morgan & Goldstein, 2004), and behavioral (Strain & Timm, 2001) skills. The benefits of involving families directly in interventions has been debated (Dunst, 1999; Mahoney et al., 1999), but a consensus exists that professionals' interactions with families should emphasize support for family members as well as intervention to promote children's skill development (Trivette & Dunst, 2000).

The empirical linkages between family support and child progress are now being established (Thompson et al., 1997), with the best example being Dunst's (1999) structural equation model analysis of family support and child outcomes. Dunst (2000) proposed a model in which social support promotes family well-being, which in turn allows families to engage in responsive interaction styles with their children, thereby providing the children with opportunities and help in learning important skills. The professionals' role in this model is to work collaboratively with families, to strengthen families by helping them secure needed supports and resources, to provide individualized and flexible help, and to capitalize on families' existing competencies and strengths (Trivette & Dunst, 2000). Families characterize professionals who provide family-centered services as (a) being positive with and about families, (b) being responsive to families' concerns and priorities, (c) having friendly interaction styles, (d) being sensitive and empathetic, and (e) focusing on the whole family rather than only the child with disabilities (McWilliam, Tocci, & Harbin, 1998). Such professionals also are competent in working with the child and know about community resources (McWilliam et al., 1998). Knowledge of community resources (e.g., informal activities and events, social services), in turn, helps professionals assist families in arranging natural learning opportunities for their child (Raab & Dunst, 2004).

Strengthening Relationships Is an Essential Feature of EI/ECSE

Establishing positive relationships between the parents (or other caregivers) and their infants/young children, among children with disabilities and their peers, and among professionals working with infants, children, and families is an essential goal of EI/ECSE. A great amount of literature exists on the importance of attachment between infants and caregivers for later development (Grossman, Grossman, & Waters, 2005). Difficulties may arise in parent–infant interactions and relationship formation for some infants with or at risk for disabilities (Vondra & Barnett, 1999). Some early intervention programs use relationship-based interventions with the goal of establishing positive relationships early in life (Mahoney & Perales, 2003). For example, for premature infants in neonatal intensive care units, teams of professionals from the Vermont Intervention Program for Low Birthweight Infants helped mothers interpret their infants' behavioral cues and appreciate their infants' temperaments to promote positive reciprocal interaction patterns (Rauh, Achenbach, Nurcombe, Howell, & Teti, 1988). This project led to positive long-term outcomes (Achenbach, Howell, Aoki, & Rauh, 1993), and similar longitudinal effects of early intervention have been found by other researchers (Boyce, Saylor, & Price, 2004; Brisch, Bechinger, Betzler, & Heineman, 2003;). For older infants with disabilities, interventions designed to promote positive interactions between mothers and infants have resulted in increases in reciprocal interactions, in parenting styles, and in collateral effects on children's development (Girolametto, Verbey, & Tannock, 1994; Heinicke, Rineman, Ponce, & Guthrie, 2001). Similarly, Bromwich (1997) described the positive outcomes of her early intervention program over a 20-year period. The unique feature of this project is that it focused intervention on promoting mutual enjoyment by the parents and infants as a basis for forming attachment before emphasizing parents' promotion of children's developmental skills.

EI/ECSE programs also emphasize relationships among peers. For all young children, establishing positive peer relationships is a critical developmental task built on peer-related social competence. Such social competence is problematic, however, for some children with disabilities (McConnell & Odom, 1999). Guralnick (2001) suggested that participating in inclusive classes may foster peer-related social competence and peer relationships. The evidence is mixed about the effectiveness of placing children in inclusive classes without specific programming to promote positive peer interactions and relationships (Wolfberg et al., 1999). Some young children with disabilities appear well accepted by peers while others are actively rejected (Harper & McCluskey, 2002; Odom, Zercher, Li, Marquart, Sandall, & Brown, 2005). Brown, Odom, and Conroy (2001) identified naturalistic approaches, social integration activities, and explicit social skills training as evidence-based interventions for children with disabilities who are socially rejected.

Relationships among professionals working in EI/ECSE programs also may have a direct impact on infants and young children with disabilities and their families. EI/ECSE is a multidisciplinary endeavor, and barriers may arise between the adults on a team. These barriers are similar to those confronting other teams and include poor communication, lack of respect, lack of time for planning, and philosophical differences (Lieber et al., 1997). Research suggests that professionals in early intervention programs prefer working in a collaborative manner (Buysse, Schulte, Pierce, & Terry, 1994) and that cohesive communication between special education and early childhood teachers in inclusive programs leads to greater engagement for children with disabilities (McCormick, Noonan, & Heck, 1998). The challenge has been to establish program features that support and enhance positive relationships among adults. One approach is to use a problem-solving strategy for team building (McWilliam, 1996). Lieber et al. (2001) described the use of such an approach in an inclusive program implemented over a 2-year period. Positive changes occurred in joint participation in program development, shared philosophy, shared ownership of children, administrative support, and positive relationships among the professionals.

Children Learn by Acting on and Observing Their Environment

Many factors influence children's learning and development, including their genetic makeup, the status of their central nervous system, their health and physiological functioning, and the risk and opportunity variables in their families and communities. However, since the early 1960s, an appreciation has grown for the power of proximal environments and children's experiences in shaping their own learning and development. Concomitant with these developments was a dramatic revision in our view of infants' competence. Whereas infants' and young children's learning was once seen as emerging from a biological base or from environmental shaping, the current perspective is that infants actively adapt to, learn about, master, control, and understand their worlds (Sameroff & Fiese, 2000). As such, their experiences—interactions with their social and physical environments—are opportunities for learning (Dunst, Hambry, Trivette, Raab, & Bruder, 2002).

The active nature of young children's learning leads to two major practice implications. Infants and young children actively engage in activities and use materials that hold interest for them (Odom et al., 2000). Such engagement leads to competence and mastery, which in turn leads to additional interests (Dunst, Herter, & Shields, 2000). Thus, attending to child interests and child-initiated interactions is important. For infants and young children, contingently responsive toys, physical environments, and a responsive parenting style of interaction are positive forces in promoting learning and development (Kim & Mahoney, 2004; Landry, Smith, Swank, Assel, & Vellet, 2001). Such exchanges teach infants and young children about how the world works and validate their sense of self-efficacy. Promoting children's engagement, therefore, is a recommended practice in EI/ECSE classes (Wolery, 2000).

To foster positive outcomes, service providers must influence large proportions of children's experiences. Hobbs (1966), in describing his ecological approach to working with children with emotional difficulties, stated that "every hour in every day, is of great importance to a child, and when an hour is neglected . . . teaching and learning go on nonetheless and the child may be the loser" (p. 1109). In home-visiting programs, part-day classes, clinic-based programs, and many inclusive classes, specialists have relatively little contact with the child. Thus, interventions must be mediated through the adults who have ongoing contact with the child (McWilliam, Wolery, & Odom, 2001). In those contexts, there may be a concern that instruction for the child is not specifically planned or implemented as it would be in more specialized settings. To counter this concern, researchers have designed interventions that are implemented in natural environments where children spend most of their time (Hunt, Soto, Maier, Liboiron, & Bae, 2004; Woods, Kashinath, & Goldstein, 2004).

Adults Mediate Children's Experiences to Promote Learning

Adults in EI/ECSE mediate children's experiences to promote learning. The term *mediate* is used to broaden the perception of teaching and instruction as an adult delivering a preplanned set of trials or body of information in a relatively restricted context. Effective adult mediation is well planned, goal directed, and systematic. Although discrete trial training and direct instruction form an effective approach for some children (Odom et al., 2003), for many children effective interventions can occur during play and other routines and activities; these should be embedded in and distributed across activities and should be contextually relevant (e.g., Horn, Lieber, Li, Sandall, & Schwartz, 2000; Woods et al., 2004). Learning is promoted by the organization of the social and physical aspects of the environment and by specialized intervention practices (Wolery, 2000).

Features of the classroom ecology may promote engagement, communication, interaction, or play. Such features include varying the number and size of play areas, establishing a predictable schedule, ensuring that activities are physically accessible, arranging the materials within each play area, specifying the rules of access to each area, and having a sufficient teacher:child ratio (Odom & Bailey, 2001). Strategies such as selecting materials based on children's preferences, rotating materials in and out of play areas, and providing choices about toys/materials result in more engagement (Gmitrova & Gmitrov, 2003; Kok, Kong, & Bernard-Optiz, 2002; Reinhartsen, Garfinkle, & Wolery, 2002). Assigning staff to areas and activities rather than to children often results in more engagement and play and less waiting (LeLaurin & Risley, 1972). Transitions between activities may be facilitated for some children by the use of pictures and visual support (Morrison, Sainato, BenChaaban, & Endo, 2002) and can be used to teach new skills (Wolery, Anthony, & Heckathorn, 1998). Providing structure to play activities by incorporating props and specifying roles during dramatic play may lead to more interactive behavior (DeKlyen & Odom, 1989), although as noted, providing opportunities for child choice after the teacher introduces the activity is important.

A variety of specialized practices have been evaluated and are recommended. As with older students, reinforcement of desired behaviors and reinforcement-based procedures are recommended in early childhood programs (Wolery, 2000) and have strong empirical support (Odom & Strain, 2002). For example, the high-probability request procedure is associated with increases in children's compliance with adult requests as well as enhanced social contacts between preschoolers (Davis, Brady, Hamilton, McEvoy, & Williams, 1994). For promoting language and communicative skills, procedures such as modeling, expanding children's statements, and incidental teaching are effective (Kaiser & Hancock, 2003). As noted, social skills are promoted through group friendship activities (McEvoy et al., 1988) and peer-mediated strategies (Odom et al., 1999). Procedures such as simultaneous prompting (Sewell, Collins, Hemmeter, & Schuster, 1998), constant time delay (Holcombe, Wolery, & Snyder, 1994), progressive time delay (Venn et al., 1993), and graduated guidance (Bryan & Gast, 2000) are effective in teaching a variety of behaviors. When these procedures are used, they should be embedded in and distributed across activities (Wolery, Anthony, Caldwell, Snyder, & Morgante, 2002).

Participation in More Developmentally Advanced Settings Is Essential

Participation in more advanced settings, as a practice, is supported most directly by the literature on situated cognition (Rogoff, Baker-Sennett, Lacasa, & Goldsmith, 1995) and legitimate peripheral participation (Lave & Wenger, 1991). From this perspective, individuals acquire important skills for specific contexts by participating in those contexts, often with assistance or guided participation from a caregiver or more competent peer. Situated learning research has been the foundation for instruction in other areas of education (see Cobb & Bowers, 1999, application to math education); it is just beginning to be applied in EI/ECSE and shows substantial promise. An example of such application is the research of Dunst, Hambry, et al. (2002), who have identified a large range of learning opportunities existing in natural settings, such as the home and community.

Learning through participation in developmentally advanced environments has long been cited as a rationale for inclusive or integrated programs (Bricker, 1978). Inclusive settings may provide a developmental press through a more cognitively, linguistically, and socially stimulating environment than occurs in nonintegrated special education settings. Given the necessary and appropriate assistance, this developmental press could lead to the acquisition of more advanced skills and successful participation in the inclusive settings. For example, the research of Guralnick and Paul-Brown (1977) documented that typically developing children reduced the complexity of their communications when interacting with classmates with disabilities, and Guralnick (1981) proposed that such adjustments may facilitate language acquisition. Similarly, Guralnick, Connor, Hammond, Gottman, and Kinnish (1996) found that children with disabilities in inclusive play groups engaged in more advanced forms of play and more frequent social interactions than when they were in groups only with peers with disabilities. For young children with autism, Strain (1983) demonstrated that increased levels of social interaction resulting from a peer-mediated intervention generalized to play settings in which typically developing children participated but not to settings in which there were only children with disabilities. As a result of this and other later research (see Odom, Vitztum, et al., 2004 for a review), a recommended practice in EI/ECSE is to place children in inclusive settings and provide the support necessary to ensure successful participation (Sandall et al., 2000). Research-based strategies for providing such support were described previously (e.g., curriculum modifications, naturalistic interventions, adult prompting, peer-mediated interventions) and have served as the basis for curricula and training in EI/ECSE (Gold, Liepack, Scott, & Benjamin-Wise, 1999; Hunt et al., 2004; Sandall, Schwartz, & Joseph, 2001).

EI/ECSE Practice Is Individually and Dynamically Goal Oriented

EI/ECSE is an inherently individualized endeavor, and a recommended practice for caregivers and service providers is to individualize goals and the strategies used to meet those goals (Wolery, 2000). This is particularly necessary in the field of EI/ECSE because of the varied characteristics of children who are eligible for services and the range of severity levels exhibited by those children. The range of disabilities with which a given

EI/ECSE professional works is broader than that of their colleagues who teach older children. The curriculum in early childhood often focuses on developmental and early academic skills (e.g., social, communication, early literacy). Thus, individualized assessment in these areas is essential (Neisworth & Bagnato, 2000). Curriculum-based measurement approaches have been developed to guide program planning and have been used as a complementary source of information for determining children's eligibility for services (Bricker, Yovanoff, Capt, & Allen, 2003). A major innovation in individualized assessment has been the development of continuous progress measurement techniques that can provide teachers with information upon which to base decisions about individual children's instruction (Carta, Greenwood, Luze, Kline, & Kuntz, 2003; Priest et al., 2001). In addition, parental input about goals is valued and often is facilitated by routines-based interviews and checklists seeking to identify problematic parts of the day (McWilliam, 1992).

Individualization is not restricted to children's intervention goals and practices but also applies to interactions with families. Families who participate in EI/ECSE are often quite different from one another in terms of family structure, family functioning, aspirations for their child, available resources and supports, history, and experiences. As a result, a one-size-fits-all approach to working with and interacting with families is counter to recommended practice in the field (Trivette & Dunst, 2000).

Program Transitions Are Enhanced by Facilitating Adults and Experience

Bronfenbrenner (1979) proposed that an ecological transition occurs when there is a change in settings and/or roles for an individual and that such transitions are both a result of and potentially an instigator of developmental processes. The developmental potential of new settings is enhanced if children make the transition with one or more individuals with whom they shared the previous setting. During the early childhood years, children with disabilities and their families experience transitions across settings and agencies, including the following: (a) neonatal intensive care unit to the home, (b) home to early intervention services provided by agencies in the state, (c) early intervention program to an inclusive or special education preschool program, and (d) preschool program to a kindergarten or traditional school-age classroom. Such transitions place new demands on and create new growth opportunities for children, their families, and care providers (Hanson et al., 2000; Odom & Chandler, 1990).

Since characteristics and demands of settings differ, preparing children with disabilities for new settings may support successful transition and learning (Hanson, 2005). In the field of EI/ECSE, there has been a long tradition of transition planning and support for infants, young children, and families through various transitions (Atwater, Orth-Lopes, Elliott, Carta, & Schwartz, 1994), and such supports have been woven into policies and laws (Rosenkoetter, Whaley, Hains, & Pierce, 2001). Service providers have attempted to promote the continuity of experiences across settings and ideally to create a seamless service system (Sainato & Morrison, 2001). Research-based strategies include identifying skills necessary for success in the new setting (Johnson, Gallagher, Cook, & Wong, 1995; McCormick & Kawate, 1982), assessing the children's skills on those essential skills and teaching them the skills needed in the next setting (Ager & Shapiro, 1995), and preparing personnel in the home or new class for the transition (Bruder & Chandler, 1996; Wyly, Allen, Pfalzer, & Wilson, 1996). Similarly, an essential component of supportive transition practices has been formal and informal interagency agreements that pave the way for infants, young children, and families to move from one program or service agency to another (Rosenkoetter et al., 2001).

Broader Ecological Contexts Influence Families and EI/ECSE Programs

Pushed by ecological systems theory, EI/ECSE professionals recognize that factors outside the immediate environment of a child and family exert an influence on development and learning (Spiker, Hebbler, & Mallik, 2005; Thurman, 1997). Bronfenbrenner conceptualized these factors as occurring at the microsystem (i.e., in a classroom or home), mesosystem (e.g., transition planning, professional collaboration, family issues), exosystem (e.g., social policy), and macrosystem (e.g., culture). With the passage of P.L. 99-457 in 1975 and continuing through subsequent reauthorizations of the law, service providers for infants and toddlers have adopted a family-centered approach, as described previously (Trivette & Dunst, 2000), broadened individualized planning to include the family through the Individualized Family Service Plan (IFSP), and accessed services in the community for children and families rather than following the classroom-based service model traditionally used for school-age children. These practices build support for families as a means of creating a more developmentally facilitative environment for infants and young children with disabilities. Trivette, Dunst, and Deal (1997) have documented the relationships between access to social support and the progress young children make on developmental objectives. Intervention approaches for providing such support for families and children are a foundation for practice in EI/ECSE.

A second important reflection of an ecological perspective has been the recognition of the importance of the cultural and linguistic diversity of children, families, and communities. Research in EI/ECSE has documented how cultural and linguistic diversity affect access to services (Hanson, Gutierrez, Morgan, Brennan, & Zercher, 1997) and the nature of services provided (Hanson et al., 1998). A central value in EI/ECSE has been to make programs culturally appropriate for infants, young children, and families (Lynch, 1998). This has occurred through the development of culturally appropriate curriculum and practices for inclusive and general early childhood programs (Catlett, Winton, & Santos, 2000; CLAS, 2002), as well as models of EI/ECSE services for children and families from specific cultural groups (Bruder, Anderson, Schutz, & Caldera, 1991).

Conclusion

From the application of different psychological and education theories, practitioners in EI/ECSE have developed, we propose, an implicit theory of practice. In this chapter, we have proposed a number of tenets for such a theory. Also, for each tenet we have provided examples of evidence-based practices associated with positive outcomes for children and families. The emphasis on grounding practice recommendations in supportive evidence is a critical direction in EI/ECSE. An important step in this direction is the recent comprehensive review of the early intervention literature from the 1990s, which served as one basis for establishing effective practices recommended by DEC (Smith, McLean, Sandall, Snyder, & Broudy, 2000). Such a review process, with the intent of providing an empirical basis for practice, is unprecedented in EI/ECSE or most other areas of special education, and undoubtedly will lead the field in positive new directions. One such new direction is the synthesis of the research literature about EI/ECSE practices conducted by Dunst, Trivette, and Cutspec (2002) and dissemination of their findings in a format that is meaningful for teachers and family members (Dunst & Trivette, 2005). Such a research-to-practice translation for consumers may well be necessary if the scientific findings about effective practices are ever to be used.

Yet, questions still exist for the field of EI/ECSE. What level or degree of evidence is necessary for declaring a practice effective? For what types of children are the specific practices effective? How does the field support the use of evidence-based techniques in everyday early intervention settings? Does a research-to-practice translation narrow the gap between recommended and actual practice? These questions await us in the future.

AUTHORS' NOTES

1. This chapter is a revision and update of an article that appeared in *The Journal of Special Education*.
2. The authors wish to thank Marci Hanson, Scott McConnell, Gerald Mahoney, Robin McWilliam, and William H. Brown for their comments on earlier drafts of this chapter.
3. This chapter is dedicated to the memory of Mary E. McEvoy, a close friend, colleague, and contributor to the field of EI/ECSE.

NOTE

By *evidence-based practice*, we mean empirical and published research that documents the relationship of practices to outcomes for children, families, professionals, and systems. The purpose of this chapter was not to conduct a synthesis of the EI/ECSE literature but, rather, to propose a theory that guides practice and to illustrate that scientifically based practices underlie this theory. In doing this, we intend not to engage the current controversy about the definition of science in education (see Jacob & White, 2002).

REFERENCES

Achenbach, T. M., Howell, C. T., Aoki, M. F., & Rauh, V. A. (1993). Nine-year outcome of the Vermont Intervention Program for low birth weight infants. *Pediatrics, 91*, 45–55.

Ager, C. L., & Shapiro, E. S. (1995). Template matching as a strategy for assessment of and intervention for preschool students with disabilities. *Topics in Early Childhood Special Education, 15,* 187–218.

Atwater, J. B., Orth-Lopes, L., Elliott, M., Carta, J. J., & Schwartz, I. S. (1994). Completing the circle: Planning and implementing transitions to other programs. In M. Wolery & J. S. Wilbers (Eds.), *Including children with special needs in early childhood programs* (pp. 167–188). Washington, DC: National Association for the Education of Young Children.

Bailey, D. B., Blasco, P. M., & Simeonsson, R. J. (1992). Needs expressed by mothers and fathers of young children with disabilities. *American Journal on Mental Retardation, 97,* 1–10.

Bandura, A. (1976). *Social learning theory.* Englewood Cliffs, NJ: Prentice Hall.

Barker, R. (1968). *Ecological psychology*. Stanford, CA: Stanford University Press.

Brisch, K. H., Bechinger, D., Betzler, S., & Heinemann, H. (2003). Early preventative attachment-oriented psychotherapeutic intervention program with parents of a very low birthweight premature infant: Results of attachment and neurological development. *Attachment and Human Development, 5*, 120–135.

Boyce, G. C., Saylor, C. F., & Price, C. L. (2004). School-age outcomes for early intervention participants who experienced intraventricular hemorrhage and low birth weight. *Children's Health Care, 33*, 257–274.

Bricker, D. (1978). A rationale for the integration of handicapped and nonhandicapped preschool children. In M. Guralnick (Ed.), *Early intervention and the integration of handicapped and nonhandicapped children* (pp. 3–27). Baltimore: University Park Press.

Bricker, D., Yovanoff, P., Capt, B., & Allen, D. (2003). Use of curriculum-based measurement to corroborate eligibility decisions. *Journal of Early Intervention, 26*, 20–31.

Bromwich, R. (1997). *Working with families and their infants at risk: A perspective after 20 years of experience*. Austin, TX: PRO-ED.

Bronfenbrenner, U. (1979). *The ecology of human development: Experiments by nature and design.* Cambridge, MA: Harvard University Press.

Brookes-Gunn, J., Berlin, L. J., & Fuligni, A. S. (2000). Early childhood intervention programs: What about the family? In J. Shonkoff & S. Meisels (Eds.), *Handbook of early childhood intervention* (2nd ed., pp. 549–588). New York: Cambridge University Press.

Brown, W. H., Odom, S. L., & Conroy, M. (2001). An intervention hierarchy for promoting preschool children's peer interactions in naturalistic environments. *Topics in Early Childhood Special Education, 21*, 162–175.

Brown, W. H., Odom, S. L., Li, S., & Zercher, C. (1999). Ecobehavioral assessment in early childhood programs: A portrait of preschool inclusion. *The Journal of Special Education, 33*, 138–153.

Bruder, M. B., Anderson, R., Schutz, G., & Caldera, M. (1991). Project profile: Niños Especiales Program: A culturally sensitive early intervention model. *Journal of Early Intervention, 15*, 268–277.

Bruder, M. B., & Chandler, L. (1996). Transition. In S. Odom & M. McLean (Eds.), *Early intervention/early childhood special education: Recommended practices* (pp. 287–307). Austin, TX: PRO-ED.

Bryan, L. C., & Gast, D. L. (2000). Teaching on-task and on-schedule behaviors to high functioning children with autism via picture activity schedules. *Journal of Autism and Developmental Disorders, 30,* 553–567.

Buysse, V., Schulte, A. C., Pierce, P. P., & Terry, D. (1994). Models and styles of consultation: Preferences of professionals in early intervention. *Journal of Early Intervention, 18*, 302–310.

Carta, J. J., Greenwood, C. R., Luze, G. J., Cline, G., & Kuntz, S. (2003). Developing a general outcome measure of growth in social skills for infants and toddlers. *Journal of Early Intervention, 26*, 91–114.

Catlett, C., Winton, P., & Santos, R. M. (2000). Resources within reason: Materials that serve culturally and linguistically diverse children and families. *Young Exceptional Children, 3*(4), 27.

CLAS. (2002). *Culturally and linguistically appropriate services early childhood research institute website.* Urbana: University of Illinois. Available at www.clas.uiuc.edu.

Cobb, P., & Bowers, J. (1999). Cognitive and situated learning perspectives in theory and practice. *Educational Researcher, 28*(2), 4–15.

Davis, C. A., Brady, M. P., Hamilton, R., McEvoy, M. A., & Williams, R. E. (1994). Effects of high-probability requests on the social interactions of young children with severe disabilities. *Journal of Applied Behavior Analysis, 27,* 619–637.

DeKlyen, M., & Odom, S. L. (1989). Activity structure and social interactions with peers in developmentally integrated play groups. *Journal of Early Intervention, 13,* 342–352.

Diamond, K. A., & Kontos, S. (2004). Families' resources and accommodations: Toddlers with Down syndrome, cerebral palsy, and developmental delay. *Journal of Early Intervention, 26*, 253–265.

Dunst, C. J. (1999). Placing parent education in conceptual and empirical context. *Topics in Early Childhood Special Education, 19*, 141–147.

Dunst, C. J. (2000). Revisiting "rethinking early intervention." *Topics in Early Childhood Special Education, 20,* 95–104.

Dunst, C. J., Bruder, M. B., Trivette, C. M., & Hambry, D. W.

(2005). Young children's natural learning environments: Contrasting approaches to early childhood intervention indicate differential learning opportunities. *Psychological Reports, 96*, 231–234.

Dunst, C. J., Hambry, D., Trivette, C. M., Raab, M., & Bruder, M. B. (2002). Young children's participation in everyday family and community activity. *Psychological Reports, 91*, 875–889.

Dunst, C. J., Herter, S., & Shields, H. (2000). Interest-based natural learning opportunities. *Young Exceptional Children Monograph, 2*, 37–47.

Dunst, C. J., & Trivette, C. M. (2005). *Research and Training Center on Early Childhood Development: Home page.* Ashville, NC: Orlena Puckett Institute. Retrieved June 13, 2005, from http://www.researchtopractice.info/index.php.

Dunst, C. J., Trivette, C. M., & Cutspec, P. A. (2002). Toward an operational definition of evidence-based practices. *Centerscope, 1*(1). Retrieved June 13, 2005, from http://www.evidencebasedpractices.org/centerscope/centerscopevol1no1.pdf.

Emde, R., & Brown, C. (1978). Adaptation to the birth of a Down's syndrome infant: Grieving and maternal attachment. *Journal of the American Academy of Child Psychiatry, 17*, 299–323.

Emde, R., & Robinson, J. (2000). Guiding principles for a theory of early intervention: A developmental-psychoanalytic perspective. In J. Shonkoff & S. Meisels (Eds.), *Handbook of early childhood intervention* (2nd ed., pp. 160–179). New York: Cambridge University Press.

Feuerstein, R. (1980). *Instrumental enrichment: Redevelopment of cognitive functions of retarded performers.* New York: University Park Press.

Fosnot, C. T. (1996). Constructivism: A psychological theory of learning. In C. Fosnot (Ed.), *Constructivism: Theory, perspectives, and practice* (pp. 8–33). New York: Teachers College Press.

Fraiberg, S. (1975). The development of human attachments in infants blind from birth. *Merrill-Palmer Quarterly, 21*, 315–334.

Gallagher, J. J. (2000). The beginnings of federal help for young children with disabilities. *Topics in Early Childhood Special Education, 20*, 3–6.

Girolametto, L., Verbey, M., & Tannock, R. (1994). Improving joint engagement in parent-child interaction: An intervention study. *Journal of Early Intervention, 18*, 155–167.

Gmitrova, V., & Gmitrov, J. (2003). The impact of teacher-directed and child-directed pretend play on cognitive competence in kindergarten children. *Early Childhood Education Journal, 20*, 241–246.

Gold, S., Liepack, S., Scott, M., & Benjamin-Wise, S. (1999). Creating inclusive classrooms: A report from the field. *Young Exceptional Children, 2*(2), 2–9.

Greene, M. (1996). A constructivist perspective on teaching and learning in the arts. In C. Fosnot (Ed.), *Constructivism: Theory, perspectives, and practice* (pp. 120–144). New York: Teachers College Press.

Greenspan, S. I., & Wieder, S. (1999). A functional developmental approach to autism spectrum disorders. *Journal of the Association for Persons with Severe Handicaps, 24*, 147–161.

Grossman, K. E., Grossman, K., & Waters, E. (2005). *Attachment from infancy to adulthood: The major longitudinal studies.* New York: Guilford.

Guralnick, M. J. (1981). Peer influences on development of communicative competence. In P. Strain (Ed.), *The utilization of peers as behavior change agents* (pp. 31–68). New York: Plenum.

Guralnick, M. J. (2001). Social competence with peers and early childhood inclusion: Need for alternative approaches. In M. Guralnick (Ed.), *Early childhood inclusion: Focus on change* (pp. 481–502). Baltimore: Brookes.

Guralnick, M. J., Connor, R. T., Hammond, M. A., Gottman, J. M., & Kinnish, K. (1996). Immediate effects of mainstreamed settings on the social interactions and social integration of preschool children. *American Journal on Mental Retardation, 100*, 359–377.

Guralnick, M. J., & Paul-Brown, D. (1977). The nature of verbal interaction among handicapped and nonhandicapped preschool children. *Child Development, 48*, 254–260.

Hadadian, A., Tomlin, A. M., & Sherwood-Puzzello, C. M. (2005). Early intervention service providers: What do they say about their infant mental health training needs? *Early Child Development and Care, 175*, 431–444.

Hanson, M. J. (2003). National legislation for early intervention in the United States. In S. Odom, M. Hanson, J. Blackman, & S. Kaul (Eds.), *Early intervention: Practices from around the world* (pp. 253–279). Baltimore: Brookes.

Hanson, M. J. (2005). Ensuring effective transitions in early intervention. In M. Guralnick (Ed.), *The developmental systems approach to early intervention* (pp. 373–398). Baltimore: Brookes.

Hanson, M. J., Beckman, P. J., Horn, E., Marquart, J., Sandall, S. R., Greig, D., & Brennan, E. (2000). Entering preschool: Family and professional experiences in this transition process. *Journal of Early Intervention, 23*, 279–293.

Hanson, M. J., Gutierrez, S., Morgan, M., Brennan, E. L., & Zercher, C. (1997). Language, culture, and disability: Interacting influences on preschool inclusion. *Topics in Early Childhood Special Education, 17*, 307–336.

Hanson, M. J., Wolfberg, P., Zercher, C., Morgan, M., Gutierrez, S., Barnwell, D., & Beckman, P. (1998). The culture of inclusion: Recognizing diversity at multiple levels. *Early Childhood Research Quarterly, 13*, 185–210.

Harper, L. V., & McCluskey, K. S. (2002). Caregiver and peer responses to children with language and motor disabilities in inclusive preschool programs. *Early Childhood Research Quarterly, 17*, 171–196.

Haywood, H. C., Brooks, P., & Burns, S. (1992). *Bright start: Cognitive curriculum for young children.* Watertown, MA: Charlesbright.

Heinicke, C. M., Rineman, N. R., Ponce, V. A., & Guthrie, D. (2001). Relation-based intervention with at-risk mother: Outcomes in the second year of life. *Infant Mental Health Journal, 22*, 431–462.

Hobbs, N. (1966). Helping disturbed children: Psychological and ecological strategies. *American Psychologist, 21*, 1105–1115.

Holcombe, A., Wolery, M., & Snyder, E. (1994). Effects of two levels of procedural fidelity with constant time delay on children's learning. *Journal of Behavioral Education, 4,* 49–73.

Horn, E., Lieber, J., Li, S., Sandall, S., & Schwartz, I. (2000). Supporting young children's IEP goals in inclusive settings through embedded learning opportunities. *Topics in Early Childhood Special Education, 20,* 208–223.

Hunt, P., Soto, G., Maier, J., Liboiron, N., & Bae, S. (2004). Collaborative teaming to support preschoolers with severe disabilities who are placed in general education early childhood programs. *Topics in Early Childhood Special Education, 24,* 123–142.

Johnson, L. I., Gallagher, R. J., Cook, M., & Wong. P. (1995). Critical skills for kindergarten: Perceptions from kindergarten teachers. *Journal of Early Intervention, 19,* 315–349.

Kaiser, A. P., & Hancock, T. B. (2003). Teaching parents new skills to support their young children's development. *Infants and Young Children, 16*(1), 9–21.

Kim, J., & Mahoney, G. (2004). The effects of mother's style of interaction on children's engagement: Implications for using responsive interventions with parents. *Topics in Early Childhood Special Education, 24,* 31–38.

Klein, P. S. (2003). A mediational approach to early intervention in Israel. In S. Odom, M. Hanson, J. Blackman, & S. Kaul (Eds.), *Early intervention: Practices from around the world* (pp. 69–89). Baltimore: Brookes.

Kok, A. J., Kong, T Y., & Bernard-Optiz, V. (2002). A comparison of the effects of structured and facilitated play approaches on preschoolers with autism: A case study. *Autism: The International Journal of Research and Practice, 6,* 181–196.

Kuhn, T. S. (1970). *The structure of scientific revolutions* (2nd ed.). Chicago: University of Chicago Press.

Landry, S. H., Smith, K. E., Swank, P. R., Assel, M. A., & Vellet, S. (2001). Does early responsive parenting have a special importance for children's development or is consistency across early childhood necessary? *Developmental Psychology, 37,* 387–403.

Lave, J., & Wenger, E. (1991). *Situated learning: Legitimate peripheral participation.* New York: Cambridge University Press.

LeLaurin, K. D., & Risley, T. R. (1972). The organization of day care environments: Zone vs. man-to-man staff assignments. *Journal of Applied Behavior Analysis, 5,* 225–232.

Lieber, J., Beckman, P. J., Hanson, M. J., Janko, S., Marquart, J. M., Horn, E., & Odom, S. L. (1997). The impact of changing roles on relationships between professionals in inclusive programs for young children. *Early Education and Development, 8,* 67–82.

Lieber, J., Wolery, M., Horn, E., Tschantz, J., Beckman, P. J., & Hanson, M. J. (2001). Collaborative relationships among adults in inclusive preschool programs. In S. Odom (Ed.), *Widening the circle: Including children with disabilities in preschools* (pp. 81–97). New York: Teachers College Press.

Lynch, E. W. (1998). Developing cross-cultural competence. In E. Lynch & M. Hanson (Eds.), *Developing cross-cultural competence: A guide for working with children and their families* (2nd ed., pp. 47–90). Baltimore: Brookes.

Mahoney, G., Kaiser, A., Girolametto, L., MacDonald, J., Robinson, C., Safford, P., & Spiker, D. (1999). Parent education in early intervention: A call for a renewed focus. *Topics in Early Childhood Special Education, 19,* 131–140.

Mahoney, G., & Perales, F. (2003). Using relationship-focused intervention to enhance the social-emotional functioning of young children with autism spectrum disorder. *Topics in Early Childhood Special Education, 23,* 77–90.

McConnell, S. R., McEvoy, M. A., & Priest, J. S. (2002). Growing measures for monitoring progress in early childhood education: A research and development process for individual growth and development indicators. *Assessment for Effective Intervention, 27*(4), 3–14.

McConnell, S. R., & Odom, S. L. (1999). Performance-based assessment of social competence for young children with disabilities. Development and initial evaluation of a multi-measure model. *Topics in Early Childhood Special Education, 19,* 67–74.

McCormick, L., & Kawate, J. (1982). Kindergarten survival skills: New directions for preschool special education. *Education and Training of the Mentally Retarded, 17,* 247–252.

McCormick, L., Noonan, M. J., & Heck, R. (1998). Variables affecting engagement in inclusive preschool classrooms. *Journal of Early Intervention, 21,* 160–176.

McEvoy, M. A., Nordquist, V. M., Twardosz, S. Heckaman, K., Wehby, J. H., & Denny, R. K. (1988). Promoting autistic children's peer interaction in an integrated early childhood setting using affection activities. *Journal of Applied Behavior Analysis, 21,* 193–200.

McWilliam, R. A. (1992). *Family-centered intervention planning: A routines-based approach.* Tucson, AZ: Communication Skill Builders.

McWilliam, R. A. (1996). How to provide integrated therapy. In R. McWilliam (Ed.), *Rethinking pull-out services in early intervention: A professional resource* (pp. 147–184). Baltimore: Brookes.

McWilliam, R. A., Tocci, L., & Harbin, G. L. (1998). Family-centered services: Service providers' discourse and behavior. *Topics in Early Childhood Special Education, 18,* 206–221.

McWilliam, R. A., Wolery, M., & Odom, S. L. (2001). Instructional perspectives in inclusive preschool classrooms. In M. Guralnick (Ed.), *Early childhood inclusion: Focus on change* (pp. 503–530). Baltimore: Brookes.

Meisels, S. J., & Shonkoff, J. P. (2000). Early childhood intervention: A continuing evolution. In J. Shonkoff & S. Meisels (Eds.), *Handbook of early childhood intervention* (2nd ed., pp. 3–31). New York: Cambridge University Press.

Morgan, L., & Goldstein, H. (2004). Teaching mothers of low socioeconomic status to use decontextualized language during storybook reading. *Journal of Early Intervention, 26,* 235–254.

Morris, E. K., & Midgley, B. D. (1990). Some historical and

conceptual foundations of ecobehavioral analysis. In S. Schroeder (Ed.), *Ecobehavioral analysis and developmental disabilities* (pp. 1–32). New York: Springer-Verlag.

Morrison, R. S., Sainato, D. M., BenChaaban, D., & Endo, S. (2002). Increasing play skills of children with autism using activity schedules and correspondence training. *Journal of Early Intervention, 25*, 58–72.

National Association for the Education of Young Children. (2005). *Principles of child development and learning that inform developmentally appropriate practice*. Washington, DC: Author. Retrieved June 10, 2005, from http://www.naeyc.org/about/positions/dap3.asp.

Neisworth, J. T., & Bagnato, S. J. (2000). Recommended practices in assessment. In S. Sandall, M. E. McLean, & B. J. Smith (Eds.), *DEC Recommended practices in early intervention/early childhood special education* (pp. 17–27). Longmont, CO: Sopris West.

Odom, S. L. (2001). Learning about the barriers to and facilitators of inclusion for young children with disabilities. In S. Odom (Ed.), *Widening the circle: Including children with disabilities in preschool programs* (pp. 1–9). New York: Teachers College Press.

Odom, S. L., & Bailey, D. B. (2001). Inclusive preschool programs: Classroom ecology and child outcomes. In M. Guralnick (Ed.), *Early childhood inclusion: Focus on change* (pp. 253–276). Baltimore: Brookes.

Odom, S. L., Brown, W. H., Frey, T., Karasu, N., Smith-Carter, L., & Strain, P. S. (2003). Evidence-based practices for young children with autism: Evidence from single subject design research. *Focus on Autism, 18*, 176–181.

Odom, S. L., & Chandler, L. (1990). Transition to parenthood for parents of technology assisted infants. *Topics in Early Childhood Special Education, 9*(4), 43–55.

Odom, S. L., Favazza, P. C., Brown, W. H., & Horn, E. M. (2000). Approaches to understanding the ecology of early environments for children with disabilities. In T. Thompson, D. Felce, & F. Symons (Eds.), *Behavioral observation: Technology and applications in developmental disabilities* (pp. 193–214). Baltimore: Brookes.

Odom, S. L., & Loftin, R. (2005). Contextualism. In M. Hersen, G. Sugai, & R. Horner (Eds.), *Encyclopedia of behavior modification and cognitive behavior therapy: Vol. 3. Educational applications* (pp. 1233–1235). Thousand Oaks, CA: Sage.

Odom, S. L., McConnell, S. R., McEvoy, M. A., Peterson, C., Ostrosky, M., Chandler, L. K., Spicuzza, R. J., Skellenger, A., Creighton, M., & Favazza, P. C. (1999). Relative effects of interventions supporting the social competence of young children with disabilities. *Topics in Early Childhood Special Education, 19*, 75–91.

Odom, S. L., & Strain, P. S. (2002). Evidence-based practice in early intervention/early childhood special education: Single subject design research. *Journal of Early Intervention 25*, 151–160.

Odom, S. L., Teferra, T., & Kaul, S. (2004). An overview of international approaches to early intervention for young children with special needs and their families. *Young Children, 59*(5), 38–43.

Odom, S. L., Vitztum, J., Wolery, R., Lieber, J., Sandall, S., Hanson, M. J., Beckman, P., Schwartz, I., & Horn, E. (2004). Preschool inclusion in the United States: A review of research from an ecological systems perspective. *Journal of Research in Special Educational Needs, 4*(3), 17–49.

Odom, S. L., Zercher, C., Li, S., Marquart, J., Sandall, S., & Brown, W. H. (2005). *Social acceptance and social rejection of young children with disabilities in inclusive classes*. Manuscript submitted for publication.

Peterson, P., Carta, J. J., & Greenwood, C. R. (2005). Teaching enhanced milieu language teaching skills to parents in multiple risk families. *Journal of Early Intervention, 27*, 94–109.

Priest, J. S., McConnell, S. R., Walker, D., Carta, J. J., Kaminski, R. A., McEvoy, M. A., Good, R. H., Greenwood, C. R., & Shinn, M. R. (2001). General growth outcomes for young children: Developing a foundation for continuous progress measurement. *Journal of Early Intervention, 24*, 163–180.

Raab, M., & Dunst, C. J. (2004). Early intervention practitioner approaches to natural environment interventions. *Journal of Early Intervention, 27*, 15–26.

Rauh, V. A., Achenbach, T. M., Nurcombe, B., Howell, C. T., & Teti, D. M. (1988). Minimizing adverse effects of low birth weight: Four-year results of an early intervention program. *Child Development, 59*, 544–553.

Reinhartsen, D. B., Garfinkle, A. N., & Wolery, M. (2002). Engagement with toys in 2-year-old children with autism: Teacher selection versus child choice. *Journal of the Association for Persons with Severe Handicaps, 27*, 175–187.

Rogoff, B. (2003). *The cultural nature of human development*. New York: Oxford University Press.

Rogoff, B., Baker-Sennett, Lacasa, P., & Goldsmith, D. (1995). Development through participation in sociocultural activity. *New Directions in Child Development, 67* (Spring), 45–65.

Rosenkoetter, S. E., Whaley, K. T., Hains, A. H., & Pierce, L. (2001). The evolution of transition policy for young children with special needs and their families: Past, present, and future. *Topics in Early Childhood Special Education, 21*, 3–15.

Sainato, D. S., & Morrison, R. S. (2001). Transition to inclusive environments for young children with disabilities: Toward a seamless system of service delivery. In M. J. Guralnick (Ed.), *Early childhood inclusion: Focus on change* (pp. 293–306). Baltimore: Brookes.

Sameroff, A. J., & Fiese, B. H. (2000). Transactional regulation: The developmental ecology of early intervention. In J. P. Shonkoff & S. J. Meisels (Eds.), *Handbook of early childhood intervention* (2nd ed., pp. 135–159). New York: Cambridge University Press.

Sandall, S., McLean, M. E., Milagros, R., & Smith, B. J. (2000). DEC's new recommended practices: The context for change. In S. Sandall, M. McLean, & B. Smith (Eds.), *DEC recommended practices in early intervention/early childhood special education* (pp. 5–16). Denver: Sopris West.

Sandall, S., Schwartz, I., & Joseph, G. (2001). A building blocks model for effective instruction in inclusive early childhood settings. *Young Exceptional Children, 4*(3), 3–9.

Schwartz, I. S., Carta, J. J., & Grant, S. (1996). Examining the use of recommended language intervention practices in early childhood special education. *Topics in Early Childhood Special Education, 16*, 251–272.

Sewell, T. J., Collins, B. C., Hemmeter, M. L., & Schuster, J. W. (1998). Using simultaneous prompting within an activity-based format to teach dressing skills to preschoolers with developmental delays. *Journal of Early Intervention, 21*, 132–145.

Shearer, M. S., & Shearer, D. E. (1972). The Portage Project: A model for early childhood education. *Exceptional Children, 39*, 210–217.

Smith, B. J., McLean, M. E., Sandall, S., Snyder, P., & Broudy, A. (2000). Methods and activities used to produce the DEC recommended practices. In S. Sandall, M. McLean, & B. Smith (Eds.), *DEC recommended practices in early intervention/early childhood special education* (pp. 107–114). Denver: Sopris West.

Spiker, D., Hebbler, K., & Mallik, S. (2005). Developing and implementing early intervention programs for children with established disabilities. In M. Guralnick (Ed.), *The developmental systems approach to early intervention* (pp. 305–349). Baltimore: Brookes.

Strain, P. S. (1983). Generalization of autistic children's social behavior change: Effects of developmentally integrated and segregated settings. *Analysis and Intervention in Developmental Disabilities, 3*, 23–34.

Strain, P. S., & Timm, M. (2001). Remediation and prevention of aggression: An evaluation of the Regional Intervention Program over a quarter century. *Behavioral Disorders, 26*, 297–313.

Thompson, L., Lobb, C., Elling, R., Herman, S., Jurkiewicz, T., & Hulleza, C. (1997). Pathways to family empowerment: Effects of family-centered delivery of early intervention services. *Exceptional Children, 64*, 99–113.

Thurman, S. K. (1997). Systems, ecologies, and the context of early intervention. In S. Thurman, J. Cornwell, & S. Gottwald (Eds.), *Contexts of early intervention: Systems and settings* (pp. 3–19). Baltimore: Brookes.

Thurman, S. K., & Widerstrom, A. H. (1990). *Infants and young children with special needs: A developmental and ecological approach* (2nd ed.). Baltimore: Brookes.

Trivette, C. M., & Dunst, C. J. (2000). Recommended practices in family-based practices. In S. Sandall, M. E. McLean, & B. J. Smith (Eds.), *DEC recommended practices in early intervention/early childhood special education* (pp. 39–46). Denver: Sopris West.

Trivette, C. M., Dunst, C. J., & Deal, A. G. (1997). Resource-based approach to early intervention. In S. K. Thurman, J. R. Cornwell, & S. R. Gottwald (Eds.), *Contexts of early intervention: Systems and settings* (pp. 73–92). Baltimore: Brookes.

Venn, M. L., Wolery, M., Werts, M. G., Morris, A., DeCesare, L. D., & Cuffs, M. S. (1993). Embedding instruction in art activities to teach preschoolers with disabilities to imitate their peers. *Early Childhood Research Quarterly, 8*, 277–294.

Vondra, J. I., & Barnett, D. (Eds.). (1999). Atypical attachment in infancy and early childhood among children at developmental risk. *Monographs of the society for research in child development, 64*(3, Serial No. 258).

Weiss, C. H. (1995). Nothing as practical as a good theory: Exploring theory-based evaluation for comprehensive community initiatives for children and families. In J. Connell, A. Kubisch, L. Schorr, & C. Weiss (Eds.), *New approaches to evaluating community initiatives: Concepts, methods, and contexts* (pp. 119–145). Washington, DC: The Aspen Institute.

Wolery, M. (2000). Recommended practices in child-focused interventions. In S. Sandall, M. E. McLean, & B. J. Smith (Eds.), *DEC recommended practices in early intervention/early childhood special education* (pp. 29–37). Denver: Sopris West.

Wolery, M., Anthony, L., Caldwell, N. K., Synder, E. D., & Morgante, J. D. (2002). Embedding and distributing constant time delay in circle time and transitions. *Topics in Early Childhood Special Education, 22*, 14–25.

Wolery, M., Anthony, L., & Heckathorn, J. (1998). Transition-based teaching: Effects on transitions, teachers' behavior, and children's learning. *Journal of Early Intervention, 21*, 117–131.

Wolfberg, P. J., Zercher, C., Lieber, J., Capell, K., Matias, S. G., Hanson, M., & Odom, S. L. (1999). "Can I play with you": Peer culture in inclusive preschool programs. *Journal of the Association for Persons with Severe Disabilities, 24*, 69–84.

Woods, J., Kashinath, S., & Goldstein, H. (2004). Effects of embedding caregiver-implemented teaching strategies in daily routines on children's communication outcomes. *Journal of Early Intervention, 26*, 175–193.

Wyly, M. V., Allen, J., Pfalzer, S. M., & Wilson, J. R. (1996). Providing a seamless system from hospital to home: The NICU training project. *Infants and Young Children, 8*(3), 77–84.

Chapter 7

Transition-Focused Education:

Foundation for the Future

Paula D. Kohler and **Sharon Field**

Most articles regarding transition education and services begin with information about poor postschool outcomes of individuals with disabilities, which were well documented in the late 1980s and early 1990s (e.g., Blackorby & Wagner, 1996; Hasazi, Gordon, & Roe, 1985; Mithaug, Horiuchi, & Fanning 1985). Although the frequency of comprehensive follow-up studies of students with disabilities has diminished in recent years, surveys of adults with disabilities conducted by the National Council on Disability through the Harris Poll indicate that individuals with disabilities continue to lag far behind individuals without disabilities in employment and other aspects of community engagement (Taylor, 1998, 2000). Over the years, the information regarding student outcomes has caused advocates, families, and educators to seriously question both the content and process of special education programming. Public recognition that youths with disabilities were not achieving high levels of quality full-time employment, independent living, success in postsecondary education, or community engagement resulted in an increased, changing focus on transition education and services.

During the past 15 years, in response to information regarding students' postschool outcomes, three specific initiatives have emerged that support this increased focus on transition education and services: (a) federal special education and disability legislation; (b) federal, state, and local investment in transition services development; and (c) effective transition practices research. In this chapter, we present a summary of these initiatives and an overview of the changing perspective related to transition-focused education. Using this perspective, we then describe and recommend specific transition-focused practices, supported by current research. Finally, we address the extent and fidelity of transition practices implementation and synthesize aspects of transition-focused education unique to special education.

Historical Initiatives

Federal Special Education and Disability Legislation

Since 1983, federal special education policy regarding transition services for students with disabilities has expanded significantly. The 1983 amendments to the Education for all Handicapped Children Act of 1975 (P.L. 98-199) authorized spending for transition-focused research and model demonstration grants and contracts. In 1990, while continuing federal support for transition-related activities, the Individuals with Disabilities Education Act (IDEA; P.L. 101-476) defined transition services and required that students' interests, preferences, and needs be considered in their development. Furthermore, IDEA required that the Individualized Education Program (IEP) for students aged 16 and older must include specific transition components, such as a statement of needed transition services and agency linkages. In one of the most important mandates related to special education, the IDEA Amendments of 1997 (P.L. 105-17) expanded the transition requirements regarding a student's IEP to include transition service needs related to the student's course of study beginning at age 14. For the first time, federal policy communicated that the content of a student's education should be focused on postschool aspirations.

The 1990 and 1997 IDEA provisions also mandated a more participatory approach to education and service planning for individuals who have disabilities. IDEA required student involvement in transition planning and mandated that students' preferences and interests be taken into account when transition services are planned. As conceptualized in the 1990 and 1997 IDEA mandates, transition planning focuses on postschool outcomes and consists of a variety of activities, coordinated in a meaningful way, that inform educational planning and decision making.

Federal, State, and Local Investment in Transition Services Development

Since 1983, the Office of Special Education Programs (OSEP) has funded more than 500 projects focused on transition education and services for students with disabilities in secondary and postsecondary education. Federal funding has supported transition system change in 46 states, as well as transition-related professional development for beginning and continuing educators. Federal resources have also provided technical assistance to support transition efforts by establishing national transition technical assistance and research centers. Projects supported by federal dollars have ranged from family-focused and interagency collaboration initiatives to dropout identification and retrieval to transition from high school to employment. Through investment in transition services development, the field gained a much better understanding of the many aspects of transition services and ways to implement transition in local contexts. Reviews of project outcomes indicated that the impact of these initiatives on program development and student skills and outcomes has been significant (Kohler & Rusch, 1995; Rusch, Kohler, & Hughes, 1992).

Effective Transition Practices Research

Important information regarding effective practices emerged from state and national follow-up studies of students with disabilities. Not only did these studies generate data regarding students' poor postschool outcomes, as mentioned previously, but they also added significantly to knowledge about potential ways to improve student outcomes. Studies generally indicated that vocational education, paid work experience, parent involvement, and/or interagency collaboration had a positive impact on student outcomes (e.g., Hasazi et al., 1985; Mithaug et al., 1985; Sitlington, Frank, & Carson, 1993). The National Longitudinal Transition Study (NLTS) extended these findings and provided additional information regarding school performance. The NLTS findings indicated that in general, vocational education, work experience, tutoring, extracurricular group activities, and parental support positively contributed to school performance and postschool outcomes (e.g., Blackorby & Wagner, 1996).

In addition to the follow-up studies, the field has investigated transition practices at both the individual student and program levels. For example, several studies that utilized students as the unit of analysis found that students who are more involved in setting their educational goals are more likely to achieve those goals (e.g., Deci & Ryan, 1991; Sheldon, Ryan, Rawsthorne, & Ilhardi, 1997). Furthermore, Wehmeyer and Schwartz (1997) found that 1 year after school completion, graduates of special education programs were more likely to be employed and have higher earnings if they had higher self-determination scores during their final year of high school. Others have sought to make sense of transition-related research across studies, in efforts to develop some general models or principles and/or generate information useful for program development (e.g., Hughes et al., 1997; Kohler, 1993; Phelps & Hanley-Maxwell, 1997). This work was important in synthesizing findings from the specific intervention and follow-up studies, and organizing and disseminating information in a way meaningful to those developing local transition services and programs. This work also provided an important link between initial theoretical models regarding transition services and the intervention studies.

The research initiative resulted in increased recognition that transition to adult roles is a complex process all youths must negotiate and that a myriad of factors work together to influence students' lives after school completion (e.g., Benz, Lindstrom, & Yovanoff, 2000; Kohler, 1993; Wehmeyer & Schwartz, 1997). The field learned that successful transition requires the development of a student's abilities through education and other experiences, specific supports that enhance or facilitate those abilities, and opportunities through which one can apply those abilities. Further, research supported the importance of students' playing a central role in planning and preparing for postschool outcomes. Research and evaluation also indicated that in some cases, educational and service systems facilitate this process but in others, either leave it to chance or actually impede the process by establishing barriers, wasting instructional time, or limiting access.

In summary, with the convergence of these three initiatives—federal legislation, investment in transition services development, and effective practices research—the emphasis on transition-focused education and services grew stronger and broader. Each initiative influenced the other in important ways, and it is imperative to recognize the interaction and interrelationships among them, as well as the importance of parent and advocate influence across them. Through these initiatives, the perspective of "transition services" also changed, and thus the investigation and implementation of effective transition practices.

A Changing Perspective of Transition Services

The changed perspective of transition services is an important outcome of the three initiatives, as well as an important consideration in the interpretation of the transition practices research. When transition services were originally conceptualized, many in the field focused on the transition of students with disabilities from one service system to another, that is, from the educational system to the adult community service system. For example, Will's (1984) original conceptualization of transition emphasized three bridges, representing levels of community services, which she theorized students with disabilities utilized to achieve postschool employment. The emphasis on services as the process of transition planning and on employment as the outcome represented a somewhat narrow interpretation of the concept.

With growing knowledge of the complexity of effective transition practices, many adopted a much broader conceptualization of transition planning and services (see Bates, 1990; Halpern, 1985; Wehman, 1992a)—what Kohler (1998) referred to as *transition-focused education.* This perspective views "transition planning" not as an add-on activity for students with disabilities once they reach age 14 or 16 but rather as a fundamental basis of education that guides the development of all educational programs. As illustrated in Figure 1, transition-focused education is directed toward adult outcomes and consists of academic, career, and extracurricular instruction and activities delivered through a variety of instructional and transition approaches and services, depending on the local context and students' learning and support needs. The concept of transition-focused education represents a shift from disability-focused, deficit-driven programs to an education and service delivery approach based upon abilities, options, and self-determination (Kohler & Rusch, 1996; Szymanski, Hanley-Maxwell, & Parker, 1990; Wehman, 1992b). This approach incorporates Halpern's (1993) quality-of-life issues, Szymanski's (1994) life-span and life-space considerations, and Repetto and Correa's (1996) suggestions for seamless transition approaches.

A Framework of Effective Transition Practices

Kohler and her colleagues (e.g., Kohler, 1993, 1996; Kohler, DeStefano, Wermuth, Grayson, & McGinty, 1994; Rusch et al., 1992) developed the Taxonomy for Transition Programming, illustrated in Figure 2, which presents a comprehensive, conceptual organization of practices through which transition-focused education and services are developed and delivered. This taxonomy emerged from several investigations that reviewed research literature (Kohler, 1993), evaluation studies (Kohler et al., 1994), and model

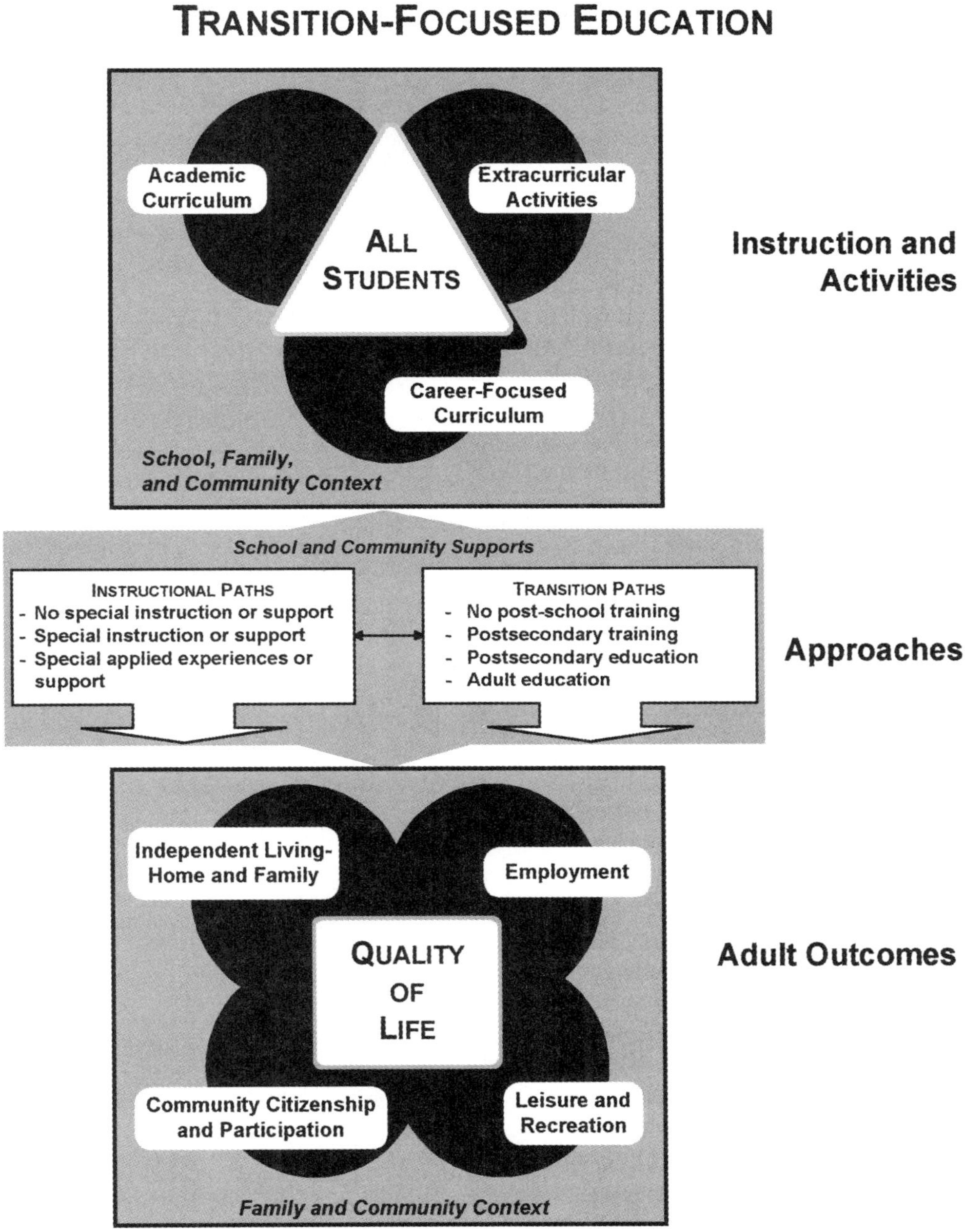

FIGURE 1. Transition-focused education. From "Effective Transition Education: It Takes a Community," by P. D. Kohler, May 1998, paper presented at Ohio's DCDT Interagency Conference, Columbus, OH. Reprinted with permission of the author.

transition project outcomes (Rusch et al., 1992). Through a three-phased research process, effective practices identified through each of these investigations were synthesized and organized into five categories:

1. student-focused planning,
2. student development,
3. interagency and interdisciplinary collaboration,
4. family involvement, and

5. program structure and attributes (Kohler, 1996).

The practices included in the model were evaluated using criteria proposed by Peters and Heron (1993) to determine "best practices." They (a) are associated with positive student outcomes, (b) have a sound basis in theory, (c) are supported in the literature, and (d) were socially validated by a national group of transition experts. More recently, Kohler and Chapman (1999) reviewed the transition literature to investigate the efficacy of an extended taxonomy model and to identify how the model might need to be expanded to remain consistent with current literature. They found that the practices reviewed in the current literature generally paralleled the practices in the model.

In summary, the practices presented and described in the taxonomy represent concrete strategies that operationalize the concept of transition-focused education; further, they represent a consumer-oriented paradigm built upon student and family involvement and students' self-determination. In the following sections, we use the taxonomy as an organizing heuristic to describe general transition practices synthesized from the research and to summarize recent research regarding these practices. In each of the five areas, we first provide a general description of the practices that emerged in each area and then describe examples of specific practices recently shown to be effective.

Student-Focused Planning

Student-focused planning practices emerging from the research include the development of student goals using relevant assessment information as a basis for planning, student participation in planning and decision making, and student evaluation of progress in meeting goals (e.g., Martin, Marshall, & Maxson, 1993; Ward & Kohler, 1996). With student-focused planning activities, students develop and strengthen self-determination skills through practice and application. In the elementary and early secondary education years,

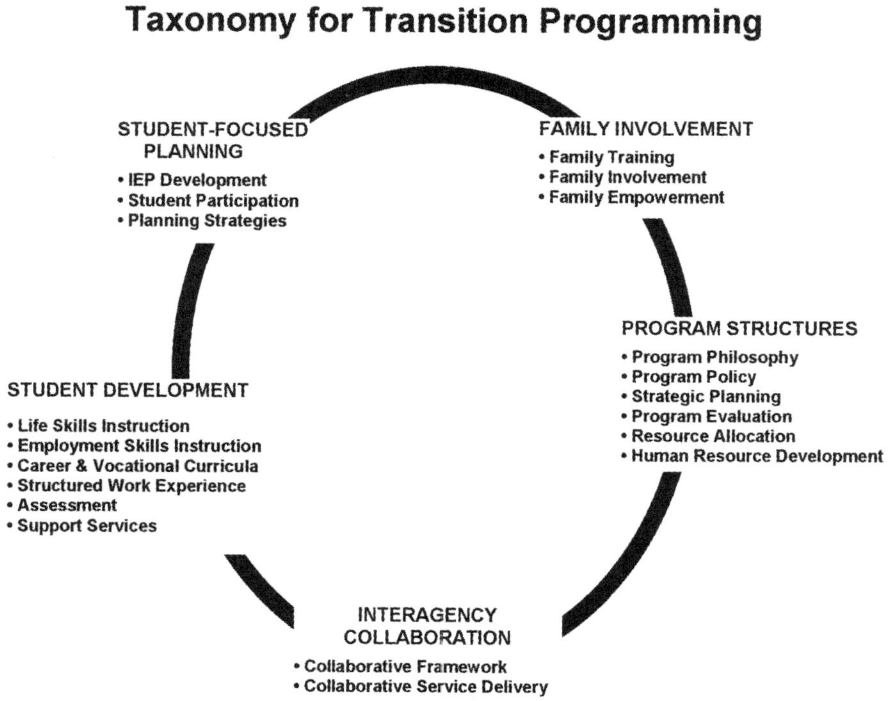

FIGURE 2. Taxonomy for Transition Programming. From "Taxonomy for Transition Programming," by P. D. Kohler. Champaign: University of Illinois, Transition Research Institute. Copyright 1996. Reprinted with permission of the author.

educators may need to guide students through the process, with the subsequent expectation that students become increasingly proficient as they progress through high school.

An important aspect of student-focused planning is that educational decisions are based on students' goals, visions, and interests. Thus, it is important to facilitate development of the student's self-awareness and use this information to set short- and long-term goals. An important strategy to help students identify their interests and preferences is to provide opportunities and experiences across curricula through which students collect and reflect on information about themselves, and use that information to set goals (Powers, Singer, & Sowers, 1996; Sands & Wehmeyer, 1996). Based on these goals, an appropriate IEP is developed in partnership with the student and his or her family. The process is continuous and cyclical—help the student reflect on his or her experiences, derive meaning particular to his or her context, use that information for future action, and begin the cycle anew.

Transition "best practices," as well as IDEA mandates, imply that students work with a variety of people during the educational planning process—school psychologists, general educators, special educators, school administrators, agency personnel, and their parents/guardians. To participate actively in this context, students must exercise self-advocacy skills so that they can express their self-awareness to others—important behaviors that are often challenging to develop and/or apply. Effective student-focused planning also includes student reflection on progress, or lack of, during the preceding year. These behaviors—self-advocacy within a group setting and self-reflection—are considered fundamental aspects of self-determination, and their application is an important component of student-focused planning (Hoffman & Field, 1995; Wehmeyer, 1992).

A variety of strategies have been shown effective in increasing students' participation in their transition planning. The Self-Directed IEP model, an 11-step process aligned with typical IEP meeting components (e.g., identification of participants, introductions, evaluation of previous goals) and multiple opportunities for practice, has been found to be effective for teaching students to participate in and/or lead their transition planning (see Allen, Smith, Test, Flowers, & Wood, 2001; Cross, Cooke, Wood, & Test, 1999; German, Martin, Marshall, & Sale, 2000). Students instructed to use the Self-Advocacy Strategy (take an inventory, provide inventory information, ask questions, respond to questions, and summarize IEP goals) identified more IEP goals and provided more information during their IEP meetings than a contrast group (Van Reusen & Bos, 1994). Through student coaching, peer mentorships, parent support, and transition staff inservice education, the TAKE CHARGE for the Future intervention model resulted in significant increases in the level of student involvement in transition planning activities and meetings, empowerment, and transition awareness (Powers et al., 2001).

Student Development

Those practices included in the student development category emphasize life, employment, and occupational skill development through school- and work-based learning experiences. They also include student assessment and accommodations, which provide a foundation for determining and evaluating these learning experiences so they result in successful transition.

Through student development activities, students develop and apply self-determination skills, as well as academic, living, social, and occupational skills; career awareness; and work-related behaviors—characteristics and behaviors associated with positive postschool outcomes (Blackorby & Wagner, 1996; Heal & Rusch, 1995; Wehmeyer & Schwartz, 1997). So that students achieve the maximum benefit from these experiences and generalize their skills to multiple environments, such experiences are provided in both school-based and community-based settings, including work-based situations. An important part of this process is to identify the accommodations or supports a student needs to participate and achieve success in educational and community settings. Effective student development practices increase students' knowledge, develop students' skills, and provide guidance and opportunities to apply those skills.

Research continues to support the importance of student development practices in preparing individuals with disabilities to assume independent adult roles. Benz, Yavonoff, and Doren (1997) found that work experience, academic skills, social skills, and job search skills, in addition to continuing postschool support, improved employment outcomes. Benz et al. (2000) found that career-related work experience and completion of student-identified transition goals were strongly associated with graduation and employment. Colley and Jamison (1998) found that work experience, occupational education, and mainstreamed academics contributed to employment. Farley and Johnson (1999) described specific strategies for improving students' decision-making confidence, career decisiveness, and job-seeking skills—skills important to student's vocational preparedness. Kohler and Troesken (1999) and Kohler and Hood (2000) identified a variety of programs that resulted in increased student skills and/or postschool outcomes and described specific examples for providing occupational training, work experience, academic development, and other aspects of student development. For example, occupational skill development and work experiences (with appropriate supports) consistently resulted in private-sector employment for students with disabilities (see Kohler & Hood, 2000). Similarly, Leuking and Fabian (2000) illustrated the positive effects of paid internships on student employment.

A number of interventions have also been shown to be effective in developing some aspects of a student's self-determination. *Steps to Self-Determination* (Field & Hoffman, 1996), an experiential curriculum that includes five major components (Know Yourself, Value Yourself, Plan, Act, and Experience Outcomes and Learn), resulted in significant increases in behaviors considered correlates of self-determination (Hoffman & Field, 1995). The *Next S.T.E.P.* curriculum (Halpern et al., 1997), which includes teacher and student demonstrations and field-related and hands-on activities focused on preparing students to participate in their transition planning, resulted in increases in students' skills related to autonomy, psychological empowerment, self-realization, and self-regulation (Zhang, 2001). Students participating in the Self-Determined Learning Model of Instruction, a three-phased curriculum model that teaches self-regulated problem-solving strategies, attained goals, exhibited increased levels of self-determination, and communicated their satisfaction (Wehmeyer, Palmer, Agran, Mithaug, & Martin, 2000). (For a complete review of research regarding self-determination interventions, see Algozzine, Browder, Karvonen, Test, & Wood, 2001.)

Collaborative Service Delivery

The collaborative practices synthesized through the taxonomy facilitate involvement of community businesses, organizations, and agencies in all aspects of transition-focused education. Collaborative service delivery is fostered by interagency agreements that clearly articulate roles, responsibilities, communication strategies, and other collaborative actions that enhance curriculum and program development and service delivery (Benz, Lindstrom, & Halpern, 1995; Blalock, 1996). Through collaborative practices, educational and adult service providers address opportunities for individual students, as well as community issues that influence opportunities and services for students in general. The purpose of these collaborative activities is to implement an integrated *system* that addresses the life-long learning and support needs of a community's members.

Devlieger and Trach (1999) found that interagency collaboration and support for individual students in transition and their families is a factor so important that when done well, it facilitates achievement of transition goals; and when done poorly, it limits or impedes those goals. Benz, Lindstrom, and Halpern (1995) found that the Community Transition Team model was effective in building school and community capacity to better serve students' transition service needs. Collet-Klingenberg (1998) also found that school-based and community-based transition teams were instrumental in introducing and implementing student-focused planning and student development practices, such as work experiences and student involvement in planning. In addition, Benz, Johnson, Mikkelsen, and Lindstrom (1995) found specific barriers identified by various stakeholders—including students and their families—to effective collaboration, including ineffective use of transition planning meetings, intimidating language, and complexity of agency procedures. Thus, addressing such issues would be important goals of initial collaborative efforts.

Family Involvement

The practices represented in the family involvement category are associated with parent and family participation in planning and delivering education and transition services, including practices that facilitate family participation. These practices focus on three aspects of family involvement: (a) participation and roles, (b) empowerment, and (c) training (Kohler, 1996, 1998). Participation practices focus on a wide array of roles through which families might be involved in planning and delivering individual and community-level transition education and services, such as assessment, decision making, policy development, and training. Empowerment strategies include practices that facilitate meaningful family involvement in transition-focused activities, such as specific methods to identify family needs. Family-focused training increases family members' ability to work effectively with educators and other service providers, and vice versa. Family involvement has been shown to improve school attendance, increase higher education attendance and assessment scores, improve students' self-esteem and confidence, and reduce dropout rates (Blackorby & Wagner, 1996; Flaxman & Inger, 1991; Newman & Cameto, 1993). Ryan and colleagues (Ryan & Lynch, 1989; Ryan, Stiller, & Lynch, 1994) found a positive link between relatedness to parents and autonomy in adolescents, a key component of self-determination. Morningstar, Turnbull, and Turnbull (1995) found that from students' perspectives, their families play important roles in the development of their self-determination and their visions for the future. Thus, student-focused planning and student development practices described previously are supported and extended through family involvement.

Whitney-Thomas and Hanley-Maxwell (1996) described specific parent concerns regarding their children's transition needs, such as economic self-sufficiency, expanding social networks, and vocational and residential options, as well as the importance of school personnel in assisting them to address these concerns. Geenen, Powers, and Lopez-Vasquez (2001) identified a variety of roles that culturally and linguistically diverse, as well as European-American, parents assume regarding their children's transition, such as teaching cultural values, helping with employment, and teaching their children to care for disability. These authors caution us that our assumptions, attitudes, and behaviors often alienate parents, who are key participants in supporting their children's transitions, thus increasing, rather than helping to decrease, their concerns.

McCarney (cited in Turnbull & Turnbull, 1990) found that direct, routine communication strategies, such as face-to-face conferences, telephone contacts, open house events, teacher notes, and classroom visits, improved educator and family interactions. Regarding planning, Hutchins and Renzaglia (1998) effectively engaged families in selecting work experiences and developing long-term job placements for students with moderate and severe disabilities through a comprehensive family vocational interview. Through the interview, educators integrated family concerns and issues into a long-term educational planning process focused on employment outcomes. Flannery et al. (2000) found that students and parents were more satisfied with IEP transition goals and teacher interactions after personal future planning strategies were used.

Suggestions generated directly from families regarding effective involvement strategies have also been identified. In a study focused on improving collaboration conducted by Benz, Johnson et al. (1995), parents suggested that better informational materials; joint training for vocational rehabilitation and school staff, parents, and students; resource fairs; a single, knowledgeable contact person; and support groups and networking opportunities would improve the transition planning process and the quality of parent involvement. Further, deFur, Todd-Allen, and Getzel (2001) found that parent-identified factors that improved their participation in transition planning were based on the development of personal, rather than bureaucratic, relationships. These families identified professionals who made a difference in their participation in transition planning as those who communicated effectively and shared information, developed collaborative partnerships, connected them with other families, and illustrated genuine care for and recognition of their children.

Program Structure

Program structures are features that relate to efficient and effective delivery of transition-focused education and services, including philosophy, planning, policy, evaluation, and resource development. The structures and attributes of a school provide the framework for implementing transition-focused education. Practices that promote outcome-based education and expanded curricular options include community-level strategic planning, cultural and ethnic sensitivity, a clearly articulated mission and values, qualified staff, and sufficient allocation of resources (Kohler, 1996). Transition-oriented schools focus also on systematic community involvement in the development of educational options; community-based learning opportunities; systematic inclusion of students in the social life of the school; and increased expectations related to skills, values, and outcomes for all students (Edgar & Polloway, 1994).

Hasazi, DeStefano, and Furney conducted several policy studies that investigated implementation of IDEA mandates and effective transition practices at both the state and local levels. Their findings reaffirmed the importance of program policies and philosophies as a foundation through which transition-focused education occurs. Through case studies of three states considered exemplary in their implementation of transition policies and services, Furney, Hasazi, and DeStefano (1997) found that shared values and beliefs regarding transition services, direct policy approaches, collaborative structures for systemic change, a commitment to basing change on research and evaluation, and capacity-building activities were characteristic of these states. These authors also conducted case studies of nine local sites across the United States, five considered model sites with national reputations for effectiveness and four considered representative sites demonstrating both progress and challenges. Hasazi, Furney, and DeStefano (1999) found substantive differences between the two types of sites and described the following factors as characteristics of the effective sites:

> (a) incorporation of systemwide, student- and family-centered strategies; (b) fostering of effective and substantive interagency collaboration; (c) facilitation of systemic professional development; (d) a visionary, supportive, and inclusive form of leadership; (e) coordination of an integrated set of reform efforts; and (f) emergence of connections among a variety of local and federal transition initiatives. (p. 558)

Again, these findings support the conclusion that program policy and philosophy provide the context within which transition-focused education is possible.

Extent of Effective Practices Implementation

Implementation of effective transition practices has progressed over the past 15 years, and attempts to identify exemplary transition practices and programs have discovered pockets of excellence scattered across the country (National Council on Disability, 2000). Although widespread systems change has not been documented, activities within states have been successful in raising stakeholder awareness, increasing parent and student participation, enhancing collaborative relationships, and establishing transition-related policies to better support services (Guy & Schriner, 1997). Further, the extent to which organizations are evaluating their transition services and students' outcomes—a fundamental requirement for identifying effective practices—seems to be increasing (see Kohler & Hood, 2000; Kohler & Troesken, 1999; Kohler & Van Beaver, 1996.)

The extent to which particular transition practices have been implemented varies widely. Wehmeyer and Schwartz (1998) examined the transition goals of 136 students with mental retardation or developmental disabilities and found that none of the goals targeted instruction related to a specific self-determination skill. In their research on student involvement in transition planning, Lehmann, Bassett, Sands, Spencer, and Gliner (1999) concluded that "ironically, many basic transition elements, often presumed in our field already to exist (e.g., transition teams, student-focused planning, and basic curricula), were selected by schools participating in this study as targeted interventions" (p. 16). In their investigation of policy compliance and best practices implementation in Ohio, McMahan and Baer (2001) determined that policy compliance was occurring with regularity, but best practice utilization was not. Everson, Zhang, and Guillory (2001) found similar results when they reviewed 329 individual transition plans in Louisiana.

Investigations of compliance with the basic IDEA transition mandates also indicate that the field has much work to do before achieving wide-scale implementation, even when using the most minimal of indicators. Williams and O'Leary (2001) analyzed OSEP monitoring reports for compliance with the 1990 IDEA transition mandates. The monitoring reports of 44 of the 54 states and entities (81.5%) monitored between 1993 and 1997 included findings regarding the transition mandates. Among their findings were that one third of the states or entities had not invited students to their IEP meeting, and about half of the IEPs reviewed by OSEP during the monitoring process did not address instruction, community experiences, or postschool objectives within the statement of transition services (Williams & O'Leary, 2001). Subsequent investigations of OSEP monitoring reports posted at their Web site (see www.ed.gov/offices/OSERS/OSEP/Monitoring) indicated only limited compliance with the 1990 and 1997 transition mandates.

What Is Special About Transition-Focused Education?

The concept of normalization has been a central construct in special education and disability services for many years. According to Nirje (1972), normalization involves "making available to [persons with disabilities] the patterns and conditions of everyday life which are as close as possible to the norms and patterns of mainstream society" (p. 363). The normalization principle has been the driving force behind the least restrictive environment provisions of special education legislation and the resulting focus on mainstreaming in the 1980s and inclusion in the 1990s. Due to the unique needs of individuals with disabilities, it was also clear that in order for persons with disabilities to participate in typical communities, individualized instruction, accommodations, and supports would be necessary. Thus, two central and enduring tenets of special education have been *normalization* and *individualization*.

Transition-focused education, through which specific transition practices are implemented, is a logical outgrowth of these two key principles. Effective transition practices emphasize the development of practical life skills that are geared toward the goals and aspirations of individual students. This emphasis on practical life skills evolved to help ensure meaningful community participation in typical settings. In other words, a primary goal of transition-focused education is to promote and facilitate normalization in postschool life. This end clearly requires that educational goals, and the resulting instruction toward those goals, be individualized to meet the specific aspirations and needs of students. Special education—and in particular the IEP—provides the means for accomplishing this end.

As noted, the research regarding effective transition practices has been conducted at both the program level and the individual student level. Follow-up studies, meta-evaluations, and research syntheses provided aggregate information that supports the importance of such practices as occupational skill development, paid work experience, and family involvement. Thus, these components are elements of effective programs. At the individual student level, specific interventions have been shown effective in developing student skills or characteristics. This work provides strategies effective in a particular context, again useful for developing transition-focused programs, curricula, or services. Effective providers establish programmatic elements, such as those included in the taxonomy, and through these elements provide *individualized* experiences, supports, and services. It is this aspect of individualization that distinguishes services authorized and provided through special education from those typically provided in general education.

For example, Devlieger and Trach (1999) described how individual needs and contexts influenced the way students mediated their transition to employment and reiterated the importance of individualized planning and services attuned to those contexts. So, although many people with disabilities might utilize community employment services, the why, when, and how of those services will vary on an individual basis. Bullis, Moran, Benz, Todis, and Johnson (2002) found that program flexibility and responsiveness to individual student needs were critical aspects of an effective transition program for students with emotional disturbances. Again, program elements were established, such as skill assessment, person-centered planning, and job placement, but they were individualized in response to students' specific preferences and needs. Case studies (cited in Kohler & Hood, 2000) illustrated the individual nature and variety of services necessary to assist students to achieve their transition goals, as well as the "ups and downs" and "stops and starts" of students' transitions. These cases also demonstrated how the intensity and timing of transition services vary from individual to individual. Thus, across transition studies, research has illustrated that *individual* supports and approaches embedded within transition-focused educational *programs* facilitate effective student transitions (e.g., Benz et al., 1997; Benz et al., 2000; Collet-Klingenberg, 1998).

Is effective transition programming peculiar to special education? The answer is both yes and no. In many cases, the context of general education, as organized currently, does not provide for significant individualization or flexibility in student programming, nor does general education funding support the range of services students might require to achieve successful transitions. For example, cooperative education is a typical approach used in career and technical education; however, services that some students with disabilities might need to access community-based employment, such as extensive job development, training, and ongoing support, are not typically provided. Special education services, and often community services, are generally necessary to help prepare students with disabilities for their transitions to adult outcomes and to help facilitate these transitions, although many students served by special education require only limited or intermittent supports. As illustrated in the other chapters in this book, the development of student characteristics and skills—and the provision of special education services—can and should certainly occur within the general education setting in many situations. Further, proven aspects of transition-focused education, such as family involvement, benefit all students.

Conclusion

This examination of the transition literature demonstrates that this work has progressed from the development of theoretical models of transition planning to the identification of generic practices associated with improved student outcomes, to the development of specific interventions that teach transition-related skills. This progression supported a broader perspective of transition planning that recognizes its complexity and the importance of multifaceted approaches. Because of this complexity, research focused on effective transition practices is not as straightforward as one would like. Transition to adult roles can be a complicated process, one that all youths must negotiate, and a myriad of factors work together to affect students' lives after school completion. Transition outcomes are strongly influenced by student and family characteristics, economic conditions, community contexts, and the availability of services. The inability to control many of these variables presents significant challenges for conducting transition practices research.

The transition practices literature recognizes that educators, service providers, and families must help students develop their skills and abilities, provide services and supports that enhance and facilitate these abilities, and develop opportunities through which students can apply those abilities. One-size-fits-all and "check-the-box transition planning" strategies do not effectively prepare students with disabilities—who all have unique needs—for successful, fulfilling adult roles. Through continued attention to establishing effective transition services, flexible enough to meet individual student needs, we can arm students with information and opportunities on which they can build their futures.

REFERENCES

Algozzine, B., Browder, D., Karvonen, M., Test, D. W., & Wood, W. M. (2001). Effects of interventions to promote self-determination for individuals with disabilities. *Review of Education Research, 71,* 49–108.

Allen, S. K., Smith, A. C., Test, D. W., Flowers, C., & Wood, W. M. (2001). The effects of self-directed IEP on student participation in IEP meetings. *Career Development for Exceptional Individuals, 24,* 107–120.

Bates, P. (1990). *Best practices in transition planning: Quality indicators.* Carbondale: Illinois Transition Project.

Benz, M. R., Johnson, D., Mikkelsen, K., & Lindstrom, L. (1995). Improving collaboration between schools and vocational rehabilitation: Stakeholder identified barriers and strategies. *Career Development for Exceptional Individuals, 18,* 133–144.

Benz, M. R., Lindstrom, L. E., & Halpern, A .S. (1995). Mobilizing local communities to improve transition services. *Career Development for Exceptional Individuals, 18,* 21–32.

Benz, M. R., Lindstrom, L., & Yovanoff, P. (2000). Improving graduation and employment outcomes of students with disabilities: Predictive factors and student perspectives. *Exceptional Children, 66,* 509–529.

Benz, M. R., Yovanoff, P., & Doren, B. (1997). School-to-work components that predict postschool success for students with and without disabilities. *Exceptional Children, 63,* 151–165.

Blackorby, J., & Wagner, M. (1996). Longitudinal postschool outcomes of youth with disabilities: Findings from the National Longitudinal Transition Study. *Exceptional Children, 62,* 399–413.

Blalock, G. (1996). Community transition teams as the foundation for services for youth with disabilities. *Journal of Learning Disabilities, 29,* 148–159.

Bullis, M., Moran, T., Benz, M., Todis, B., & Johnson, M. (2002). Description and evaluation of the ARIES Project: Achieving rehabilitation, individualized education, and employment success for adolescents with emotional disturbance. *Career Development for Exceptional Individuals, 25,* 41–58.

Collet-Klingenberg, L. (1998). The reality of best practices in transition: A case study. *Exceptional Children, 65,* 67–78.

Colley, D., & Jamison, D. (1998). Post school results for youth with disabilities: Key indicators and policy implications. *Career Development for Exceptional Individuals, 21,* 145–160.

Cross, T., Cooke, N. L., Wood, W. M., & Test, D. W. (1999). A comparison of the effects of MAPS and ChoiceMaker on student self-determination skills. *Education and Training in Mental Retardation and Developmental Disabilities, 34,* 499–510.

Deci, E., & Ryan, R. (1991). A motivational approach to self: Integration in personality. In R. Dienstbier (Ed.), *Nebraska Symposium on Motivation: Vol. 38. Perspectives on motivation* (pp. 31–49). New York: Plenum Press.

deFur, S. H., Todd-Allen, M., Getzel, E. E. (2001). Parent participation in the transition planning process. *Career Development for Exceptional Individuals, 24,* 19–36.

Devlieger, P., & Trach, J. (1999). Meditation as a transition process: The impact on postschool employment outcomes. *Exceptional Children, 65,* 507–523.

Edgar, E., & Polloway, E. A. (1994). Education for adolescents with disabilities: Curriculum and placement issues. *The Journal of Special Education, 27,* 438–452.

Education for All Handicapped Children Act of 1975, 20 U.S.C. § 1400 *et seq.* (1975) (amended 1983).

Everson, J. M., Zhang, D., & Guillory, J. D. (2001). A statewide investigation of individualized transition plans in Louisiana. *Career Development for Exceptional Individuals, 24,* 37–49.

Farley, R., & Johnson, V. A. (1999). Enhancing the career exploration and job-seeking skills of secondary students with disabilities. *Career Development for Exceptional Individuals, 22,* 43–54.

Field, S., & Hoffman, A. (1996). *Steps to self-determination: A curriculum to help adolescents learn to achieve their goals.* Austin, TX: PRO-ED.

Flannery, B., Newton, S., Horner, R., Slovic, R., Blumberg, R., & Ard, W. K. (2000). The impact of person-centered planning on the content and organization of individual supports. *Career Development for Exceptional Individuals, 23,* 123–137.

Flaxman, E., & Inger, M. (1991). Parents and schooling in the 1990s. *The ERIC Review, 1*(3), 2–6.

Furney, K., Hasazi, S., & DeStefano, L. (1997). Transition policies, practices, and promises: Lessons from three states. *Exceptional Children, 63,* 343–355.

Geenen, S., Powers, L., & Lopez-Vasquez, A. (2001). Multicultural aspects of parent involvement in transition planning. *Exceptional Children, 67,* 265–282.

German, S. L., Martin, J. E., Marshall, L. H., & Sale, P. R. (2000). Promoting self-determination: Using *Take Action* to teach goal attainment. *Career Development for Exceptional Individuals, 23,* 27–38.

Guy, B., & Schriner, K. (1997). Systems in transition: Are we there yet? *Career Development for Exceptional Individuals, 20,* 141–163.

Halpern, A. S. (1985). Transition: A look at the foundations. *Exceptional Children, 51,* 479–486.

Halpern, A. S. (1993). Quality of life as a conceptual framework for evaluating transition outcomes. *Exceptional Children, 59,* 486–498.

Halpern, A. S., Herr, C. M., Wolf, N. K., Lawson, J. D., Doren, B., & Johnson, M. D. (1997). *Next S.T.E.P.* Austin, TX: PRO-ED.

Hasazi, S. B., Furney, K. S., & DeStefano, L. (1999). Implementing the IDEA transition mandates. *Exceptional Children, 65,* 555–566.

Hasazi, S. B., Gordon, L. R., & Roe, C. A. (1985). Factors associated with the employment status of handicapped youth exiting high school from 1979 to 1983. *Exceptional Children, 51,* 455–469.

Heal, L. W., & Rusch, F. R. (1995). Predicting employment for students who leave special education high school programs. *Exceptional Children, 61,* 472–487.

Hoffman, A., & Field, S. (1995). Promoting self-determination through effective curriculum development. *Intervention in School and Clinic, 30,* 134–141.

Hughes, C., Hwang, B., Kim, J., Killian, D. J., Harmer, M. L., & Alcantara, P. R. (1997). A preliminary validation of strategies that support the transition from school to adult life. *Career Development for Exceptional Individuals, 20,* 1–14.

Hutchins, M. P., & Renzaglia, A. (1998). Interviewing families for effective transition to employment. *Teaching Exceptional Children, 30*(4), 72–78.

Individuals with Disabilities Education Act of 1990, 20 U.S.C. § 1400 *et seq.* (1990) (amended 1997).

Kohler, P. D. (1993). Best practices in transition: Substantiated or implied? *Career Development for Exceptional Individuals, 16,* 107–121.

Kohler, P. D. (1996). *Taxonomy for transition programming: Linking research and practice.* Champaign: University of Illinois at Urbana-Champaign, Transition Research Institute.

Kohler, P. D. (1998). Implementing a transition perspective of education: A comprehensive approach to planning and delivering secondary education and transition services. In F. R. Rusch & J. Chadsey (Eds.), *High school and beyond: Transition from school to work* (pp. 179–205). Belmont, CA: Wadsworth.

Kohler, P. D., & Chapman, S. (1999). *Literature review on school-to-work transition.* Retrieved October 31, 2001, from http://www.ed.uiuc.edu/sped/tri/2stwresearch.htm

Kohler, P. D., DeStefano, L., Wermuth, T., Grayson, T., & McGinty, S. (1994). An analysis of exemplary transition programs: How and why are they selected? *Career Development for Exceptional Individuals, 17,* 187–202.

Kohler, P. D., & Hood, L. (2000). *Improving student outcomes: Promising practices and programs for 1999–2000.* Champaign: University of Illinois at Urbana-Champaign, Transition Research Institute.

Kohler, P. D., & Rusch, F. R. (1995). School to work transition: Identification of employment related outcome and activity indicators. *Career Development for Exceptional Individuals, 18,* 33–50.

Kohler, P. D., & Rusch, F. R. (1996). Secondary education programs and transition perspectives. In M. C. Wang, M. C. Reynolds, & H. J. Walberg (Eds.), *Handbook of special and remedial education: Research and practice* (2nd ed., pp. 107–130). Tarrytown, NY: Elsevier Science.

Kohler, P. D., & Troesken, B. (1999). *Improving student outcomes: Promising practices and programs.* Champaign: University of Illinois at Urbana-Champaign, Transition Research Institute.

Kohler, P. D., & Van Beaver, S. M. (1996). Implementing transition practices: A search for effective strategies. In P. D. Kohler, (Ed.), *Taxonomy for transition programming: Linking research and practice* (pp. 72–77). Champaign: University of Illinois at Urbana-Champaign, Transition Research Institute.

Lehmann, J., Bassett, D., Sands, D., Spencer, K., & Gliner, J. (1999). Research translated into practices for increasing student involvement in transition-related activities. *Career Development for Exceptional Individuals, 22,* 3–19.

Leuking, R. G., & Fabian, E. S. (2000). Paid internships and employment success for youth in transition. *Career Development for Exceptional Individuals, 23,* 205–221.

Martin, J. E., Marshall, L. H., & Maxson, L. L. (1993). Transition policy: Infusing self-determination and self-advocacy into transition programs. *Career Development for Exceptional Individuals, 16,* 53–61.

McMahan, R., & Baer, R. (2001). IDEA transition policy compliance and best practice: Perceptions of transition stakeholders. *Career Development for Exceptional Individuals, 24,* 169–184.

Mithaug, D. E., Horiuchi, C. N., & Fanning. P. N. (1985). A report on the Colorado statewide follow-up survey of special education students. *Exceptional Children, 51,* 395–404.

Morningstar, M., Turnbull, A., & Turnbull, H. R. (1995). What do students with disabilities tell us about the importance of family involvement in the transition from school to adult life? *Exceptional Children, 62,* 249–260.

National Council on Disability. (2000). *Transition and post-school outcomes for youth with disabilities: Closing the gaps to post-secondary education and employment.* Retrieved September 10, 2001, from National Council on Disabilities Reports, http://www.ned.gov/newsroom/publications/transition_11-1-00.html._

Newman, L., & Cameto, R. (1993). *What makes a difference? Factors related to postsecondary school attendance for young people with disabilities.* Menlo Park, CA: SRI International.

Nirje, B. (1972). The right to self-determination. In W. Wolfensberger (Ed.), *Normalization* (pp. 176–193). Toronto: National Institute on Mental Retardation.

Peters, M. T., & Heron, T. E. (1993). When the best is not good enough: An examination of best practice. *The Journal of Special Education, 26,* 371–385.

Phelps, L. A., & Hanley-Maxwell, C. (1997). School-to-work transitions for youth with disabilities: A review of outcomes and practices. *Review of Educational Research, 67,* 176–226.

Powers, L. E., Singer, G. H. S., & Sowers, J. (1996). *On the road to autonomy: Promoting self-competence in children and youth with disabilities.* Baltimore: Brookes.

Powers, L. E., Turner, A., Westwood, D., Matuszewski, J., Wilson, R., & Phillips, A. (2001). *TAKE CHARGE* for the Future: A controlled field-test of a model to promote student involvement in transition planning. *Career Development for Exceptional Individuals, 24,* 89–104.

Repetto, J., & Correa, V. (1996). Expanding views on transition. *Exceptional Children, 62,* 551–563.

Rusch, F. R., Kohler, P. D., & Hughes, C. (1992). An analysis of OSERS-sponsored secondary special education and transitional services research. *Career Development for Exceptional Individuals, 15,* 121–143.

Ryan, R. M., & Lynch, J. (1989). Emotional autonomy versus detachment: Revisiting the vicissitudes of adolescence and young adulthood. *Child Development, 60,* 340–356.

Ryan, R. M., Stiller, J., & Lynch, J. H. (1994). Representations of relationships to teachers, parents, and friends as predictors of academic motivation and self-esteem. *Journal of Early Adolescence, 14,* 225–249.

Sands, D. J., & Wehmeyer, M. L. (1996). *Self-determination across the life span: Independence and choice for people with disabilities.* Baltimore: Brookes.

Sheldon, K., Ryan, R., Rawsthorne, L., & Ilhardi, B. (1997). Trait self and true self: Cross-role variation in the Big Five traits and its relations with authenticity and subjective well-being. *Journal of Personality and Social Psychology, 73,* 1380–1393.

Sitlington, P. L., Frank, A. R., & Carson, R. (1993). Adult adjustment among high school graduates with mild disabilities. *Exceptional Children, 59,* 221–233.

Szymanski, E. M. (1994). Transition: Life-span and life space considerations for empowerment. *Exceptional Children, 60,* 402–410.

Szymanski, E. M., Hanley-Maxwell, C., & Parker, R. M. (1990). Trans-disciplinary service delivery. In F. R. Rusch (Ed.), *Supported employment: Models, methods, and issues* (pp. 199–214). Sycamore, IL: Sycamore.

Taylor, H. (1998). *Americans with disabilities still pervasively disadvantaged on a broad range of key indicators.* Harris Poll 56. Retrieved September 28, 2001, from http://www.harrisinteractive.com/harris_poll/index.asp?PID=152.

Taylor, H. (2000). *Many people with disabilities feel isolated, left out of their communities and would like to participate more.* Harris Poll 34. Retrieved September 29, 2001, from http://www.harrisinteractive.com/harris_poll/index.asp?PID=97.

Turnbull, A. P., & Turnbull, R. H. (1990). *Families, professionals, and exceptionality: A special partnership* (2nd ed.). Columbus, OH: Merrill.

Van Reusen, A. K., & Bos, C. S. (1994). Facilitating student participation in individualized education programs through motivation strategy instruction. *Exceptional Children, 60,* 466–475.

Ward, M. J., & Kohler, P. D. (1996). Promoting self-determination for individuals with disabilities: Content and process. In L. E. Powers, G. H. S. Singer, & J. Sowers (Eds.), *On the road to autonomy: Promoting self-competence in children and youth with disabilities* (pp. 275–290). Baltimore: Brookes.

Wehman, P. (1992a). *Life beyond the classroom: Transition strategies for young people with disabilities.* Baltimore: Brookes.

Wehman, P. (1992b). Transition for young people with disabilities: Challenges for the 1990's. *Education and Training in Mental Retardation, 27,* 112–118.

Wehmeyer, M. L. (1992). Self-determination and the education of students with mental retardation. *Education and Training in Mental Retardation, 27,* 302–314.

Wehmeyer, M. L., Palmer, S. B., Agran, M., Mithaug, D. E., & Martin, J. E. (2000). Promoting causal agency: Self-Determined Learning Model of Instruction. *Exceptional Children, 66,* 439–453.

Wehmeyer, M., & Schwartz, M. (1997). Self-determination and positive adult outcomes: A follow-up study of youth with mental retardation or learning disabilities. *Exceptional Children, 63,* 245–255.

Wehmeyer, M., & Schwartz, M. (1998). The self-determination focus of transition goals for students with mental retardation. *Career Development for Exceptional Individuals, 21,* 75–86.

Whitney-Thomas, J., & Hanley-Maxwell, C. (1996). Packing the parachute: Parents' experiences as their children prepare to leave high school. *Exceptional Children, 63,* 75–87.

Will, M. (1984). *OSERS programming for the transition of youth with disabilities: Bridges from school to working life.* Washington, DC: U.S. Department of Education, Office of Special Education and Rehabilitative Services.

Williams, J. M., & O'Leary, E. (2001). What we've learned and where we go from here. *Career Development for Exceptional Individuals, 24,* 51–71.

Zhang, D. (2001). The effect of *Next S.T.E.P.* instruction on the self-determination skills of high school students with learning disabilities. *Career Development for Exceptional Individuals, 24,* 121–132.

Chapter 8

Developments in Curriculum-Based Measurement

Stanley L. Deno

The special characteristics of learners with disabilities have long driven the development of alternative specialized methods for assessing those needs. Perhaps the classic example of this phenomenon is the work of Alfred Binet, who as Minister of Public Instruction in France worked with Theodore Simón to explore the possibility of using different structured tasks to differentially diagnose and prescribe educational programs for students who might not profit from regular classroom instruction. Although Binet's work subsequently was subverted by other efforts to scale intelligence, it is important to remember that Binet's purpose was to identify more effective programs for educating students rather than excluding them. The innovation in assessment described in this chapter—curriculum-based measurement (CBM; Deno, 1985)—also has as its purpose the improvement of educational programs.

Background

CBM was developed to test the effectiveness of a special education intervention model called Data-Based Program Modification (DBPM; Deno & Mirkin, 1977). That model rested on the idea that special education teachers could use repeated measurements of student performance to formatively evaluate their instruction and improve the effectiveness of their efforts to intervene. To empirically test teacher use of DBPM, a research and development program was conducted for 6 years through the federally funded University of Minnesota Institute for Research on Learning Disabilities (IRLD).

One result of the IRLD formative evaluation research was the development of a generic set of progress-monitoring procedures in reading, spelling, and written expression. Those procedures included specification of (a) the core outcome tasks on which performance is measured; (b) the stimuli used in assessment, directions for administration, and the rules for scoring; and (c) the decision rules regarding when to modify programs. Ultimately, criteria were specified that could be used to establish the technical adequacy of the measures, the treatment validity or utility of the measures, and the logistical feasibility of the measures (Deno & Fuchs, 1987). Since then, CBM data have been used across a wide range of assessment activities, including screening, prereferral evaluation, placement in remedial and special education programs, formative evaluation, and evaluation of reintegration and inclusion. Recently, research has explored the use of CBM data to predict success on high-stakes assessments and to measure growth in content areas in secondary school programs and in early childhood special education. The continued application of CBM to assess student growth and to make educational decisions resulted in the development of the National Center on Student Progress Monitoring (2003), a major university research institute (Research Institute on Progress Monitoring, 2003), a large number of Web sites, and a number of commercial ventures. As an innovation in assessment, CBM was sufficiently unique that the original paper describing its development was identified as one of the 10 most significant articles published in special education during the past 50 years (McCleskey,

2004). The remainder of this chapter describes the characteristics of CBM and illustrates the wide range of its applications to make educational decisions.

The CBM Formative Evaluation Model

The CBM formative evaluation model was designed for teachers to systematically monitor student progress and make judgments about instructional effectiveness throughout the school year (Wesson et al., 1988). This formative evaluation is intended to produce changes in instruction that "form" a student's program throughout the year in such a way that it increases program success. An important assumption on which formative evaluation is based is that selecting or designing programs is not something that we can do with certain knowledge that they will produce intended outcomes (Deno, 1990). Because of this uncertainty, we are obliged to conduct ongoing evaluation of our activities, reforming them while the program is in progress if the data indicate a need to do so.

The primary instrument used in this formative evaluation model is the student progress graph displayed in Figure 1. The graph is important to both teacher and student because it clearly and simply reveals many useful items of information regarding the student's performance and the effectiveness of that student's instructional program.

Consider the following key items:

Initial level of performance is easily obtained by selecting the median of the first three scores. In the example shown, the first three scores are 43, 31, and 42 words read correctly; thus, the initial level of performance is 42 words read aloud correctly in 1 minute. Using the median of three scores is good practice because it increases the reliability of the initial performance estimate.

Peer comparison is possible with CBM through normative peer sampling. Very often school or district norms for peer performance are established through careful representative sampling using stimulus material drawn from the curriculum. A simpler approach for individual teachers involves selecting a random sample of students (about eight) from a student's home classroom and scoring their performances on the same CBM task. The median score of the sample, then, becomes the standard for peer comparison. In Figure 1, that peer level of performance is displayed as a horizontal dotted line above the student's current level of performance. That dotted line, at 140 words correct, reveals clearly and directly the magnitude of the student's reading deficiency—the student's peers are reading approximately three times as many words correctly in the same amount of time.

Current (final) level of performance is readily available and is computed in the same fashion as initial performance level. In the example, the last three scores are 104, 102, and 110; thus, the current level of performance is expressed as 104—the median of those three scores.

The goal to be attained through instruction has been established at 120 words read aloud correctly, and the goal line (a dotted diagonal line in Figure 1) connects initial performance with the goal score at the date for goal attainment. In this instance, the goal was established at a level somewhat lower than that for current peer performance. This is because it is important to set goals that seem reasonably attainable so that both teacher and student are not needlessly frustrated. The goal line is useful because it visually establishes the rate of progress and the weekly scores that must be attained to achieve the goal.

Rate of growth in performance is the key piece of information available for evaluating program effectiveness, and it can be reliably estimated because of repeated measurement. In Figure 1, the rate of student growth is visually represented by the line drawn through the student's scores during each intervention. Drawing in the growth lines makes it clear that the student's progress during the first intervention was flatter than the slope of the goal line. Based on that trend, a prediction could be made that the student would not reach his goal. In the example provided in Figure 1, the first vertical line represents the first change (intervention) made after the initial level of performance was established; the second line represents a new intervention that occurred in response to the student's insufficient growth rate. From examining the data we might predict that the second intervention would lead to goal attainment; however, the current growth rate and level of per-

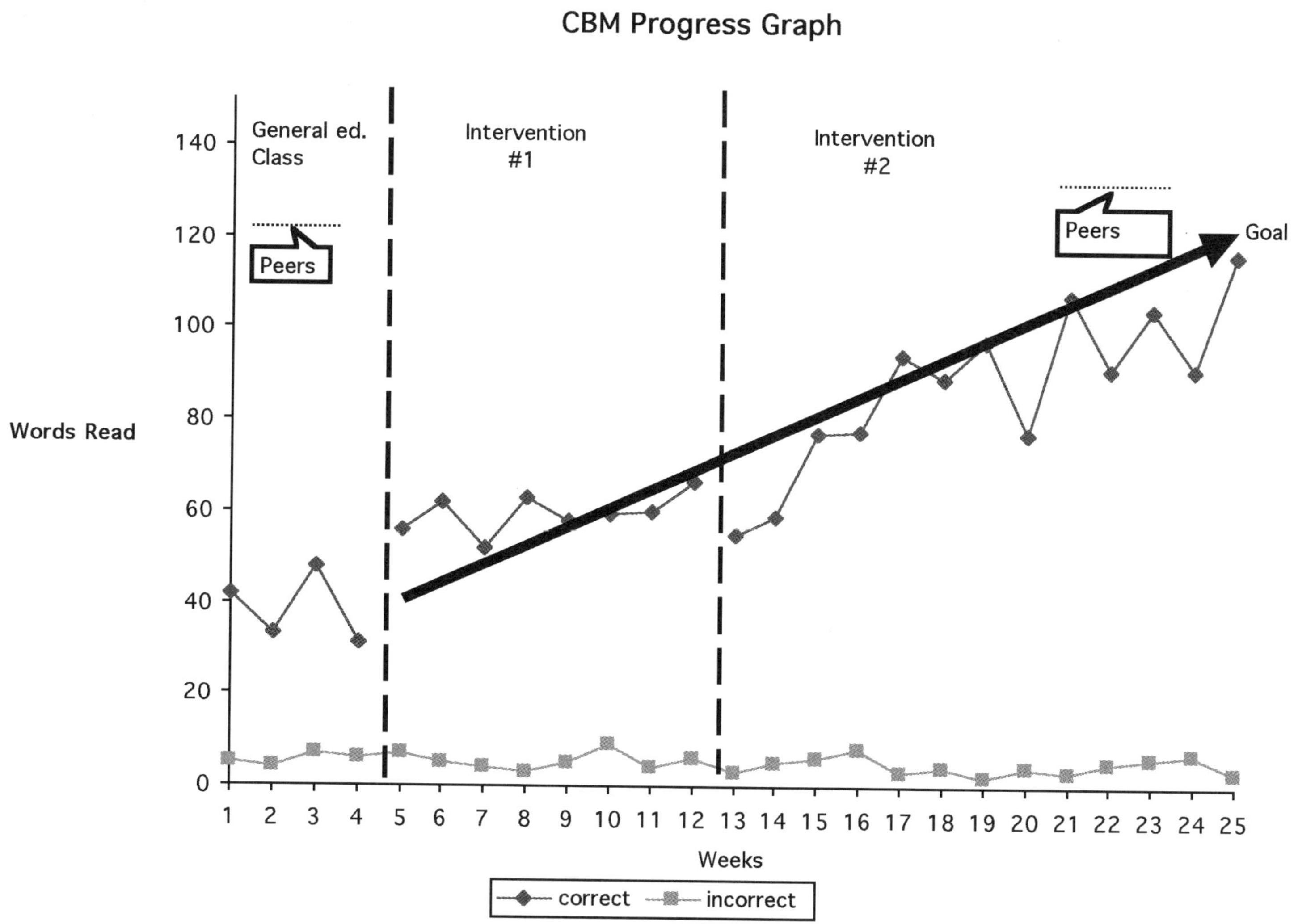

FIGURE 1. Curriculum-based measurement (CBM) student progress graph.

formance leave some doubt about whether that will occur.

Considerable research evidence is now available confirming that teachers can learn to use the graphically displayed CBM data to formatively evaluate their instruction and increase the academic progress rates of their students (e.g., L. S. Fuchs, Deno, & Mirkin, 1984).

Characteristics of CBM

When the generic procedures for measurement are employed with stimulus materials drawn directly from the instructional materials used by teachers in their classrooms, the assessment procedures are referred to as "curriculum-based" (L. S. Fuchs & Deno, 1994). Evidence has been developed that the same procedures can be used successfully with stimulus materials drawn from other sources, so the generic procedures have been referred to as General Outcomes Measures (GOMs; L. S. Fuchs & Deno, 1994) or Dynamic Indicators of Basic Skills (DIBS; Shinn, 1998). In contrast to the term *curriculum-based assessment* (CBA), which has been used in reference to a wide range of informal assessment procedures, CBM refers to a specific set of standard procedures that include the following characteristics.

Technically Adequate

CBM procedures have produced data of consistently high reliability and validity through using standardized observational procedures for repeatedly sampling performance on core reading, writing, and arithmetic skills. Unlike typical "informal" measures used in CBA, the psychometric concepts of reliability and validity are primary characteristics of CBM (e.g., Good & Jefferson 1998; Shinn, 1989). At the present time, more than 250 empirical articles on CBM exist, many of which demonstrate the technical adequacy of those procedures (Research Institute on Progress Monitoring, 2003).

Criterion Valid

To an important extent, effective use of CBM data requires empirical evidence that those data possess a high degree of criterion validity. Criterion validity evidence enables us to answer the question, "Can we use the CBM data to better predict a student's standing on other important criteria?" In the initial CBM research, we hypothesized that CBM scores would help us to predict scores on commercial norm-referenced achievement tests (Deno, Marston, & Mirkin, 1982; Deno, Mirkin, & Chiang, 1982). The results of this early research established that the CBM data were, indeed, closely associated with standardized achievement test scores (Marston, 1989).

Standard Measurement Tasks ("What to Measure")

The standard tasks identified for use in CBM include *reading aloud from text* and *selecting words deleted from text* ("maze") in reading, *writing word sequences when given a story starter or picture* in writing, *writing letter sequences from dictation* in spelling, and *writing correct answers/digits in solving problems* in arithmetic. Extensive research has been conducted on these tasks, but most of the early research and development focused on measuring growth in the elementary school years. For that reason, the U.S. Department of Education saw fit to fund a program of research to extend the research to other ages and other areas of the curriculum (Research Institute on Progress Monitoring, 2003).

Prescriptive Stimulus Materials

Given that the materials used for assessment in CBM may be obtained from the instructional materials used by the local school, specifications are provided for materials selection (e.g., Shinn, 1989). Key factors in this selection process are the representativeness and equivalence of the stimulus materials. Both factors are addressed to increase the utility of the procedures for making instructional decisions.

Administration and Scoring ("How to Measure")

CBM procedures include specification of sample duration, administration, student directions, and scoring procedures. Combining the prescriptive selection of stimulus materials with standardization of the procedures is necessary to ensure sufficient reliability and utility of the data for individual and group comparisons across time. Standardization also enables summarization of group data for developing local norms and for general descriptions of program effects across students (Shinn, 1995).

Performance Sampling

In CBM, academic performance is sampled through the use of direct observation procedures. All CBM scores are obtained by counting the number of correct and incorrect responses made in a fixed time period. In reading, for example, the most commonly used measure requires a student to read aloud from text for 1 minute and have an observer count the number of correctly and incorrectly pronounced words.

Multiple Equivalent Samples

One of the most distinctive and important features of CBM is that performance is *repeatedly sampled* across time. The repeated observations of performance are structured so that students respond to different but equivalent stimulus materials that are drawn from the same general source. For example, on the first occasion in measuring reading proficiency, students are asked to read aloud for 1 minute from a text passage that they have not previously read. On the next occasion, the students read again from the same book, but from a different, unfamiliar, and equally difficult text passage. In this way, task difficulty is held constant and inferences can be drawn regarding the generalizability of student proficiency at reading comparable, but unfamiliar, text.

Time Efficient

CBM is designed for efficiency. Multiple performance sampling requires that measures be short. CBM performance samples are 1–3 minutes in duration depending on the skill being measured and the number of samples necessary to maximize reliability.

Easy to Teach

Another logistical consideration in using CBM is the ease with which professionals, paraprofessionals, and parents can learn to use the procedures in such a way that the data are reliable.

Common Uses of CBM

Improving Individual Instructional Programs

The original purpose of CBM was to provide teachers with practical progress measurement tools to systematically evaluate their instruction. The approach to systematic formative evaluation was illustrated previously in Figure 1. The primary hypothesis driving the original CBM research was that teachers using progress measurement tools would effect higher levels of achievement by their students if they would learn to use these procedures. Evidence has developed that, indeed, this is the case (see, e.g., L. S. Fuchs et al., 1984; Stecker & Fuchs, 2000). Teachers can learn to use systematic formative evaluation based on CBM to produce greater achievement on the part of their students. In addition, CBM has also been used to produce data informing other important educational decisions. The remainder of this section of the chapter discusses some of the most common extensions of CBM.

Predicting Performance on High-Stakes Assessment

In the intervening years, commercially available standardized achievement tests have been challenged and, to a degree, replaced by state-developed high-stakes assessment procedures as the criterion validity standard. At both federal and state levels, pressure is being applied to schools to "step up" to the challenge of reform movements rooted in testing. Schools are being placed on "probation" and threatened with the prospect of "reconstitution" (i.e., disbursement and replacement of the existing school staff) as a result of low scores and lack of improvement on these high-stakes tests. In this environment, the annual high-stakes summative evaluations have become a kind of Sword of Damocles hanging over the heads of teachers and administrators. Whatever one might think about this approach to improving education, one rational response has been to seek progress-monitoring data that enable school staff to formatively evaluate programs and revise them when they appear to be unsuccessful in moving students toward passing the annual high-stakes tests. For that reason, additional research was conducted on the criterion validity of CBM data for making judgments about whether students will achieve mandated levels of performance on benchmark tests. In a variety of studies, high correlations (.65–.85) have been obtained between CBM scores for reading and math and performance on high-stakes assessments (e.g., Deno, Reschly-Anderson, Lembke, Aorka, & Callender, 2002; Good, Simmons, & Kameenui, 2001; Muyskens & Marston, 2002).

A related, noteworthy aspect of the research and development in this area has been the movement from computing simple correlations to identifying criterion levels of performance on the CBMs that teachers can use as targets for performance. Evidence has accumulated, for example, regarding the relationship between CBM reading scores and pass rates on state assessments. Students reading at least 40 words correctly in 1 minute by the end of first grade are on a trajectory to succeed in learning to read, and students reading more than 110 words correctly in 1 minute by the beginning of third grade are most likely to pass their state assessments in Oregon (Good et al., 2001). Eighth-grade students who can read at least 145 words correctly in 1 minute from local newspaper passages are almost certain to pass the *Minnesota Basic Skills Test* in reading (Muyskens & Marston, 2002). Preliminary research has been, and continues to be, conducted to identify criterion levels of performance on the CBM maze and math measures, as well.

Predicting Performance on Other Important Criteria

All of the measures used in CBM possess relatively high criterion validity coefficients (L. S. Fuchs, Fuchs, & Maxwell, 1988; Marston, 1989). For that reason, CBM data not only can be used to evaluate instruction, but can also be used to classify age and grade developmental status (Deno, 1985; Shinn, 2002), predict and improve upon teacher judgments regarding student proficiency (Marston, Mirkin, & Deno, 1984), and discriminate between students achieving typically and those in compensatory programs (Marston & Magnusson, 1988). Recent research efforts have been successfully directed to establishing reasonable *growth standards* for purposes of setting both individual and program standards (Deno, Fuchs, Marston, & Shin, 2001).

Enhancing Teacher Instructional Planning

Several related outcomes are also produced through a formative evaluation model based on CBM. In the study by L. S. Fuchs et al. (1984), teachers of reading were asked near the end of the school year whether they could identify their students' reading goals. Those teachers using CBM in formative evaluation were more accurate in identifying their students' goals. In a related study, when teachers used CBM within a formative evaluation model, it significantly affected both the frequency and quality of the instructional changes they made as they responded to unsatisfactory student progress (L. S. Fuchs, Fuchs, & Hamlett, 1993; L. S. Fuchs, Fuchs, Hamlett, & Stecker, 1991).

Developing Norms

CBM can be used to develop norms for decision making when the same CBMs are administered to normative peer samples. In Figure 1, individual performance can be compared to the average peer performance, represented by the line well above the target student's level during baseline and at the end of the year. This reference is important because it reveals the magnitude of the difference between the level of individual students and that of their peers on the same stimulus materials. Teachers can create their own peer reference by sampling the performance of other students in the same classroom. Because CBM is standardized, it has also been effectively used to create school and district norms. When local norms are created, peer references are more broadly representative of students in the same grade, in the same school, or across schools within a district (e.g., Marston & Magnusson, 1988; Shinn, 2002). Using CBM to create *local norms* has been especially useful in urban school districts, where concerns exist regarding the degree to which the norms of commercially available standardized tests reflect the rapidly changing diversity of student populations.

Increasing Ease of Communication

The CBM graph, with its multiple references, creates opportunities for clearer communication. It has now become common practice for teachers to use the CBM data in parent conferences and at multidisciplinary team meetings to provide a framework for communicating individual student status. All types of professional educators (e.g., administrators, general education teachers) and parents easily use and understand the CBM data graph because little or no interpretation of the scores is necessary (Shinn, Habedank, & Good, 1993). This contrasts sharply with the complexities related to communicating the results of commercially available standardized test scores. A simple illustration of both the ease and effectiveness of communicating around CBM data can be found in the results of the teacher planning study mentioned earlier (L. S. Fuchs et al., 1984). In that study, students as well as teachers were asked whether they knew their annual reading goals and were asked to specify those goals. Those students whose teachers were using CBM and formative evaluation not only expressed that they knew those goals but also were able to accurately specify their target reading scores.

Screening to Identify Students Academically at Risk

An increasingly common use of CBM is to screen students who are "at risk" for academic failure. As mentioned previously, because CBM procedures are standardized, they can be used to contrast individual performance to that of the group. The use of local norms is common for this purpose, but norms are not required. In a study by Deno et al. (2002), all of the students in a large urban elementary school were given three standard CBM maze passages, and their performances were aggregated within and across grades. The lowest 20% of the students on the CBM maze (multiple-choice cloze) measure in each grade was considered sufficiently at risk to require progress monitoring every other week with the more conventional CBM oral reading measure. Identification of high-risk students has now become commonplace among schools practicing CBM (Marston & Magnusson, 1988).

Evaluating Classroom Prereferral Interventions

The cost and the consequences of special education are recurring issues in the special education literature. Of particular concern is the possibility that students are being referred and placed in special education when they might succeed in regular class programs with greater accommodation by classroom teachers. One approach to addressing this issue is to require that classroom teachers conduct prereferral interventions to establish that such accommodations are insufficient. A problem with this approach has been that little useful data has been available to appraise the effects of those prereferral data. Because CBM data are sensitive to the effects of program changes over relatively short time periods, they can be used to aid in the evaluation of prereferral interventions. The use of CBM in evaluating prereferral interventions is the first component of the Problem Solving Model (Deno, 1989), which has been implemented at both the state and district levels (Shinn, 1995; Tilly & Grimes, 1998). The Problem Solving Model enables general and special educators to collaborate in the early stages of child study to determine with some validity whether the problems of skill development faced by a student are more than "instructional failures." Documentation that the problem is not readily solvable by the classroom teacher becomes the basis for special education eligibility assessment.

Reducing Bias in Assessment

The Problem Solving Model using CBM has attracted attention as a means for reducing bias in the assessment process. Because teachers typically are the source of referrals to special education, their validity as "tests" of student success in the classroom is an issue that has been examined using CBM (Shinn, Tindal, & Spira, 1987). Indeed, in one big city school system, the Office of Civil Rights joined forces with the district to examine whether the CBM data used as part of the Problem Solving Model could diminish the likelihood that students of color were being inappropriately placed in special education (Minneapolis Public Schools, 2001). Data from that school district revealed that the proportion of non-White students referred and placed in special education did not substantially change, but subsequent to implementation of the model, it became more likely that problems would be addressed through regular classroom intervention rather than placement in special education. In addition, students who were placed in special education demonstrated lower achievement test scores than prior to the introduction of the Problem Solving Model.

Offering Alternative Special Education Identification Procedures

Widespread dissatisfaction exists with traditional approaches to identifying students for special education that rely on standardized tests of ability, achievement, or both (Reschly, 1988). Despite this dissatisfaction, few alternatives have been offered to replace those more conventional procedures. Over the past 20 years, the use of CBM within a systematic decision framework has been explored as a basis for developing alternative identification procedures (Marston & Magnusson, 1988; Marston et al., 1984; Shinn, 1989). Recently, the use of CBM to test students' responsiveness to treatment (L. S. Fuchs & Fuchs, 1998) has gained favor within policy-making groups. For example, the President's Commission on Excellence in Special Education (2002) recommended the responsiveness-to-treatment (RTI) approach as an alternative to traditional standardized testing for identifying students with learning disabilities. That approach is an extension of prereferral evaluation and the Problem Solving Model to evaluate increased levels of intensity in instructional intervention and relies on CBM. For example, if a student fails to increase his or her rate of growth in response to several regular classroom interventions, then that student might be considered as eligible for special education. This alternative approach to eligibility determination rooted in the Problem Solving Model has created an entirely different perspective on the concept of disability (Tilly, Reschly, & Grimes, 1999).

Recommending and Evaluating Inclusion

As increased emphasis has been placed on inclusion of students with disabilities in regular classrooms, and as laws and regulations have required schools to assure access to the regular class curriculum, the need to evaluate the effects of these changes on the academic development of students with disabilities has increased. CBM has proved to be a very useful tool for those accountable for the progress of students with disabilities as they seek to provide education of these students in the mainstream curriculum. The general strategy employed when CBM is used to evaluate inclusion has been to collect data before and after integration into regular class instruction, and then to continue monitoring student progress to assure that reintegration of students is occurring responsibly (Fuchs, Roberts, Fuchs, & Bowers, 1996; Powell-Smith & Stewart, 1998). The results of the research in this area provide clear evidence that both special educators and classroom teachers can use CBM to provide ongoing documentation of student progress and signal the need for increased intensification of instruction when inclusive programs are unsuccessful.

Measuring Growth in Secondary School Programs and Content Areas

CBM was developed initially to help teachers at the elementary school level increase the achievement of students struggling to learn basic skills in reading, writing, and arithmetic. As development in those areas has proceeded, teachers in secondary school programs have become interested in the application of similar formative evaluation approaches with their students. For that reason, technical work has proceeded on establishing CBM progress-monitoring methods for assessing student growth both in advanced academic skills and in content area learning (Espin & Foegen, 1996; Espin, Scierka, Skare, & Halvorson, 1999; Espin & Tindal, 1998; Espin, Wallace, Lembke, & Long, 2004). The technical developments in using CBM methods to assess growth in reading and writing at the secondary level have generated outcomes that are promising. Attempts to establish the criterion validity of the same reading and writing measures that have been used at the elementary level have revealed that those measures do correlate with important criteria (e.g., test scores, grade-point average, teacher judgment), but it is unclear whether the correlations are as strong as those found for elementary-grade students. Recent work (Espin et al., 2003; Muyskens & Marston 2002) obtained relatively high correlations for eighth-grade students in reading and tenth-grade students in writing. Further research should determine the upper levels at which ordinary CBMs are effective (Research Institute on Progress Monitoring, 2003).

Assessing English Language Learning Students

A particular problem confronting schools in the United States is the dramatically increasing proportion of students whose first language is not English and who are still learning to speak English while simultaneously learning to read and write in English. Commercially available standardized tests have not been useful because they have not included the full range of languages represented among English language learning (ELL) students within their normative samples. More significantly, many achievement tests draw heavily on background knowledge of the Anglo-American culture in structuring questions. Among other problems that exist because of the lack of technically adequate procedures is how to distinguish ELL students who are having difficulty learning because of their lack of proficiency in English from ELL students whose struggles may stem in part from special disabilities.

An increasing number of studies have explored the use of CBM to overcome the problems of assessing ELL students and for monitoring their progress in mainstream classrooms. Early work by Baker and colleagues (Baker & Good, 1995; Baker, Plasencia-Peinado, & Lezcano-Lytle, 1998) focused primarily on using CBM reading scores for monitoring the progress of Spanish-speaking ELL students in regular class programs. That research provided preliminary evidence that the levels of reliability and validity for CBM procedures with ELL students in both their native and English languages are comparable to those of native speakers of English. Further, individual growth analyses revealed that students who began with comparable proficiency in English often progressed at very different rates. More recently, research has demonstrated the potential utility of CBM procedures for young ELLs in Grade 1 (Graves, Plasencia-Peinado, & Deno, 2005). CBM also has been used to predict differences in the success rates of middle school ELL students on state assessments as a function of their level or reading proficiency (Muyskens & Marston, 2002). CBM oral reading measures have also been compared with CBM maze reading measures as predictors of performance on state standards tests with no apparent advantage for the maze comprehension measure (Ives-Wiley & Deno, 2005). This finding is important because questions are often raised regarding the degree to which the oral reading measures are reflective of growth in reading comprehension for ELLs.

The apparent technical adequacy of CBM for use with ELLs has led urban schools to use CBM procedures for developing norms across reading, writing, and arithmetic for the purposes of making educational placement and progress evaluation decisions for their ELL students (Robinson, Larson, & Watkins, 2002). Additionally, research has been conducted using CBM with students in countries where languages other than English are spoken. The evidence from this body of research indicates that the procedures and tasks to be used for measurement need to be consistent with formal differences in the language. For example, oral reading can be used to measure growth in other phonetic languages, such as Korean, but the maze procedure appears to be more appropriate for measuring growth in an iconic language, such as Chinese (Yeh, 1992).

Predicting Success in Early Childhood Education

The criterion validity of CBM oral reading scores has been sufficiently established to become an important criterion for establishing the predictive validity of prereading measures and the effectiveness of early literacy interventions. With the ascendant interest in the role played by phonological skills in learning to read, the utility of scores from measures of phonological skill has been established by examining their accuracy in predicting beginning oral reading scores (Kaminski & Good, 1996). As noted earlier, Good et al. (2001) have suggested that CBM oral reading performance at the end of first grade is a significant indicator of subsequent reading success. Research in this area has established important linkages between measures of phonological skill in kindergarten, oral reading performance in Grades 1–3, and success on state assessments. More recent research has been conducted in an attempt to extend the CBM growth measurement procedures to even earlier ages (McConnell, Priest, Davis, & McEvoy, 2002). That research has demonstrated that the same generic procedures can be used to develop measurement tools that will enable early childhood educators to screen preliterate students for the purpose of identifying those at risk of early problems in learning to read.

Frequency of Use

At least two studies have been conducted to examine the factors that can function as barriers to CBM implementation (Wesson, Deno, & King, 1984; Yell, Deno, & Marston, 1992). More than 20 years ago, Wesson et al. found that nearly 85% of the 300 teachers surveyed reported that they were aware of direct and frequent measurement of student progress; yet, only half of those familiar with the procedures were using them. In the study by Yell et al., only teachers using CBM were surveyed. Teachers in both studies consistently identified "time" as the single most important barrier to implementing the measurement procedures. An interesting related finding was that teachers using CBM estimated that it took less than 10% of their instructional time to conduct the measurement. Nevertheless, given the time constraints under which teachers operate, they seem, inevitably, to believe that any additional activity cannot be accommodated in their daily schedule.

A Uniquely Special Education Development

CBM is a procedure that was developed by special educators for special educators. With that said, it is important to recognize that related work both inside and outside of special education served as a basis for CBM and supports the use of CBM in general education. All of the CBM procedures involve the direct observation of behavior and use the single-case analytical procedures that are characteristic of applied behavior analysis (ABA; Deno, 1997). ABA is a system developed for use with any behavior in any setting. Thus, much of the work of ABA has addressed behavior in the mainstream of ordinary life. In that sense, the roots of CBM include procedures derived from sources outside of special education. At the same time, the most extensive applications of ABA have been in special education, and the early applications of ABA to academic instruction occurred most often within special education (e.g., Lovitt, 1976).

The use of CBM to measure growth in reading has relied extensively on time-limited samples of oral reading. In the general literature of reading development, the speed with which students are able to translate text into spoken language is viewed as one of the most significant characteristics of skillful reading (Adams, 1990). In addition, psychologists interested in the study of reading have long viewed "automatic" responding as an essential element in reading comprehension (Laberge & Samuels, 1974). While speed and accuracy of word recognition is not always viewed as the definition of oral reading fluency, that use of the term is sufficiently widespread that the recommendations from the National Reading Panel (2000) regarding fluency have been interpreted to mean speed and accuracy of oral reading. However defined, the current broad interest in oral reading "fluency" has contributed to the rapid dissemination of CBM reading procedures. As continued research on the relationship between rapid and accurate reading of words and comprehension reveals the close connection between these key elements of reading (L. S. Fuchs, Fuchs, Hosp, & Jenkins, 2001; Jenkins, Fuchs, van den Broek, Espin, & Deno, 2002), CBM is likely to find an ever increasing source of interest from special and regular educators alike. Whether similar accelerated interest in CBM will occur for other basic skills remains to be seen.

Having said that the roots of CBM are deep within the literature inside and outside of special education, I must add a closing comment. Almost certainly, the most effective uses of CBM in the formative evaluation of individual student programs occurs in settings where individual (e.g., special education) teachers have the time and skills to respond to the charted progress of individual students. Special educators designed the formative evaluation model, which has been demonstrably effective in improving the achievement of individual students for use in special education. Initially, this meant evaluating the success of teachers at accelerating the progress of their special education students in the mainstream curriculum. As caseload limits for special educators have been raised or eliminated, and as inclusive education has become the emphasis, teachers have increasingly had insufficient time and too many students to use CBM effectively in formative evaluation.

The shift, then, has been to use CBM to support general educators' efforts to accommodate the increased diversity in classrooms produced, in part, by inclusion of students with disabilities (L. S. Fuchs, Fuchs, Hamlett, Phillips, & Bentz, 1994). CBM has proved to be a useful tool for this purpose. L. S. Fuchs and Fuchs (1998) have provided an interesting and important illustration of the efforts required to tailor CBM for use in the general education classroom. Their work demonstrates clearly the effort that must be made to effect CBM implementation with teachers who are working with large groups of students in regular classrooms. Even as those efforts are successful, it is unlikely that CBM with large groups can contribute to improved student achievement to the degree that it does when it is used to tailor individual student programs. In those settings where special education is organized for individual students, the unique contributions of CBM most certainly will be the greatest.

REFERENCES

Adams, M. J. (1990). *Beginning to read: Thinking and learning about print.* Cambridge: MIT Press.

American Institutes of Research. (2003). *National Center on Student Progress Monitoring.* Washington, DC: Author.

Baker, S. K., & Good, R. H. (1995). Curriculum-based measurement of English reading with bilingual Hispanic students: A validation study with second-grade students. *School Psychology Review, 24,* 561–578.

Baker, S. K., Plasencia-Peinado, J., & Lezcano-Lytle, V. (1998). The use of curriculum-based measurement with language-minority students. In M. R. Shinn (Ed.), *Advanced applications of curriculum-based measurement* (pp. 175–213). New York: Guilford Press.

Deno, S. L. (1985). Curriculum-based measurement: The emerging alternative. *Exceptional Children, 52,* 219–232.

Deno, S. L. (1989). Curriculum-based measurement and alternative special education services: A fundamental and direct relationship. In M. R. Shinn (Ed.), *Curriculum-based measurement: Assessing special children* (pp. 1–17). New York: Guilford Press.

Deno, S. L. (1990). Individual differences and individual difference: The essential difference of special education. *The Journal of Special Education, 24,* 160–173.

Deno, S. L. (1997). "Whether" thou goest: Perspectives on progress monitoring. In E. Kameenui, J. Lloyd, & D. Chard (Eds.), *Issues in educating students with disabilities* (pp. 77–99). Mahwah, NJ: Erlbaum.

Deno, S. L., & Fuchs, L. S. (1987). Developing curriculum-based measurement systems for databased special education problem solving. *Focus on Exceptional Children, 19*(8), 1–16.

Deno, S. L., Fuchs, L. S., Marston, D. B., & Shin, J. (2001). Using curriculum-based measurement to establish growth standards for students with learning disabilities. *School Psychology Review, 30,* 507–524.

Deno, S. L., Marston, D. E., & Mirkin, P. K. (1982).Valid measurement procedures for continuous evaluation of written expression. *Exceptional Children, 48,* 368–371.

Deno, S. L., & Mirkin, P. K. (1977). *Data-based program modification: A manual.* Reston, VA: Council for Exceptional Children.

Deno, S. L., Mirkin, P. K., & Chiang, B. (1982). Identifying valid measures of reading. *Exceptional Children, 49,* 36–45.

Deno, S. L., Reschly-Anderson, A., Lembke, E., Zorka, H., & Callender, S. *A model for school wide implementation: A case example.* Paper presented at the annual meeting of the National Association of School Psychology, Chicago.

Espin, C. A., & Foegen, A. (1996). Validity of general outcome measures for predicting secondary students' performance on content area tasks. *Exceptional Children, 62,* 497–514.

Espin, C. A., Scierka, B. J., Skare, S. S., & Halvorson, N. (1999). Criterion-related validity of curriculum-based measures in writing for secondary students. *Reading and Writing Quarterly, 15,* 5–28.

Espin, C. A., & Tindal, G. (1998). *Curriculum-based measurement for secondary students. In M. R. Shinn (Ed.), Advanced applications of curriculum-based measurement* (pp. 214–253). New York: Guilford.

Espin, C. A., Wallace, T., Lembke, E., Campbell, H., Ticha, R., Long, J., & Pickert, M. (2003, February). *Creating a progress monitoring system: Preparing secondary-school students for success on the Minnesota Basic Standards Skills Tests.* Paper presented at the Pacific Coast Research Conference, La Jolla, CA.

Espin, C. A., Wallace, T., Lembke, E., & Long, J. (2004). *Teacher implementation of a progress monitoring system: Effects on student achievement and teacher instruction.* Paper presented at the Pacific Coast Research Conference, Coronado, CA.

Fuchs, D., Roberts, P. H., Fuchs, L. S., & Bowers, J. (1996). Reintegrating students with learning disabilities into the mainstream: A 2-year study. *Learning Disabilities Research and Practice, 11,* 214–229.

Fuchs, L. S., & Deno, S. L. (1994). Must instructionally useful performance assessment be based in the curriculum? *Exceptional Children, 61,* 15–24.

Fuchs, L. S., Deno, S., & Mirkin, P. (1984). Effects of frequent curriculum-based measurement and evaluation on pedagogy, student achievement, and student awareness of learning. *American Educational Research Journal, 21,* 449–460.

Fuchs, L. S., & Fuchs, D. (1998). Treatment validity: A unifying concept for reconceptualizing the identification of learning disabilities. *Learning Disabilities Research and Practice, 13,* 204–219.

Fuchs, L. S., Fuchs, D., & Hamlett, C. L. (1993). Technological advances linking the assessment of students' academic proficiency to instructional planning. *Journal of Special Education Technology, 12,* 49–62.

Fuchs, L. S., Fuchs, D., Hamlett, C. L., Phillips, N. B., & Bentz, J. (1994). Class-wide curriculum-based measurement: Helping general educators meet the challenge of student diversity. *Exceptional Children, 60,* 518–537.

Fuchs, L. S., Fuchs, D., Hamlett, C. L., & Stecker, P. M. (1991). Effects of curriculum-based measurement and consultation on teacher planning and student achievement in mathematics operations. *American Educational Research Journal, 28,* 617–641.

Fuchs, L. S., Fuchs, D., Hosp, M., & Jenkins, J. R. (2001). Oral reading fluency as an indicator of reading competence: A theoretical, empirical, and historical analysis. *Scientific Studies of Reading, 5,* 239–256.

Fuchs, L. S., Fuchs, D., & Maxwell, L. (1988). The validity of informal reading comprehension measures. *Remedial and Special Education, 9,* 20–28.

Good, R. H., & Jefferson, G. (1998). Contemporary perspectives on curriculum-based measurement validity. In M. R. Shinn (Ed.), *Advanced applications of curriculum-based measurement* (pp. 61–88). New York: Guilford Press.

Good, R. H., Simmons, D. C., & Kameenui, E. J. (2001). The importance and decision-making utility of a continuum of fluency-based indicators of foundational reading skills for third-grade high stakes outcomes. *Scientific Studies of Reading, 5,* 257–288.

Graves, A. W., Plasencia-Peinado. J., Deno, S. L., & Johnson, J. R. (2005) Formatively evaluating the progress of first-grade English learners. *Remedial and Special Education, 26,* 215–225

Ives-Wiley, H. I., & Deno, S. L. (2005) Oral reading and maze measures as predictors of success for limited English–proficient students on a state standards assessment. *Remedial and Special Education, 26,* 207–213.

Jenkins, J. R., Fuchs, L. S., van den Broek, P., Espin, C. A., & Deno, S. L. (2002). *Reading fluency: Criterion validity and sources of individual difference.* Unpublished manuscript.

Kaminski, R. A., & Good, R. H. (1996). Toward a technology for assessing early literacy skills. *School Psychology Review, 25,* 215–227.

Laberge, D., & Samuels, S. J. (1974). Toward a theory of automatic information processing in reading. *Cognitive Psychology, 6,* 293–323.

Lovitt, T. C. (1976). Applied behavior analysis techniques and curriculum research: Implications for instruction. In N. G. Haring & R. L. Schiefelbush (Eds.), *Teaching special children* (pp. 112–156). New York: McGraw-Hill.

Marston, D. B. (1989). Curriculum-based measurement: What it is and why do it? In M. R. Shinn (Ed.), *Curriculum-based measurement: Assessing special children* (pp. 18–78). New York: Guilford Press.

Marston, D. B., & Magnusson, D. (1988). Curriculum-based assessment: District-level implementation. In J. Graden, J. Zins, & M. Curtis (Eds.), *Alternative educational delivery systems: Enhancing instructional options for all students* (pp. 137–172). Washington, DC: National Association of School Psychologists.

Marston, D. B., Mirkin, P. K., & Deno, S. L. (1984). Curriculum-based measurement: An alternative to traditional screening, referral, and identification. *The Journal of Special Education, 18,* 109–117.

McCleskey, J. (2004). Classic articles in special education: Articles that shaped the field, 1960 to 1996. *Remedial and Special Education, 25,* 79–87.

McConnell, S., Priest, J., Davis, S., & McEvoy, M. (2002). Best practices in measuring growth and development for preschool children. In A. Thomas & J. Grimes (Eds.), *Best practices in school psychology IV* (pp. 1231–1246). Washington, DC: National Association of School Psychologists.

Minneapolis Public Schools. (2001). *Report of the external review committee on the Minneapolis Problem Solving Model.* Minneapolis: Author.

Muyskens, P., & Marston, D. B. (2002). *Predicting success on the Minnesota Basic Skills Test in reading using CBM.* Unpublished manuscript, Minneapolis Public Schools.

National Center on Student Progress Monitoring. (2003).

USDOE (OSEP) Award No. 326WO30003. American Institutes for Research, Washington, DC. Retrieved August 15, 2005, from http://www.studentprogress.org.

National Reading Panel. (2000). *Teaching children to read: An evidence-based assessment of the scientific research literature on reading and its implications for reading instruction: Reports of the subgroups.* Bethesda, MD: National Institutes of Health.

Powell-Smith, K. A., & Stewart, L. H. (1998). The use of curriculum-based measurement on the reintegration of students with mild disabilities. In M. R. Shinn (Ed.), *Advanced applications of curriculum-based measurement* (pp. 254–307). New York: Guilford Press.

President's Commission on Excellence in Special Education. (2002). *A new era: Revitalizing special education for children and their families.* Retrieved November 15, 2003, from http://www.ed.gov/inits/commissionsboards/whspecialeducation/reports/index.html.

Reschly, D. (1988). Special education reform: School psychology revolution. *School Psychology Review, 17,* 459-475.

Research Institute on Progress Monitoring. (2003). USDOE (OSEP) Grant H324HO3003. University of Minnesota, Minneapolis. Retrieved August 15, 2005, from http://www.progressmonitoring.org.

Robinson, M., Larson, N., & Watkins, E. (2002). *What if they don't speak Spanish? Assessing low incidence speakers for SLD.* Paper presented at Council for Learning Disabilities International Conference, Denver, CO.

Shinn, M. R. (Ed.). (1989). *Curriculum-based measurement: Assessing special children.* New York: Guilford.

Shinn, M. R. (1995). Best practices in curriculum-based measurement and its use in a problem-solving model. In J. Grimes & A. Thomas (Eds.), *Best practices in school psychology III* (pp. 547–568). Silver Spring, MD: National Association of School Psychologists.

Shinn, M. R. (Ed.). (1998). *Advanced applications of curriculum-based measurement.* New York: Guilford.

Shinn, M. R. (2002). Best practices in using curriculum-based measurement in a problem-solving model. In A. Thomas & J. Grimes (Eds.), *Best practices in school psychology IV* (pp. 671–697). Silver Spring, MD: National Association of School Psychologists.

Shinn, M. R., Habedank, L., & Good, R. H. (1993). The effects of classroom reading performance data on general education teachers' and parents' attitudes about reintegration. *Exceptionality, 4,* 205–228.

Shinn, M. R., Tindal, G., & Spira, D. (1987). Special education referrals as an index of teacher tolerance: Are teachers imperfect tests? *Exceptional Children, 54,* 34–40.

Stecker, P. M., & Fuchs, L. S. (2000). Effecting superior achievement using curriculum-based measurement: The importance of individual progress monitoring. *Learning Disabilities Research and Practice, 15,* 128–134.

Tilly, W. D., & Grimes, J. (1998). Curriculum-based measurement: One vehicle for systematic educational reform. In M. R. Shinn (Ed.), *Advanced applications of curriculum-based measurement* (pp. 32–88). New York: Guilford Press.

Tilly, W. D., Reschly, D. J., & Grimes, J. (1999). Disability determination in problem-solving systems: Conceptual foundations and critical components. In D. J. Reschly, W. D. Tilly, & J. Grimes (Eds.), *Special education in transition: Functional assessment and noncategorical programming* (pp. 221–254). Longmont, CO: Sopris West.

Wesson, C., Deno, S. L., & King, R. (1984). Direct and frequent measurement of student performance: If it's good for us, why don't we do it? *Learning Disability Quarterly, 7,* 45–48.

Wesson, C., Deno, S. L., Mirkin, P. K., Maruyama, G., Skiba, R., King, R. P., & Sevcik, B. (1988). A causal analysis of the relationships among ongoing curriculum-based measurement and evaluation, the structure of instruction, and student achievement. *The Journal of Special Education, 22,* 330–343.

Yeh, C. (1992). *The use of passage reading measures to assess reading proficiency of Chinese elementary school students.* Unpublished doctoral dissertation, University of Minnesota.

Yell, M., Deno, S. L., & Marston, D. E. (1992). Barriers to implementing curriculum-based measurement. *Diagnostique, 18,* 99–105.

Chapter 9

What Is Special About the Preparation of Special Education Teachers?

A Review of the Research

Paul T. Sindelar, Anne G. Bishop, and **Mary T. Brownell**

In this chapter, we review special education teacher education research and attempt to identify what distinguishes it from teacher education research generally. It will come as little surprise to readers of this literature that empirical research on special education teacher education practices is scarce and that the practices that have been studied in a special education teacher education context do not set us clearly apart from general teacher education. The paucity of research on teacher education practices—in both disciplines, actually—results in part from that fact that teacher education is an extended and complex process. Its chief outcome—teacher quality—is difficult to define and measure, and beginning teachers may not realize their full potential until long after their programs are complete and their development as professionals has been shaped by the schools where they teach. Participants in studies of teacher preparation practices are heterogeneous on many dimensions, and they cannot be assigned to experimental or control groups. Furthermore, how well they perform on assessments of their teaching may be as much a function of the schools and classrooms in which they work as of their knowledge or skill. How one overcomes these problems and conducts definitive research on teacher education practices remains a problem in search of solution.

Special education is a young and maturing field, and special education teacher preparation is younger still. *Teacher Education and Special Education* (TESE), the journal of the Teacher Education Division (TED) of the Council for Exceptional Children, is in its 27th volume; the *Journal of Teacher Education* has been in print nearly 30 years longer. For many years, research in special education focused primarily on developing strategies for teaching and managing students with disabilities, as it should have. As we have grown confident about findings from intervention research, our attention has turned to the impact it has had on practice.

That teacher education figures prominently in the discussion of research-to-practice dissemination—as part of the problem as well as a potential solution—has led us to believe that the field may be turning at least some of its attention now to the preparation of practitioners. If so, this chapter would be easy to write in 20 years; today, because we have little to work with, it is not. Nonetheless, we review empirically supported, effective techniques used by special education teacher educators. There is less research—and less rigorous research—on teacher education practices than for the other disciplines reviewed in this text, and less is known about the degree to which such techniques are used or the fidelity of implementation. Yet there is interesting, important, and more methodologically rigorous research on teacher education topics, which we also consider in this review. Thus, our chapter is divided into three sections: studies of special education teacher education pedagogy, the relationship of this literature to the teacher education literature base, and other empirical work in special education teacher education. In synthesizing studies of pedagogy, we build upon a review the first author conducted some years ago as coeditor of TESE.

What Kind of Research Is Being Done in Teacher Preparation?

To commemorate the 75th anniversary of the founding of the Council for Exceptional Children, TESE published a topical issue (volume 19, issue 3) with a historical theme. That issue included a content analysis of papers published in the journal from its inception in 1975 through 1995, some 18 volumes (Tulbert, Sindelar, Correa, & La Porte, 1996). In this analysis, the authors classified both topics and the kinds of papers published. We now have extended this initial analysis through 2004, examining 9 additional TESE volumes. We begin this section by summarizing the results from the 1996 study, then compare these findings with trends that have emerged during the past 9 years. In doing our update, we used the same methods as the original authors and categorized papers into specific research types.

The original 1996 analysis led the authors to call for more empirically based work in teacher education. They suggested that the paucity of research and researchers' overreliance on small-scale surveys of expert opinion placed teacher education in a vulnerable position given a policy context in which accountability and high-stakes decision making loomed large. From 1978 through 1995, the most common paper types were survey research, which represented 24% of all papers; models and guidelines; program descriptions (distinguished from program evaluations by the absence of data); position papers; and program evaluations. From 1996 through 2004, the most common paper types were program descriptions, survey research, models and guidelines, and two new types: narrative literature reviews and qualitative studies. In the 1996 paper, the five most common paper types made up more than three fourths of TESE titles. In the more recent sample, the top five constitute two thirds.

We noted two significant changes. First, the number of qualitative studies increased dramatically from 5 between 1978 and 1995 to 26 between 1996 and 2004. Second, in spite of the increase in the number of qualitative studies, the overall percentage of empirically based papers declined. Between 1980 and 1995, the percentage of data-based papers ranged from 35% in 1981 to 80% in 1994. By contrast, during the current period of analysis, empirical work accounted for as little 20% in 1996 and as much as 55% in 1999. The difference may be accounted for by a one-third decrease in the number of survey studies.

Our current analysis suggests that teacher education may not yet be an important focus for many special education researchers. Nonempirical work continues to dominate the literature. This finding is disconcerting in light of the fact that teacher education has taken center stage in the policy spotlight, and its effectiveness has been called into question (Hess, 2001; Walsh, 2001). On the other hand, we see cause for optimism in the emergence of qualitative research, long a mainstay of general teacher education research. Given the complexity and duration of the process of teacher education and the qualitative tradition within teacher education research generally, this change seems logical. With qualitative methods, researchers are able to answer questions that cannot be addressed with quantitative methods. Thus, although the volume of teacher education research may not be increasing, the kind of empirical work being done seems to be changing. To our way of thinking, more qualitative studies and fewer surveys of expert opinion represent an improvement in the quality of our literature base.

Practice as Pedagogy: Teacher Education Practices in Special Education

Only 7% of the articles published during the 9-year period we analyzed were devoted to special education pedagogy, and those studies tended to be small scale and limited to single institutions. This literature struck us as idiosyncratic, with little systematic research on any particular pedagogical practice. In fact, only five practices—peer coaching, collaboration, reflective teaching, case method instruction (or problem-based learning), and technology-based learning—were studied more than once. We also noted variation in the frameworks underlying the five approaches and in the research methods used to assess them. Whereas peer coaching studies adhere consistently to a positivist view of teacher preparation and often involve single-subject designs, case method and problem-based instruction, collaboration, and reflective teaching align with a constructivist approach and have been studied most commonly with qualitative methods.

Peer Coaching

Peer coaching surfaced as a pedagogical strategy in the early 1980s (Joyce & Showers, 1982) and has been investigated as a technique for use with preservice teachers (Englert & Sugai, 1983; Rolider, Pierce, & Van Houten, 1985). It involves working in ongoing teacher support groups and requires peer observations of teaching behaviors, feedback sessions, and the implementation of new or different teaching techniques based on feedback (Peterson & Hudson, 1989). Peer coaching was designed to promote skill transfer from courses to field experiences and to increase the amount of observation and feedback trainees receive—without adding to the cost of supervision.

Mallette, Maheady, and Harper (1999) investigated the effects of reciprocal peer coaching on both preservice teachers and the children they tutored. Mallette et al. noted an increase in the frequency of peer coaching interactions and improvements in both the accuracy with which tutors implemented a complex instructional intervention and tutees' reading comprehension. In a second study, Tschantz and Vail (2000) conducted a peer coaching experiment in an inclusive preschool. Three early childhood special education teachers, paired with Head Start teachers, targeted change in specific behaviors. The authors reported improved teaching behaviors for all the Head Start teachers and emphasized the value of peer coaching as a means for promoting collaborative teaching.

Collaboration

The call for collaboration in preparing general and special education teachers dates back to the first issue of TESE, and although collaborative teacher preparation seems like an innovation, descriptions of collaborative programs date back nearly 20 years (Feden & Clabaugh, 1986). Much of the earlier work was descriptive (e.g., Blanton, Griffin, Winn, & Pugach, 1997), and evidence of the effectiveness of collaborative programs was lacking. However, our review yielded three empirical studies of collaborative teacher preparation, all describing initial attempts to integrate the preparation of general and special education teachers.

Nowacek and Blanton (1996) used group experimental methodology to examine the effects of a collaborative instructional model on preservice teachers' attitudes and knowledge of students with mild disabilities. After a 10-week course, few differences between groups were found, and the authors described the difficulties they encountered in establishing a more unified, collaborative program. Corbett, Kilgore, and Sindelar (1998) examined preservice students participating in the beginning stages of a unified elementary and special education teacher education program. By observing field placement performances, interviewing candidates, and reviewing student teacher documents, Corbett and her colleagues determined that differences between the perspectives of special and general education faculty enhanced student teachers' ability to address all students' needs. This finding dispelled the authors' concern that dramatic differences in instructional orientation might confuse students and limit their ability to adapt instruction meaningfully. Using survey methodology, Richards, Hunley, Weaver, and Landers (2003) studied the development of a teacher preparation model involving collaboration between secondary and special education preservice teachers at university and school sites. These authors reported that their model fostered the development of both positive attitudes toward collaboration and collaborative and problem-solving skills.

Reflective Teaching

Reflective teaching emerged in the teacher education literature in the 1990s (Clift, Houston, & Pugach, 1990) as an important pedagogical practice and a means for changing preservice teachers' beliefs and attitudes. Simply defined, reflective teaching involves making "rational and ethical choices about what and how to teach and assuming responsibility for those choices" (Ross, Bondy, & Kyle, 1993, p. 3). Reflective teaching clearly derives from a constructivist framework, in which students are thought to construct new knowledge and teachers assess and build upon what students know.

Special education research has focused on the problem of obtaining reliable and valid assessments of reflection. For example, Dieker and Monda-Amaya (1995) described procedures for analyzing the contents of preservice students' reflective journals, and Griffin and Kilgore (1995) examined interns' problem-solving abilities through reflection. More recently, in a course designed to prepare teachers to teach in diverse and inclusive classrooms, Kolar and Dickson (2002) analyzed the use of structured reflective logs. These researchers determined that the logs were critical multipurpose tools that provided students with opportunities to express, synthesize, and analyze their thoughts. According to the authors, the logs promoted reflective practice and helped students make connections among course concepts.

Case Method Instruction or Problem-Based Learning

Experiential approaches, which include Case Method Instruction (CMI) and Problem-Based Learning (PBL), provide prospective teachers opportunities to practice and apply their knowledge to real-life situations and have emerged as pedagogical tools in special education teacher education. CMI provides preservice professionals realistic problem-solving activities designed to bridge the theory-to-classroom-practice gap (G. E. Greenwood, Fillmer, & Parkay, 1999). PBL is similar but requires a more learner-centered approach, with students generating their own problems and applying their knowledge to resolve dilemmas. Both CMI and PBL may be particularly appropriate for special education, due to the scope and complexity of what special educators need to know and be able to do. These tools provide realistic opportunities for prospective teachers to understand the uniqueness of children with disabilities.

We found six studies of experiential or simulated learning interventions, four of which used case method instruction or problem-based learning as the intervention. Hutchinson and Martin (1999) used dilemma cases with preservice teachers to promote inclusive beliefs and practices. Their program evaluation suggested the combination of field-based courses and student-generated cases enhanced preservice students' ability to reflect on exceptional learners and their beliefs about inclusion.

Levin, Hibbard, and Rock (2002) used quantitative and qualitative methodology to assess what they described as a problem-based learning activity designed to help prospective general education teachers learn about teaching students with special needs. An initial problem was posed asking students to consider an offer from a principal to teach an inclusion class. Students participated in activities over a semester to gain the knowledge and skills necessary to make an educated decision. Results indicated that PBL contributed to helping teachers gain the skills, knowledge, and attitudes needed to work with students with special needs in inclusive settings.

Werts, Mamlin, and Pogoloff (2002) studied simulation, an instructional approach related to CMI and PBL. They engaged students in role-playing and Web-based forums to provide them opportunities to integrate and apply new knowledge related to the Individualized Education Program (IEP) process. Ensign's (2002) "Klutz Experience," also a simulation, allowed students in an introductory special education course to experience learning difficulties. Ensign found that this approach to understanding students with special needs resulted in empathy for students in addition to mastery of course content.

Case method instruction is the only practice highlighted in this review about which we have some sense of the degree of implementation. Elksnin (1998) surveyed 257 TED members and found that 87% of them used case method instruction in their teaching. Respondents cited many advantages, such as the application of theory to practice, the enhancement of problem-solving skills, the opportunity to collaborate, and high levels of student engagement. McNaughton, Hall, and Maccini (2001) interviewed 15 teacher educators and CMI users who cited as important benefits opportunities to explore real-life problems, opportunities to generalize skills, and the necessity of considering multiple perspectives. Disadvantages included the time that CMI required and the difficulty of finding appropriate cases (Elksnin, 1998).

CMI has been used in methods and assessment classes, and training has focused on families, administration, classroom management, early intervention, reading, deafness, inclusion, the multicultural classroom, and, more generally, students with special needs. Yet, despite the popularity of CMI, only a handful of studies provide empirical evidence of its effectiveness.

Technology-Based Learning

Over the past decade, the emergence of technology has dramatically affected instructional delivery in teacher education. Distance learning has emerged as a viable instructional tool, particularly as districts struggle to address shortages and meet the "highly qualified" requirement in the No Child Left Behind Act of 2001 (NCLB). Distance learning occurs when learners are connected with learning resources and opportunities while separated from the instructor (Caywood & Duckett, 2003). This instructional practice has great potential to provide access to coursework for preservice teachers, particularly in remote areas. Technology-enhanced instruction has emerged in course design, and the eight empirically based studies that appear in TESE capture the new roles of distance education and technology-enhanced practices.

In an early empirical study of technology applications, Langone, Malone, and Clinton (1999) investigated what they termed *anchored instruction,* the use of experiential learning activities and videodiscs to supplement lectures. Langone et al. reported that although there were no differences between groups on an immediate posttest of lecture content mastery, the group receiving anchored instruction outperformed the control group on a posttest administered 8 weeks later.

Caro, McLean, Browning, and Hains (2002) reported qualitative and quantitative findings from an evaluation of a distance education course offered across six university campuses in Wisconsin. After participating in a course in early childhood education, both faculty and students reported improved technology skill, and students felt highly successful in mastering course content. Caywood and Duckett (2003) compared online versus on-campus delivery of a behavior management course and reported no significant differences between the two delivery modes on multiple-choice test performance and classroom observations of behavior management skills. In a similar study, Beattie, Spooner, Jordan, Algozzine, and Spooner (2002) analyzed course evaluations from distance and traditional delivery courses; their results also indicated no differences in overall ratings.

Pindiprolu, Peck Peterson, Rule, and Lignugaris/Kraft (2003) combined distance learning and case method instruction to develop functional behavioral assessment skills with preservice teachers. A group experimental design was used to evaluate online learning environments consisting of an information group (in which online cases were completed individually), a chat group (which required individualized interaction between the student and instructor), and a student interaction group (in which groups of three or four students completed the online cases together). The authors reported that all three approaches were effective in teaching functional behavioral assessment skills but expressed concern that their findings might have been influenced by either students' inexperience with technology use or inadequate technology.

Welch and Brownell (2002) investigated the effectiveness of a course in professional collaboration, Professionals Ready for Educational Partnerships (PREP), enhanced with technology applications. These enhancements included documentary videos with break-out activities and CD quizzes for all instructional modules. Students exposed to these technology enhancements made significant gains from pretest to posttest on cognitive and skill measures. Scores on an attitudinal measure also improved, but those gains were not consistently significant. Phillips and Halle (2004), like Welch and Brownell, also studied a multifaceted intervention. These researchers used a single-subject design to assess an intervention to teach student teachers to use environmental arrangement strategies and delayed prompts with students with severe language delays. The training model, which incorporated videotape demonstrations, simulated role plays, reflection, and coaching, had a positive effect on interns' use of naturalistic communication strategies. This study is an exemplar of how multiple teacher education approaches may be combined and studied simultaneously.

In our review of empirically based articles in TESE, by necessity, we accepted findings uncritically. Although few studies met accepted standards for experimental rigor, we came away from the review optimistic about the potential of experiential methods and technology applications to address some of the knottier problems in our field. We noted and grew interested in the hybridization of special education and teacher education research traditions. We recognized studies of peer coaching, on the one hand, with their behavioral methods and positivistic frameworks, as having clear special education roots. On the other hand, the increasing use of qualitative methods and constructivist frameworks provided common ground with our general teacher education counterparts, who think about and conduct their work consistently from this perspective. We sensed that special education teacher education research may be following the same developmental course as research in general teacher education—but it is lagging behind. After all, early work in both fields was positivistic in concept and behavioral in methodology. Furthermore, although special education has been slow to adopt and study constructivist (e.g., reflective teaching) pedagogy and to use qualitative methods in the process, such research has become increasingly commonplace in our literature. Now teacher education has responded to the policy challenge of demonstrating its warrant through large-scale, systematic studies of teacher education outcomes—and special education has not.

The Teacher Education Literature: Research on Teacher Education Pedagogy

Studies of teacher education pedagogy represent a large portion of the research on teacher education. In the 1960s and 1970s, behavioral and social learning theories dominated the research in teacher education. Studies were largely experimental or quasi-experimental, as researchers sought to determine the most effective strategies for training teachers in effective teaching behaviors identified in process–product research (Zeichner, 1999). Among the hundreds of studies conducted to establish a scientific basis of teaching, microteaching was the most frequently examined pedagogy (Kennedy, 1991).

Microteaching is based on a behavioral and Bandurian view of learning. Researchers examining this pedagogy believed that effective instructional systems could be identified and teachers could be trained to apply them in their classrooms (Joyce, 1988). Joyce, Weil, and Wald (1981) asserted that microteaching must include four instructional components: (a) intensive study of underlying theory, (b) demonstrations, (c) opportunities to practice, and (d) videotaped self-feedback.

By the late 1970s, researchers began to question the utility of behaviorism and social learning theory as the foundation for teacher education pedagogy (Carter, 1990; Popkewitz, Tabachnick, & Zeichner, 1979). They argued that research had not established whether teachers maintained the skills they learned during experiments and cited the failure of research to contribute insight into the cognitive processes underlying teachers' learning over time. Moreover, some teacher education researchers began to question the long-term effectiveness of teacher education, suggesting that what students learned in their education courses was washed out by preservice students' enduring beliefs about teaching and learning, the dogmatic views that student teachers confront in schools, and the fragmented nature of teacher preparation generally (Stofflett & Stoddart, 1992; Zeichner & Gore, 1990; Zeichner & Tabachnick, 1981).

In the early 1980s, interest turned to the practices and experiences that would change how teachers thought about instruction (e.g., Bird, Anderson, Sullivan, & Swidler, 1993; Feiman-Nemser, 1983; Powell, 2000; Weinstein, 1990). At this point, researchers began to examine the influence of particular pedagogical approaches, courses, and field experiences on teachers' abilities to think about classroom problems and to reflect on their practice. Case-based instruction, cognitive self-instruction, social roletaking, guided reflection, and action research were studied (e.g., Gore & Zeichner, 1991; Hazareesingh & Bielawski, 1991; Powell, 2000; Reiman, 1999).

Although many teacher educators have asserted that constructivist pedagogy is necessary to change preservice and inservice teachers' beliefs, research offers little support for that presumption. In fact, research on constructivist pedagogy suffers some of the same shortcomings as the behavioral research of the 1960s and 1970s. For the most part, this research has examined short-term effects of narrowly defined pedagogical approaches (e.g., Wideen, Mayer-Smith, & Moon, 1998), sometimes in experimental or quasi-experimental designs. Researchers in this tradition have failed to demonstrate an effect on preservice teachers' beliefs and behavior over time.

Since the mid to late 1990s, teacher education research has reverted to a more performance-based training approach as researchers responded to policy concerns related to the effectiveness of teacher education programs (Cochran-Smith, 2003). Policymakers called for evidence that links preparation to teacher effectiveness, as measured by the achievement of K–12 students. A summary of peer-reviewed research on teacher preparation, commissioned by the U.S. Department of Education, provided some answers to concerns relating to subject matter and pedagogical preparation, clinical training, policy influences, and alternative certification (Wilson, Floden, & Ferrini-Mundy, 2001). Wilson et al. also called for large-scale, cross-institutional studies of teacher preparation and studies of the components of teacher preparation that make it effective. Researchers have begun to respond to this call by designing studies that evaluate programmatic components. Examples of those studies are reviewed in the following section.

Research on the Components of Effective Teacher Education: Practice as Program

Research has shown that teacher education makes a difference in what beginning teachers know and can do, as well as in their ability to influence student achievement. Teachers who are fully certified compared to those who are not produce higher achievement scores in mathematics and reading (Darling-Hammond, 2000b; Felter, 1999; Hawk, Coble, Swanson, 1985; Laczko & Berliner, 2001). Teacher education also appears to have a value-added effect on what teachers do and on the performance of their students. Teachers with subject matter preparation in math and science accompanied by related pedagogical courses are better able than teachers with subject matter preparation only to influence student achievement in those subject areas (Monk, 1994). Studies have demonstrated that teachers with pedagogical and content preparation are better able to engage students in the learning process (Kennedy, 1999; Wilson et al., 2001). Furthermore, teachers attribute their knowledge of instruction and management to their preservice education experience (Adams & Krockover, 1997; Grossman & Richert, 1988; Grossman et al., 2000).

Although comparisons of teachers with and without teacher education have established the effectiveness of teacher preparation generally, such studies have not provided information about the elements of effective preparation. Teacher education programs vary widely from institution to institution in terms of structure, requirements, and effectiveness. Because of the variability among programs, researchers must understand what characterizes effective teacher education. Although the research base in this area is limited, one recent literature review and three comparative studies of teacher education programs offer some insight into the characteristics of programs that produce positive changes in the knowledge, beliefs, and skills of their graduates.

In a review of 97 studies, Wideen et al. (1998) identified 15 studies of programmatic interventions in teacher education that produced changes in preservice teachers' views of teaching and diversity. Although these studies involved single institutions, four common program features produced conceptual change in preservice students: (a) the use of a pedagogy that helps preservice students examine their beliefs, (b) a strong programmatic vision that fosters program cohesion, (c) small program size with a high degree of faculty–student collaboration, and (d) carefully constructed field experiences in which university and school faculty collaborate extensively. As important as these findings seem to be, many studies stop short of demonstrating effects on teachers' practices. Furthermore, research has yet to establish whether changes in beliefs are accompanied by changes in practice.

Three comparative studies support the findings of Wideen et al. (1998) about features of effective programs (Darling-Hammond, 2000a; National Center for Research on Teacher Learning

[NCRTL], 1991; National Commission on Excellence in Elementary Teacher Preparation for Reading Instruction [NCEETPRI], 2003). These studies also demonstrate that graduates of effective programs practice their craft differently from other beginning teachers. In a study of 11 preservice, teacher induction, and inservice programs, researchers at the NCRTL found that teachers' conceptions of classroom practice, diverse learners, and subject matter were largely a function of their entering beliefs and knowledge about writing and mathematics. However, these researchers found that teacher education students' beliefs do change under certain conditions and that those conditions had less to do with program structure (e.g., length of program, amount of field experience) than with program orientation. Programs that adopted a constructivist orientation, marked by well-articulated goals shared by instructors and attended to carefully in courses and fieldwork, produced the most conceptual change. In these programs, teachers had repeated opportunities to consider why new practices were better than more conventional approaches, to see examples of new practices, to experiment with new practices as learners and teachers, and to receive on-site support and assistance to implement the new practices. NCRTL researchers also found that mentor teachers who knew how to help novice teachers learn and reflect were essential to program success.

Two studies of exemplary teacher education programs support and extend these findings (Darling-Hammond, 2000a; NCEETPRI, 2003). The Association of American Colleges of Teacher Education (AACTE) studied seven undergraduate and graduate teacher education programs preparing elementary or secondary teachers (Darling-Hammond, 2000a). These programs were selected on the basis of their reputation for preparing teachers who were well prepared to serve diverse learners. Case studies of these institutions involved interviews with faculty, observations of courses, and analysis of program documents. Researchers surveyed and interviewed program graduates and other beginning teachers, interviewed principals to determine their perceptions of graduates, and observed graduates in their classrooms. In a similar study sponsored by the International Reading Association (IRA), researchers studied eight undergraduate teacher education programs recognized for their excellence in preparing teachers with reading expertise. These researchers conducted document analyses and followed graduates of those programs into their first 3 years of teaching. Faculty from each program outlined features that contributed to overall effectiveness and described how those features were integrated into the program. Researchers conducted interviews with graduates and compared graduates of the reading programs to graduates from same institutions' elementary education programs.

An analysis of the AACTE and IRA comparative studies (Darling-Hammond, 2000a; NCEETPRI, 2003) reveals five features common to exemplary programs in teacher education. First, in exemplary programs, faculties develop a common program vision that shapes goals, objectives, and instructional activities for courses and field experience. Second, faculty carefully design courses and fieldwork and use active pedagogy to link theory and practice and to promote reflection. Third, field experiences play a critical role in connecting course concepts to practice. They are best when developmental in nature, well supervised, and extensive. In all the programs, students spent considerable time in field experiences designed to help them experiment with the concepts and strategies they learned in courses. Fourth, graduates of exemplary programs are expected to demonstrate the attitudes and abilities of competent beginning teachers and to work successfully with diverse learners. Finally, exemplary programs may be characterized as collaborative communities of practice. Teacher educators and other stakeholders collaborate to plan, evaluate, and revise their teacher education programs. Students proceed through programs in cohorts designed to foster the dialogue necessary for reflection about what students are learning and doing in courses and classrooms.

Other Special Education Research

No comparable programmatic research in special education exists or, to the best of our knowledge, is under way. However, current political and policy contexts make undertaking such research imperative. After all, such studies address the question of the value of teacher education, currently the subject of heated debate. In special education, students with disabilities are entitled to a free, appropriate public education (FAPE). We sincerely believe that FAPE requires competent teachers, and competent teachers require good preparation, even though no definitive special education research has yet linked teacher preparation and beginning teacher competence. On the other hand, thanks largely to the Office of Special Education Programs and the research it supports, special education has generated important information on critical policy issues, and it is to that research that we now turn. We briefly consider research on supply and demand, retention and attrition, alternative certification, and sustainability of innovations. In doing so, we rely heavily on three recent articles (Billingsley, 2004; McLeskey, Tyler, & Flippin, 2004; Rosenberg & Sindelar, 2005) and a topical issue of *Teacher Education and Special Education* on the research-to-practice gap and its implications for teacher preparation (C. R. Greenwood, 2001).

Supply and Demand

The supply of and demand for special education teachers has been the subject of research for 2 decades, due largely to chronic shortages of special education teachers. Using *Schools and Staffing Survey* (SASS) data, Boe and his colleagues conducted a series of supply-and-demand analyses. Although these analyses are not limited to special education teachers, they have commonly been published in the special education literature (Boe, Bobbitt, & Cook, 1997; Boe, Cook, Bobbitt, & Terhanian, 1998; Boe, Cook, Kauffman, & Danielson, 1996), perhaps because shortage is felt so sharply in our field. A synthesis of these analyses led McLeskey et al. (2004) to conclude that shortages of special education teachers are serious, widespread, and likely to worsen.

Shortages vary dramatically by state and specialization, with shortages in the area of emotional disturbance being most severe (McLeskey et al., 2004). Furthermore, although 38% of students in special education are culturally and linguistically diverse, only 14% of their teachers are. Thus, another important aspect of the teacher shortage problem in special education is recruiting a teaching workforce that reflects the diversity of the students it serves. According to McLeskey et al., supply and demand have been affected by overall K–12 enrollment growth; growth in special education enrollments, which has exceeded general enrollment growth; and attrition, which may be the result of many factors, including working conditions.

Research has shown that the supply of new graduates from teacher education programs is inadequate to meet the demand for special education teachers. In fact, Boe et al. (1996) established that a reserve pool of unemployed teachers is the single most important source of new teacher hires, constituting about 50% of annual demand. Analyses of data from the 1993–1994 SASS administration led some to suggest that the reserve pool may even be shrinking. The U.S. Department of Education, for one, in its *20th Annual Report to Congress*, conjectured that "graduates from teacher preparation programs must serve as the major source of supply in the future" (1998, p. III-19). However, more recent analyses from the 1999–2000 SASS administration paint a different picture: That year, 61% of all newly hired teachers were reserve pool members (Cook & Boe, 2004).

Attrition

Attrition—teachers leaving the special education workforce—contributes substantially to the demand for teachers and has been the subject of a substantial research effort in special education. In the 1990s, the Office of Special Education Programs (OSEP) funded four studies of attrition, three with a focus on city schools (Billingsley, Pyecha, Smith-Davis, Murray, & Hendricks, 1995; Levine, Campeau, Doorlag, & Cegelka, 1994; Morvant, Gersten, Gillman, Keating, & Blake, 1995). In addition, Miller, Brownell, and Smith (1999) and Boe (Boe et al., 1997) have provided estimates of attrition from state and national perspectives. It is important to note that in attrition research, the choice of the unit of analysis affects estimates dramatically. For example, if the unit of analysis is the nation as a whole, a teacher who moves from Florida to Georgia but who remains in teaching is not counted as attrition; when the state (Florida, in this case) is the unit of analysis, however, the same change is regarded as attrition. It is also important to keep in mind that attrition definitions differ from study to study. Thus, a teacher who moves from special education to general education may be counted toward attrition in some studies but not in others where teaching is defined more broadly.

Boe and his colleagues (1997) have estimated that 13% of all special education teachers leave the workforce annually, although about half remain in education. Billingsley (2004) noted that attrition is related to (a) teachers' age and experience, where younger and less experienced teachers and older teachers (nearing retirement) are more likely to leave the field; and (b) to certification, with less than fully qualified teachers being more likely to leave. Furthermore, a number of school and district variables, among them salaries, school climate, and administrative support, also relate to attrition. Higher salaries, more positive climates, and stronger support have been shown to reduce attrition and mitigate intent to leave. Job-related stress has also been shown to relate to attrition and intent to leave. Research has demonstrated that increasing job satisfaction will reduce attrition; other studies have associated commitment to the field with reduced risk of attrition.

Alternative Routes of Licensure

In the special education literature, Rosenberg and Sindelar (2005) found 10 studies of alternative routes to special education licensure. These studies suggest that alternative routes (ARs) can produce competent teachers, but AR graduates are not always as competent as graduates of traditional teacher education programs. Furthermore, most successful AR programs were offered collaboratively by teacher education programs and school districts, and successful programs were long and substantive—quite different from the streamlined training envisioned in NCLB. Successful programs also tended to make use of both university and site-based supervision.

Among these 10 studies, 2 comparative studies stand out. Sindelar, Daunic, and Rennells (2004) compared beginning teachers who had completed either AR or traditional programs. The AR programs were of two types: those offered by teacher education programs and districts collaboratively and those offered by districts alone. The authors analyzed observations of teaching and conducted surveys regarding graduates' sense of preparedness and principals' satisfaction. (For classroom observations, Sindelar et al. used PRAXIS III, a beginning teacher-assessment process involving paper-and-pencil measures and interviews, in addition to direct observations, with teachers rated on 19 criteria.) Findings were mixed; whereas traditional graduates were rated higher on several PRAXIS criteria, graduates of all programs met minimal standards. Furthermore, principals preferred graduates of AR programs, perhaps because they were more likely to be familiar with the schools where they worked and were generally more school savvy. The authors also found differences between different AR program types: Specifically, when collaborative program graduates and graduates of district-only programs were found to differ, those differences consistently favored the collaborative group.

Nougaret, Scruggs, and Mastropieri (2005) also studied graduates of traditional and AR programs. The teachers were observed in their classroom (using a process similar to PRAXIS III) and asked to complete a self-assessment of teaching competence. In this study, the AR participants were teaching on the basis of emergency certification and had completed no more than six credits at the time of the study. Nougaret et al. reported that traditionally trained teachers scored significantly higher than AR participants on the observation scores, but on self-reports of preparedness, the two groups did not differ. Taken together, these two studies suggest that graduates of traditional teacher preparation programs are likely to outperform AR graduates on measures of teaching performance and that some ARs are more effective than others.

Rosenberg and Sindelar (2005) subsequently expressed concern about the proliferation of AR programs, noting that the programs studied empirically might well represent only the tip of the AR iceberg; the proliferation of ARs might also reflect the politicization of teacher preparation since NCLB. As policymakers and politicians have ratcheted up standards governing traditional programs, they have eased entry to teaching by fostering the development of ARs.

This allows them to both claim the high ground on teacher preparation and trumpet their concern for increasing the supply of new teachers. Furthermore, although we know that ARs are often designed for nontraditional populations of prospective teachers, little is known about the effect of AR training on teacher supply—the variable it is intended to affect.

Bridging the Research-to-Practice Gap

In the late 1990s, the Office of Special Education Programs funded two cohorts of "research-to-practice" projects in which researchers studied how research-based innovations are developed and sustained as classroom practices. In the TESE topical issue, bridging the research-to-practice gap was considered from the perspective of teachers' professional development. Boudah, Logan, and Greenwood (2001) synthesized the findings from these studies and offered guidelines about effective professional development. They noted that successful professional development required up-front commitment from all participants, including trainers and trainees alike. Such work was intensive, extensive, and sustained. By "intensive," Boudah et al. meant that the trainers in these studies typically demonstrated innovations, coached teachers in their classrooms, guided study groups, and consulted with individual teachers. By "extensive and sustained," they meant that effective professional development took time and occurred over time. These assertions corroborate the work of Guskey (1995) and others in the general teacher education literature. Boudah et al. concluded that effective professional development is not cheap, as its intensive and extensive nature suggests. They noted that schools typically have little to spend on professional development and that too often what is available is spent on one-time workshops for large groups of teachers who may or may not need what the trainer is providing.

Conclusion

Teacher education research in special education is a hybrid; it derives in part from the behavioral tradition in special education and in part—and perhaps increasingly—from the teacher education research tradition. Although teacher education research went through a period in which behavioral methods prevailed, increasingly it has used qualitative methods and focused on teachers' beliefs and cognitions. Also, perhaps in response to a challenging policy context, teacher education has undertaken large-scale studies of effectiveness. We strongly believe that special education must do the same. Such research is needed to address critics of teacher education as well as to guide effective practice. In special education, teacher education researchers also bear the burden of demonstrating the cost-effectiveness of a substantial annual federal subsidy.

Although research on special education teacher education pedagogical practices does not set us apart from the enterprise of teacher education writ large, our literature is distinct in many important ways. For one, we struggle with teacher shortages, which are an issue for only a few general education disciplines (science, mathematics, and English as a Second Language). As a result, much of the attention of researchers of special education teacher training has focused on understanding this problem and the factors that contribute to it. We have focused on the problem of providing an adequate supply of competent teachers and have not yet addressed the question of how to prepare an exemplary workforce. Yet without data to substantiate the warrant of special education teacher preparation, we are vulnerable to both our critics and to policymakers who must decide how best to expend the limited resources available for training.

REFERENCES

Adams, P. E., & Krockover, G. H. (1997). Beginning science teacher cognition and its origins in the preservice science teacher program. *Journal of Research in Science Teaching, 34*, 633–653.

Beattie, J. R., Spooner, F., Jordan, L., Algozzine, B., & Spooner, M. (2002). Evaluating instruction in distance learning classes. *Teacher Education and Special Education, 25*, 124–132.

Billingsley, B. S. (2004). Special education teacher retention and attrition: A critical analysis of the literature. *The Journal of Special Education, 38*, 39–57.

Billingsley, B., Pyecha, J., Smith-Davis, J., Murray, K., & Hendricks, M. B. (1995). *Improving the retention of spe-*

cial education teachers: Final report. Raleigh, NC: Research Triangle Institute.

Bird, T., Anderson, L., Sullivan, B., & Swidler, S. (1993). Pedagogical balancing acts: Attempts to influence prospective teachers' beliefs. *Teaching and Teacher Education, 9,* 253–267.

Blanton, L., Griffin, C., Winn, J., & Pugach, M. (Eds.). (1997). *Teacher education in transition: Collaborative programs to prepare general and special educators*. Denver: Love.

Boe, E. E., Bobbitt, S., & Cook, L. (1997). Whither didst thou go? Retention, reassignment, migration, and attrition of special and general education teachers from a national perspective. *The Journal of Special Education, 30,* 371–389.

Boe, E. E., Cook, L., Bobbitt, S., & Terhanian, G. (1998). The shortage of fully certified teachers in general and special education. *Teacher Education and Special Education, 21,* 1–21.

Boe, E. E., Cook, L., Kauffman, M., & Danielson, L. (1996). Special and general education teachers in public schools: Sources of supply in national perspective. *Teacher Education and Special Education, 19,* 1–16.

Boudah, D. J., Logan, K. R., & Greenwood, C. R. (2001). The research to practice projects: Lessons learned about changing teacher practice. *Teacher Education and Special Education, 24,* 290–303.

Caro, P., McLean, M., Browning, E., & Hains, E. (2002). The use of distance education in a collaborative course in early childhood special education. *Teacher Education and Special Education, 25,* 333–341.

Carter, J. (1990). Teachers' knowledge and learning to teach. In W. R. Houston, M. Haberman, & J. Sikula (Eds.), *Handbook of research on teacher education* (pp. 291–310). New York: Macmillan.

Caywood, K., & Duckett, J. (2003). Online vs. on-campus learning in teacher education. *Teacher Education and Special Education, 26,* 98–105.

Clift, R., Houston, W. R., & Pugach, M. (1990). *Encouraging reflective practice in education: An analysis of issues and programs*. New York: Teachers College Press.

Cochran-Smith, M. (2003). Teacher education's Bermuda Triangle: Dichotomy, mythology, and amnesia. *Journal of Teacher Education, 54,* 275–280.

Cook, L. H., & Boe, E. E. (2004). *From whence didst thou come: National trends in the sources of supply of teachers in special and general education*. Philadelphia: University of Pennsylvania, Center for Research and Evaluation in Social Policy.

Corbett, N. L., Kilgore, K. L., & Sindelar, P. T. (1998). "Making sense" in a collaborative teacher education program: Lessons from Project PART students. *Teacher Education and Special Education, 21,* 293–305.

Darling-Hammond, L. (2000a). *Studies of excellence in teacher education*. Washington, DC: AACTE.

Darling-Hammond, L. (2000b). Teacher quality and student achievement: A review of state policy evidence. *Education Policy Analysis Archives, 8*. Available at http://epaa.asu.edu/epaa/v8n1/

Dieker, L. A., & Monda-Amaya, L. E. (1995). Reflective teaching: A process for analyzing journals of preservice educators. *Teacher Education and Special Education, 18,* 240–252.

Elksnin, L. (1998). Use of the case method of instruction in special education teacher preparation programs: A preliminary investigation. *Teacher Education and Special Education, 21,* 95–108.

Englert, C. S., & Sugai, G. (1983). Teacher training: Improving performance through peer observation and observation system technology. *Teacher Education and Special Education, 6,* 7–17.

Ensign, J. (2002). Weaving experiential education into a preservice special education course: The Klutz experience. *Teacher Education and Special Education, 25,* 105–113.

Feden, P. D., & Clabaugh, G. K. (1986). The "new breed" educator: A rationale and program for combining elementary and special education teacher preparation. *Teacher Education and Special Education, 9,* 180–189.

Feiman-Nemser, S. (1983). Learning to teach. In L. Shulman & G. Sykes (Eds.), *Handbook of teaching and policy* (pp. 150–170). New York: Longman.

Felter, M. (1999). High school staff characteristics and mathematics test results. *Education Policy Analysis Archives, 7*. Available at http://epaa.asu.edu/epaa/v7n9.html

Gore, J. M., & Zeichner, K. M. (1991). Action research and reflective teaching in preservice teacher education: A case study from the United States. *Teaching and Teacher Education, 7,* 119–136.

Greenwood, C. R. (2001). Bridging the gap between research and practice in special education: Issues and implications for teacher preparation. *Teacher Education and Special Education, 24,* 273–275.

Greenwood, G. E., Fillmer, H. T., & Parkey, F. W. (1999). *Educational psychology cases for teacher decision making*. Upper Saddle River, NJ: Merrill/Prentice Hall.

Griffin, C. C., & Kilgore, K. L. (1995). Framing the problems of practice: The effects of self-assessment in a study of special education students' internships. *Teacher Education and Special Education, 18,* 56–71.

Grossman, P. L., & Richert, A. E. (1988). Unacknowledged knowledge growth: A reexamination of the effects of teacher education. *Teaching and Teacher Education, 4,* 53–62.

Grossman, P. L., Valencia, S., Evans, K., Thompson, C., Martin, S., & Place, N. (2000). Transitions into teaching: Learning to teach writing in teacher education and beyond. *Journal of Literacy Research, 32,* 631–662.

Guskey, T. R. (1995). Professional development in education: In search of the optimal mix. In T. R. Guskey & M. Huberman (Eds.), *Professional development in education: New paradigms and practices* (pp. 114–134). New York: Teachers College Press.

Harmon, J., Hendrick, W., Martinez, M., Perez, B., Strecker, S., & Fine, J. C. (2001). *Features of excellence of reading teacher preparation programs*. Unpublished manuscript.

Hawk, P. P., Coble, C. R., & Swanson, M. (1985). Certification: It does matter. *Journal of Teacher Education, 36,* 13–15.

Hazareesingh, N., & Bielawski, L. (1991). The effects of cognitive self-instruction on student teachers' perceptions of control. *Teaching and Teacher Education, 7,* 383–393.

Hess, F. M. (2001). *Tear down this wall: The case for a radical overhaul of teacher certification.* Washington, DC: Progressive Policy Institute. Retrieved May 11, 2004, from http://www.ppionline.org/documents/teacher_certification.pdf.

Hutchinson, N. L., & Martin, A. K. (1999). Fostering inclusive beliefs and practices during preservice teacher education through communities of practice. *Teacher Education and Special Education, 22,* 234–250.

Joyce, B. R. (1988). Training research and preservice teacher education: A reconsideration. *Journal of Teacher Education, 39,* 32–36.

Joyce, B. R., & Showers, B. (1982). *Transfer of training: The contribution of coaching.* Eugene, OR: Center for Educational Policy and Management.

Joyce, B. R., Weil, M., & Wald, R. (1981). Can teachers learn repertoires of models of teaching? In B. R. Joyce, L. Peck, & C. Browne (Eds.), *Flexibility in teaching* (pp. 141–156). New York: Longman.

Kennedy, M. M. (1991). *Research genres in teacher education* (Issue Paper 91-1). East Lansing: Michigan State University, National Center for Research on Teacher Learning.

Kennedy, M. M. (1999). Approximations to indicators of student outcomes. *Educational Policy and Analysis, 21,* 345–363.

Kolar, C., & Dickson, S. V. (2002). Preservice general educators' perceptions of structured reflective logs as viable learning tools in a university course on inclusionary practices. *Teacher Education and Special Education, 25,* 395–406.

Laczko, I., & Berliner, D. C. (2001, April). *The effects of teacher certification on student achievement: An analysis of the Stanford Nine.* Paper presented at the annual meeting of the American Educational Research Association, Seattle, WA.

Langone, J., Malone, D. M., & Clinton, G. N. (1999). The effects of technology-enhanced anchored instruction on the knowledge of preservice special educators. *Teacher Education and Special Education, 22,* 85–96.

Levin, B., Hibbard, K., & Rock, T. (2002). Using problem-based learning as a tool for learning to teach students with special needs. *Teacher Education and Special Education, 25,* 278–290.

Levine, R., Campeau, P., Doorlag, D., & Cegelka, P. (1994, November). *Attrition of special education and regular education teachers in California: Analyses of CBEDS data.* Paper presented at the annual meeting of the Teacher Education Division of the Council for Exceptional Children, San Diego, CA.

Mallette, B., Maheady, L., & Harper, G. F. (1999). The effects of reciprocal peer coaching on preservice general educators' instruction of students with special learning needs. *Teacher Education and Special Education, 22,* 201–216.

McLeskey, J., Tyler, N, C., & Flippin, S. S. (2004). The supply and demand of special education teachers: The nature of the chronic shortage of special education teachers. *The Journal of Special Education, 38,* 5–21.

McNaughton, D., Hall, T. E., & Maccini, P. (2001). Case-based instruction in special education teacher preparation: Practices and concerns of teacher educator/researchers. *Teacher Education and Special Education, 24,* 84–94.

Miller, D., Brownell, M. T., & Smith, S. (1999). Factors that predict teachers staying in, leaving, or transferring from the special education classroom. *Exceptional Children, 65,* 201–218.

Monk, D. H. (1994). Subject area preparation of secondary mathematics and science teachers and student achievement. *Economics of Education Review, 13,* 125–145.

Morvant, M., Gersten, R., Gillman, J., Keating, T., & Blake, G. (1995). *Attrition/retention of urban special education teachers: Multifaceted research and strategic action planning.* Final performance report (Vol. 1). Eugene: Oregon Research Institute. (ERIC Document Reproduction Service No. ED 338 154)

National Center for Research on Teacher Learning. (1991). *Findings from the teacher education and learning to teach study.* East Lansing: Michigan State University College of Education, National Center for Research on Teacher Learning.

National Commission on Excellence in Elementary Teacher Preparation for Reading Instruction. (2003). *Prepared to make a difference.* Newark, DE: International Reading Association.

No Child Left Behind Act of 2001, 20 U.S.C. 70 § 6301 *et seq.* (2002).

Nougaret, A. A., Scruggs, T. E., & Mastropieri, M. A. (2005). Does teacher education produce better special education teachers? *Exceptional Children, 71,* 217–229.

Nowacek, E. J., & Blanton, L. P. (1996). A pilot project investigating the influence of a collaborative methods course on preservice elementary education teachers. *Teacher Education and Special Education, 19,* 298–312.

Peterson, S. K., & Hudson, P. J. (1989). Coaching: A strategy to enhance preservice teacher behaviors. *Teacher Education and Special Education, 12,* 56–60.

Phillips, B., & Halle, J. (2004). The effects of a teacher-training intervention on student interns' use of naturalistic language teaching strategies. *Teacher Education and Special Education, 27,* 81–96.

Pindiprolu, S. S., Peck Peterson, S. M., Rule, S., & Lignugaris/Kraft, B. (2003). Using web mediated experiential case-based instruction to teach functional behavioral assessment skills. *Teacher Education and Special Education, 26,* 1–16.

Popkewitz, T., Tabachnick, B. R., & Zeichner, K. M. (1979). Dulling the senses: Research in teacher education. *Journal of Teacher Education, 30,* 52–60.

Powell, R. (2000). Case-based teaching in homogeneous teacher education contexts: A study of preservice teachers' situative cognition. *Teaching and Teacher Education, 16,* 389–410.

Reiman, A. (1999). The evolution of the social roletaking and guided reflection framework in teacher education: Recent theory and quantitative synthesis of research. *Teaching and Teacher Education, 15,* 597–612.

Richards, S. B., Hunley, S., Weaver, R., & Landers, M.

(2003). A proposed model for teaching collaboration skills to general and special education preservice candidates. *Teacher Education and Special Education, 26,* 246–250.

Rolider, A., Pierce, M. M., & Van Houten, R. (1985). The effects of a comprehensive feedback component on the preparation of preservice educators. *Teacher Education and Special Education, 8,* 17–24.

Rosenberg, M. S., & Sindelar, P. T. (2005). The proliferation of alternative routes to certification in special education: A critical review of the literature. *The Journal of Special Education, 39,* 117–127.

Ross, D. D., Bondy, E., & Kyle, D. (1993). *Reflective teaching for student empowerment.* New York: Macmillan.

Sindelar, P. T., Daunic, A., & Rennells, M. S. (2004). Comparisons of traditionally and alternatively trained teachers. *Exceptionality, 12,* 209–223.

Stofflett, R., & Stoddart, T. (1992, April). *Patterns of assimilation and accommodation in traditional and conceptual change teacher education courses.* Paper presented at the annual meeting of the American Educational Research Association, San Francisco, CA.

Tschantz, J. M., & Vail, C. O. (2000). Effects of peer coaching on the rate of responsive teacher statements during a child-directed period in an inclusive preschool setting. *Teacher Education and Special Education, 23,* 189–201.

Tulbert, B., Sindelar, P. T., Correa, V. I., & La Porte, M. M. (1996). Looking in the rear view mirror: A content analysis of teacher education and special education. *Teacher Education and Special Education, 19,* 248–261.

U.S. Department of Education. (1998). *Twentieth annual report to Congress.* Washington, DC: Author.

Walsh, K. (2001). *Teacher certification reconsidered: Stumbling for quality.* Baltimore: The Abell Foundation. Retrieved May 11, 2004, from http://www.abell.org/publications/detail.asp?ID=59.

Weinstein, C. S. (1990). Prospective elementary teachers' beliefs about teaching: Implications for teacher education. *Teaching and Teacher Education, 6,* 279–290.

Welch, M., & Brownell, K. (2002). Are professionals ready for educational partnerships? The evaluation of a technology-enhanced course to prepare educators for collaboration. *Teacher Education and Special Education, 25,* 133–144.

Werts, M. G., Mamlin, N., & Pogoloff, S. M. (2002). Knowing what to expect: Introducing preservice teachers to IEP meetings. *Teacher Education and Special Education, 25,* 413–418.

Wideen, M., Mayer-Smith, J., & Moon, B. (1998). A critical analysis of the research on learning to teach: Making the case for an ecological perspective on inquiry. *Review of Educational Research, 68,* 130–178.

Wilson, S. M., Floden, R. E., & Ferrini-Mundy, J. (2001). *Teacher preparation research: Current knowledge, gaps, and recommendations.* Seattle: University of Washington Press.

Zeichner, K. M. (1999). The new scholarship in teacher education. *Educational Researcher, 28,* 4–15.

Zeichner, K. M., & Gore, J. M. (1990). Teacher socialization. In W. R. Houston (Ed.), *Handbook of research on teacher education* (pp. 329–348). New York: Macmillan.

Zeichner, K. M., & Tabachnick, B. R. (1981). Are the effects of teacher education washed out by school experience? *Journal of Teacher Education, 32,* 7–11.

Chapter 10

Where Should Students With Disabilities Receive Special Education Services?

Is One Place Better Than Another?

Naomi Zigmond

The question of *where* special education students should be educated is not new. Lloyd Dunn raised the question in 1968 and response to his article spurred the adoption of resource room services in place of special day classes in the 1970s. The question was raised again with the passage of P.L. 94-142, the Education of All Handicapped Children Act (EHA, 1975), and its balanced support for a continuum of services on the one hand and for placement in the least restrictive environment on the other. P.L. 94-142 required that procedures be established

> to assure that, to the maximum extent appropriate, handicapped children . . . are educated with children who are not handicapped and that . . . removal of handicapped children from the regular educational environment occurs only when the nature or severity of that handicap is such that education in regular classes with the use of supplemental aids and services cannot be achieved satisfactorily. (EHA, 1975, Part B, Section 612(5)(B))

The first annual report to Congress (U.S. Department of Health, Education, and Welfare, 1979) provided a succinct summary of this balanced position. The argument went as follows. The courts, in 1819, in *McCulloch v. Maryland*, maintained that government's purpose is served with as little imposition on the individual as possible, and if less dramatic means for achieving the same basic purpose can be found, the less dramatic means are to be taken. Years later, with respect to students with disabilities, this court decision was interpreted to mean that children with disabilities should be educated in as normal a setting as possible. That interpretation was supported by the wave of civil rights litigation in the late 1960s and early 1970s, most notably *Brown v. Board of Education* (1954) and *Pennsylvania Association for Retarded Citizens (PARC) v. Commonwealth of Pennsylvania* (1972). PARC, and the subsequent *Mills v. Board of Education of the District of Columbia* (1972) case, established the proposition that, given two or more alternative educational settings, children with disabilities should be placed in the least drastic or most normal setting appropriate, with as little interference and as normal an educational process as possible.

Court cases established the principle of least restrictiveness, but they were only part of the story. State and federal legislation reiterated the principle. Well before the federal legislation became effective, the principle of least restrictiveness embodied in the PARC agreement was clearly established in the laws, statutes, or regulations of at least 20 states. In fact, the first annual report to Congress (U.S. Department of Health, Education, and Welfare, 1979) proudly proclaimed that even in 1976–77, the school year preceding full implementation of the new federal law, "many handicapped children are already receiving their education in a regular classroom setting and appropriate alternative placements are in most cases available to accommodate children with special needs" (p. 39). Over the next decades, efforts would be made to move services for students with disabilities from separate schools to regular schools, with students with disabilities integrated (mainstreamed) into regular education classes for part of the school day and provided pull-out itinerant, resource, or part-time special class special education services for the rest of the day.

The question of *where* students with disabilities should be educated was hotly debated again in the mid-1980s, as essays on the failure of pull-out special education began to proliferate. The theme was consistent: Fundamental changes in the delivery model for special education were needed to increase the accomplishments of students with disabilities. Even Madeline Will, then Assistant Secretary of Education and head of the Office of Special Education Programs, joined the fray. "Although well intentioned, the so-called 'pull out' approach to the educational difficulties of students with learning problems has failed in many instances to meet the educational needs of these students," she wrote in 1986 (p. 413). Will and other advocates of the Regular Education Initiative (REI) called for completely integrated educational experiences for children with learning problems to achieve "improved educational outcomes" (Will, p. 413), "academic growth" (Gartner & Lipsky, 1989, p. 21), and "better outcomes" (National Association of State Boards of Education, 1992, p. 4).

In the 1997 reauthorization of the Individuals with Disabilities Education Act of 1990 (IDEA Amendments of 1997), the question of *where* was raised again, but with a new urgency. Whereas earlier definitions of "restrictiveness" had focused on *access* of students with disabilities *to nondisabled peers*, the new focus defined restrictiveness in terms of *access to the general education curriculum*. With the additional requirement that students with disabilities participate in (and perform respectably on) statewide assessments, pressures to favor one kind of placement (inclusion in the general education *classroom*) over any other (providing pull-out services in some other place) mounted.

McKinney and Hocott (1988) a decade earlier had explained that "part of the rationale for totally integrated [as compared to pull-out] programs for mildly handicapped students is based on research that questions the efficacy of special education" (p. 15). But how solid is the research evidence indicating that any one particular place, or service delivery model, can achieve better outcomes for students with disabilities? In this article I will review research studies and research reviews that address the question of *place*. I will argue, as many others have before me, that research evidence on the relative efficacy of one special education *placement* over another is scarce, methodologically flawed, and inconclusive. But I will also argue that, in practical terms, "Where should students with disabilities be educated?" is the wrong question to ask. The question is antithetical to the kind of individualized planning that should be embodied in decision making for and with students with disabilities. And the question fails to specify "where, for what, and for whom?" I will argue for new ways of thinking about the problem and of conducting research before progress can be made on improving results for students with disabilities.

One caveat before proceeding. Although I will limit myself to the research literature in which students with "mild" and "moderate" disabilities are studied, I strongly believe that the arguments I will make have merit across the entire range of students with disabilities promoted and protected by IDEA.

Efficacy Studies on Place

For more than 3 decades, special education researchers and scholars have researched, and synthesized research, on the relative usefulness of one place or another for serving students with disabilities. On the basis of a half-dozen studies conducted in the 1960s and a review of research published by Kirk in 1964, Dunn (1968) concluded that there was no empirical support for educating students with mild disabilities in special classes. "Retarded pupils make as much or more progress in the regular grades as they do in special education [and] efficacy studies on special day classes for other mildly handicapped children, including the emotionally handicapped, reveal the same results" (p. 8). Although Dunn called for the abandonment of special day classes for students with mild disabilities, he argued persuasively for part-time pull-out special education services to meet their specialized educational needs.

Ten years later, in a narrative review of 17 studies, Sindelar and Deno (1978) concluded that resource rooms were more effective than regular classrooms in improving academic achievement of students with learning disabilities (LD). At about the same time, a meta-analysis of efficacy studies completed by Carlberg and Kavale (1980) reported more complex results. Carlberg and Kavale's calculations of effect sizes showed that students with mental retardation in special class placements performed as well, academically, as those placed in regular grades. But they also showed a modest academic advantage for students with learning or behavior disorders in special classes (both self-contained and resource programs) over those remaining in the regular class. Leinhardt and Pallay (1982) also concluded from their research review that resource rooms were better than regular placements for students with LD. And 1 year later, Madden and Slavin (1983) reviewed seven studies on the efficacy of part-time resource placements compared to full-time special education classes and full-time placement in the mainstream, and they concluded that if increased academic achievement is the desired outcome, "the research favors placement in regular classes . . . *supplemented by well designed resource programs*" (p. 530, emphasis added).

Research support for supplemental resource room services was, however, overlooked in the national frenzy to reshape special education that swept the country in the mid-1980s. With the introduction of newer, more inclusive service delivery models, the early research comparing special pull-out placements with regular class placements seemed dated and irrelevant. In those earlier studies, it was easy to draw stark contrasts between regular class placements, where no special services were available to students with disabilities, and pull-out services staffed by trained teachers who provided special instruction. In the newer service delivery models, particularly the full inclusion models for students with mild/moderate disabilities, which utilized special education teachers in consulting or coteaching roles, students with disabilities were supposed to be receiving specially designed instruction or supplemental aids and services right in the general education classroom without having to be pulled out. Research documenting student progress in these new inclusive settings was needed, and it proliferated.

Some studies seemed to show positive trends when students were integrated into general education classrooms (see Affleck, Madge, Adams, & Lowenbraun, 1988; Baker, Wang, & Walberg, 1995; Deno, Maruyama, Espin, & Cohen, 1990; Schulte, Osborne, & McKinney, 1990; Walther-Thomas, 1997). Some researchers found that full-time placement in a general education classroom resulted in student academic progress that was just as good as that achieved by students in separate settings in elementary schools (see Banerji & Dailey, 1995; Bear & Proctor, 1990). But others reported academic and social achievement results from inclusion models that were disappointing or unsatisfactory (see Fox & Ysseldyke, 1997; Saint-Laurent, Dionne, Glasson, Royer, Simard, & Pierard, 1998; Sale & Carey, 1995; Vaughn, Elbaum, & Boardman, 2001; Zigmond & Baker, 1990; Zigmond et al., 1995). It should come as no surprise, then, that in a review of research on these newer special education service delivery models, Hocutt (1996) reported equivocal findings. She concluded, "Various program models, implemented in both general and special education, can have moderately positive academic and social impacts for student with disabilities" (p. 77). However, no intervention in the research literature eliminated the impact of having a disability. That is, regardless of the place of the intervention, students with disabilities did not achieve even at the level of low-achieving nondisabled peers. And no model was effective for *all* students with disabilities.

Manset and Semmel (1997) compared eight inclusion models for elementary students with mild disabilities, primarily LD, reported in the research literature between 1984 and 1994. They reiterated Hocutt's conclusions: Inclusive programs can be effective for *some* although not *all* students with mild disabilities. Waldron and McLeskey (1998) appeared to agree. In their research, students with severe LD made comparable progress in reading and math in pull-out and inclusion settings, although students with mild LD were more likely to make gains commensurate with those of nondisabled peers when educated in inclusive environments than when they were receiving special education services in a resource room.

Holloway (2001) reviewed five studies conducted between 1986 and 1996 comparing traditional pull-out services to fully inclusive service delivery models and models that combined in-class services with pull-out instruction. His conclusions did not offer strong support for the practice of full inclusion. Reading progress in the combined model was significantly better than in either the inclusion-only model or the resource room-only models.

In very recent research, Rea, McLaughlin, and Walther-Thomas (2002) used qualitative and quantitative methods to describe two schools and their special education models, one fully inclusive and one with more traditional supplemental pull-out services. Results showed that students served in inclusive schools earned higher grades, achieved higher or comparable scores on standardized tests, committed no more behavioral infractions, and attended more school days than students in the more traditional schools with pull-out programs.

In a review of coteaching as the inclusive service delivery model, Zigmond and Magiera (2002) found only four studies that focused on academic achievement gains. In the three elementary studies, coteaching was just as effective in producing academic gains as resource room instruction or consultation with the general education teacher; in the high school study, students' quiz and exam grades actually worsened following the coteaching experiment. Murawski and Swanson (2002), in their meta-analysis of the coteaching research literature, found six studies from which effect sizes could be calculated; dependent measures included grades, achievement scores, and social and attitudinal outcomes. Murawski and Swanson reported effect sizes for individual studies ranging from low to high, with an average total effect size in the moderate range. Both literature reviews on coteaching concluded that despite the current and growing popularity of coteaching as a service delivery model, further research is needed to determine whether it is an effective service delivery option for students with disabilities, let alone a preferred one.

Conclusions Derived From the Empirical Research Base

There would appear to be no simple and straightforward answer to the question of *where* students with disabilities should receive their special education instruction. The more than 3 decades of efficacy research reviewed here provides no compelling research evidence that *place* is the critical factor in the academic or social progress of students with mild/moderate disabilities. There are probably lots of reasons for reaching this conclusion, but I will suggest at least two. The first has to do with the body of research evidence itself. The second has to do with the appropriateness of the question.

Explanation 1: Research on Place Is Scarce, Methodologically Flawed, and Inconclusive

Even though the efficacy research literature on the *places* in which special education services are provided spans more than 3 decades, and even though dozens of studies have been reported in refereed special education journals, Murawski and Swanson (2002) are right to ask, "Where are the data?" (p. 258). Studies worthy of consideration in a meta-analysis or narrative literature review, with appropriate controls and appropriate dependent measures, are few and far between. Of course, research on the efficacy of special education placements is hard to conduct, let alone to conduct well. For example, definitions of service delivery models or settings vary from researcher to researcher and descriptions of the treatments being implemented in those models or settings are woefully inadequate. Random assignment of students to treatments is seldom an option, and appropriately matched (sufficiently alike) samples of experimental and control students and teachers are rare. As a result, *place* is not a phenomenon that lends itself to precise investigation, and funding for research studies and publication of results in refereed journals are difficult to achieve.

Methodologically Flawed Research. Research designs used to explore the effectiveness of different service delivery models often employ pre–post treatment group designs. The limitations of these research designs for studying the efficacy of special education have been reported in numerous previous research reviews, most notably in Kirk (1964) and Semmel, Gottleib, and Robinson (1979). Some studies use control groups, often samples of students experiencing "traditional" programs (sometimes referred to as business-as-usual) in nonexperimental schools. In some studies, the researchers manage to achieve random assignment of students to treatments, but most use intact groups of students assigned to the teacher or the school building who volunteered to participate in the experimental treatment program. Often the experimental treatment is well described, although degree of implementation is not. Descriptions of the control treatment and its degree of implementation (if indeed a control group is used) are rarely provided. Most often, treatment is not described sufficiently, nor is its implementation monitored sufficiently to make replication possible. So, even if reliable achievement changes are demonstrated in one research study, difficulty in identifying critical treatment variables makes replicability impossible in virtually all cases. Achievement gains, or lack thereof, cannot be related to replicable interventions, and the fundamental question of whether Place A is better than Place B cannot actually be answered.

Inconclusive Research. The accumulated evidence to date produces only one unequivocal finding. Languishing in a regular education class where nothing changes and no one pays you any attention is not as useful to students with mild/moderate learning and behavior disorders as getting some help, though it does not seem to matter for students with mild mental retardation. All other evidence on whether students with disabilities learn more, academically or socially, and are happier in one school setting or another is at best inconclusive. Resource programs are more effective for some students with disabilities than self-contained special education classes or self-contained general education classes, but they are less effective for other students with similar disabilities. Fully inclusive programs are superior for some students with disabilities on some measures of academic or social skills development, and inferior for other students or on other measures. The empirical research not only does not identify one best place, but also often finds equivalent progress being made by students with disabilities across settings; that is, the research reports nonsignificant differences in outcomes. Interpreting nonsignificant findings can be tricky. Do we conclude that the proverbial cup is half full or half empty? Do we acknowledge that it doesn't matter where students receive their special education services and allow parents or school personnel wide latitude in making choices? Or do we proclaim that one setting is preferred over another for philosophical or moral reasons with empirical evidence that it "doesn't hurt?"

Explanation 2: Efficacy Studies Have Been Asking the Wrong Question

Failure to Specify "Best for Whom?" Special education has evolved as a means of providing specialized interventions to students with disabilities based on individual student progress on individualized objectives. The bedrock of special education is instruction focused on *individual* need. The very concept of "one best place" contradicts this commitment to individualization. Furthermore, results of research on how *groups* of students respond to treatment settings do not help the researcher or practitioner make an individualized decision for an individual student's plan. A better question to ask, if we dare, is "best for whom?" or, for which individual students with which individual profiles of characteristics and needs? An answer to this question would require that we abandon the rhetoric in which we call for *all* students to do this, *all* students to learn that, or *all* students be educated in this place or that one.

Special educators understand about individual differences. Special educators understand that no matter how hard they try or how well they are taught, there are some students who will never be able to learn on the same schedule as most others, there are some students who will take so long to learn some things that they will have to forego learning other things, and there are some students who will need to be taught curricular content not ordinarily taught. Special educators understood this when they fought hard for the legal requirement of the Individualized Education Program for children with disabilities, to permit formulation of unique programs of instruction to meet unique individual needs. By continuing to frame the research question as "what's the best place?" we are ignoring what we know.

Reframing the question to "best for whom?" would also require new research designs and data analysis. A first step in that direction might be to reanalyze group design data at the individual student level. For example, in Zigmond et al. (1995), the researchers collected achievement test data for 145 students with LD in three full inclusion programs, as well as data on many of their nondisabled classmates. Rather than reporting average growth of the students with LD, the researchers reported the number and percentage of students with LD who made reliably significant gains (i.e., gains exceeded the standard error of measurement of the reading test) during the experimental year. They also reported on the number and percentage of students with LD whose reading gains matched or exceeded the average gain of their grade-level peers. And finally, they reported on the number and percentage of students with LD whose achievement status (i.e., their relative standing in the grade-level peer group) had improved during the school year. These analytic techniques allowed for the exploration of setting effects individual by individual. Waldron and McLeskey followed this same tactic in their 1998 study. Unfortunately, neither group of researchers took the final step of describing individual participants in sufficient detail to permit generalization of the findings or extrapolation of the findings to the individual case. Nevertheless, this approach seems more promising than more traditional approaches in terms of answering the question "best for whom?"

Failure to Specify "Best for What?" Different settings offer different opportunities for teaching and learning. The general education classroom allows for access to students who do not have disabilities, access to curricula and textbooks to which most other students are exposed, access to instruction from a general education teacher whose training and expertise are quite different from those of a special education teacher, access to subject matter content taught by a subject matter specialist, and access to all of the stresses and strains associated with the preparation for, taking of, and passing or failing the statewide assessments. If the goal is to have students learn content subject information, or learn how to interact with nondisabled peers, the general education setting is the place to do that.

Pull-out settings allow for smaller teacher–student ratios and flexibility in the selection of texts, choice of curricular objectives, pacing of instruction, scheduling of examinations, and assignment of grades. Special education pull-out settings allow students to learn different "stuff" in different ways and on a different schedule. If students need instruction in basic academic skills that is a lot more intensive than that being provided to their nondisabled peers, if students need explicit instruction in controlling behavior or interacting with peers and adults, or if students need to learn anything that is not customarily taught to everyone else, a pull-out special education setting may be more appropriate.

If educators value "different" and "special" and want to preserve that feature of special education, it is legitimate to ask whether the general education classroom can be transformed to support it. Or, as D. Fuchs and Fuchs (1995, p. 528) asked, "Can general education become special education?" Their experience (and mine) suggests strongly that the answer to this question is "no." Attempts to transport teaching methods developed and validated in special education to general education settings have not been successful. Instructional practices that focus on individual decision making for individual students and improve outcomes of students with severe learning problems are not easily transposed into practices that can survive in a general education classroom. General educators will make instructional adaptations in response to students' persistent failure to learn, but the accommodations are typically oriented to the group, not to the individual, and are relatively minor in substance, with little chance for helping students with chronically poor learning histories (Zigmond & Baker, 1995).

Over and over again, researchers and staff development personnel have come to recognize that general education teachers carry with them a different set of assumptions about the form and function of education than do special educators. General educators cannot imagine focusing intensively on the individual student, so that different instructional activities for different students are being implemented at the same time. This is simply impractical in a classroom of 25 to 35 students. Moreover, special education's most basic article of faith, that instruction must be individualized to be truly effective, is rarely contemplated, let alone observed, in most general education classrooms. Mainstream teachers must consider the good of the group and the extent to which the learning activities they present maintain classroom flow, orderliness, and cooperation. And they generally formulate teaching plans that result in a productive learning environment for 90% or more of their students. General education settings are best for learning what "everyone" needs to learn.

For many of the remaining 10% of students, however, a different orientation is likely to be needed. These students need to learn something different because they are clearly not learning what everyone else is learning. Interventions that might be effective for this group of students require a considerable investment of time and effort, as well as extensive support. Special education in a pull-out setting, with its emphasis on empirically validated practices and its use of data-based decision making to tailor instruction to the individual student's needs, might be better for the learning these students need to do.

Conclusion

As early as 1979, federal monitoring of state programs was put into place not only to guard against too much segregation of students with disabilities but also to guard against "inappropriate mainstreaming" (U.S. Department of Health, Education, and Welfare, 1979, p. 39). Although most would agree that students with mild and moderate disabilities should spend a large proportion of the school day with peers without disabilities, research does not support the superiority of any one service delivery model over another. Furthermore, effectiveness depends not only on the characteristics and needs of a particular student but also on the quality of the program's implementation. A poorly run model with limited resources will seldom be superior to a model in which there is a heavy investment of time, energy, and money. Good programs can be developed in any setting; so can bad ones. *Setting is less important than what is going on in the setting.*

So, reflecting on the present review of 35 years of efficacy research on the settings in which special education is delivered, what do we know? We know that what goes on in a place is what makes the difference, not the location itself. We know that you learn what you spend time on, and that most students with disabilities will not learn to read or to write or to calculate if not explicitly taught. We know that some instructional practices are easier to implement and more likely to occur in some settings than in others. We know that we need more research that asks better and more focused questions about who learns what best where. And, we know that we need to explore new research designs and new data analysis techniques that will help us bridge the gap between efficacy findings and decision making on placements for individual students.

In response to the query of what is special about special education, I can say with some certainty that *pla*ce is not what makes special education "special" or effective. Effective teaching strategies and an individualized approach are the more critical ingredients in special education, and neither of these is associated solely with one particular environment. That said, educators must also remember that typical general education environments have been shown in research not to be supportive places in which to implement what are known to be effective teaching strategies for students with disabilities (e.g., Zigmond, 1996). On the basis of research evidence to date, placement decisions must continue to be made by determining whether a particular placement option will support those effective instructional practices that are required for a particular child to achieve his or her individual objectives and goals.

The search for the best place in which to receive special education services has tended to be fueled by passion and principle rather than by reason and rationality. Until educators are ready to say that receiving special education services in a particular setting is good for some students with disabilities but not for others; that different educational environments are more conducive to different forms of teaching and learning; that different students need to learn different things in different ways; and that traditional group research designs may not capture these individual differences in useful ways, we may never get beyond the equivocal findings reported here. We may even fail to realize that, in terms of the best place to receive special education and related services, we have probably been asking the wrong questions.

REFERENCES

Affleck, J., Madge, S., Adams, A., & Lowenbraun, S. (1988). Integrated classroom versus resource model: Academic viability and effectiveness. *Exceptional Children, 54,* 339–348.

Baker, E. T., Wang, M., & Walberg, H. J. (1995). The effects of inclusion on learning. *Educational Leadership, 53*(4), 33–35.

Banerji, M., & Dailey, R. (1995). A study of the effects of an inclusion model on students with specific learning disabilities. *Journal of Learning Disabilities, 28,* 511–522.

Bear, G. G., & Proctor, W. A. (1990). Impact of a full-time integrated program on the achievement of non-handicapped and mildly handicapped children. *Exceptionality, 1,* 227–238.

Brown v. Board of Education, 347 U.S. 483 (1954).

Carlberg, C., & Kavale, K. (1980). The efficacy of special versus regular class placement for exceptional children: A meta-analysis. *The Journal of Special Education, 14,* 295–309.

Deno, S., Maruyama, G., Espin, C., & Cohen, C. (1990). Educating students with mild disabilities in general education classrooms: Minnesota alternatives. *Exceptional Children, 57,* 150–161.

Dunn, L. M. (1968). Special education for the mildly retarded—Is much of it justifiable? *Exceptional Children, 35,* 5–22.

Education of All Handicapped Children Act of 1975, 20 U.S.C. § 1400 *et seq.* (1975).

Fox, N. E., & Ysseldyke, J. E. (1997). Implementing inclusion at the middle school level: Lessons from a negative example. *Exceptional Children, 64,* 81–98.

Fuchs, D., & Fuchs, L. (1995). What's "special" about special education? *Phi Delta Kappan, 76,* 522–530.

Gartner, A., & Lipsky, D. K. (1989). *The yoke of special education: How to break it.* Washington, DC: National Center on Education and the Economy.

Hocutt, A. M. (1996). Effectiveness of special education: Is placement the critical factor? *The Future of Children, 6,* 77–102.

Holloway, J. (2001). Inclusion and students with learning disabilities. *Educational Leadership,* 57(6), 86–88.

Individuals with Disabilities Education Act of 1990, 20 U.S.C. § 1400 *et seq.* (1990) (Amended 1997).

Kirk, S. A. (1964). Research in education. In H. A. Stevens & R. Heber (Eds.), *Mental retardation: A review of research* (pp. 57–99). Chicago: University of Chicago Press.

Leinhardt, G., & Pallay, A. (1982). Restrictive educational settings? Exile or haven. *Review of Educational Research, 52,* 557–578.

Madden, N. A., & Slavin, R. E. (1983). Mainstreaming students with mild handicaps: Academic and social outcomes. *Review of Educational Research, 53,* 519–569.

Manset, G., & Semmel, M. I. (1997). Are inclusive programs for students with mild disabilities effective? A comparative review of model programs. *The Journal of Special Education, 31,* 155–180.

McCulloch v. Maryland, 4 Wheat 316, U.S. Ed. 579 (1819).

McKinney, J. D., & Hocott, A. M. (1988). Policy issues in the evaluation of the Regular Education Initiative. *Learning Disabilities Focus, 4*(1), 15–23.

Mills v. Board of Education of the District of Columbia, 348 F. Supp. 866, 880 (1972).

Murawski, W. W., & Swanson, H. L. (2002). A meta-analysis of co-teaching research: Where are the data? *Remedial and Special Education, 22,* 258–267.

National Association of State Boards of Education. (1992). *Winners all: A call for inclusive schools.* Alexandria, VA: Author.

Pennsylvania Association for Retarded Citizens v. Commonwealth of Pennsylvania, 343 F. Supp. 279, Consent Agreement (1972).

Rea, P. J., McLaughlin, V. L., & Walther-Thomas, C. (2002). Outcomes for students with learning disabilities in inclusive and pull-out programs. *Exceptional Children, 68,* 203–222.

Saint-Laurent, L., Dionne, J., Glasson, J., Royer, E., Simard, C., & Pierard, B. (1998). Academic achievement effects of an in-class service model on students with and without disabilities. *Exceptional Children, 64,* 239–253.

Sale, P., & Carey, D. M. (1995). The sociometric status of students with disabilities in a full-inclusion school. *Exceptional Children, 62,* 6–19.

Schulte, A. C., Osborne, S. S., & McKinney, J. D. (1990). Academic outcomes for students with learning disabilities in consultation and resource programs. *Exceptional Children, 57,* 162–172.

Semmel, M. I., Gottlieb, J., & Robinson, N. (1979). Mainstreaming: Perspectives in educating handicapped children in the public schools. In D. Berliner (Ed.), *Review of research in education* (pp. 223–279). Itaska, IL: Peacock.

Sindelar, P. T., & Deno, S. L. (1978). The effectiveness of resource programming. *The Journal of Special Education, 12,* 17–28.

U.S. Department of Health, Education, and Welfare. (1979). *Progress toward a free appropriate public education: A report to Congress on the implementation of Public Law 94-142, the Education for All Handicapped Children Act.* Washington, DC: U.S. Government Printing Office.

Vaughn, S., Elbaum, B. E., & Boardman, A. G. (2001). The social functioning of students with learning disabilities: Implications for inclusion. *Exceptionality, 9,* 47–65.

Waldron, N. L., & McLeskey, J. (1998). The effects of an inclusive school program on students with mild and severe learning disabilities. *Exceptional Children, 64,* 395–405.

Walther-Thomas, C. (1997). Co-teaching experiences: The benefits and problems that teachers and principals report over time. *Journal of Learning Disabilities, 30,* 395–407.

Will, M. C. (1986). Educating children with learning problems: A shared responsibility. *Exceptional Children, 52,* 411–415.

Zigmond, N. (1996). Organization and management of general education classrooms. In D. Speece & B. Keogh (Eds.), *Research on classroom ecologies: Implications for inclusion of children with learning disabilities* (pp. 163–190). Hillsdale, NJ: Erlbaum.

Zigmond, N., & Baker, J. M. (1990). Mainstreaming experiences for learning disabled students (Project MELD): Preliminary report. *Exceptional Children, 57,* 176–185.

Zigmond, N., & Baker, J. M. (1995). Concluding comments: Current and future practices in inclusive schooling. *The Journal of Special Education, 29,* 245–250.

Zigmond, N., & Magiera, K. (2002). Co-teaching. *Current Practice Alerts, 6,* 1–4.

Zigmond, N., Jenkins, J., Fuchs, L., Deno, S., Fuchs, D., Baker, J. N., Jenkins, L., & Coutinho, M. (1995). Special education in restructured schools: Findings from three multi-year studies. *Phi Delta Kappan, 76,* 531–540.

Chapter 11

Critical Dimensions of Experimental Studies and Research Syntheses That Help Define Effective Practices

John Wills Lloyd, Paige C. Pullen, Melody Tankersley, and **Patricia A. Lloyd**

The No Child Left Behind Act of 2001 (NCLB) stipulates that federally funded educational programs and practices must be grounded in scientifically based research "that involves the application of rigorous, systematic, and objective procedures to obtain reliable and valid knowledge relevant to education activities and programs" (NCLB, p. 126). This mandate, which was extended by language in the 2004 revision of the Individuals with Disabilities Education Act (Individuals with Disabilities Education Improvement Act of 2004), begs two questions: (a) How do we know if a research study involves rigorous, systematic, and objective procedures; and (b) how do we use the results of such research studies to identify educational practices that are effective for improving student outcomes?

Through empirical research, the field of special education has accumulated vast knowledge and achieved significant outcomes that have helped shape public policy and guide educational services for students with exceptional learning needs (for a discussion see Mostert & Crockett, 1999–2000). As with other areas of education, however, special education research has been a battleground for advocates of different philosophical persuasions (see, e.g., Crockett, 2001; Stanovich, 2003). Phenomenologists in various guises level criticisms at empiricists in their diverse costumes and vice versa. In educational scholarship, differences in philosophy align—not perfectly, but substantially—with major classes of research: Phenomenology and qualitative research cohabit while empiricism and quantitative research comingle. Our purpose in this chapter is not to take sides in that battle (though some may accuse us of bias), but to offer criteria by which to judge the utility of studies in creating a knowledge base about effective practices—those that lead to improved outcomes for students with disabilities. We then discuss the need for establishing a system to synthesize the results of such studies so that teachers of students with disabilities and other stakeholders (e.g., students, parents, teacher educators, administrators, legislators) can identify practices that provide the best evidence for effectiveness. We argue that establishing effective practices is a two-step process: (a) identify studies that meet critical criterion for assessing practices' efficacy and (b) determine whether specific practices have sufficient empirical support regarding their efficacy and utility, as indicated by the results of syntheses of a body of research, to warrant designation as effective practice.

The foundation for our argument is that improving outcomes for students with disabilities is not just a worthwhile endeavor but the foremost purpose of special education. To be sure, there are other scientifically and socially important purposes for research in special education and disabilities. Different types of research methods are essential for addressing the different types of questions that are important for building and documenting effective practices (Odom et al., 2005). However, in this chapter we are simply addressing questions about whether those practices have demonstrated efficacy.

To address the question "What practices are effective for improving student outcomes?" we must identify those studies that answer the question. Plainly put, teachers need to know what practices to institute Monday morning, parents want to determine whether their children are receiving effective education in their educational programs, teacher educators must instruct future teachers how to implement the most effective practices, and administrators should require effective practices as standard practices in their districts. Some research is more valuable in guiding how we determine effective educational practice than other research. By determining which research studies most reliably address the question of whether an educational intervention works and then synthesizing results from multiple research studies on a particular practice, we can evaluate the general efficacy of that practice.

One purpose of this chapter is to explicate where—within the extensive, broad, and diverse body of research about special education and disabilities—one should look for evidence that has the strongest implications for practice. We argue that there are three critical dimensions along which effectiveness studies differ and that studies that fall at one end of these dimensions are the most valuable to include in research syntheses used to determine effective practices. The second focus of the chapter is on research syntheses, the results of which can be evaluated against professional guidelines to establish whether specific practices are effective and warrant broad-scale implementation.

Determining Efficacy: Three Critical Dimensions of Research Design

In simplified fashion, we think it is sensible to consider three dimensions along which empirical research can vary that are critical to helping us know whether a given study can contribute to determining the effectiveness of a given practice. In this section we describe these three dimensions—credibility of measurement, representivity of sample, and falsifiability of questions—as a way of setting the stage for discussing what constitutes empirical research that can serve as the basis of our knowledge about practices that improve students' outcomes. By choosing to discuss design issues, we do not mean to denigrate the importance of other aspects of research. For example, replication across studies is critical in establishing the robustness and generality of findings (e.g., see Justice & Pullen, 2003; Lonigan, Elber, & Johnson, 1998). It deserves a discussion of its own, in fact. We have simply elected to focus on aspects of research design within studies that make some more valuable in contributing to the knowledge base of effective practice than others.

Credibility of Measurement

Although there is ample debate about the goals of education, we believe that a consensus of educators and researchers would agree with a focus on academic and social competence. People will disagree about whether any one given test reflects those outcomes adequately. We doubt that one does. For example, we could agree that reading competence is a desirable academic outcome for the vast majority of children in U.S. schools, but not be able to settle on whether Test M, Test N, or Test O is the best measure of reading competence. However, it is not necessary to settle the issue at such a specific level. Rather, we suggest that direct measures of reading performance, whether reported as a standard score or in a more molecular fashion (e.g., words read correctly per minute), yield more valuable results for determining the effects of a practice than measures that report tangential or related variables (e.g., teachers' ratings of students' reading competence, students' self-reports of their reading competence, students' central auditory processing competence). In general, measures that more directly and explicitly describe performance on tasks representative of consensus outcomes are more credible and, thus, are more valuable for identifying improved outcomes for students (see Table 1 for examples of more and less credible measures).

The dimension of credibility of measurement represents an amalgam of several related concepts. Not only does the dimension represent the importance of directly measuring the outcomes of concern, but it also refers to familiar concepts from psychometrics (reliability and validity) and the importance of using multiple outcome measures as opposed to only one measure. Studies that examine effects on several different outcomes—especially outcomes that show gen-

TABLE 1. Examples of Studies on the Dimension of Credibility of Measurement

Continuum placement	Description of measurement
Less credible measures	• Among other measures, researchers investigating a social skills program examined children's self-reported social competence (Weiner & Harris, 1997). • Researchers interviewed teachers to gain their perceptions of how cooperative learning benefits students (Jenkins, Antil, Wayne, & Vadasy, 2003).
Intermediate	• Researchers assessed correct academic responses per minute by analyzing students' written products and on-task behavior by determining the percentage of intervals when students were observed to be engaged in writing or other appropriate motor behavior (Miller, Gunter, Venn, Hummel, & Wiley, 2003).
More credible measures	• Dependent measures included (a) words read correctly per minute from grade-level material and (b) percentage of observation intervals when the student was engaged in academic tasks, measured with high inter-observer agreement (Burke, Hagan-Burke, & Sugai, 2003). • To assess reading competence, researchers used a battery of reliable, objective measures assessing performance on (a) timed phonological awareness tasks, (b) subtests of a standardized reading achievement test, (c) reading fluency, and (d) spelling words drawn from a standardized test (O'Connor, Notari-Syverson, & Vadasy, 1998). • Researchers assessed academic performance using the *Dynamic Indicators of Basic Early Literacy Skills* (DIBELS) and behavioral performance with the *Systematic Screening for Behavior Disorders* (SSBD), or *Early Screening Project,* which are well-recognized assessments with known reliability and validity (Kamps et al., 2003).

eralization or limitation of effects—help educators understand more about the benefits of intervention procedures than do studies that report only one outcome (Gersten, Baker, & Lloyd, 2000). Certainly, research that demonstrates outcome effectiveness is important, but it answers only one basic question—whether the practice improves performance. Research that demonstrates outcome effectiveness and documents how a practice affects or does not affect other related variables (e.g., measures of similar outcomes) helps even more.

We hasten to note that measures all along this continuum are informative. Certainly, there is benefit in knowing about teachers' perceptions of the effects of interventions such as cooperative learning, as illustrated in the report by Jenkins, Antil, Wayne, and Vadasy (2003). Indeed, even behaviorists have championed more subjective measures as having utility (Kazdin, 1977; Wolf, 1978). Social validity measures—participants' and others' acceptance of the goals, procedures, and outcomes of interventions—have been shown to be positively related to treatment fidelity, and treatment fidelity has a significant influence on outcomes (see Telzrow & Beebe, 2002).

Relatively subjective measures may be useful for a variety of legitimate purposes (see Gersten, this volume). For example, they may help special educators understand the nuances of variation among individuals, the social context of alternative actions, the chances of getting people to use effective practices, and even people's perceptions and use of interventions. However, because they do not directly measure the behavior or performance of students with disabilities—the defining outcome that determines the effectiveness of an educational intervention—they cannot be used to establish whether or the degree to which an instructional practice is effective.

Measures that fall closer to the more credible end of this continuum provide more valuable information for identifying the effects of practice

TABLE 2. Examples of Studies on the Dimension of Representivity of Sample

Continuum placement	Description of sample
Less representative	• Participant was one third-grade student; attended a suburban elementary school; Pacific Northwest (Burke, Hagan-Burke, & Sugai, 2003). • Participants were 19 pairs of biological siblings (*N* = 38), one with and one without a disability; 16 boys and 3 girls, ages 8–13 years; participants were from a medium-size, West Coast, metropolitan Canadian city (Dyson, 2003).
Intermediate	• Participants were 99 children, 4–6 years old (50 girls and 49 boys); located in southern California; represented low to upper middle class income levels (Mann & Foy, 2003). • Participants were 984 parents/primary caregivers and 698 general and special education teachers, randomly selected from two schools systems in one mid-Atlantic state (*n* = 496 who responded to survey); teachers and parents of students between the ages of 16 and 21; two urban school districts (Grigal, Neubert, Moon, & Graham, 2003).
More representative	• Participants were 3,356 students, ages 6–12 years during the 1999–2000 school year, randomly selected nationally, who received special education services from local education agencies (SEELS, 2004). • Sample included 827 first-grade classrooms in 747 schools in 32 states (National Institute of Child Health and Human Development, 2002).

because they tell us about how performance differs or changes in relation to the practice. Claims of effectiveness, then, can be related to direct changes in outcomes. To improve outcomes, we must know that performance differs or changes in the presence of the practice. Outcome measures that are objective, reliable, and valid provide this type of information.

Representivity of Sample

There are two critical issues related to the representivity of a sample: sample size and unbiased representation of the people to whom the methods apply. Study samples vary across a wide range (see Table 2 for examples of studies of various sample sizes). A study may have as few as one or as many as thousands or more participants. Furthermore, these participants may be included in a study based on various selection techniques: participants volunteer (self-selected), participants are available (convenience sample), or participants are selected randomly from either a small population (one classroom) or from the general population. Although a large number of participants selected randomly from a large population results in the most representative sample possible, random selection from the general population rarely, if ever, occurs in special education research.

It is quite reasonable to conduct a study of only one participant. Studies employing only one participant come from diverse traditions, including psychiatry, behavior analysis, and other areas. Regardless of the tradition from which an idiographic study emerges, it may provide valuable information about the effects of practice provided that it includes explicit measures of performance and falls more toward the experimental end of the continuum discussed next. That is, a small number of participants is not, by itself, a limiting factor in whether a study provides useful information. For example, we have learned about effective treatments for students with attention-deficit/hyperactivity disorder through a series of studies with relatively small samples, some employing single-subject methods (DuPaul & Eckert, 1997; Horner et al., 2005).

In contrast to idiographic research, other research in special education employs very many participants and also comes from many different traditions. In an analysis relevant to educational policy, Colarusso, Keel, and Dangle (2001), for example, examined more than 6,000 eligibility reports in their study of the contribution of eligibility criteria to proportional racial representation in learning disabilities. In contrast, Serna, Nielsen, Mattern, and Forness (2003) conducted an intervention study in which they examined the effects of an intervention delivered by teachers on the mental health status of 98 preschool children. Both of these studies employed larger numbers, and the study by Colarusso et al. had far more participants than the one reported by Serna et al. However, the number of participants in a study does not, by itself, make a study more or less valuable. Whereas the Colarusso et al. study was not about improving outcomes, the Serna et al. study was. Despite the larger number of participants in the Colarusso et al. study, its descriptive nature results in a lesser contribution for examining the effects of practices related to student outcomes. We will focus more on this issue in the next dimension, falsifiability of questions.

Regardless of whether only one, a few, or many students participate in a study, consumers of the research might legitimately wonder about the representivity of the participants. In fact, the importance of the number of participants is moderated by how representative the participants are of larger populations, particularly the population to which one hopes to generalize the results. When only one or a few participate in a study, representivity is achieved through replication (Johnston & Pennypacker, 1992). When many participate, representivity is achieved by randomly sampling from a population.

Despite these competing concerns, many people may champion large- or small-scale studies. Our view is that the number of participants alone is not the critical or deciding factor about whether a study can contribute to determining the effectiveness of specific practices. It is one of several important factors. Generally, as the number of participants increases, the chance of results having broad implications for practice also increases. However, the extent to which this general rule holds depends on the representivity of the sample and other factors, including the measurement dimension already discussed and especially the extent to which the design of a study allows one to test a true–false research question.

Falsifiability of Questions (Design)

Studies differ in purpose. In simple terms, some studies seek to describe how things are (i.e., descriptive) and others seek to determine change wrought by practice (i.e., experimental). To be sure, people might characterize studies as raising other sorts of questions: Do certain features of phenomena correspond? Why are things this way? Even these different characterizations of study purposes, we think, fall along a continuum ranging from descriptive to experimental research (see National Research Council, 2002; see Table 3 for examples of research questions in relation to this continuum).

Ethnographies, case studies (regardless of whether the case is an individual student or a statewide program), surveys, and correlational designs generally describe the conditions that exist. They usually examine research questions similar to those described in the section of Table 3 devoted to more descriptive studies. Ethnographic or case studies cannot make strong causal statements about the effects of interventions; they may present information related to outcome, but the holistic description of the process or group, not the magnitude of their outcome, is generally the focus of these designs.

Survey research aims to describe population characteristics (e.g., opinions, aptitudes, attitudes, beliefs, knowledge). Knowing what skills teachers think are important to teach, understanding the change in societal opinion of acceptable disciplinary procedures over time, documenting differences among parents' perceptions of Individualized Education Program (IEP) goals, and similar purposes of research are vital to the continued development and progress of the field. Descriptive studies (e.g., surveys) help with these issues. Although descriptive information about special education is important, it does not allow statements about effectiveness of interventions.

Correlational research is often called associational research, because the relationships between two or more variables are studied without

TABLE 3. Examples of Studies on the Dimension of Falsifiability

Continuum placement	Research question
More descriptive	• How do families' abilities to pay fees for services affect their control over decisions about the frequency and duration of services, and what are the consequences of paying for services on other aspects of their daily lives? (Shannon, Grinde, & Cox, 2003) • Do ratings of students with and without emotional disturbance differ on the major characteristics of emotional disturbance, and do those differences interact with other relevant variables, such as demographics? (Cullinan, Evans, Epstein, & Ryser, 2003)
Intermediate	• How well does fluency in naming letters and reading pseudo-words predict subsequent reading ability? (Speece, Mills, Ritchey, & Hillman, 2003) • Is the level of aggression in first-grade classrooms related to individual aggression in later years? (Kellam, Ling, Merisca, Brown, & Ialongo, 1998)
More experimental	• Do children having difficulty learning to read and randomly assigned to the "word building" intervention have greater decoding, phonemic awareness, and passage comprehension scores than controls assigned to a waiting-list condition? (McCandliss, Beck, Sandak, & Perfetti, 2003) • Does classwide instruction in following directions, sharing, and problem-solving skills improve children's outcomes on measures of mental health risk in Head Start children? (Serna, Nielsen, Lambros, & Forness, 2000)

an attempt to influence them. In fact, correlational studies are often conducted to determine what variables predict various outcomes. For example, correlational research has established a clear relationship between fluency in naming letters (LNF) in young children and later reading achievement (e.g., Speece, Mills, Ritchey, & Hillman, 2003; Speer & Lamb, 1976). This relationship alone, identified through correlational studies, does not establish a causal connection between the two variables—LNF and reading achievement. It is possible that increased LNF caused improved reading achievement, but it is also possible that improved reading performance caused enhanced LNF (or, possibly, that another variable caused both heightened reading achievement and LNF). Correlational studies may identify useful assessments and may provide the impetus for investigating whether a relationship is causal by conducting experimental studies. In the example of LNF and reading achievement, due to subsequent experimental investigations, we now have evidence that students receiving instruction in phonological awareness perform better than students who do not receive such instruction (e.g., McCandliss, Beck, Sandak, & Perfetti, 2003), but promoting LNF does not have to be part of the instruction.

As the previous example demonstrates, correlational studies have an important role in special education research. However, as with other nonexperimental designs, these studies do not explicitly demonstrate causal relationships about the effects of interventions. To promote social and academic outcomes, we need studies that investigate cause–effect relationships and, specifically, cause–effect relationships between interventions and student outcomes.

Experimental studies, those that randomly assign participants to experimental and control conditions, provide more powerful evidence of effects because they rule out other explanations for the results (Campbell & Stanley, 1963). For example, if a school adopts a new curriculum for fourth-grade science and finds that students with disabilities have significantly higher scores at the end of the year than they had at the beginning, no one can make a strong case that the growth was caused by the new curriculum. Perhaps the students would have had comparable growth with another curriculum or even no curriculum. To make sure that the curriculum caused the growth, one would need to have some of the students—randomly determined—receive the old curriculum (Old), the new curriculum (New), and another good curriculum (Good); then one can compare the growth for Old versus New, Old versus Good, and New versus Good.

By distinguishing between descriptive and experimental types of research, we are not proposing a broad value judgment. Studies all along this dimension can promote greater general understanding of a variety of phenomena related to special education. We propose that studies that fall farther toward the experimental end of the continuum provide results that lead more directly to understanding effectiveness of practice in relation to student outcome variables, but this proposal does not mean that educators might not learn something valuable from descriptive studies. For example, a descriptive study might reveal a strong correlation between some aspect of curricula and students' positive peer interactions. However, an experimental comparison of the presence and absence of that particular aspect of the curriculum would provide more valuable evidence about its effectiveness. The extent to which the experimental comparison controlled for alternative explanations would, of course, focus and refine the value of the evidence.

In general, the results of studies that compare performance under different conditions that are experimentally determined (see Campbell & Stanley, 1963) make it possible for educators to make statements about the effectiveness of practices. In establishing effectiveness, then, a study showing that students who receive a given method of instruction gain in their reading ability is not as beneficial as a study showing that students who receive that given method of instruction gain even more than other students who receive an alternative method of instruction (Gersten et al., 2000).

Determining Efficacy

Educators who seek to identify practices that are effective on the basis of research will find studies that show a wide variety of characteristics. Some of these studies contribute to the understanding of practices; however, only a select subset of these studies expressly establishes the extent to which the practice improved student outcomes. That subset can be defined by the three dimensions that we presented here: credibility of measurement, representivity of the sample, and falsifiability (design) of questions.

Nearly all studies will fall somewhere on the continua of these three dimensions. Figure 1 illustrates these three dimensions and lists characteristics on each end of the continua. Where a study falls on each continuum will determine, to a substantial degree, its contribution to our knowledge of the effects of practices for students with disabilities. A study that falls toward the right end of the credibility of measurement continuum is more valuable because it measures the specific outcomes in question and does so with measures that are trustworthy (see Table 1 for examples). Studies that include a larger, more representative sample—the right end of the second dimension—provide more opportunity to affect change because the methods tested can be applied to a greater number of individuals and a more specific population (see Table 2 for examples). Finally, studies that employ an experimental design eliminate or substantially reduce alternative explanations for changes in the study's outcomes, which results in greater certainty that a practice or procedure caused change (see Table 3 for examples).

Taken in aggregate, the arguments we have advanced here lead to the conclusion that some studies provide evidence that is valuable for identifying the effects of practices. Studies that have credible measures, larger samples, and use experimental designs allow us to have greater confidence in identifying the extent to which a practice resulted in greater outcomes for students on critical variables (social and academic measures). It is, then, to these studies we turn when seeking to accumulate evidence for determining practices that improve student outcomes. The next section of this chapter is devoted to discussing methods for synthesizing the empirical base of specific educational practices in order to determine which are effective for students with disabilities.

Credibility of Measurement

Less Credible	More Credible
Subjective **Lower or no reliability/validity reported**	**Direct measures of desired outcomes** **Objective** **Reliable** **Valid**

Representivity of the Sample

Less Representative	More Representative
***N* = 1** **Case studies** **No random sampling**	**Large sample size** **Random sampling from population**

Falsifiability of the Design

Descriptive	Causal
Observational **Correlational** **No random assignment to group**	**Experimental design** **Strong internal validity** **Random assignment to group**

FIGURE 1. Critical dimensions of research shown as continua with illustrative descriptors on the extremes.

Determining Effective Practices Through Synthesis

Although an individual study that has credible outcome measures, uses a representative sample, and permits clear causal conclusions provides more trustworthy evidence of the effects of practice than single studies not imbued with these characteristics, the results of any one study cannot fully determine whether a practice is effective and should have widespread implementation. In order to determine whether a practice is effective, professionals must develop guidelines for making decisions about the results of a body of knowledge—whether there is sufficient and strong evidence to endorse the practice as effective.

If a research question addresses the efficacy of a practice, the first step is to identify studies that have investigated the effects of that practice. Once the research is accumulated, criteria such as those outlined previously—employs credible outcome measures, uses representative samples, and permits clear causal conclusions—should be applied to identify studies to include in a synthesis. The final step is to amass a corpus of those studies and evaluate the results against professional guidelines for determining whether the practice is effective. Unfortunately, although there are general guidelines (e.g., Cooper & Hedges, 1994), to date special educators have not agreed on methods for determining how to synthesize studies and what guidelines to follow (see Vaughn & Dammann, 2001).

Methods for Synthesizing Studies

Although there are many approaches to synthesizing research (Cooper & Hedges, 1994), identifying effective practices requires that the knowledge base regarding a specific practice be aggregated in such a way that it can be used to determine whether the practice merits designation as effective. To our way of thinking, there are two ways to approach research synthesis for this purpose: (a) through statistical integration of the results (e.g., effect sizes) of individual studies and analyses investigating the effects of the practice and determining the overall level of effect of the practice or (b) by applying a criterion-based framework to the literature base and qualitatively determining that a sufficient number of methodologically sound studies indicating effectiveness of the practice have been conducted. These are not mutually exclusive methods; in fact, they are best when combined. It is important to note that for both of these methods, we maintain that the first step is identifying the studies of a particular practice that meet the criteria outlined here and including only those studies in the synthesis.

Statistical Integration (Meta-Analysis). In 1976, Glass presented a statistical method to integrate and summarize findings from a collection of individual studies. He called this method *meta-analysis*. Meta-analysis is applicable to collections of empirical studies that investigate comparable questions, produce quantitative results, examine the same constructs, and have findings that can be configured in a comparable statistical form. It provides one technique for statistically integrating research results.

The effect size is the key to meta-analysis. Effect size (*ES*) can be conceptualized as a standardized difference of means between groups. Any standardized index can serve as an effect size as long as it is comparable across studies, is independent of sample size, and represents the magnitude and direction of the relationship of interest. Mean effect sizes are calculated across the different investigations of a particular practice and categorized in relation to the statistical power of the overall mean. For example, Cohen (1988) described mean effect sizes of .20 as small, .50 as medium, and .80 as large. Figure 2 illustrates these effect sizes graphically using the familiar normal curve.

Using these same categories, researchers have conducted meta-analytic reviews of many specific practices in special education. For example, in a summary of 24 meta-analyses for effect size, Forness (2001) presented results that showed small effect sizes for eight practices, such as social skills training (*ES* = .20; Quinn, Kavale, Mathur, Rutherford, & Forness, 1999) and modality-based instruction (*ES* = .14; Kavale & Forness, 1987); medium effect sizes for eight practices, such as word recognition strategies (*ES* = .57; Swanson, 1999) and stimulant medication (*ES* = .67; Crenshaw, Kavale, Forness, & Reeve, 1999); and large effect sizes for four practices, such as Direct Instruction (*ES* = .84; White, 1988) and reading comprehension strategies (*ES* = 1.13; Talbott, Lloyd, & Tankersley, 1994).

With meta-analysis, effective practices can be identified using systematic and objective criteria that summarize results across studies investigating student outcome, the results of which can be compared to professional guidelines of effectiveness. By investigating the results of meta-analytic studies, teachers and other stakeholders can determine the impact of a particular practice across an entire body of research studies. As Forness (2001) pointed out in the conclusion of his review, based on the results of meta-analysis, teachers who use Direct Instruction and reading comprehension strategies, for example, should expect better student outcomes than teachers who use social skills training and modality-based instruction.

Criterion-Based Framework. A second approach to research synthesis is to apply a criterion-based framework to the body of research surrounding a practice. As with meta-analytic procedures, the first step is to identify and examine each study that has investigated the effects of a particular practice and to include for further consideration only results of studies that meet methodological criteria (i.e., employ direct measures of outcomes, have a representative sample, and test falsifiable questions). When the literature regarding a particular practice is exhausted, and the studies that meet the methodological criteria are identified, the results of those studies are synthesized and the level of effectiveness for that practice is determined.

Many professions have or are in the process of developing frameworks for establishing effec-

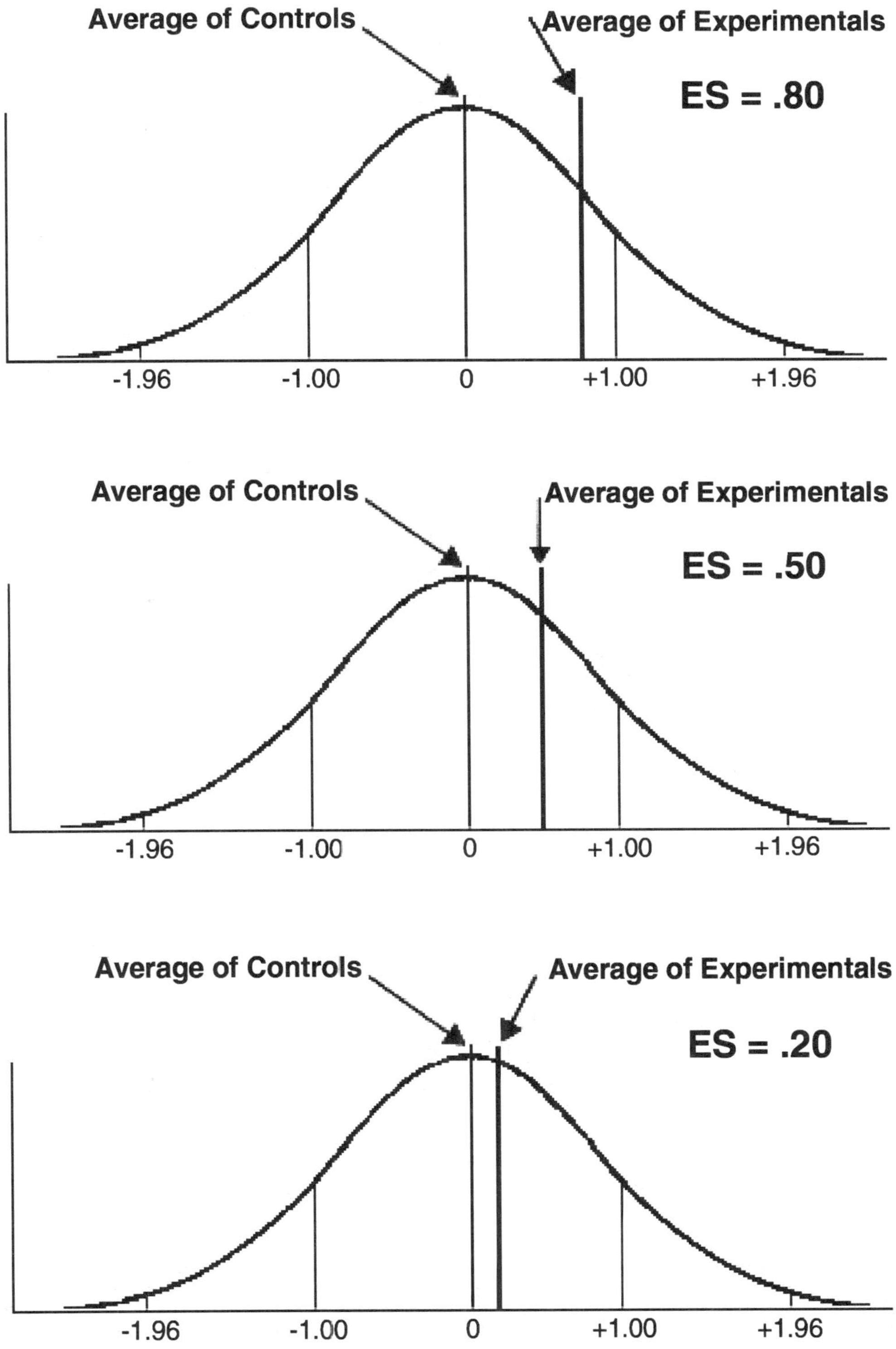

FIGURE 2. Cohen's standards for effect sizes. Normal curve represents the distribution of scores for the control conditions and the relative standing of the average score for the experimental condition (heavier line).

tive or evidence-based practices based on a set of criteria (Mosteller & Boruch, 2002; National Research Council, 2002; Stoiber & Kratochwill, 2000). For example, a criterion-based framework for establishing which treatments and practices warrant implementation, promotion, and dissemination was first developed in 1993 by the Division 12 Task Force of the American Psychological Association (APA). Two sets of criteria were established for defining a treatment as empirically supported: *well established* and *probably efficacious* (Chambless et al., 1998). To be identified as well established, a practice had to meet one of the following criteria:

> 1. At least two good between-group design experiments demonstrating efficacy in one or more of the following ways: (a) superior (statistically significantly so) to pill or psychological placebo or another treatment, (b) equivalent to an already established treatment in studies with adequate sample sizes.
> 2. A large series of single case design experiments ($n > 9$) demonstrating efficacy. These experiments must have (a) used good experimental designs and (b) compared the intervention to another treatment. (p. 4)

Further criteria for both 1 and 2 require that (a) studies be conducted with treatment manuals, (b) characteristics of the client samples must be clearly specified, and (c) effects must have been demonstrated by at least two different investigators or investigating teams. Moreover, the preponderance of evidence must be in favor of the practice's efficacy, with two positive studies (in the absence of contravening evidence) a minimum.

The work by Division 12 of APA is only one recent effort to promote the use of methodological criteria of research to determine effective practices. Other professional organizations also employ or are considering similar techniques for summarizing their knowledge base (e.g., Council for Exceptional Children, the Task Force on Evidence-Based Interventions in School Psychology, U.S. Department of Education's Institute of Education Sciences). The frameworks they use have established or will establish their specific methodological criteria and coding structures for determining which practices have sufficient empirical support to be deemed effective. Although all of the frameworks established across the different organizations may use different methodological criteria, most of the established coding structures provide support for our argument that only studies providing falsifiable tests can be used to determine effectiveness of a practice. For example, in all of the work group criteria reviewed by Chambless and Ollendick (2001), only experimental designs and series of single-case design experiments were considered to determine effective and efficacious outcomes.

Applying methodological criteria to a literature base results in the identification of effective practices that can be used to guide stakeholders' decision making. For example, in applying the Division 12 criteria, Chambless and Ollendick (2001) identified 108 empirically supported treatments for adults and 37 for children. These practices have been recommended as (a) the best methods for treating patients, (b) the foundations for training programs for psychologists, (c) the impetus for research, and (d) evidence for educating stakeholders and the public about the current knowledge base of psychology.

To date, the field of special education has yet to agree upon a criterion-based framework for identifying practices that are effective for improving the outcomes of students with disabilities (see Odom et al., 2005). However, in the fall of 2004 the Council for Exceptional Children's Division for Research published a report of their Task Force on Quality Indicators for Special Education. The executive summary of the task force presented quality indicators for research and guidelines for evidence-based practice (the executive summary is available online at http://interact.uoregon.edu/dr/Quality_Indicators.pdf). The resulting guidelines using experimental and quasi-experimental group designs are divided into two sets: evidence-based practices and promising practices. To be determined as an *evidence-based practice*, two or more high-quality studies (*high-quality studies* are defined by meeting all quality indicators—such as strong conceptualization of the study, well-defined participants, clear description of accurate implementation of the intervention, systematic use of appropriate outcome measures, accurate analysis of the data—specific to the research design) or four or more acceptable-quality studies (*acceptable-quality studies* meet the majority of quality indicators), with mean weighted effect sizes significantly different from zero, must support the effectiveness of the practice. *Promising practices* are those that have some evidence that supports their efficacy, but the accumulated evidence is still emerging. The number of studies necessary to meet the guidelines for identification as a promising practice is two or more high-quality studies or four or more acceptable-quality studies that support the practice with a 20% confidence interval for the weighted effect size that is greater than zero.

Similar guidelines were proposed for identifying evidence-based practices from single-subject designs. Specifically, five or more single-subject design studies that (a) document the effectiveness of a particular intervention; (b) meet the acceptable criteria (i.e., practice is operationally defined, context and outcomes are clearly described, practice is implemented with documented fidelity, practice is functionally related to outcomes); (c) have been published in a peer-reviewed journal; and (d) have been systematically replicated by three different research teams in three different geographic locations are required for a practice to be identified as evidence based. Moreover, the body of studies must collectively include 20 or more participants (Division for Research, 2004).

At the time we wrote this chapter, the quality indicators and guidelines proposed by the Division for Research have yet to be applied to specific interventions to determine which meet evidence-based or promising practices designations. Yet, there is growing consensus that professional guidelines must be established and applied. And, once criteria are established, recommendations to teachers and other stakeholders can be made.

Issues Related to Identifying Effective Practices Through Synthesis

The benefit of synthesizing the research base seems clear. By identifying the most effective practices through the synthesis of multiple, high-quality studies, teachers, parents, teacher educators, administrators, legislators, and others can be confident in their implementation and support of those practices—which, ultimately, affords students with disabilities the best chance for improved outcomes. However, as strongly as we advocate for synthesis, we understand that many issues need to be acknowledged and addressed.

Publication Bias. Regardless of the type of research synthesis employed, the results of a synthesis are no better than the methods of the primary studies on which it is based. As we have stressed throughout this chapter, only studies that employ credible outcome measures, use representative samples, and permit clear causal conclusions should be included in the synthesis process. However, identifying *all* studies that meet these criteria can be an issue of concern.

A major threat to the validity of research synthesis is publication bias. Although there are many selection processes that may cause studies to be accepted or rejected for publication, publication bias is a phenomenon in which statistically significant findings are more likely to be published than nonsignificant findings (Preston, Ashby, & Smyth, 2004). Studies that meet the methodological criteria may have been conducted and not published due, in part perhaps, to nonsignificant findings. This practice is likely to skew the findings of syntheses in the direction of positive results. Statistical corrections can help mitigate the effects of publication bias, but concerted efforts to conduct comprehensive searches of the literature must be the main defense (Cooper & Hedges, 1994).

Number of Studies Required. The term *research synthesis* implies that results from many studies will be collectively analyzed to yield general findings about the intervention of focus. But how many primary studies must be involved for the synthesis to be meaningful? There is no absolute number of studies required for conducting a meta-analysis. In fact, there are no well-established guidelines regarding the minimum number of studies that must be included in a meta-analysis (Cooper & Hedges, 1994). The number of studies included in the 24 meta-analyses Forness (2001) reviewed ranged from 18 to 180, with a mean of 58 and a median of 49. Clearly, syntheses of 18 studies will yield results that are less stable and open to less detailed analysis than syntheses of 180 studies; one would hope to find most syntheses using larger numbers.

Likewise, some criterion-based frameworks may establish how many studies are required for the synthesis, but others may not be as clearly defined. For example, the criteria established by Division 12 of the APA states minimum numbers of studies required for a practice to be identified as well established (i.e., minimum of two between-group design or nine single-case design studies). However, noting that "the preponderance of evidence must be in favor of the efficacy of the practice" and that "two positive studies (in the absence of contravening evidence) is minimum" (Chambless et al., 1998, p. 4) is not exactly unequivocal guidance.

Although specific guidelines may not yet be identified for all types of research syntheses, researchers generally recognize that more is better. When each effect size is considered as a unit of analysis in meta-analyses, outlying units can have less impact on results if more units are included in the calculation of the mean effect. And when criterion-based frameworks are used, identifying greater numbers of studies that demonstrate positive effects provides more credibility to the claim of effectiveness. It is important to remember that the results of research syntheses are not prescriptions to be followed, but rather, they offer guidelines that allow educators to make professional judgments based on the known effects of practices.

Practice and Subject Characteristics. The first decisions made at the onset of research synthesis relate the purpose of the synthesis product. In general, the synthesis product is a determination of the effectiveness of a specific practice for learners who may share similar characteristics. To achieve a meaningful synthesis product, both the practice and the learners must be defined at the onset of the synthesis.

Special education researchers who investigate the effectiveness of a specific intervention, strategy, curriculum, or treatment—what we have been terming collectively as a *practice*—are required to describe the practice so that others can identify and replicate it. Yet, practices are not always uniformly identified and, even when identified by the same name, they could include different elements or procedures during implementation. For example, *self-recording* is a practice that has been investigated extensively for the past 20 years (see Cole & Bambara, 2000, for a review), yet studies often identify the practice with different terms, such as *self-monitoring* and *self-evaluation*. Moreover, the procedural implementation of the practice varies across investigations. For example, some studies incorporated prompts to signal students to monitor their behaviors (e.g., Lloyd, Bateman, Landrum, & Hallahan, 1989), but others included self-initiated prompts (e.g., Heins, Lloyd, & Hallahan, 1986).

The issue of how practice is identified and investigated in the primary studies is an important consideration for interpreting the results of a research synthesis. Indeed, the scope of the synthesis is narrowed or broadened by the decision of how to approach it. To address this issue, Chorpita (2003) suggested aggregating practices that share a majority of essential components and theoretical underpinnings for the purposes of synthesis. Although such a suggestion would require that essential components of practices be delineated and defined, it is a task that can be accomplished through professional agreement.

In addition to defining the practice, to achieve a meaningful synthesis, the learners for whom the practice is being evaluated also need to be identified clearly. In special education research, participants are typically described in relation to such variables as their diagnosed disability (e.g., learning disability), achievement or aptitude scores (e.g., below grade level in math achievement), deficit areas (e.g., poor reading), or symptomatic behavior (e.g., inattentive). Such designations of participants may be important for establishing the need for the practice or to reduce the variance of the group in individual studies. For example, Swanson and colleagues (e.g., Swanson, 1988, 1999, 2001; Swanson, Carson, & Sachse- Lee, 1996; Swanson & Deshler, 2003; Swanson & Hoskyn, 1998) have systematically synthesized intervention literature to identify effective instructional practices for students with learning disabilities.

However, as Gersten (this volume) described in his discussion of aptitude-treatment research, to date we have no evidence that specific practices are more or less effective for students of specific disability categories. That is, specific practices (e.g., Direct Instruction) have not been identified as effective for only one designation of learner (e.g., individuals with learning disabilities). In fact, it is frequently the case that investigators seek to demonstrate generalizability of practices by evaluating the effects of practice with students of different learning characteristics.

As with identifying practices, one way to address concerns related to participant characteristics for the purpose of synthesis is to define learners through broad terms (e.g., reading achievement) rather than only at levels of specificity (e.g., disability condition). Such groupings may serve to broaden the scope of the synthesis and provide direction for effective practices in relation to instructional focus. Until research has fully established different learning patterns of development for various groups of student (see Gersten, this volume), the most useful way to identify effective practices appears to be in relation to broader learning characteristics of students.

Efficacy Versus Effectiveness. We have used the terms *efficacy* and *effectiveness* interchangeably to refer to the results of research syntheses examining questions about the impact of practices. However, we should clarify that *efficacy* refers to how well a practice is known to bring about change in dependent variables of concern through empirical research, whereas *effectiveness* refers to how well a practice brings about change in natural, real-world settings (Chorpita, 2003).

Most syntheses of the research base actually assess the efficacy of practices. However, the difference between effectiveness and efficacy of practices in special education research might not be as clear-cut as with other disciplines. Most special education research about the effects of practice takes place in classrooms, with real teachers and real students. In many ways, the results are identifying effectiveness of practice. However, when researchers enter into relationships with schools and teachers to conduct investigations of the effects of practice, the resources that are brought to bear on those schools and classrooms may alter the natural arrangement of the setting. In fact, many researchers have noted that when resources are removed from schools and classrooms, even the most effective of practices are not maintained (e.g., Fuchs & Fuchs, 2001).

Currently, a new focus in research is bringing practices to scale—evaluating the effectiveness of practices as they are used by teachers and other professionals in their own schools and districts—without external resources (e.g., university personnel and support; Fuchs & Fuchs, 1998, 2001). When interpreting the results of research syntheses, consumers need to be aware of whether the results speak to the efficacy or the effectiveness of a particular practice. That is, if the majority of the primary studies involved in a research synthesis were conducted in a laboratory setting or with external supports not present in typical educational environments—although we can be confident that the practice of focus may work in similar ways in these conditions—we cannot be confident that the practice will work or is feasible to implement under typical circumstances (e.g., without atypical levels of support). Interpreting the results of research syntheses in relation to efficacy or effectiveness of the practice needs to be a consideration in the recommendation of practices.

Addressing Issues in Research Synthesis

Many issues, such as those identified here, need to be addressed as we synthesize the extant research base regarding educational practices for students with disabilities and apply the results of those syntheses. Yet in acknowledging issues, we must remember that the purpose of research synthesis for determining effective practices is to serve as a guide to stakeholders who seek to improve outcomes for students with disabilities. Any guide will include criteria that are somewhat arbitrary and subjective in nature, and research synthesis criteria and procedures will be no exception. Because integrating research requires professional judgments at all points of the process, it will never be a completely objective, precise task (Kavale, 2001).

Exercising sound professional judgment in developing criteria for determining effectiveness, implementing the procedures, and evaluating the products of research syntheses is critical. As professionals, educators must seek extensive information about the effects of practice, not simply rely on outcomes from one or even a few studies. More evidence about the effects of a practice provides better guidance than fewer pieces of evidence. Researchers should synthesize research in meaningful ways so that the results are useful for stakeholders and accurately communicate the characteristics of the practices, the students who were studied, and the implementation procedures used in the primary studies. Research synthesis is a scientific process, and science provides the most reliable and objective means for determining practices' efficacy and effectiveness.

Determining Effective Practices

Determining effective practices requires that professionals make decisions about acceptable ways of synthesizing the experimental research base of specific practices. As a profession, we should have guidelines for identifying which practices constitute the best chances for improving outcomes for students with disabilities. Without guidelines, we cannot make trustworthy recommendations to teachers, parents, teacher educators, school administrators, policymakers, or other interested people regarding practices. The results of syntheses provide a perspective for determining, advocating, and legislating effective practices.

However, synthesis results will not answer all of our questions about effective practices. Even with practices that garner strong recommendations of effectiveness, there are certainly students for whom those practices will not work (Landrum & Tankersley, 2004). But systematic synthesis of research, guided by professional decision making, provides us with clear directions regarding practices that have the best potential for improving student outcomes. Indeed, although the processes and results of research syntheses are not completely objective or precise, conclusions about the effectiveness of practices based on the results of research synthesis will provide the highest levels of objectivity and precision for identifying what works in special education (Kauffman, 1999). As the state of knowledge improves, future syntheses taking into account that improvement will be able to provide more precise and robust guidance.

We have proposed only one purpose for research synthesis—to determine effective practices. We have simply emphasized the need to integrate experimental studies into syntheses. Synthesis can serve many functions and will, therefore, include different types of primary studies. The purpose of the synthesis is to drive decisions about the criterion for including studies. For example, a research synthesis examining the relationship between achievement and socioeconomic status would include predominantly, if not solely, correlational studies. However, if one is seeking to determine the effectiveness of a practice, only certain types of research (e.g., experimental, quasi-experimental, or single-subject studies) should be considered.

Conclusion

Our purpose in this chapter was to provide guidelines for defining and synthesizing effective practices. Although many types of research questions are important in special education, determining the effects of practice relies on one question: Does the practice meaningfully increase important student outcomes? To answer this question, we must employ studies that have credible measures, use representative samples, and permit clear causal conclusions about use of the practice. The results from these studies should then be integrated and synthesized to establish the effectiveness of the practice clearly.

U.S. law (e.g., NCLB) requires that practices be grounded in scientifically based research. There is much to be done to establish the scientific basis of special educational practices and achieve this edict. Systematically integrating results from high-quality experimental studies will provide the best means for identifying, implementing, and promoting practices that meaningfully increase important student outcomes.

REFERENCES

Burke, M. D., Hagan-Burke, S., & Sugai, G. (2003). The efficacy of function-based interventions for students with learning disabilities who exhibit escape-maintained problem behaviors: Preliminary results from a single-case experiment. *Learning Disability Quarterly, 26,* 15–27.

Campbell, D., & Stanley, J. (1963). *Experimental and quasi-experimental designs for research.* Boston: Houghton Mifflin.

Chambless, D. L., Baker, M. J., Baucom, D. H., Beutler, L. E., Calhoun, K. S., Crits-Christoph, P., Daiuto, A., DeRubeis, R., Detweiler, J., Haaga, D. A. F., Johnson, S. B., McCurry, S., Mueser, K. T., Pope, K. S., Sanderson, W. C., Shoham, V., Stickle, T., Williams, D. A., & Woody, S. R. (1998). Update on empirically validated therapies: II. *The Clinical Psychologist, 51,* 3–16.

Chambless, D. L., & Ollendick, T. H. (2001). Empirically supported psychological interventions: Controversies and evidence. *Annual Review of Psychology, 52,* 685–716.

Chorpita, B. F. (2003). The frontier of evidence-based practice. In A. E. Kazdin & J. R. Weisz (Eds.), *Evidence-based psychotherapies for children and adolescents* (pp. 42–59). New York: Guilford.

Cohen, J. (1988). *Statistical power analysis of the behavioral sciences* (2nd ed.). Hillsdale, NJ: Erlbaum.

Colarusso, R. P., Keel, M. C., & Dangle, H. L. (2001). A comparison of eligibility criteria and their impact on minority representation in LD programs. *Learning Disabilities Research and Practice, 16,* 1–7.

Cole, C. L., & Bambara, L. M. (2000). Self-monitoring: Theory and practice. In E. S. Shapiro & T. R. Kratochwill (Eds.), *Behavioral assessment in schools* (2nd ed., pp. 202–232). New York: Guilford.

Cooper, H., & Hedges, L. V. (Eds.). (1994). *The handbook of research synthesis.* New York: Russell Sage Foundation.

Crenshaw, T. M., Kavale, K. A., Forness, S. R., & Reeve, R. E. (1999). Attention deficit hyperactivity disorder and the efficacy of stimulant medication: A meta-analysis. In T. Scruggs & M. Mastropieri (Eds.), *Advances in learning and behavioral disabilities* (Vol. 13, pp. 135–165). Greenwich, CT: JAI Press.

Crockett, J. B. (Ed.). (2001). The meaning of science and empirical rigor in the social sciences [Special issue]. *Behavioral Disorders, 27*(1).

Cullinan, D., Evans, C., Epstein, M. H., & Ryser, G. (2003). Characteristics of emotional disturbance of elementary school students. *Behavioral Disorders, 28,* 94–110.

Division for Research, Council for Exceptional Children. (2004, Fall). *Quality indicators for research in special education and guidelines for evidence-based practice.* Retrieved May 9, 2005, from http://interact.uoregon.edu/dr/Quality_Indicators.pdf.

DuPaul, G. J., & Eckert, T. L. (1997). The effects of school-based interventions for children with attention deficit hyperactivity disorder: A meta-analysis. *School Psychology Review, 26,* 5–27.

Dyson, L. L. (2003). Children with learning disabilities within the family context: A comparison with siblings in global self-concept, academic self-perception, and social competence. *Learning Disabilities Research and Practice, 18,* 1–9.

Forness, S. R. (2001). Special education and related services: What have we learned from meta-analysis? *Exceptionality, 9,* 185–197.

Fuchs, D., & Fuchs, L. S. (1998). Researchers and teachers working together to adapt instruction for diverse learners. *Learning Disabilities Research and Practice, 13,* 126–137.

Fuchs, D., & Fuchs, L. S. (2001). One blueprint for bridging the gap: Project PROMISE (Practitioners and researchers orchestrating model innovations to strengthen education). *Teacher Education and Special Education, 24,* 304–314.

Gersten, R., Baker, S., & Lloyd, J. W. (2000). Designing high-quality research in special education: Group experimental design. *The Journal of Special Education, 34,* 2–18.

Glass, G. V. (1976). Primary, secondary, and meta-analysis of research. *Educational Researcher, 5,* 3–8.

Grigal, M., Neubert, D. A., Moon, M. S., & Graham, S. (2003). Parents' and teachers' views of self-determination for secondary students with disabilities. *Exceptional Children, 70,* 97–112.

Heins, E. D., Lloyd, J. W., & Hallahan, D. P. (1986). Cued and noncued self-recording of attention to task. *Behavior Modification, 10,* 235–254.

Horner, R. H. Carr, E. G., Halle, J., McGee, G., Odom, S., & Wolery, M. (2005). The use of single-subject research to identify evidence-based practices in special education. *Exceptional Children, 71,* 165–179.

Individuals with Disabilities Education Improvement Act of 2004, 20 U.S.C. § 1400 *et seq.* (2004) (reauthorization of the Individuals with Disabilities Education Act of 1990).

Jenkins, J. R., Antil, L. R., Wayne, S. K., & Vadasy, P. F. (2003). How cooperative learning works for special education and remedial students. *Exceptional Children, 69,* 279–292.

Johnston, J. M., & Pennypacker, H. S. (1992). *Strategies and tactics of human behavioral research* (2nd ed.). Hillsdale, NJ: Erlbaum.

Justice, L. M., & Pullen, P. C. (2003). Promising interventions for promoting emergent literacy: Three evidence-based interventions. *Topics in Early Childhood Special Education, 23,* 99–113.

Kamps, D. M., Wills, H. P., Greenwood, C. R., Thorne, S., Lazo, J. F., Crockett, J. L., Akers, J. M., & Swaggart, B. L. (2003). Curriculum influences on growth in early reading fluency for students with academic and behavioral risks: A descriptive study. *Journal of Emotional and Behavioral Disorders, 11,* 211–224.

Kauffman, J. M. (1999). Commentary: Today's special education and its messages for tomorrow. *The Journal of Special Education, 32,* 244–254.

Kavale, K. A. (2001). Meta-analysis: A primer. *Exceptionality, 9,* 177–183.

Kavale, K. A., & Forness, S. R. (1987). Substance over style: A quantitative synthesis assessing the efficacy of modality testing and teaching. *Exceptional Children, 54,* 228–234.

Kazdin, A. E. (1977). Assessing the clinical or applied importance of behavior change through social validation. *Behavior Modification, 1,* 427–452.

Kellam, S. G., Ling, X., Merisca, R., Brown, C. H., & Ialongo, N. (1998). The effect of the level of aggression in the first grade classroom on the course and malleability of aggressive behavior in middle school. *Development and Psychopathology, 10,* 165–185.

Landrum, T. J., & Tankersley, M. (2004). Science at the schoolhouse: An uninvited guest. *Journal of Learning Disabilities, 37,* 207–212.

Lloyd, J. W., Bateman, D. F., Landrum, T. J., & Hallahan, D. P. (1989). Self-recording of attention versus productivity. *Journal of Applied Behavior Analysis, 22,* 315–323.

Lonigan, C., Elber, J., & Johnson, S. (1998). Empirically supported interventions for children: An overview. *Journal of Clinical Child Psychology, 27,* 138–145.

Mann, V. A., & Foy, J. G. (2003). Speech development, phonological awareness, and letter knowledge in preschool children. *Annals of Dyslexia, 53,* 149–173.

McCandliss, B., Beck, I. L., Sandak, R., & Perfetti, C. (2003). Focusing attention on decoding for children with poor reading skills: Design and preliminary tests of the word building intervention. *Scientific Studies in Reading, 7,* 75–104.

Miller, K. A., Gunter, P. A., Venn, M. L., Hummel, J., & Wiley, L. P. (2003). Effects of curricular and materials modification on academic performance and task engagement of three students with emotional or behavioral disorders. *Behavioral Disorders, 28,* 130–149.

Mosteller, F., & Boruch, R. (Eds.). (2002). *Evidence matters: Randomized trials in education research.* Washington, DC: Brookings.

Mostert, M. P., & Crockett, J. B. (1999–2000). Reclaiming the history of special education for more effective practice. *Exceptionality, 8,* 133–143.

National Institute of Child Health and Human Development. (2002). The relation of global first-grade classroom environment to structural classroom features and teacher and student behaviors. *The Elementary School Journal, 102,* 367–387.

National Research Council, Committee on Scientific Principles for Educational Research, Shavelson, R. J., & Towne, L. (Eds.). (2002). *Scientific research in education.* Washington, DC: Center for Education, National Academy Press.

No Child Left Behind Act of 2001, 20 U.S.C. 70 § 6301 *et seq.* (2002).

O'Connor, R. E., Notari-Syverson, A., & Vadasy, P. (1998). First-grade effects of teacher-led phonological activities in kindergarten for children with mild disabilities: A follow-up study. *Learning Disabilities Research and Practice, 13,* 43–52.

Odom, S. L., Brantlinger, E., Gersten, R., Horner, R. H., Thompson, B., & Harris, K. R. (2005). Research in special education: Scientific methods and evidence-based practices. *Exceptional Children, 71,* 137–148.

Quinn, M. N., Kavale, K. A., Mathur, S. R., Rutherford, R. B., & Forness, S. R. (1999). Meta-analysis of social skills interventions for children with mental or behavioral disorders. *Journal of Emotional and Behavioral Disorders, 7,* 54–64.

Preston, C., Ashby, D., & Smyth, R. (2004). Adjusting for publication bias: Modeling the selection process. *Journal of Evaluation in Clinical Practice, 10,* 313–322.

SEELS. (2004). *The children we serve: The demographic characteristics of elementary and middle school students with disabilities and their households.* Retrieved May 10, 2005, from http://www.seels.net/info_reports/children _we_serve.htm.

Serna, L., Nielsen, E., Lambros, K., & Forness, S. (2000). Primary prevention with children at risk for emotional and behavioral disorders: Data on a universal intervention for Head Start classrooms. *Behavioral Disorders, 26,* 70–84.

Serna, L. A., Nielsen, E., Mattern, N., & Forness, S. (2003). Primary prevention in mental health for Head Start classrooms: Partial replication with teachers as intervenors. *Behavioral Disorders, 28,* 124–129.

Shannon, P., Grinde, L. R., & Cox, A. W. (2003). Families' perceptions of the ability to pay for early intervention services. *Journal of Early Intervention, 25,* 164–172.

Speece, D. L., Mills, C., Ritchey, K. D., & Hillman, E. (2003). Initial evidence that letter fluency tasks are valid indicators of early reading skill. *The Journal of Special Education, 36,* 223–233.

Speer, O. B., & Lamb, G. S. (1976). First grade reading ability and fluency in naming verbal symbols. *The Reading Teacher, 29,* 572–576.

Stanovich, K. E. (2003). Understanding the styles of science in reading. *Scientific Studies of Reading, 7,* 105–126.

Stoiber, K. C., & Kratochwill, T. R. (2000). Empirically supported interventions and school psychology: Rationale and methodological issues—Part I. *School Psychology Quarterly, 15,* 75–105.

Swanson, H. L. (1988). Toward a metatheory of learning disabilities. *Journal of Learning Disabilities, 21,* 196–209.

Swanson, H. L. (1999). Reading research for students with LD: A meta-analysis of intervention outcomes. *Journal of Learning Disabilities, 32,* 504–532.

Swanson, H. L. (2001). Research on interventions for adolescents with learning disabilities: A meta-analysis of outcomes related to higher-order processing. *The Elementary School Journal, 101,* 331–348.

Swanson, H. L., Carson, C., & Sachse-Lee, C. M. (1996). A selective synthesis of intervention research for students with learning disabilities. *School Psychology Review, 25,* 370–391.

Swanson, H. L., & Deshler, D. (2003). Instructing adolescents with learning disabilities: Converting a meta-analysis to practice. *Journal of Learning Disabilities, 36,* 124–135.

Swanson, H. L., & Hoskyn, M. (1998). Experimental intervention research on students with learning disabilities: A meta-analysis of treatment outcomes. *Review of Educational Research, 68,* 277–321.

Talbott, E., Lloyd, J. W., & Tankersley, M. (1994). Effects of reading comprehension interventions for students with learning disabilities. *Learning Disability Quarterly, 17,* 223–232.

Telzrow, C. F., & Beebe, J. J. (2002). Best practices in facilitating intervention adherence and integrity. In A. Thomas & J. Grimes (Eds.), *Best practices in school psychology* (Vol. 4, pp. 503–516). Bethesda, MD: National Association of School Psychologists.

Vaughn, S., & Dammann, J. E. (2001). Science and sanity in special education. *Behavioral Disorders, 27,* 21–29.

White, W. A. T. (1988). A meta-analysis of effects of direct instruction in special education. *Education and Treatment of Children, 11,* 364–374.

Wiener, J., & Harris, P. J. (1997). Evaluation of an individualized, context-based social skills training program for children with learning disabilities. *Learning Disabilities Research and Practice, 12,* 40–53.

Wolf, M. M. (1978). Social validity: The case for subjective measurement or how applied behavior analysis is finding its heart. *Journal of Applied Behavior Analysis, 11,* 203–214.

Chapter 12

Relationship Between the Quality of the Research Design and the Quality of the Evidence for Improvement of Special Education Practice

Russell Gersten

The 1990s was a rather bleak decade for scientific research in special education. At the beginning of the decade, the noted educational historian Larry Cuban (1990) wrote eloquently about the havoc that widely promoted "reform" solutions brought to the field of education in general. He documented the profound cynicism that abounded in educational professions, including special education. Although every field—from medicine to anthropology—is plagued with cynicism about research, the cynicism in education about the utility and validity of research was extraordinary when compared to other professions. At that time, many seriously questioned the paradigms underlying scientific research as outdated in our postmodernist era (Heshusius, 1991; Poplin, 1988).

In many ways, the situation has changed dramatically since then. In 2001, Congressman Michael Castle (cited in National Research Council [NRC], 2002) issued a press release on recent legislation: "Education research is broken in this country . . . and Congress must work to make it more useful . . . Research needs to be conducted on a more scientific basis. Educators and policy makers need objective, reliable research" (p. 28). At about this time, the NRC released a report on scientific research in education. The NRC report concluded that "the guiding principles for scientific research in education are the same as those in the social, physical and life sciences" (NRC, 2002, p. 80). In other words, they stated that the field of education, like the field of physical science in the 17th and 18th centuries or the field of medicine in the 20th century, can evolve from a profession that relies primarily on craft knowledge and tradition to a field that relies primarily on a scientific knowledge base gained by systematic observation and valid assessments and guided by principles of scientific research, such as experimental design principles and mathematical models. They also noted, however, that "the ways that those principles are instantiated . . . depend on the specific features of what is being studied . . . Each field has features that influence what questions are asked, how research is designed, how it is carried out, and how it is interpreted and generalized" (p. 80).

In other words, educational science will not apply precisely the same principles as physical science or scientific psychology or sociology. However, it can—and hopefully will—utilize and adapt relevant features from these diverse disciplines. If this scenario unfolds, it will also share with these disciplines the concept that theories that do not fit the data need to be rejected and that alternative theories need to be developed and evaluated on the basis of empirical research.

Despite the clear intent of the U.S. Congress to make educational research (including special education research) more rigorous, objective, and scientific and the conclusion by the experts on the NRC panel that rigorous research in education is achievable and feasible, skepticism about the value of scientific research in education remains. Although many state and local educational agencies indicate that they now rely on scientific research as a basis for curriculum selection and instructional approaches (at least in the field of reading), it seems clear that some profess adherence because of the language of recent federal legislation concerning funding, as opposed to a true belief that the answers to educational problems lie in the painstaking, dispassionate methodology of the sciences. The profession continues to lack depth of knowledge of what scientific research really entails and of what evidence-based practice really means.

I have been working on this issue for 28 years, but particularly in the past 10 years. I served as a member of several different work groups formed by the Division for Research of the Council for Exceptional Children (CEC), the Research-to-Practice Division of the Office of Special Education Programs (OSEP), and the National Center for Learning Disabilities. The major focus of each group has been delineating standards for quality research, encouraging more rigorous intervention research, and translating research into classroom practice for special education students. This work has resulted in several articles that discussed the purposes of various types of research designs (Gersten, 2001), issues to consider in designing strategies for translating research into practice (Gersten, Vaughn, Deshler, & Schiller, 1997), issues to consider in designing high-quality special education research studies (Gersten, Baker, & Lloyd, 2000), and quality indicators in special education research (Gersten et al., 2005). In a sense, this chapter updates these various pieces by describing an array of issues relating to scientific research in the field of special education. The chapter begins with a series of questions; the remainder of the text begins to provide some answers and to articulate relevant issues. Among the issues addressed are the following: (a) the purposes of varying types of special education research methodologies, (b) quality indicators to use in evaluating a research article on the effectiveness of an intervention, (c) how we determine that a special education practice is evidence based, and (d) implications of these issues for special education professionals.

This chapter seeks to create greater awareness in special education professionals of the issues to consider when they are trying to determine if a study demonstrates the effectiveness of an approach. This knowledge can be critical in the increased professionalism of the field. In particular, it can make special educators more effective in their work in that they will know which practices really are evidence based and which types of research evidence to consider seriously in evaluating effectiveness.

Guiding Questions

The chapter is guided by a series of questions:

- What are the basic types of research designs in special education intervention research?
- Is there a set of quality indicators that educators can use to determine the degree to which special education intervention research provides valid and reliable evidence that a given approach is effective for teaching special education students?
- What types of research are useful for understanding problems in implementing evidence-based practices and guiding professional development?
- What types of research are useful for understanding *why* special education research interventions are effective?
- What types of research help us understand how to conceptualize an intervention for struggling learners?
- What can be special about special education research?

To address these questions, I will provide a brief overview of the purposes of various types of research designs, present a recently developed set of quality indicators for special education intervention research, and discuss how special education research can address some of the issues of individualization and personalization of instruction.

Types of Research Designs: An Overview

Two types of designs can be used to evaluate the effectiveness of a special education intervention in a rigorous fashion. The first is randomized trials, and the second is regression discontinuity design. Along with single-subject research designs (see Horner et al., 2005), these are the only types of research designs that allow you to say that an intervention causes positive effects on students.

Randomized Trials. In experimental studies involving randomized trials, participants (students, teachers, or other interventionists) are assigned to either the intervention or a comparison condition by a random process. The NRC (2002) is clear that "from a scientific perspective, randomized trials . . . are the idea for establishing whether one or more factors caused change in an outcome because of their strong ability to enable fair comparisons" (p. 110). Only with random assignment can we be sure that the two groups do not systematically differ in important ways that could influence the results.

Regression Discontinuity Designs. There is another design that offers a valid means of understanding intervention effects, but it is rarely used. The *regression discontinuity design* has great implications for special education research, including studies of early intervention. This design requires that "the selection process be completely known and perfectly measured" (Shadish, Cook, & Campbell, 2002, p. 224). For example, let us say a school provided early intervention to any first grader with a score on a measure of phonological processing less than 90 and that this rule was implemented with virtually no exceptions. Using this information, we could estimate, using regression techniques, what outcomes would look like if the intervention were ineffective and use statistics (in this case, regression analyses or analysis of covariance) to discern whether the intervention consistently provides significant benefit to students who score below the cutoff. In this case, we could see if students initially scoring between 70 and 90 on the phonological processing measure received the same scores after an intervention has been applied as those children who originally scored 90 to 110. If so, we would conclude that this intervention was successful because it consistently led to higher performance than one would expect based on entry skills. Regression allows for precise calculations of how students in the "at-risk" category would normally perform and whether these students are consistently performing at a higher level as a result of the intervention than one would anticipate otherwise.

Regression discontinuity designs seem counterintuitive, yet they are consistently regarded as one of the most valid means to gauge effectiveness of interventions (Shadish et al., 2002). In order to understand the logic underlying regression discontinuity analysis, it is helpful to think of it as a way to test whether students whose screening scores indicate they will experience difficulties consistently perform in the average or above-average range after the introduction of an intervention. Shadish et al. have provided a detailed and thorough explanation of the approach.

Quasi-Experimental Designs. In quasi-experimental designs, two (or more) groups that appear to be comparable are selected; one receives the intervention, and the other does not. Often intact classes or schools are used as the basis for assignment. In these studies, the researcher can attempt to control for any differences in important background variables (e.g., student's initial reading ability, parent education) between the groups by statistical methods. However, we must assume that the researchers picked the right background variables to equate the groups statistically. There may in fact be other differences (e.g., in student motivation for a study of after-school programs) that would not necessarily be discerned in advance. With quasi-experiments, we never can be sure that the differences in outcomes between the groups are due to the intervention, because they may actually be due to preexisting differences between the groups for which the researcher did not statistically control. Thus, readers of reports of quasi-experimental research need to be cautious in interpreting findings. Experts in the field continue to disagree on the ultimate value—and validity—of findings from quasi-experimental research (Shadish et al., 2002). Generally we assume that for a finding from a quasi-experimental design to be considered as valid, we need to see replications. For this reason, in many ways, randomized trials are a more efficient means of addressing educational questions and problems.

Quality Indicators for Special Education Intervention Research

With all the emphasis on improving the rigor and scientific basis of educational research, CEC's Division for Research felt that providing a set of quality indicators would be useful for those interested in designing rigorous research studies. The work group from CEC's Division for Research reasoned that any given study would have definite strengths and weaknesses. Thus, we decided to develop sets of *essential* and *desirable* quality indicators. We discussed each of these quality indicators for experimental research (including true experiments and quasi-experimental studies) in Gersten et al. (2005). If an experimental study is deficient in more than one of the essential indicators, its results and conclusions are likely to be suspect, and we would not recommend treating the study as serious evidence of effectiveness. Readers wishing to pursue these issues in greater depth might also consult any of the major texts in educational research or social science research (Boruch, 1997; Gall, Borg, & Gall, 2002; Shadish et al., 2002). The reader should also consult the more elaborate criteria specified in *What Works Clearinghouse Study Design and Implementation Assessment Device* (Valentine & Cooper, 2003), developed for the U.S. Department of Education. Gersten et al. summarized the rationale for the quality indicators as follows:

> We intentionally chose to look at quality indicators, rather than a set of "yes/no" standards, because evaluating a research design always entails weighing the relative strengths and weaknesses in a set of domains . . . Our hope is that our set of indicators will be field tested and refined, and . . . considered useful by journal editors and reviewers of Federal grant proposals. (Gersten et al., 2005, p. 150)

The set of essential and desirable quality indicators for experimental research, developed by the work group following 18 months of discussion, is presented in Tables 1 and 2. Note that parallel sets of quality indicators for single-subject research, correlational research, and qualitative research also appear in the same issue of *Exceptional Children* as the Gersten et al. article (2005) and that the single-subject quality indicators are equally important for assessing the quality of evidence to support a given educational approach.

Rather than review the entire set of quality indicators, I will focus on one to give the reader a flavor of the type of analysis that goes into evaluating the scientific merit of research findings. This indicator, *"Valid arguments supporting the proposed intervention as well as the nature of the comparison group are presented,"* does not require detailed knowledge of statistics or measurement. Every experimental research study compares learners under two or more conditions. The nature of the comparison condition is directly related to how we calculate the effect size, a measure of effectiveness. There are studies in which researchers compare an innovative condition to a pure control group. For example, a researcher might compare performance on a fractions test between students taught with a new instructional approach and students taught a different topic in mathematics altogether. This is a relatively "soft" or easy criterion in that the researcher is simply asking whether this intervention is better than doing nothing. This type of comparison is most useful when we have virtually no information on how to approach a problem.

More often, we try to contrast the outcomes of students taught with the innovative approach to those of students taught for exactly the same amount of time using the same material, but with a more traditional textbook approach, the design we used in Kelly, Gersten, and Carnine (1990). Here, the criterion for effectiveness is not as easy. A design with this type of comparison provides much more valid information as to effectiveness because the effect cannot be attributed to the amount of time devoted to the topic, but rather to some instructional variable.

Typically, we most highly value results from studies where the comparison group and intervention group receive the same amount of instruction on the same topics because this is the more stringent gauge of effectiveness. Providing a clear rationale for why the various comparison

TABLE 1. Essential and Desirable Quality Indicators for Group Experimental and Quasi-Experimental Research Proposals

Essential Quality Indicators

Conceptualization Underlying the Study

1. Is a compelling case for the importance of the research made? Is the conceptualization based on well-designed studies and does it reflect the scope of extant knowledge?
2. If an innovative approach is proposed, is it based on a sound conceptualization formed from sound research?
3. Are the research questions appropriate and stated clearly for the purposes of this study? Are valid arguments supporting the nature of intervention in the comparison group(s) presented?

Participants/Sampling

1. Will appropriate procedures be used to ensure that participants are comparable across intervention conditions on relevant characteristics? If random assignment is used, will information about participants prior to the intervention be made available to ensure that samples are comparable on salient characteristics?
2. Will sufficient information be provided to determine (or confirm) whether the participants demonstrated the disability(ies) or learning/social learning difficulties presented?
3. Will appropriate procedures be used to increase the probability that teachers or interventionists will be comparable across conditions?

Implementation of the Intervention and the Nature of Comparison Condition(s)

1. Is the intervention clearly described?
2. Are procedures for ensuring and assessing fidelity of implementation described?
3. Is the nature of instruction/services provided in comparison conditions described?

Outcome Measures

1. Will multiple measures be used to provide an appropriate balance between measures closely aligned with the intervention and measures of generalized performance?
2. Is evidence of reliability for the outcome measures provided? If not, will it be calculated?

Quality Indicators for Data Analysis

1. Are the data analysis techniques appropriate and linked to key research questions and hypotheses?
2. Is the variability within each sample accounted for either by sampling techniques (e.g., restricting range) or statistical techniques (blocking, analysis of covariance, growth curve analysis)?
3. Is a power analysis provided to describe the adequacy of the minimum cell size?

Desirable Quality Indicators

1. Are data collectors and/or scorers blind to study conditions and equally (un)familiar to examinees across study conditions?
2. Does the study provide not only internal consistency reliability but also test–retest reliability and inter-rater reliability (when appropriate) for outcome measures?
3. Are outcomes for capturing the intervention's effect measured beyond an immediate posttest?
4. Is evidence of the validity of the measures provided? If not, will it be estimated based on data from the proposed study or with data collected from other samples?
5. Will the research team assess more than surface features of fidelity implementation (e.g., number of minutes allocated to the intervention or teacher/interventionist following procedures specified)? Additionally, will the research team examine the quality of implementation?
6. Will the research include actual audio- or videotape excerpts that capture the nature of the intervention?
7. Does the researcher conduct power analyses proper for varying levels of statistical analysis? For example, if data will be analyzed at a classroom or day care center level, are analyses at that level sensitive enough to detect effects?

Note. From "Quality Indicators for Group Experimental and Quasi-Experimental Research in Special Education," by R. Gersten, L. S. Fuchs, D. Compton, M. Coyne, C. Greenwood, & M. Innocenti, 2005, *Exceptional Children, 71*(2), 2005, p. 151. Copyright 2005 by the Council for Exceptional Children. Adapted by permission.

TABLE 2. Desirable Quality Indicators for Group Experimental and Quasi-Experimental Research Studies

Indicator
1. Was data available on attrition rates among intervention samples? Was severe overall attrition documented? If so, is attrition comparable across samples? Is overall attrition less than 30%?
2. Did the study provide not only internal consistency reliability but also test–retest reliability and interrater reliability (when appropriate) for outcome measures? Were data collectors and/or scorers blind to study conditions and equally (un)familiar to examinees across study conditions?
3. Were outcomes for capturing the intervention's effect measured beyond an immediate posttest?
4. Was evidence of the criterion-related validity and construct validity of the measures provided?
5. Did the research team assess not only surface features of fidelity implementation (e.g., number of minutes allocated to the intervention or teacher/interventionist following procedures specified), but also examine quality of implementation?
6. Was any documentation of the nature of instruction or series provided in comparison conditions?
7. Did the research report include actual audio- or videotape excerpts that capture the nature of the intervention?

Note. From "Quality Indicators for Group Experimental and Quasi-Experimental Research in Special Education," by R. Gersten, L. S. Fuchs, D. Compton, M. Coyne, C. Greenwood, & M. Innocenti, *Exceptional Children, 71*(2), 2005, p. 152. Copyright 2005 by the Council for Exceptional Children. Adapted by permission.

conditions were chosen is, thus, a critical feature of any experimental design. We also need to know something about the nature of instruction in the comparison group, be it from seeing a sample lesson or reading a glimpse of instruction from transcribed audiotapes or videotapes. Only designs with clear rationales for the comparison conditions, measurement of the quality of instruction in the comparison condition, and reasonable control for time and access to content provide valid answers to questions about effectiveness. At times, researchers contrast theoretically opposed or divergent interventions. This, too, is legitimate, especially when the contrast is focused and of high interest. There are occasions when a researcher is broaching a new topic and simply wants to know if it leads to change. These would be the only instances where a no-treatment comparison group would be appropriate. Designs may also include multiple groups or subtle contrasts (e.g., same intervention taught by an interventionist or teacher vs. a paraprofessional, same intervention with or without progress monitoring).

Understanding Problems in Implementing Evidence-Based Practices and Guiding Professional Development

Descriptive studies are invaluable for helping us understand educational phenomena, such as common implementation problems and how we need to structure or restructure professional development. A vast array of descriptive and correlational methodologies are available for this purpose, ranging from those utilizing relatively low inference measures of classroom instructional variables (e.g., Foorman & Schatschneider, 2003; Gersten, Carnine, & Williams, 1982) to rating scales that encapsulate key features of desirable implementation (e.g., Vadasy, Jenkins, Antil, Phillips, & Pool, 1997) to more in-depth qualitative examinations of implementation of innovative approaches to teaching (e.g., Beck, McKeown, Sandora, Kucan, & Worthy, 1996; Marks & Gersten, 1998). For example, from descriptive studies, we have learned that teachers typically cannot learn more than two complex teaching strategies in a given year (Kline, Deshler, & Schumaker, 1992) and that almost invariably inservice demonstrations and training need to be followed by in-class observations and informal discussions (Gersten, Morvant, & Brengelman, 1995; Goldenberg & Gallimore, 1991). We have also learned that it is often not until the second year of use that teachers begin to really use a new approach with comfort and ease (Hall & Hord, 2001) and that most teachers crave concrete, specific examples in order to understand the more theoretical research underpinnings of the intervention (Gersten et al., 1995; McLaughlin, 1990). Although this type of research is shunned by many as prosaic, I believe it will increasingly become a prominent area because findings can allow us to understand specific means for breaking down the gap between research and special education practice. These types of studies can lead to radical improvements in how we provide professional development to teachers and in how special educators communicate with other teachers at their schools.

Understanding Why Special Education Research Interventions Are Effective

At times, researchers have correlated level of implementation with relative growth in learning outcomes to understand which components of an intervention are the most important for accelerating learning (e.g., Gersten, Woodward, & Darch, 1986). They also have linked observed performance with data on teachers' perceptions of the strengths and weaknesses of the intervention and/or measures of teacher knowledge of the principles and research underlying the intervention. Sometimes, they have found that several of the components highly valued by developers (e.g., use of hand signals in SRA Reading Mastery) are not well linked to student outcomes (Gersten et al., 1982).

Qualitative methods can also enhance our understanding of why interventions work. These can include analyses of discourse during a lesson, classroom observational studies to discern patterns of use, and in-depth teacher interviews to understand why teachers follow some aspects of the intervention and not others. They can also explore students' understandings of the material and/or strategies taught to them by use of think-aloud procedures, in which children express how they approached solving a problem.

Mixed-methods methodology (Chatterji, 2004) is an attempt to embed qualitative methods within quantitative intervention research studies. The potential benefits are that one can both learn a good deal about the effects of the intervention and point to reasons for success or failure. However, there is some debate about this approach. For one thing, researchers may be invested in the intervention, and qualitative research does not provide the type of constraints against bias that quantitative experimental designs provide. In addition, Cook (cited in *Education Week,* Feb. 7, 2005) notes that in his large-scale evaluation of the Comer Process for school improvement, the qualitative analyses did not reveal much information that could not be obtained from the quantitative analysis.

Understanding How to Conceptualize an Intervention for Struggling Learners

A key aspect of the quality of an intervention research study is the richness of the underlying conceptualization. This goes beyond the rigor of the study, the measurement and experimental design issues typically covered in texts and university courses. It is linked to, but also goes beyond, the quality of the case built for the intervention in terms of prior research or theory. Richness of conceptualization refers to how well the intervention addresses real issues in the field; that is, how sensitive it is to the realities of special education students and those who teach them. Developing insightful, well-grounded, imaginative interventions requires extensive development work and field-testing. Educational research has recognized the importance of rich field-testing and revision of intervention plans based on formative data over the past decade (A. L. Brown, 1992; Gersten et al., 2000).

Use of Design Experiments to Refine an Intervention. In their study of technology use in the classroom, Reinking and Pickle (1993) described the unanticipated changes and compromises they needed to make for successful implementation: "As the school year progressed, we found ourselves in a seemingly endless cycle of compromises that threatened the control required in a true experiment . . . Each compromise seemed like a defeat in a war we were quickly losing." They then noted, however, that their "need to maintain control of extraneous variation was a barrier to finding and understanding the most relevant aspects of implementing the intervention and the effects it might have on the educational environment" (pp. 266–267). In other words, they suggested that often some extensive field research must be done in order to shape the intervention to fit the demands of the actual teaching situation and to ensure that instructional objectives are being met.

These types of studies are often called *design experiments* (A. L. Brown, 1992), or teaching experiments (Lesh & Kelly, 2000), and are increasingly used prior to the initiation of a formal intervention study involving randomized trials. We have used them, for example, in our work on teaching history to students with learning disabilities (LD) in inclusive settings (Gersten, Baker, Smith-Johnson, Peterson, & Dimino, 2003) and found that they are an excellent means for refining interventions, removing unnecessary procedures, and discerning curricula gaps. They can—and have—led to subsequent experimental studies (e.g., Brown, Pressley, Van Meter, & Schuder, 1996; Gersten, Baker, Smith-Johnson, Dimino, & Peterson, in press).

Use of Programmatic Intervention Research to Refine an Intervention. Of course, interventions can also be improved through programmatic intervention research, a series of systematic studies that rigorously assess the value of specific components of a comprehensive intervention. One excellent example is the large number of experimental studies conducted by Lynn Fuchs and colleagues on peer-assisted learning in mathematics. In their earlier research studies (e.g., Fuchs & Deno, 1991), students were placed into heterogeneous pairs, and the more proficient student tutored the less proficient student, who was often a student with LD or attention-deficit/hyperactivity disorder (ADHD) or who experienced difficulties in mathematics. Extrapolating from their ongoing research in reading, they modified the system so that each student served in the role of tutor and tutee. Though the idea is counterintuitive, when the less proficient students serve as tutors, they carefully watch the steps and strategies used by a more proficient peer to solve problems and carefully attend to these models so that, as tutors, they can correct any errors. This fine-tuning of the approach yielded positive results.

Interventions can be rich and vibrant in many ways. One way is the insightful, craft-wisdom reflected in the strategy being evaluated. For example, as part of a series of programmatic research studies, Englert, Raphael, Anderson, Anthony, and Stevens (1991) developed an intervention for teaching fifth graders to write expository text using basic text structures such as compare–contrast. To stimulate brainstorming, students were taught to use "think sheets." Englert et al. designed the intervention so that the think sheets did not become mere "worksheets" to be filled out, but rather were seen by students as "note-taking tools with prompts to remind students of the thinking strategies and dialogue that good writers used" (p. 352). They did not modify the expectations for the special education students, but realized that they would need a good deal of extra support in terms of guidance, help with spelling and grammar, and extended time to practice the writing strategy. Another innovative feature of the approach was the intervention component used to help students develop their own writing style. When presenting a highly structured organizer for writing essays, the researchers found that the students tended to write well-organized and developed essays, but they were deadly boring. Therefore they added a component of peer feedback on writing style, where peers gave each other a sense of what was monotonous about the writing style and discussed suggestions for improvements. Not until the addition of this small but important step did the formal experiment indicate that the intervention was successful for special education students, as well as their peers.

What Is Special About Special Education Research?

Special education research does not and should not use paradigms that are radically different from those used in other types of educational or social science research. However, a critical issue in contemporary special education research is the determination of better operational definitions of various types of disabilities in mathematics, reading, writing, and social skills, as well as an understanding of which types of interventions are likely to be effective for particular students. This search for aptitude–treatment interactions has a long history in special education research (Cronbach & Snow, 1977). Sadly, many of the earlier attempts to determine, for example, if a student was a visual or auditory learner and then teach to his or her strengths were conceptualized on the basis of simplistic notions of learning and lacked any empirical support (Kavale & Mattson, 1983). Furthermore, theorists disagreed as to whether to teach to a student's strengths or weaknesses. That theories of reading development and reading instruction were much more primitive than current conceptions also likely contributed to the inability to identify aptitude–treatment interactions.

We now have begun to develop and validate much more sensitive measures of factors that seem to impede learning of mathematics, reading, and social skills development. Advances in cognitive science have led to more refined theories of development of academic abilities and skills. The field has a better sense of which areas and topics need to be taught to students in order for them to learn how to read and is beginning to develop a sense of the types of roadblocks that occur in reading or mathematics development for various groups of children (Gersten, Jordan, & Flojo, in press; National Reading Panel [NRP], 2000).

In addition, more sophisticated models of statistical analysis, such as hierarchical linear modeling, allow for in-depth longitudinal analysis of how various groups of students develop—or fail to develop—adequate social skills, reading proficiency (Schatschneider, Fletcher, Francis, Carlson, & Foorman, 2004), and competence in arithmetic (Hanich, Jordan, Kaplan, & Dick, 2001). Developments in this area are likely to have a profound effect on how special education services are delivered. Thus, we can envision, in the near future, some clear-cut rules of thumb for providing appropriate interventions to students.

We also can envision important practical results emanating from the increasing number of response-to-intervention studies being conducted by Fuchs and colleagues (D. Fuchs & Fuchs, 2001) and Vaughn and colleagues (2003). Hopefully these studies are beginning to address a question broached 30 years ago by Cronbach and Snow (1977): For which students do specific interventions work? If so, there could be a quantum leap in special education practice and the scientific, professional knowledge base.

Many years ago, at the end of a vital decade of scientific research on teaching, the founder of the modern movement, Nate Gage, wrote a book titled *The Scientific Basis of the Art of Teaching* (Gage, 1978). This was a brilliant title in that Gage recognized the battle between the scientific/objectivist wing of professional educators and those like his colleague Elliot Eisner (1991), who stressed the artistry involved in good teaching. In the book, Gage reviews the decade of research on effective teaching and clearly indicates that research merely serves as a foundation for solid, professional practice. It cannot and should not straitjacket educators; rather, it should inform them of techniques or strategies or curricula approaches that are likely to be successful. Research cannot be totally prescriptive; it should point professional educators in sensible directions—directions likely to benefit the children and youth they teach.

AUTHOR'S NOTE

This is an adaptation of the article by Gersten, Baker, and Lloyd (2000) that appeared originally in *The Journal of Special Education.*

REFERENCES

Beck, I. L., McKeown, M. G., Sandora, C., Kucan, L., & Worthy, J. (1996). Questioning the author: A yearlong classroom implementation to engage students with text. *The Elementary School Journal, 96,* 385–414.

Boruch, R. F. (1997). *Randomized experiments for planning and evaluation: A practical guide.* Thousand Oaks, CA: Sage.

Brown, A. L. (1992). Design experiments: Theoretical and methodological challenges in creating complex interventions in classroom settings. *The Journal of Learning Sciences, 2*(2), 141–178.

Brown, R., Pressley, M., Van Meter, P., & Schuder, T. (1996). A quasi-experimental validation of transactional strategies instruction with low-achieving second grade readers. *Journal of Educational Psychology, 88,* 18–37.

Chatterji, M. (2004). Evidence on "what works": An argument for extended-term mixed-method (ETTM) evaluation designs. *Educational Researcher, 33*(9), 3–13.

Cronbach, L. J., & Snow, R. E. (1977). *Aptitudes and instructional methods: A handbook for research on interactions.* New York: Irvington.

Cuban, L. (1990). Reforming again, again, and again. *Educational Researcher, 19*(1), 3–13.

Eisner, E. (1991). *The enlightened eye: Qualitative inquiry and the enhancement of educational practice.* New York: Macmillan.

Englert, C. S., Raphael, T. E., Anderson, L. M., Anthony, H. M., & Stevens, D. D. (1991). Making strategies and self-talk visible: Writing instruction in the regular and special education classrooms. *American Educational Research Journal, 28,* 337–372.

Foorman, B., & Schatschneider, C. (2003). Measurement of teaching practices during reading/language arts instruction and its relation to student achievement. In S. R. Vaughn & K. L. Briggs (Eds.), *Reading in the classroom: Systems for the observation of teaching and learning* (pp. 1–30). Baltimore: Brookes.

Fuchs, L. S., & Deno, S. L. (1991). Paradigmatic distinctions between instructionally relevant measurement models. *Exceptional Children, 57,* 488–500.

Fuchs, D., & Fuchs, L. S. (2001). Principles for the prevention and intervention of mathematics difficulties. *Learning Disabilities Research and Practice, 16*(2), 85–95.

Gage, N. L. (1978). *The scientific basis of the art of teaching.* New York: Teachers College Press.

Gall, M. D., Borg, W. R., & Gall, J. P. (2002). *Educational research: An introduction* (7th ed.). White Plains, NY: Pearson/Allyn & Bacon.

Gersten, R. (2001). Sorting out the roles of research in the improvement of practice. *Learning Disabilities Research and Practice, 16,* 45–50.

Gersten, R., Baker, S., & Lloyd, J. W. (2000). Designing high quality research in special education: Group experimental design. *The Journal of Special Education,* 34, 2–18.

Gersten, R., Baker, S., Smith-Johnson, J., Dimino, J., & Peterson, A. (in press). Eyes on the prize: Teaching history to students with learning disabilities in inclusive settings. *Exceptional Children.*

Gersten, R., Baker, S., Smith-Johnson, J., Peterson, A., & Dimino, J. (2003). *Providing meaningful access to the general curriculum through use of design experiments* (Technical Report 03-02). Long Beach, CA: Instructional Research Group.

Gersten, R., Carnine, D., & Williams, P. (1982). Measuring implementation of a structured educational model in an urban setting: An observational approach. *Educational Evaluation and Policy Analysis, 4,* 67–79.

Gersten, R., Fuchs, L. S., Compton, D., Coyne, M., Greenwood, C., & Innocenti, M. (2005). Quality indicators for group experimental and quasi-experimental research in special education. *Exceptional Children, 71,* 149–164.

Gersten, R., Jordan, N., & Flojo, J. (in press). Early identification and interventions for students with mathematics difficulties. *Journal of Learning Disabilities.*

Gersten, R., Morvant, M., & Brengelman, S. (1995). Close to the classroom is close to the bone: Coaching as a means to translate research into classroom practice. *Exceptional Children, 62,* 52–66.

Gersten, R., Vaughn, S., Deshler, D., & Schiller, E. (1997). What we know about using research findings: Implications for improving special education practice. *Journal of Learning Disabilities, 30,* 466–476.

Gersten, R., Woodward, J., & Darch, C. (1986). Direct instruction: A research-based approach for curriculum design and teaching. *Exceptional Children, 53,* 17–36.

Goldenberg, C., & Gallimore, R. (1991). Changing teaching takes more than a one-shot workshop. *Educational Leadership, 49*(3), 69–72.

Hall, G. E., & Hord, S. M. (2001). Implementing change: Patterns, principles, and potholes. Boston: Allyn & Bacon.

Hanich, L., Jordan, N., Kaplan, D., & Dick, J. (2001). Performance across different areas of mathematical cognition in children with learning disabilities. *Journal of Educational Psychology, 93,* 615–626.

Heshusius, L. (1991). Curriculum-based assessment and direct instruction: Critical reflections on fundamental assumptions. *Exceptional Children, 57,* 315–328.

Horner, R. H., Carr, E. G., Halle, J., McGee, G., Odom, S., & Wolery, M. (2005). The use of single-subject research to identify evidence-based practice in special education. *Exceptional Children, 71,* 165–180.

Kavale, K., & Mattson, D. P. (1983). "One jumped off the balance beam": Meta-analysis of perceptual-motor training. *Journal of Learning Disabilities, 16,* 165–173.

Kelly, B., Gersten, R., & Carnine, D. (1990). Student error patterns as a function of curriculum design: Teaching fractions to remedial high school students with learning disabilities. *Journal of Learning Disabilities, 23,* 23–29.

Kline, F. M., Deshler, D. D., & Schumaker, J. B. (1992). Implementing learning strategy instruction in class settings: A research perspective. In M. Pressley, K. R. Harris, & J. T. Guthrie (Eds.), *Promoting academic competence and literacy in school* (pp. 361–406). San Diego, CA: Academic Press.

Lesh, R. A., & Kelly, A. E. (2000). Multitiered teaching experiments. In A. E. Kelly & R. A. Lesh (Eds.), *Handbook of research design in mathematics and science education* (pp. 17–34). Mahwah, NJ: Erlbaum.

Marks, S. U., & Gersten, R. (1998). Understanding engagement and disengagement between special and general educators: An application of Miles and Huberman's cross-case analysis. *Learning Disability Quarterly, 21,* 34–56.

McLaughlin, M. (1990). The Rand change agent study revisited: Macro perspectives and micro realities. *Education Research, 19*(9), 11–16.

National Reading Panel. (2000). *Teaching children to read: An evidence-based assessment of the scientific literature on reading and its implications for reading instruction.* Washington, DC: National Institute for Literacy.

National Research Council. (2002). Design principles for fostering science in a federal education research agency. In Committee on Scientific Principles for Educational Research, R. J. Shavelson, & L. Towne (Eds.), *Scientific research in education* (pp. 127–157). Washington, DC: Center for Education, National Academy Press.

Poplin, M. S. (1988). Holistic/constructivist principles of the teaching/learning process: Implications for the field of learning disabilities. *Journal of Learning Disabilities, 21,* 401–416.

Reinking, D., & Pickle, J. M. (1993). Using a formative experiment to study how computers affect reading and writing in classrooms. In C. Z. Kinzer & D. J. Leu (Eds.), *Examining central issues in literacy research, theory, and practice* (pp. 263–270). Chicago: National Reading Conference.

Schatschneider, C., Fletcher, J., Francis, D. J., Carlson, C. D., & Foorman, B. (2004). Kindergarten prediction of reading skills: A longitudinal comparative analysis. *Journal of Educational Psychology, 96,* 265–282.

Shadish, W. R., Cook, T. D., & Campbell, D. T. (2002). *Experimental and quasi-experimental designs for general causal inference.* Boston: Houghton Mifflin.

Vadasy, P. F., Jenkins, J. R., Antil, L. R., Phillips, N. B., & Pool, K. (1997). The research-to-practice ball game: Classwide peer tutoring and teacher interest, implementation, and modifications. *Remedial and Special Education, 18,* 143–156.

Valentine, J. C., & Cooper, H. (2003). *What Works Clearinghouse Study Design and Implementation Assessment Device* (Version 1.0). Washington, DC: U.S. Department of Education.

Vaughn, S., Kim, A., Sloan, C., Hughes, M., Elbaum, B., & Sridhar, D. (2003). Social skills interventions for young children with disabilities: A synthesis of group design studies. *Remedial and Special Education, 24,* 2–15.

Chapter 13

Bridging the Research-to-Practice Gap:

Maintaining the Consistent Implementation of Research-Based Practices

Jeanne Wanzek and **Sharon Vaughn**

Perhaps the most important issue in education, certainly in special education, is determining effective practices and the means for implementing them in schools. Determining effective practices in special education is no easy matter. We are continually bombarded with new materials, techniques, and policies, making it difficult to "keep up," much less assess the relative effectiveness of these new ideas.

Educators face the growing challenge of assimilating new knowledge about practices, deciding how to implement these practices, and documenting the effectiveness with their own students. Teachers need to be able to discriminate between new techniques that show promise for student learning and techniques with little or no merit. Unlike medicine and pharmacology, the field of education has no governing body to approve particular techniques or practices. It is often up to teachers to make decisions about the effectiveness of instructional practices to be implemented in the classroom. For special education teachers, these challenges are greater because often the research on effectiveness involves neither students with disabilities nor students who have characteristics similar to those of the students they teach. Yet, the use of evidence-based practices could not be more important than in special education, because teachers are serving students who have already demonstrated difficulties in learning. Thus, the additional burden for special education teachers often includes knowing the research and for whom it has been documented, implementing the research, and determining its effectiveness with their own students.

However, there seems to be a mismatch between the research findings and classroom-level implementation of the practices associated with these findings. That is, the instructional techniques that research has shown to be most effective are seldom implemented in schools, and many practices with little research backing are routinely implemented. This gap suggests that effective research practices may not be widely known, understood, or implemented in schools. For example, converging evidence from research on beginning reading suggests that many students at risk for reading difficulties can acquire the necessary skills to become successful readers when provided with effective instruction or intervention (Torgesen et al., 1999; Vellutino et al., 1996). Some evidence suggests that only 2% to 6% of students still struggle with reading after receiving effective instruction or intervention (Torgesen, 2000). However, the recent National Assessment of Educational Progress (NAEP) report indicated that 69% of students in the United States are unable to read at proficient levels by fourth grade, and 37% of fourth graders cannot read at even a basic level (National Center for Education Statistics, 2003). The NAEP report findings have remained relatively stable over the past 10 years. Clearly, the instruction occurring in our nation's schools and classrooms differs in some significant ways from the instructional practices validated by research.

The question remains, then, how can we ensure that findings from research (research-based practices) are successfully transitioned into practice, and how can these practices be sustained? The answer is undoubtedly complex. However, a research base has emerged to provide guidance for successfully bridging the gap between research and practice.

What Practices Should Be Translated Into Practice?

How much research is needed to provide enough evidence to suggest educational change? What information does the design of the study provide in terms of the intervention effectiveness? How should educators proceed with new practices that have not yet been proven in the research? These questions are directly related to determining which research findings should be implemented as part of a school's or district's practice. Researchers and educators need to consider these questions when determining whether practices studied in the research literature are sufficiently supported and are appropriate for their populations—as well as whether they are feasible for implementation. This is a big task for practicing teachers and educational leaders to tackle alone.

Recently, the What Works Clearinghouse (WWC) was established to provide a means to systematically review the scientific evidence supporting educational interventions. A group of outcome evaluators apply predetermined criteria to individual studies and determine the extent to which the study provides evidence of causal validity. In addition, study results are reported by topic to present the amount and type of evidence available to support specific interventions. The information offered by the WWC is designed to provide an organized mechanism for educators seeking information on the research base of instructional techniques.

Educators may learn of interventions that have not been submitted to the WWC for evaluation. Using criteria similar to those of the WWC, an educator can examine several key areas to determine the quality of evidence for a particular intervention or instructional technique. The strongest indication of an intervention being deemed effective and ready for implementation in practice is converging evidence from multiple experimental studies demonstrating the intervention's influence. However, it can take years of research to build this evidence base for a specific intervention or intervention type. It may be inappropriate to withhold promising, though unproven, interventions from students who could benefit from their application, particularly students with learning difficulties or disabilities. Examination of individual studies—specifically, the participants, design, and implementation—can provide essential information on the potential effectiveness of a new intervention.

Information regarding the participants of a study can allow educators to establish the population of students to which the intervention effects can be generalized. At a very basic level, the participants in the intervention study should be comparable to the students for whom the intervention will be implemented in practice. In other words, the strongest evidence for a third-grade teacher of students with externalizing behavior disorders is found in a research study that provides the results of the intervention when used with third-grade students with externalizing behavior disorders. Studies providing detailed information about the participants (e.g., age, gender, ethnicity, disability) allow educators to make informed decisions about the intervention's potential effectiveness for their own students.

High-quality research design and methods are imperative for an unreplicated study to demonstrate intervention potential, that is, consideration for use with students. High-quality intervention research includes comparison groups and detailed descriptions of the treatment intervention and the instruction the comparison groups receive (Gersten, Baker, & Lloyd, 2000; Pressley & Harris, 1994; Zigmond, 1996). These descriptions allow analyses of the differences between the treatment and comparison groups to better interpret the results. The reader can assess whether the treatment intervention was stronger in comparison to no intervention or to other commonly used interventions. In addition, information on controls for possible threats to validity can provide further evidence that the treatment and comparison groups differed only in the intervention they received and, therefore, that the results can be attributed to implementation of the intervention rather than other differences between the groups (e.g., one group receiving additional interventions conducted by the school). Finally, descriptions of the intervention and its implementation allow analysis of the practicality and feasibility of applying the technique in a specific educational environment.

In addition to detailed implementation descriptions, evidence that the intervention was carried out as designed is beneficial when one is interpreting results (Gersten, Baker, & Lloyd, 2000; Pressley & Harris, 1994). This is commonly referred to as *treatment fidelity* or *validity*. Information on treatment fidelity is one assurance for educators that replication of the intervention as described would produce similar results. Educators can have greater confidence in a study's outcomes if the research involves multiple dependent measures—some broad measures of the constructs and some narrow measures of skills aligned with the intervention—to demonstrate the full capabilities of the intervention (Gersten et al., 2005). Evidence of the validity and reliability of the measures is also important for providing evidence that teachers will see meaningful differences in student outcomes if they implement the detailed intervention.

When research findings from several high-quality studies demonstrate significant outcomes in favor of the treatment condition, research-to-practice implications are more obvious. However, what are educational leaders and teachers to do if there is insufficient evidence to support these promising practices for the students they are teaching? A reasonable solution that could be implemented at the district, school, or classroom level is to document the effectiveness of the promising practice through classroom-based measures of students' response to the intervention. There may be no more important activity than for teachers to use classroom-based measures to document the effectiveness of interventions. In this way, teachers can confirm effectiveness and alter treatments to assure the most effective outcomes for students. The practice of using classroom-based student progress monitoring is effective when teachers monitor student progress frequently and examine the individual student data to verify whether the new intervention is having the intended effect (Stecker & Fuchs, 2000). Student response to the intervention that is positive and in line with findings from the research study is evidence for continuing a promising practice.

In summary, converging evidence, including studies with randomized controlled trials, provides the strongest scientific base for generalizing a research intervention into practice. When multiple studies using these designs yield positive outcomes, implementation of an intervention is clearly warranted. In instances in which a convergent body of clearly validated interventions cannot be found, educators should use evidence from a single high-quality research study to guide their selection of teaching techniques. When these interventions are carefully implemented with frequent monitoring of student progress, the interventions are likely to have positive outcomes in practice. Table 1 provides guiding questions for educators to use when examining a research study.

Factors in Translating Research to Practice

In recent years, sustainability has been a prominent topic in special education (e.g., Crockett, 2004). Specifically, authors have discussed factors necessary to assist in implementing and sustaining effective practices for students with disabilities. These discussions and the limited research examining effective ways of sustaining research-based practices provide considerations for improving implementation and sustainability of research-based practices in classrooms.

Planning for Implementation of New Interventions

Planning for sustained implementation of a new practice is required even during the beginning stages of implementation in classrooms. It is in the initial implementation of a new practice that teachers decide whether they will continue or discontinue its use. Appropriate planning, including consideration of how to assure teacher mastery and comfort with the new practice, can set the stage for sustained implementation of the new practice.

It is probably not surprising to find that a new practice is more likely to be sustained if teachers have mastered implementation of the

TABLE 1. Key Questions for Teachers and Educational Leaders to Consider in Determining the Quality of Individual Intervention Studies

Participant information	Design and implementation	Findings and practice implications
1. What is the ethnicity of the participants? 2. What is the gender of the participants? 3. What are the ages of the participants? 4. Were students with disabilities included? Exceptionality:	1. Is a comparison group included? If yes, are students randomly assigned to the treatment(s) and comparison groups? 2. Is the implementation of the intervention clearly described to allow transfer to practice? 3. Is the instruction for the comparison group described? 4. Is there evidence the treatment and comparison groups are comparable (e.g., similar amount of time in instruction, comparable teachers)? 5. Is evidence of the validity and reliability of outcome measures provided?	1. How effective was the treatment? If effect sizes are reported, consider ES of .20 or higher as sufficient to make change in your practice. 2. Are effect sizes reported for the students with disabilities? If yes, are these effect sizes the same as or different than those of other students?

practice. Teachers who fully understand the implementation of a practice, including many of the underlying conceptual foundations for the approach, are more likely to use the practice effectively within their classroom (Gersten & Dimino, 2001; Klingner, Ahwee, Pilonieta, & Menendez, 2003). One reason for this may be the ability of a master teacher to make appropriate adaptations to the practice to fit his or her students. If teachers understand the underlying principles of the practice, they are less likely to inadvertently change the key components of the practice—the components associated with improved outcomes.

Therefore, it is useful to consider how to make the underlying principles of an effective intervention apparent to teachers when they are initially learning the new approach. Including teachers in problem-solving the aspects of the intervention that can be modified and working with them to determine when and how to modify the approach is likely to yield high dividends in terms of sustaining the intervention and implementing it with fidelity. This more active involvement in the change process appears to be more successful for long-term implementation (Gersten, Morvant, & Brengelman, 1995). With this type of assistance, teachers gain the knowledge necessary to make future adaptations and to assist other teachers with implementing the practice.

Mastering implementation of a new practice may actually begin with a teacher's beliefs about how students learn and how instruction should be delivered (Wong, 1997). Although it is difficult to know whether changes in teachers' beliefs yield changes in the teachers' instructional practices or whether successfully implementing a new practice can lead to changes in beliefs, the sustainability of the practice is most likely related to both: a belief in the practice and proficiency of implementation.

Kennedy (1991) has previously noted researchers' lack of attention to the strong beliefs teachers may have about their practice. In fact, teachers have as their experience thousands of days of instruction and observed student responses to that instruction. If a new intervention does not immediately fit within this prior knowledge of "what works," a teacher may be skeptical. In addition to learning skills to implement a new intervention, teachers must be persuaded that the new intervention is more effective than the instruction already occurring (Vaughn, Klingner, & Hughes, 2000). Simply learning the instructional techniques is not likely to change beliefs. Rather, time and effort spent in helping educators understand the basis for the intervention and the reasons why the techniques work are likely to be more effective. As with mastery, an understanding of the underlying principles and "why it works" may assist in developing a belief in the practice (Richardson, 1994). This requires planning to provide teachers with more than just training in the use of the intervention.

A belief in a new intervention suggests a level of commitment to the practice. Fuchs and Fuchs (2001) reported that sustained, schoolwide implementation of a new math intervention seemed to depend on the commitment of a key individual in the school who was able to assist in allocating resources and training new personnel. This sense of ownership by the teacher allowed for maintenance of the intervention after researchers had finished initial implementation of the intervention. If the practice is owned by researchers and not the teachers or administrators, it is unlikely teachers will have either the belief or the mastery of the new intervention to sustain the intervention after the research is completed (Englert & Tarrant, 1995; Wong, 1997).

However, having only one key individual in the school committed to the intervention may be problematic if that person leaves the school. This is an all too common occurrence and can bring an end to full implementation of new practices. Gersten, Chard, and Baker (2000) suggested the necessity of "grassroots" supports in sustaining new practices. A solid core of persons within a school who are committed to a practice and have developed mastery of implementation is more likely to allow sustainability of the practice (Fuchs & Fuchs, 2001; Greenwood & Delquadri, 1993). As new faculty come and go, there is always someone to continue the practice, train new people, and develop new master teachers (Fuchs & Fuchs, 2001).

Gersten and colleagues (Gersten & Brengelman, 1996; Gersten, Chard, & Baker, 2000; Gersten & Dimino, 2001; Gersten, Vaughn, Deshler, & Schiller, 1997) have suggested that certain types of interventions may lend themselves to ease of mastery and sustainability. These authors reported that concrete and specific interventions are more likely to be sustained, as are interventions with a sufficient scope and magnitude. For example, interventions should have clear procedures and teaching techniques that can affect the learning of a number of students. However, practices with extremely detailed implementation procedures are often not maintained (Berman & McLaughlin, 1976). Essentially, overly prescriptive interventions do not fit well with most teachers' environments and instructional styles, and, therefore, may not be seen as feasible for long-term application. When implementing a new practice, teachers prefer a practice wherein the implementation and application are clear, but there is enough flexibility to fit into an already existing context (Arguelles, Vaughn, Boardman, Hughes, & Klingner, in press).

The feasibility of a new practice cannot be ignored in planning for implementation, regardless of the significance of student outcomes shown in the research. Feasibility is largely dependent upon whether teachers find that the practice can be readily integrated into their teaching routine and does not require an inordinate amount of time or preparation. Thus, if a new practice produces slightly better student outcomes than an old practice but requires an excessive amount of teacher time or a large shift in teaching style, it is unlikely that teachers will sustain the practice. Vaughn, Klingner, and Hughes (2000) referred to this as the *cost–benefit ratio of the new practice*. Translating research-based practices to classroom realities requires adaptations to fit teacher styles and school contexts (Ball, 1995; Gersten & Dimino, 2001). Teachers are unlikely to use a practice that cannot be readily adapted to meet their specific classroom or student needs (Gersten et al., 1997).

Support During Implementation of New Practices

Achieving mastery and commitment to a new intervention requires time (Gersten, Chard, & Baker, 2000). Mastery of most effective interventions is unlikely to happen following a one-session inservice. In fact, similar to student development of skills, teachers may be at very different stages in their learning or implementation of new practices. Researchers and key school personnel need to recognize varying levels of professional development in order to meet the needs of individual teachers and to support these teachers in reaching mastery (Gersten, Chard, & Baker, 2000).

Several factors are likely to lead to improved teacher knowledge and classroom instruction. First, access to high-quality professional development opportunities is necessary. This includes time to participate in professional development activities as well as opportunities to receive feedback on implementation of the practice. Assistance for the implementation of the practice also comes from peers and administrators (Bays, 2004; Bullough, Kauchak, Crow, Hobbs, & Stokes, 1997). A significant factor in sustained use of practices is a collaborative school atmosphere where teachers have input in decision making and where problem solving is utilized to address implementation difficulties (Clement & Vandenberghe, 2001; Renyi, 1998). These crucial factors give teachers support for learning and integrating new practices in their classrooms.

Bos (1995) summarized several common characteristics of successful professional development related to teacher change in beliefs or practice. These characteristics summarize the critical factors suggested above. One common characteristic is creating ownership with collaborative and supportive contexts. This is similar to the collaborative school atmosphere and problem-solving character of schools cited earlier. A second common characteristic is the development of a common language among colleagues related to the new practice. As with the need for collaboration and the need for feedback on implementation, a common language empowers teachers to improve instruction as part of a community rather than feeling isolated in their quest. The third commonality among successful professional development models is the integration of teachers' personal knowledge with new, additional knowledge. This connection brings meaning to research practices and their relationship to the classroom context teachers live in each day.

As discussed previously, the currently held beliefs of teachers are linked to implementation of practices. As a result, professional development activities must take into account the sometimes deeply held belief systems of individual teachers if the change process is to take place (Gersten & Brengelman, 1996). Adult learning may be mitigated by such factors as lack of awareness of learning needs, disillusionment, distrust, pessimism, comfort with current practices, stress, fear of failure, impatience, preoccupation with other concerns, or even time management difficulties (Duke, 1993). These same factors relate to the learning involved in professional development activities (Bell & Gilbert, 1994; Duke, 1993).

Support networks may provide one way of effectively addressing currently held beliefs and changes in practice. Support networks provide teachers with the opportunity to discuss their beliefs, implementation issues, and student outcomes, thus improving the likelihood they will sustain efforts (Gersten, Chard, & Baker, 2000). Strong professional networks can also provide the support teachers need to stay committed to implementing new instructional practices. The power of professional networks for assisting in changing practice, merging old and new ideas, and providing support have made these networks an important form of professional development (Abbott, Walton, Tapia, & Greenwood, 1999; Gersten & Brengelman, 1996).

Providing teachers with feedback and support on implementation of the new practice develops confidence and skills needed to gain mastery of a new technique. These follow-up sessions, including in-class coaching and discussions focused on student outcomes, are tailored to teachers' classrooms and students and give teachers the opportunities to learn about the practice within their own classroom and their own environment—again increasing the likelihood for sustained implementation. When teachers can see demonstrations of the practice and try new techniques with support and feedback, implementation is improved (Gersten et al., 1995; Showers, Joyce, & Bennett, 1987). Seeing how the procedure is applied in a classroom setting with actual students appears to improve teachers' perceptions of an intervention's feasibility, thereby enhancing the likelihood that teachers will sustain their use of it.

A final, somewhat obvious, necessity for translating research into practice is support in the form of resources (Arguelles et al., in press; Fuchs & Fuchs, 2001). Adequate resources are imperative for effective implementation of any practice. Resources can include the actual materials or money to purchase the materials needed to implement the intervention, but may also consist of personnel for implementation or even time for additional planning and preparation. During initial implementation, teachers often cite time as a barrier to success (Klingner et al., 2003; Vaughn, Klingner, & Hughes, 2000). This suggests that one valuable resource to consider is how to provide teachers with adequate time for learning the practice, planning for the practice, and networking with their colleagues about the practice. For many schools, lack of appropriate resources may be a major reason a practice is not sustained, particularly when specific planning related to resource needs and allocation does not occur. As with the feasibility of the practice, it may be necessary to adapt practices from research according to the resources available within a particular school.

Student Outcomes

A common finding from research on sustaining research-based practices is that teachers need to be able to determine that the practices are associated with positive student outcomes (Fuchs & Fuchs, 2001; Stanovich & Stanovich, 1997; Vaughn, Klingner, & Hughes, 2000). When teachers see that a new practice improves student outcomes, they are more likely to implement that practice (Wong, 1997). This link between practice and outcome may be the catalyst that leads teachers to adjust their beliefs about "what works" and, therefore, encourages sustained use of the practice (Gersten & Brengelman, 1996). Teachers who conclude that the new practice is no more effective than a previous method are unlikely to sustain the new practice and may return to a technique they are more comfortable implementing.

Teachers' self-efficacy in achieving outcomes influences their acceptance and sustained use of new practices (Sparks, 1988; Wong, 1997). Teachers who associate their teaching with student learning are more apt to implement a new practice. Alternatively, teachers who do not see their teaching as a means to improving student learning are reluctant to implement new practices.

Explicitly linking student data to instructional practices may be one avenue toward building self-efficacy. A few studies have incorporated teacher training in interpreting student data into the implementation of new practices. This appears to be a successful practice for building links between instruction and student outcomes (e.g., Simmons, Fuchs, Fuchs, Mathes, & Hodge, 1995). The use of student data may be particularly helpful in the stages of implementation in which student gains often are subtle and not easily observed in day-to-day lessons. If teachers can learn to use data to see the subtle changes occurring, they may be more likely to see the benefits of a new practice and continue its use. The data may help teachers see that their effort in implementing the new practice is "worth it." In fact, if teachers perceive a new practice to be stronger than what they are already doing, they are more likely to sustain the new practice (Vaughn, Klingner, & Hughes, 2000).

Bridging Research and Practice: An Example

In an effort to demonstrate the practical implications for bridging research and practice, let's take a look at a specific research-based practice and how the above suggestions might be utilized to assist in improving the chances the practice will be effectively implemented and sustained. Peer-assisted learning has been documented as a practice that raises achievement for all students, including students with disabilities (Vaughn, Gersten, & Chard, 2000). As discussed in this chapter, several factors need to be considered to plan for and support implementation of this practice.

Planning for Implementation of New Interventions

Planning for implementation requires examining the concreteness, specificity, scope, and magnitude of the practice. For initial implementation, one way of making peer-assisted learning more concrete and specific is to choose one subject area for implementation. Additionally, specifying a program or instructional sequence for implementing peer-assisted learning will provide a concrete and specific objective. For example, Math PALS (see Fuchs & Fuchs, 2001) provides specific roles for the tutor and tutee in peer-assisted learning. When the materials are not available for purchase, the school or teachers may need to prepare the specific materials needed for implementing the chosen technique.

Once the technique has been chosen and specified, initial training in the technique can be provided. Initial training should provide the information and materials needed to begin implementation of peer-assisted learning. Teachers need to learn the procedures for the technique, such as how to partner students effectively, how to teach the students the procedures, how to plan the lessons, and what role the teacher should take during the peer learning. It also is important to begin the process of understanding the underlying principles of the technique by including information about the important aspects of the technique and what each component contributes to student learning. It is possible that follow-up training focused on planning and adapting the technique so that it best fits within the school or classroom context will be needed before implementation begins. Teachers should be involved in choosing the techniques as well as any follow-up planning in order to be sure they own the strategies. It is important to simplify the planning and implementation of the peer-assisted learning as much as possible so teachers will feel that the improved student outcomes are worth the effort.

Finally, plans for providing materials are needed. Initial materials may include a specific program or training manual for teachers. Additional materials may include copies of learning sheets students will use during the peer-assisted learning. Decisions need to be made about how these copies will be produced and distributed as well as about budget needs for the additional copies.

Support During Implementation of New Practices

Translating research into practice within the school requires ongoing professional development consisting of in-class support, feedback, and collegial discussions. Plans for follow-up professional development during initial implementation of peer-assisted learning are needed. An educator who is familiar with implementing peer-assisted learning can work with teachers in their classrooms during the first days of implementation to assist with and model implementation. Once a teacher has implemented the practice for several days or weeks, this coach can provide further assistance in the classroom and feedback to assist the teacher in mastering the implementation of peer-assisted learning.

In addition, regular meetings of teachers implementing the peer-assisted learning should be planned to allow teachers time to discuss implementation issues. As teachers progress in their implementation, it also may be helpful to provide additional information regarding the underlying principles of peer-assisted learning, including the roles of the tutor and tutee and the type of learning material most beneficial for students engaged in peer-assisted learning. These meetings, or study groups, are a way in which teachers can examine student data, discuss improvements, and determine changes needed to improve individual student outcomes. Including student outcomes in these meetings is essential to provide an explicit connection between the change in practice and any changes in student outcomes. During initial learning, it may be helpful to have an educator familiar with peer-assisted learning available to help with suggestions for adaptations and to provide reasons why the adaptations would assist in implementation but preserve the strength of the intervention. If the school does not have the resources for follow-up professional development from experts in the practice, including in-class assistance and facilitation of teacher discussions, the school may want to "grow" its own experts by training teachers interested in the technique to implement peer-assisted learning. These teachers would then become the experts to assist other teachers in implementation.

Maintaining Implementation

Once teachers have fully implemented peer-assisted learning, maintenance of the resources, collegial networks for problem solving, and continual examination of student outcomes are needed. It may also be appropriate to provide training in peer-assisted learning strategies in a second subject area if teachers are interested. This could also assist teachers in further understanding the principles behind the instructional technique, as they see the components that remain constant and the components that are adapted to meet the demands of a different instructional area.

TABLE 2. Key Considerations for Planning and Implementing Sustainable Practices

Planning for implementation	Support for implementation
Build teacher mastery of the practice. Build teacher commitment to the practice. Teach the underlying principles of the practice. Consider teachers' previous beliefs in relation to the practice. Select concrete and specific practices. Select practices with sufficient scope and magnitude. Consider feasibility of the practice.	Provide access to continued professional development. Provide opportunities for feedback on implementation. Develop collaborative atmosphere. Develop support networks. Provide resources required to implement practice. Outcomes: • Evaluate student outcomes related to the practice. • Use student data throughout the implementation to match teacher changes in instruction to student outcomes.

Conclusion

Several factors seem to be related to sustained use of research practices in the classroom. A commitment to and mastery of the practice is necessary for sustained teacher implementation. Careful consideration of the type of intervention, including such aspects as its feasibility and fit with the teacher as well as the support provided in initial implementation, can assist teachers in reaching mastery. When teachers link the implemented practice to improved student outcomes, they may be more likely not only to sustain the practice, but also to develop the necessary commitment to the practice.

Although these variables appear to have implications for future professional development and implementation of practices, it is important to note the paucity of research specifically examining these variables and their subsequent outcomes. Much of the literature available on sustainability relies on hypotheses of possible barriers to sustaining practices or examinations of extant intervention data and methods. Thus, the literature provides the field with recurring themes but little in the way of empirically validated processes for translating research into practice. More experimental research examining the impacts of specific types of professional development and/or implementation assistance is needed in order to better ascertain how to promote the connection between research and practice. Table 2 provides a planning checklist for educators considering the adoption of research-based techniques.

REFERENCES

Abbott, M., Walton, C., Tapia, Y., & Greenwood, C. R. (1999). Research to practice: A "blueprint" for closing the gap in local schools. *Exceptional Children, 65*, 339–352.

Arguelles, M. E., Vaughn, S., Boardman, A. G., Hughes, M., & Klingner, J. (in press). Special education teachers' views on research-based practices. *The Journal of Special Education.*

Ball, D. L. (1995). Blurring the boundaries of research and practice. *Remedial and Special Education, 16*, 354–363.

Bays, D. A. (2004). Science in the schoolhouse: The critical role of the school leader. *Journal of Learning Disabilities, 37*, 256–261.

Bell, B., & Gilbert, J. (1994). Teacher development as professional, personal, and social development. *Teaching and Teacher Education, 10*, 483–497.

Berman, P., & McLaughlin, M. (1976). Implementation of educational innovations. *Educational Forum, 40*, 345–370.

Bos, C. S. (1995). Professional development and teacher change. *Remedial and Special Education, 16*, 379–382.

Bullough, R. V., Kauchak, D., Crow, N. A., Hobbs, S., & Stokes, D. (1997). Professional development schools: Catalysts for teacher and school change. *Teaching and Teacher Education, 13*, 153–169.

Clement, M., & Vandenberghe, R. (2001). How school leaders can promote teachers' professional development: An account from the field. *School Leadership and Management, 21*(1), 43–57.

Crockett, J. (Ed.). (2004). Supporting science in the schoolhouse [Special series]. *Journal of Learning Disabilities, 37*(3).

Duke, D. L. (1993). Removing barriers to professional growth. *Phi Delta Kappan, 74*, 702–704, 710–712.

Englert, C. S., & Tarrant, K. L. (1995). Creating collaborative cultures for educational change. *Remedial and Special Education, 16*, 325–336, 353.

Fuchs, L. S., & Fuchs, D. (2001). Principles for sustaining research-based practice in the schools: A case study. *Focus on Exceptional Children, 33*, 1–14.

Gersten, R., Baker, S., & Lloyd, J. W. (2000). Designing high-quality research on special education: Group experimental design. *The Journal of Special Education, 34*, 2–18.

Gersten, R., & Brengelman, S. U. (1996). The quest to translate research into classroom practice. *Remedial and Special Education, 17*, 67–74.

Gersten, R., Chard, D., & Baker, S. (2000). Factors enhancing sustained use of research-based instructional practices. *Journal of Learning Disabilities, 33*, 445–457.

Gersten, R., & Dimino, J. (2001). The realities of translating research into classroom practice. *Learning Disabilities Research and Practice, 16*, 120–130.

Gersten, R., Fuchs, L. S., Compton, D., Coyne, M., Greenwood, C. R., & Innocenti, M. S. (2005). Quality indicators for group experimental and quasi-experimental research in special education. *Exceptional Children, 71*, 149–164.

Gersten, R., Morvant, M., & Brengelman, S. (1995). Close to the classroom is close to the bone: Coaching as a means to translate research into classroom practice. *Exceptional Children, 62*, 52–66.

Gersten, R., Vaughn, S., Deshler, D., & Schiller, E. (1997). What we know about using research findings: Implications for improving special education practice. *Journal of Learning Disabilities, 30*, 466–476.

Greenwood, C. R., & Delquadri, J. (1993). Current challenges to behavioral technology in the reform of schooling: Large-scale, high quality implementation and sustained use of effective educational practices. *Education and Treatment of Children, 16*, 401–440.

Kennedy, M. M. (1991). Following through on follow through. In E. A. Ramp & C. S. Pederson (Eds.), *Follow through: Program and policy issues*. Washington, DC: U.S. Department of Education.

Klingner, J. K., Ahwee, S., Pilonieta, P., & Menendez, R. (2003). Barriers and facilitators in scaling up research-based practices. *Exceptional Children, 69*, 411–429.

National Center for Education Statistics. (2003). *National assessment of educational progress*. Retrieved January 21, 2005, from http://nces.ed.gov/nationsreportcard/reading/results2003

Pressley, M., & Harris, K. (1994). Increasing the quality of educational intervention research. *Educational Psychology Review, 6*, 191–208.

Renyi, J. (1998). Building learning into the teaching job. *Educational Leadership, 55*, 70–74.

Richardson, V. (1994). Conducting research into practice. *Educational Researcher, 23*, 5–10.

Showers, B., Joyce, B., & Bennett, B. (1987). Synthesis of research on staff development: A framework for future study and state-of-the-art analysis. *Educational Leadership, 45*, 77–87.

Simmons, D. C., Fuchs, L., Fuchs, D., Mathes, P., & Hodge, J. P. (1995). Effects of explicit teaching and peer tutoring on the reading achievement of learning disabled and low-performing students in general education. *The Elementary School Journal, 95*, 387–408.

Sparks, G. (1988). Teacher attitudes toward change and subsequent improvements in classroom teaching. *Journal of Educational Psychology, 80*(1), 111–117.

Stanovich, P. J., & Stanovich, K. E. (1997). Research into practice in special education. *Journal of Learning Disabilities, 30*, 477–481.

Stecker, P. M., & Fuchs, L. S. (2000). Effecting superior achievement using curriculum-based progress monitoring. *Learning Disabilities Research and Practice, 15*, 128–134.

Torgesen, J. K. (2000). Individual differences in response to early interventions in reading: The lingering problem of treatment resisters. *Learning Disabilities Research and Practice, 15*, 55–64.

Torgesen, J. K., Wagner, R. K., Rashotte, C. A., Rose, E., Lindamood, P., Conway, T., et al. (1999). Preventing reading failure in young children with phonological processing disabilities: Group and individual responses to instruction. *Journal of Educational Psychology, 91*, 579–593.

Vaughn, S., Gersten, R., & Chard, D. J. (2000). The underlying message in LD intervention research: Findings from research. *Exceptional Children, 67*, 99–114.

Vaughn, S., Klingner, J., & Hughes, M. (2000). Sustainability of research-based practices. *Exceptional Children, 66*, 163–171.

Vellutino, F. R., Scanlon, D. M., Sipay, E. R., Small, S. G., Pratt, A., Chen, R., et al. (1996). Cognitive profiles of difficult-to-remediate and readily remediated poor readers: Early intervention as a vehicle for distinguishing between cognitive and experiential deficits as basic causes of specific reading disability. *Journal of Educational Psychology, 88*, 601–638.

Wong, B. Y. L. (1997). Clearing hurdles in teacher adoption and sustained use of research-based instruction. *Journal of Learning Disabilities, 30*, 482–485.

Zigmond, N. (1996). Educational intervention research and students with learning disabilities. *Learning Disabilities: A Multidisciplinary Journal, 7*, 69–73.

Chapter 14

Conclusion: An Overview and Analysis of the Role of Evidence-Based Practices in Special Education

Bryan G. Cook and **Barbara R. Schirmer**

What is special about special education? This question, in one form or another, has been associated with efforts to educate children and youth with disabilities since soon after the inception of special education classes in U.S. public schools. To address the atypical needs and often unresponsive nature of the students that it serves, special education has traditionally involved providing something "extra" and "different." For example, higher levels of resources have been allocated for students in special education, teaching techniques not often used with nondisabled students have been developed and utilized, labels have been applied to designate students served, and students have been placed in separate environments with specially trained teachers. In an effort to justify the specialized—and often expensive and potentially stigmatizing—treatment of students with disabilities, special educators have long sought to address the question of whether their field is truly special, and, if so, to specify what those unique and effective characteristics and practices are (e.g., D. Fuchs & Fuchs, 1995; Hockenbury, Kauffman, & Hallahan, 1999–2000; Kirk, 1953; Lord, 1952; Mastropieri & Scruggs, 1997).

As the 2004 reauthorization of the Individuals with Disabilities Education Act (IDEA) and the preceding discussions have brought the future of serving students with disabilities under increased public scrutiny, the legitimacy of special education has been pointedly and repeatedly questioned. For example, Bolick (2001) claimed, "A powerful toxin infects our nation's education system, imperiling the ability of every public school to fulfill its mission. It is . . . the federal Individuals with Disabilities Education Act" (p. 56). Finn and Rotherham (2001) reported that "special education has become not a road to life but a cul-de-sac where they [students] are stopped before they get the help they need to do as well as they can" (p. B13). And Fisher (2001) went so far as to claim that "special-ed is the gold-plated garbage can of American schooling" (p. B1). More recently, Hettleman (2005) commented on "the illusion and broken promises of special education instruction" (p. 32), suggesting that "ineffective and unlawful practices . . . cause and conceal the system's failures" (p. 30). Although these criticisms of special education seem to be particularly caustic, skepticism regarding special education is by no means new (e.g., Milofsky, 1974). As early as 1929, Fiorello La Guardia, mayor of New York City, remarked, "There is nothing more repulsive to me and nothing more unwarranted than to single out little tots, under 12, put them in a separate room and label them" (cited in Lazerson, 1983, p. 15).

Contemporary critiques suggest that special education, among other things, is unnecessarily and unfairly overrepresentative of minority students; grows at a faster rate than the school-age population in general; is expensive, resulting in the redirection of funds away from general education and other programs; uses labels and categories that are without educational merit and result in stigmatization and decreased expectations; creates a double standard, especially in the area of discipline; employs a wait-until-they-fail philosophy; emphasizes process compliance over outcomes; and is generally ineffective (e.g., Bolick, 2001; Finn & Rotherham, 2001; Fisher, 2001; "Help for Poor Readers," 2001; Hettleman, 2005; Horn & Tynan, 2001; Malkin, 2001; Rotherham, 2001). For many critics, dismantling or radically altering special education and IDEA are necessary remedies for a system that "is costly and, even worse, ineffective" (Horn & Tynan, 2001, p. 47).

Special education, like any other service or profession, is admittedly imperfect. There are, no doubt, many individuals who have not been served well by special education. In short, there is at least some support for the criticisms leveled against the field. However, there is equally little doubt that special education is beneficial and truly special for some students with disabilities (e.g., Kauffman, Bantz, & McCullough, 2002). Thus, it appears that the justification of special education hangs in the balance between the validity of its benefits and "specialness," on the one hand, and the legitimacy of the charges made in regard to its shortcomings and the damage it incurs, on the other. In this book, we examine one side of this equation: how and to what degree contemporary special education is truly special. In light of proliferating proposals that special education harms students with (and without) disabilities, it is critical that consideration be given to what is special or "right" about the provision of special services in order to make an informed and balanced judgment on the justifiability of the field. So, what constitutes truly special education?

Historical Perspective on What Is Special About Special Education

Most scholars mark the work of Jean Marc Gaspard Itard with Victor, the Wild Boy of Aveyron, in 1801 as the beginning of modern special education (see Lane, 1976). The basic principles of his work influenced a new generation of special educators (e.g., Gallaudet, Howe, Seguin) who spread the practice of educating people with disabilities throughout Europe, and eventually into the United States, in the early- and mid-19th century. Hallahan and Kauffman (2006) summarized seven aspects of these pioneers' beliefs and practices that formed the basis of special education: (a) individualized instruction, (b) carefully sequenced series of tasks, (c) emphasis on stimulation and awakening of the child's senses, (d) meticulous arrangement of the child's environment, (e) immediate reward for correct performance, (f) tutoring in functional skills, and (g) belief that every child should be educated to the greatest extent possible.

The work of Elizabeth Farrell, who taught the first special education classrooms in New York City schools and who later became the first president of the Council for Exceptional Children (CEC), echoes many of these same principles regarding what made special education special. For example, Farrell (1908–1909) noted (in regard to her first "ungraded" classrooms) that "we take the child where we find him" (individualization; p. 94); "we offer much more work in the manual and physical arts than is given in regular grades" (functional skills; p. 94); and "special cases are bathed as often as necessary to relieve irritation and equalize the circulation" (stimulation; p. 95). In her first annual report on these classrooms, Farrell (1907) also suggested that systematic ordering of related tasks could capitalize on a boy's interest in marbles and result in an understanding of the world's pottery markets (sequencing; cited in Phillips, 1935).

As the number of children served by special education swelled in the mid-20th century, new questions regarding the technical aspects of teaching students with disabilities (e.g., assessment, curriculum, classroom management) were raised, and a "tremendous conflict over the presumed benefits of special education" ensued (Lazerson, 1983, p. 38). It was in this context that a series of invited papers appeared in *Exceptional Children* in 1952 and 1953 on the following question: What is special about special education? (see Lord, 1952). Samuel Kirk (1953), writing on what is special about special education for "the child who is mentally handicapped," delineated eight features that distinguished special from general education: special class organization, special materials, special diagnosis, special clinical teaching procedures, intensive use of learning principles, systematic instruction, individualized instruction, and parent education. By the 1950s, then, special education had come to incorporate a variety of specific school-related techniques and configurations based on the foundational pedagogical philosophies of the field.

In these formative years of special education, the focus appears to have been on instituting unique techniques and philosophies that theoretically met the distinctive needs of children and youth with disabilities and distinguished special from general education. Scant attention was paid to empirical validation of these practices in historical discussions of what made special education special. These emphases helped to generate and reinforce a unique identity among special educators in past decades (and likely contributed to the field's separateness from general education). However, in the absence of evidence that what made special education unique was also effective, the field was susceptible to being perceived as a political, legal, and administrative arrangement rather than as a force for improving student outcomes. Instead of proactively asserting the mission and efficacy of special education, special educators frequently found themselves defining its form and future in reaction to social forces and external reproach.

Recent Perspectives on What Is Special About Special Education

As D. Fuchs and Fuchs (1995) pointed out, "the coup de grace" in contemporary critiques of special education "is the contention that the enterprise flat out doesn't work" (p. 523). In response, special education scholars have endeavored to show that special education, although it cannot and does not produce optimal outcomes for all students with disabilities, generally provides an added value to the educational opportunities and outcomes of the students it serves. For example, Hockenbury et al. (1999–2000) suggested, "One thing that is right about special education is that it includes devising and testing empirically validated methods of instruction that are effective with atypical students" (p. 6). The authors specifically noted that such instructional practices as direct instruction, self-monitoring, mnemonic instruction, strategy training, curriculum-based measurement, applied behavior analysis, and functional assessment are effective techniques utilized in special education. D. Fuchs and Fuchs (1995) similarly commented that in their view, "the use of empirically validated procedures" (p. 527) is a primary component of what makes special education special. They cited curriculum-based measurement (CBM) as an example of an effective practice that embodies special education's traditional emphasis on individualization. In addition to noting specific, empirically validated instructional techniques, these authors stressed that although it was possible for the effective practices described to be applied in general education settings, in reality many are almost never used in this environment and are, in essence, unique to special education (see also Mastropieri & Scruggs, 1997).

> Many practices validated by special educators for use in special education settings, like CBM, do not transfer easily to most mainstreamed classrooms, where teachers have many students and often a different set of assumptions about the form and function of education . . . Special education's most basic article of faith—that instruction must be individualized to be effective—is rarely contemplated, let alone observed, in most general education classrooms. (D. Fuchs & Fuchs, 1995, pp. 528–529)

The work of these and other scholars in conceptualizing and illustrating the effectiveness and uniqueness of instructional practices associated with special education constitutes a critical initial step in assessing the "specialness" of special education. Recent syntheses and analyses of the special education research literature (e.g., Gersten, Schiller, & Vaughn, 2000) represent continued and vital progress in this area. Our primary focus in this book is to take another stride toward developing a broad and detailed understanding of empirically validated practices in different areas of special education. The field is so multifaceted and expansive that a single list of effective techniques is inevitably incomplete and even misleading. For example, effective practices for infants and toddlers with disabilities are quite different than those for young adults with disabilities involved in the transition from school to work. Furthermore, reviews and analyses of any knowledge base must build upon and update previous work in order to provide a current and accurate perspective on what works—so there is constantly the need for new synthesis and analysis of research findings.

We also believe, as others before us have asserted, that to be truly special, special education must provide services and techniques that are unique. Even if techniques associated with special education are effective, if they are just as easily and effectively implemented in typical settings without special educators, then special education is not truly special and may not be justified. Additionally, the degree of implementation and fidelity of implementation must be examined in assessing the legitimacy of special education. It is possible that techniques are unique to special education and empirically validated, but are not implemented very often by special educators, are not implemented as designed and validated, or both. If this is the case, the potential benefits of these effective practices for students with disabilities would remain unrealized and special education could not be considered truly special.

Thus, we asked leaders in their respective areas of special education to (a) identify the empirically supported, effective techniques in their area of special education; (b) ascertain whether these techniques are widely implemented and implemented with fidelity; and (c) determine whether these techniques are unique to special education settings, unique to students with disabilities, or unique to the competencies of special education teachers. In addition, we invited the authors to examine issues related to making special education more special or effective through the implementation of evidence-based practices. In other words, what can be culled from the extant literature to address areas identified as limiting the degree to which special education is truly special (i.e., effective)?

What Is Special About Special Education

One theme that clearly emerged from the chapters in the first two sections of the volume is the large number of effective practices developed for students with a wide range of disabilities throughout the educational span of birth through transition to adult roles. The chapters in this book included literally dozens of techniques found to be effective for students with disabilities. Thus, we can begin to answer the question of what is special about special education by providing substantial and compelling evidence of effective practices developed by special educators for students with disabilities. This finding is particularly important given the emphasis placed in the No Child Left Behind Act of 2001 on instructional strategies that have been shown to be effective through scientifically based research. At the very least, then, special education has the knowledge base and potential to improve upon the educational outcomes and lives of children and youth with disabilities.

A second theme that emerged from the chapters involves the frequency and fidelity with which these effective practices are implemented in special education. In terms of frequency, the precise degree to which these techniques are being used does not appear to be known. The literature reviewed offers little clarity regarding the extent to which techniques are implemented throughout educational programs but, rather, focuses largely on the effects and outcomes of specific techniques and practices. However, informal reports lend support to the belief that they are not widely implemented. If and when teachers endeavor to implement research-based practices, it appears that the difficult process of translating research into practice customarily (a) proves overwhelming, resulting in teachers implementing the technique without fidelity or abandoning their attempts to use the new technique altogether (e.g., Gersten, Morvant, & Brengelman, 1995) or (b) limits the implementation of the most effective practices to teachers who are extraordinarily skilled, dedicated, or both. Given the lack of research on extent of use, it is not surprising that little is known about fidelity of use, either. Again, though, informal reports indicate that even when empirically validated practices are used, they are often not implemented with integrity and therefore may not maintain the level of effectiveness achieved in the studies reviewed. Thus, we cannot say that what is special about special education is the consistent and conscientious use of effective techniques.

The third theme emerging from these chapters involves the connection between effective practices and special education. Techniques that are effective for students with disabilities are generally effective for all students. The techniques, practices, procedures, and in many cases, content, are appropriate for most, if not all, learners. There is little inherent, then, in the content of the particular effective practices that make special education special. Instead, what is unique about special education is, as Vaughn and Linan-Thompson noted in this book, the delivery of instruction. The majority of the effective techniques reviewed in this volume are unlikely to be used with all students because many teachers in general education do not recognize the need for them, do not know how to implement them, or both. Furthermore, many of the techniques are too time-consuming to be used with all students. Indeed, whereas learners without disabilities will likely succeed without these instructional techniques, learners with disabilities will likely fail without them. Thus, we can answer our third question by affirming that these techniques are, de facto, unique to special education settings, unique to students with disabilities, and unique to the competencies of special education teachers. As Zigmond wrote in this book:

> Effective teaching strategies and an individualized approach are the more critical ingredients in special education, and neither of these is associated with one particular environment. That said, educators must also remember that typical general education environments have been shown in research not to be supportive places in which to implement what are known to be effective teaching strategies for students with disabilities. (p. 133)

How to Make Special Education More Special

As discussed by authors in the first two sections, a number of effective practices exist in special education. However, they are not routinely used, and when used, they are infrequently implemented with fidelity. The consequence is that many students with disabilities receive less than optimally effective instruction. Two recommendations for addressing this issue emerge from the chapters in the third section: (a) Effective practices must be clearly distinguished from practices without research support, and (b) techniques for facilitating and supporting teachers in adapting evidence-based practices should be implemented.

Readers will, we hope, come away from reading chapters in the first two sections with an understanding of techniques that are effective in a range of areas in special education and among a diverse population of students with disabilities. These and other literature reviews can provide useful guides for educators in identifying effective practices. However, different reviews can be expected to yield disparate viewpoints on which practices are most effective. Such discrepancies may stem from a variety of sources, including differences in (a) specific studies reviewed, (b) procedures used to determine effectiveness, and (c) outcomes considered. Further, marked differences in what "experts" assert to be an effective practice can be expected when claims are based on personal experience or philosophical disposition, rather than research findings. Regardless of the cause of differing viewpoints, they can lead to confusion (Mostert & Crockett, 1999–2000) and a distrust of scholarship and research altogether (see Gersten, 2001) that appears to be at least partially responsible for the existing gap between research and practice.

Lloyd, Pullen, Tankersley, and Lloyd (this book) suggest that a broadly endorsed system or model for determining what are, and are not, evidence-based practices in special education should be instituted so that teachers and other stakeholders will have a definitive answer to the question, "What are the most effective practices?" For such a process to be meaningful, Gersten (this book) and Lloyd et al. (this book) suggest, first, that only certain types of research (e.g., high-quality studies that exhibit experimental control) be considered as providing "evidence" for effective practice, and second, that criteria for evaluating the evidence base of practices be standardized and logical. The Division for Research of

CEC took important steps in this direction by (a) developing quality indicators for four research methodologies in special education, including those that can be used to determine whether a practice is effective (i.e., experimental and quasi-experimental designs and single-subject research designs; see Odom et al., 2004; Graham, 2005), and (b) proposing logical criteria for establishing a practice as evidence-based in the field of special education based on the findings of experimental and quasi-experimental research studies (Gersten et al., 2005) and single-subject research studies (Horner et al., 2005).

Specifically, Gersten et al. (2005) proposed that for a practice that has been investigated experimentally to be considered evidence based, two criteria must be met:

1. At least four acceptable (meeting all but one of the essential quality indicators and demonstrating at least one of the desirable quality indicators) or two high-quality (meeting all but one of the essential quality indicators and demonstrating at least four of the desirable quality indicators) experimental studies have been conducted that demonstrate the positive effect of the practice on student outcomes.
2. The weighted effect size of experimental studies examining the practice in question is significantly greater than zero.

Horner et al. (2005) specified three criteria for identifying a practice as evidence based that has been assessed in the context of single-subject research studies:

1. At least five single-subject studies published in peer-reviewed journals that meet methodological criteria and document experimental control exist.
2. The studies are conducted by at least three different researchers and in at least three different locations.
3. The studies collectively include at least 20 participants.

As plans for endorsing and implementing a model for determining the evidence base of practices in special educations are formulated, it should be recognized that carrying out the task will be a time-consuming endeavor. It will, at a minimum, involve (a) sifting through an extensive literature base spanning a multitude of instructional practices to identify studies utilizing research designs that address the question of whether a practice is effective (i.e., experimental/quasi-experimental and single-subject research designs), (b) critically evaluating those studies against agreed-upon quality standards or indicators, and (c) conducting new high-quality research exhibiting experimental control to establish the effectiveness of instructional practices about which there is currently insufficient evidence. Such a significant expenditure of time and effort may seem unnecessary, given the main theme in the first two sections of the book that research findings indicate the effectiveness of a number of practices in special education. However, establishing practices as evidence based through a more standardized and broadly endorsed process should not only provide teachers and other stakeholders with a more objective and complete indication of which practices can be considered evidence based, but may also begin to change teachers' (and public policymakers') perceptions regarding the trustworthiness and relevance of educational research.

As promising as the establishment of a process for determining evidence-based practices appears, it will be virtually meaningless unless teachers implement the identified practices with greater frequency (and greater fidelity) than is currently the case. Dissemination of which practices are (and are not) evidence based should therefore (a) be extensive and multifaceted (so that any teacher, administrator, or parent can easily access them) and (b) include information on how to implement and adapt the practice written in non-technical language. However, it is unlikely that even the best prepared dissemination products will be sufficient to change the practices of many teachers in the absence of ongoing support.

Wanzek and Vaughn (this book) summarize supports that have been associated with teachers adopting evidence-based practices. Many of these are labor intensive and will force both teachers and teacher educators to rethink their roles and relationships with one another. Unfortunately, examples of intensive, collaborative involvement of teacher educators with teachers in schools and classrooms resulting in the adoption of evidence-based practices appear to be relatively isolated and often supported through external funding. Professional development schools (PDS), sometimes referred to as partner schools, might also provide the kind of collaborative and supportive environments in which teachers adopt and maintain their use of evidence-based practices. According to the National Council for the Accreditation of Teacher Education (NCATE, 2005), on its Web site, the mission of PDSs is "the preparation of new teachers, faculty development, inquiry directed at the improvement of practice, and enhanced student achievement." If successful, these and other efforts to involve teacher educators intensely and collaboratively in schools would not only serve to ground the instruction and scholarship of teacher educators, but would also facilitate novice and veteran teachers in adopting and maintaining the use of evidence-based practices.

Recommendations for Future Action and Research

The most unequivocally positive outcome of the chapters in this book is the identification of empirically validated practices for students with different disabilities in a range of areas of special education. Yet it should be recognized that this constitutes only a preliminary and informal look at the research base of special education. Models for determining the evidence base of practices in special education have been proposed (Gersten et al., 2005; Horner et al., 2005), and similar models are being employed in related fields (e.g., Chambless et al., 1998). It appears that the models proposed for use in special education by Gersten et al. and Horner et al. are logical and would serve the field of special education well if implemented. Although it is possible that the proposed models might benefit from fine-tuning and field-testing or that alternative models should be adopted, it appears critical to us that the field of special education (a) reach consensus on the specific model or models to be used in determining the evidence-based nature of practices in special education and (b) apply that model to generate an inventory of practices that are and are not evidenced based. In short, we have no shortage of functional models. It is time to mobilize the field to select a model and get to the arduous business of applying it.

In order to apply criteria and meaningfully assess the effectiveness of any specific practice in special education, a robust body of research that addresses the question of whether the practice is effective for students with disabilities (e.g., experimental studies incorporating the quality indicators described by Gersten et al., 2005, single-subject research studies utilizing the quality indicators described by Horner et al., 2005) must exist. However, there are many practices about which researchers have not conducted multiple, high-quality studies exhibiting experimental control. Thus, any logical set of criteria for determining the evidence base of practices will deem these practices as not evidence based, even though they might be potentially effective. Increased emphasis and resources, then, need to be brought to bear to improve and expand the body of high-quality, experimental research documenting the effectiveness of instructional practices with students with disabilities. Moreover, more studies utilizing other research designs (e.g., correlational, qualitative/descriptive) are also needed to determine issues related to the implementation of evidence-based practices, such as the degree to which they are implemented with fidelity, attitudes of students and teachers, and ecobehavioral classroom factors.

Of course, identifying effective practices is only meaningful to the extent that they are applied (and applied with fidelity) with children and youth with disabilities. A list of effective practices provides no real benefit to students with disabilities unless the practices are frequently and appropriately used. Given the lack of relevant empirical evidence available regarding the degree to which many practices are implemented and implemented with fidelity by teachers in typical conditions, an improved research base in this area is clearly needed. Just as a measure of central tendency is not interpretable without an accompanying measure of variance, so a report on the efficacy of an instructional technique is incomplete without also determining the degree to which the practice is likely to be adopted by teachers and applied as designed. Research gauging the level and fidelity of implementation should be an important component of the empirical literature base on each instructional practice.

In addition to an expanded research focus regarding the frequency and fidelity with which evidence-based practices are implemented, it appears to be even more critical that methods for improving the regularity and reliability of implementing effective practices be investigated. A nascent literature base (see Wanzek & Vaughn, this book) suggests that specific supports and processes are associated with implementation and maintenance of research-based teaching techniques. Examples include mentors or coaches—skilled teacher educators who are familiar with schools and teaching as well as the literature on evidence-based practices and the supports needed for teachers to adopt such practice—providing frequent and concrete feedback based on classroom observations. As Wanzek and Vaughn note, the research base regarding practices that support teachers in the adoption of evidence-based practices is just emerging. More research is needed to evaluate the impact of the various supports to determine which are most beneficial, as well as the frequency and intensity of implementation needed for sustainable classroom implementation of evidence-based practices.

The field should also continue to explore new and increasingly efficient ways to widely disseminate information about evidence-based practices and develop approaches that support teachers who have no connection to colleges of education or professional development schools in the implementation of such practices. The labor-intensive and expensive nature of the supportive practices identified in the literature (Sindelar & Brownell, 2001) may pose a significant obstacle in the broad-scale application of evidence-based practices. Continued efforts toward developing and investigating models for "scaling up" implementation of effective practices (e.g., D. Fuchs & Fuchs, 1998; L. S. Fuchs & Fuchs, 2001) in order to expand their use beyond the level of individual teachers to entire schools and school systems may help to address this problem. Another possible alternative for improving the support of teachers in implementing evidence-based practices may be found in Web-based supports, which can provide many of the same benefits as face-to-face supports and would allow teacher educators to be involved with multiple schools at the same time.

Systemic change may also be needed in how teachers are prepared to ensure that they are well versed in evidence-based practices, committed to career-long continuous learning about new practices, and skilled in recognizing the difference between instructional fads and research-proven practices.

Conclusion

One theme of this book deals with the degree to which the effective practices discussed are unique to special education. The authors indicate that there is little inherent in the practices themselves that make them applicable only to special education settings, special education teachers, or students with disabilities. Yet the authors also propose that due to the population of students served in general education, the group focus of general educators, the background and training of general educators, and the competing pressures associated with general education (e.g., high-stakes testing), it is unrealistic to expect these practices to be consistently and effectively applied in the absence of special education. Thus, the provision of special education appears to be an important component of contemporary educational environments that support meeting the individualized needs of students with disabilities. Although it is impossible to forecast precisely how conditions in education and schooling will change in the future, we postulate that there will always be children and youth whose learning needs and characteristics deviate from the norm in meaningful ways and who, therefore, will require some form of individualized special education to receive appropriate instruction.

So, is special education special? The answer is "yes" if we consider only two of the criteria we deemed necessary for special education to be considered truly special. First, we asserted that special education must have developed a number of effective practices for improving the educational outcomes of students with disabilities. Certainly there is more work to be done in summarizing, synthesizing, expanding, and updating the research literature on effective practices for students with disabilities, but the criterion of having developed effective techniques appears to have been met. We also claimed that these effective practices must be unique to special education. In other words, if special education is not needed for these techniques to be utilized with students with disabilities, it may not be necessary. The authors in this book indicated that it was conceivable for general educators to use the identified effective practices with students with disabilities without involving special education. However, they generally concluded that the context and individualized focus of special education contributed significantly to implementing effective practices needed by students with disabilities. Thus, the effective practices reviewed may also be considered unique to special education.

The final criterion we proposed for determining the "specialness" of special education had to do with the utilization of the effective practices. Despite the effectiveness and uniqueness of the techniques, if they are not used (and used as designed), they do not make a difference in the education and lives of children and youth with disabilities. Unfortunately, the evidence does not clearly show that the most effective teaching techniques are routinely used as designed in special education. It is, then, the inability of the field to persistently apply empirically validated practices with fidelity that most jeopardizes the specialness and justifiability of special education. Certainly the potential exists to make real improvements in the lives of children and youth with disabilities through special education—and that potential is being achieved in particular schools, with specific teachers, and for individual students. Yet it is apparent that for special education to completely realize its promise, to wholly fulfill its moniker (i.e., *special* education), and to more fully justify itself, the field needs to implement what we know to work with greater regularity and integrity. When this is accomplished, special education will, in our view, become truly special.

As to how to make special education more special by increasing the level of implementation of effective practices, it appears that much of the groundwork has been set. In the earlier history of special education, much of the field's energies seem to have been focused on developing and delivering unique practices and programs to meet the individualized needs of students with disabilities. This focus on individualized education benefited an untold number of children and youth with disabilities whose unique learning characteristics would not have otherwise been addressed. As the efficacy of the practices utilized in special education have been called into question in more recent years, special education, like other fields, has begun to devote more time and energy to establishing the empirical validity of the techniques and practices used in the field in order to guide the decision making of teachers and improve the effectiveness of instruction. However, in special education these efforts have been largely fragmented and have not, to date, had the desired effect of broad changes in teaching practice. It appears, then, time to take the next developmental steps in special education research and practice toward the broad-scale identification and implementation of evidence-based practices.

The first step will be achieving consensus on and broadly endorsing a model for determining the evidence base of practices in special education. Fortunately, commendable models specifying the amount and type of research evidence necessary for identifying a practice as evidence based in special education have already been developed and proposed (Gersten et al., 2005; Horner et al., 2005). Leading individuals and organizations in the field must come together to (a) officially endorse a model, (b) develop a plan for how that model can be implemented, and (c) secure resources to generate an authoritative and comprehensive inventory of the evidence base of practices in special education.

The next step will entail promoting widespread adoption of practices designated as evidence based. The same process used to assess an instructional practice should be used to determine how to best support teachers in implementing evidence-based teaching techniques. As Heward (2003) has noted, "The same attitudes of science that helped us discover effective teaching practices can help us learn how to improve the application of these practices in the schools" (p. 201). High-quality research utilizing experimental control should, then, be conducted regarding the impact of these supports on teachers' use of evidence-based practices, and that research synthesized and evaluated using a broadly endorsed model for determining the evidence base of the supportive practices. By clearly defining what works in special education and identifying the most effective methods for supporting teachers' adoption of those practices, special education will become more completely special by increasing its effectiveness and improving the outcomes of the students it serves.

It should be remembered, though, that even the identification and application of evidence-based practices is not a panacea. The outcomes of students with disabilities will, on the whole, undoubtedly be raised by implementing an evidence-based practice, but research can never guarantee that any particular technique will work for every child in every instance. In essence, no evidence-based practice will be effective for every student. Thus, while special education strives to increase its effectiveness by advancing an agenda to establish and implement evidence-based practices, the original focus of the field on individualizing education for students with disabilities must be retained. For example, if and when an extensive inventory of well-established, evidence-based practices exists, skilled special educators must utilize professional judgment in selecting which evidence-based practice to implement for a particular child based on a complex amalgam of individualized considerations (e.g., the child's unique learning goals and needs; the school and classroom environment; the teacher's supports, experiences, and skills). Additionally, even when implementing an evidence-based practice, special educators should frequently and consistently monitor the individual progress of their students. If and when these assessments indicate that the student is not making adequate progress, changes in learning conditions, increased intensity and/or frequency in the application of the evidence-based practice, and/or implementation of additional or alternative evidence-based practices are necessitated. By concurrently maximizing the potential for increasing students' outcomes through the faithful application of evidence-based practices and maintaining a focus on individualization, special education can become truly special.

REFERENCES

Bolick, C. (2001, September 5). A bad IDEA is disabling public schools. *Education Week,* pp. 56, 63.

Chambless, D. L., Baker, M. J., Baucom, D. H., Beutler, L. E., Calhoun, K. S., Crits-Christoph, P., Daiuto, A., DeRubeis, R., Detweiler, J., Haaga, D. A. F., Johnson, S. B., McCurry, S., Mueser, K. T., Pope, K. S., Sanderson, W. C., Shoham, V., Stickle, T., Williams, D. A., & Woody, S. R. (1998). Update on empirically validated therapies, II. *The Clinical Psychologist, 51,* 3–16.

Farrell, E. K. (1908–1909). Special classes in the New York City schools. *Journal of Psycho-Asthenics, 13,* 91–96.

Finn, C. E., Jr., & Rotherham, A. J. (2001, December 26). Give special ed a road map to success. *Los Angeles Times,* p. B13.

Fisher, M. (2001, December 13). Students still taking the fall for D.C. schools. *Washington Post,* p. B1.

Fuchs, D., & Fuchs, L. S. (1995). What's "special" about special education? *Phi Delta Kappan, 76,* 522–530.

Fuchs, D., & Fuchs, L. S. (1998). Researchers and teachers working together to adapt instruction for diverse learners. *Learning Disabilities Research and Practice, 13,* 126–137.

Fuchs, L. S., & Fuchs, D. (2001). Principles for sustaining research-based practice in the schools: A case study. *Focus on Exceptional Children, 33*(6), 1–14.

Gersten, R. (2001). Sorting out the roles of research in the improvement of practice. *Learning Disabilities Research and Practice, 16,* 45–50.

Gersten, R., Fuchs, L. S., Compton, D., Coyne, M., Greenwood, C., & Innocenti, M. S. (2005). Quality indicators for group experimental and quasi-experimental research in special education. *Exceptional Children, 71,* 149–164.

Gersten, R., Morvant, M., & Brengelman, S. (1995). Close to the classroom means close to the bone: Coaching as a means to translate research into classroom practice. *Exceptional Children, 62,* 52–67.

Gersten, R., Schiller, E. P., & Vaughn, S. (Eds.). (2000). *Contemporary special education research: Syntheses of the knowledge base on critical instructional issues.* Mahwah, NJ: Erlbaum.

Graham, S. (Ed.). (2005). Criteria for evidence-based practice in special education [Special issue]. *Exceptional Children, 71*(2).

Hallahan, D. P., & Kauffman, J. K. (2006). *Exceptional learners: Introduction to special education* (10th ed.). Boston: Allyn & Bacon.

Help for poor readers often comes too late. (2001, September 6). *USA Today,* p. A14.

Hettleman, K. R. (2005, March 9). Commentary: The illusion and broken promises of special education. *Education Week,* pp. 30, 32.

Heward, W. L. (2003). Ten faulty notions about teaching and learning that hinder the effectiveness of special education. *The Journal of Special Education, 36,* 186–205.

Hockenbury, J. C., Kauffman, J. K., & Hallahan, D. P. (1999–2000). What is right about special education. *Exceptionality, 8,* 3–11.

Horn, W. F., & Tynan, D. (2001). Time to make special education "special" again. In C. E. Finn, Jr., A. J. Rotherham, & C. R. Hokanson, Jr. (Eds.), *Rethinking special education for a new century* (pp. 23–51). Washington, DC: Fordham Foundation.

Horner, R. H., Carr, E. G., Halle, J., McGee, G., Odom, S., & Wolery, M. (2005). The use of single-subject research to identify evidence-based practice in special education. *Exceptional Children, 71,* 165–179.

Individuals with Disabilities Education Improvement Act of 2004, 20 U.S.C. § 1400 *et seq.* (1990) (reauthorization of the Individuals with Disabilities Education Act of 1990).

Kauffman, J. K., Bantz, J., & McCullough, J. (2002). Separate and better: A special public school class for students with emotional and behavioral disorders. *Exceptionality, 10,* 149–170.

Kirk, S. A. (1953). What is special about special education? The child who is mentally handicapped. *Exceptional Children, 19,* 138–142.

Lane, H. T. (1976). *The wild boy of Aveyron.* Cambridge: Harvard University Press.

Lazerson, M. (1983). The origins of special education. In J. G. Chambers & W. T. Hartman (Eds.), *Special education policies: Their history, implementation, and finance* (pp. 15–47). Philadelphia: Temple University Press.

Lord, F. E. (1952). What is special about special education? *Exceptional Children, 19,* 95–96.

Malkin, M. (2001). Special-ed idea bad for special-ed kids. *Human Events, 57*(16), 13.

Mastropieri, M. A., & Scruggs, T. E. (1997). What's special about special education? A cautious view toward full inclusion. *The Educational Forum, 61,* 206–211.

Milofsky, C. D. (1974). Why special education isn't special. *Harvard Educational Review, 44,* 437–458.

Mostert, M. P., & Crockett, J. B. (1999–2000). Reclaiming the history of special education for more effective practice. *Exceptionality, 8,* 133–143.

National Council for the Accreditation of Teacher Education. (2005). *What is a professional development school?* Retrieved June 8, 2005, from http://www.ncate.org/public/pdswhat/asp?ch=133.

No Child Left Behind Act of 2001, 20 U.S.C. 70 § 6301 *et seq.* (2002).

Odom, S. L., Brantlinger, E., Gersten, R., Horner, R. D., Thompson, B., & Harris, K. (2004). *Quality indicators for research in special education and guidelines for evidence-based practice.* Division for Research, Council for Exceptional Children. Retrieved June 4, 2005, from http://interact.uoregon.edu/dr/Quality_Indicators.pdf.

Phillips, H. C. (1935). Elizabeth E. Farrell. *Exceptional Children, 1,* 72–76.

Rotherham, A. (2001, October 31). Students poorly served by special education program. *Atlanta Journal-Constitution,* p. A15.

Sindelar, P. T., & Brownell, M. T. (2001). Research to practice dissemination, scale, and context: We can do it, but can we afford it? *Teacher Education and Special Education, 24,* 348–355.

About the Editors

Bryan G. Cook is an associate professor in the Department of Special Education at the University of Hawaii. Dr. Cook received his PhD in special education from the University of California at Santa Barbara and taught at Kent State University for 9 years before moving to Hawaii. His primary interests lie in the areas of inclusion, evidence-based practices, and students with disabilities in higher education. In recent years, Dr. Cook has worked with a number of local school systems on the adoption of evidence-based practices, such as curriculum-based measurement, classwide peer tutoring, and self-monitoring. In addition to coediting this book, he is coauthor, with Phillip Rumrill, of *Research in Special Education*.

Barbara R. Schirmer is vice president for academic affairs and provost and professor of education at the University of Detroit–Mercy. After receiving her doctorate in education at the University at Buffalo, State University of New York, she was involved in deaf education teacher preparation at the University of Wisconsin–Milwaukee and Lewis & Clark College. Subsequently, she was a department chair at Kent State University and a dean at Miami University. Her research involving the literacy development of deaf and other struggling readers has been published in numerous journal articles, book chapters, and two books, *Language and Literacy Development in Children Who Are Deaf* and *Psychological, Social, and Educational Dimensions of Deafness*. Dr. Schirmer has received the best paper award three times from the Research on the Education of Deaf Persons special interest group of the American Educational Research Association.

About the Authors

Margarita Bianco received her EdD in exceptional student education from Florida Atlantic University in 2003 and is currently an assistant professor in the School of Education at Colorado State University. She is also consulting with the Colorado Department of Education and presenting statewide teacher-training workshops dealing with identifying twice-exceptional students. Her research interests include identification of and services for gifted students from underrepresented populations, special education teacher preparation, and professional development for in-service teachers. Her teaching interests are in the areas of learning disabilities, twice-exceptional students, English as a second language, and multicultural education. In 2004, Dr. Bianco was honored with the Outstanding Researcher of the Year Award from the Council for Learning Disabilities

Anne G. Bishop is an assistant scholar at the University of Florida and serves as project coordinator for the Center on Personnel Studies for Special Education (COPSSE) and Project RITE, Building Capacity for Research in Teacher Education. Her research interests include assessing and defining teacher quality, with a focus on beginning special education teachers of reading. She has also conducted research in early literacy assessment. Dr. Bishop teaches reading courses in the Unified Elementary Program. She has 26 years of experience as a teacher and administrator at the school and district levels. Dr. Bishop was chosen as the 2003 Teacher of the Year for the University of Florida's College of Education and received the 2002 Outstanding Researcher Award from the Council for Learning Disabilities and the 2005 Early Career Publication Award from the Division for Research of the Council for Exceptional Children.

Diane M. Browder is the Snyder Distinguished Professor of Special Education at the University of North Carolina at Charlotte. She currently serves as vice president of the Research Division of the Council for Exceptional Children. Dr. Browder has dedicated more than 2 decades of research and writing on assessment and instruction for students with severe disabilities. Recently, she has focused on alternate assessment and linking both assessment and instruction to the general curriculum. She is principal investigator for an OSEP-funded reading and mental retardation research center to evaluate an experimental curriculum for teaching students with moderate and severe disabilities to read. She also works with Dr. Claudia Flowers as a partner in the National Center on Alternate Assessment, focusing on the alignment of alternate assessment with the general curriculum.

Mary T. Brownell is a professor in the Department of Special Education at the University of Florida. Her research interests in special education include teacher preparation and teacher quality, teacher attrition, teacher collaboration, and professional development. To conduct this research, Dr. Brownell and her colleagues have secured more than $7 million in federal research grants. Currently, Dr. Brownell is the codirector of the Center on Personnel Studies in Special Education, for which she directs a multisite study examining the practices and knowledge base of effective elementary special education teachers and how these relate to the academic achievement of students with reading disabilities. Through this research, Dr. Brownell and her colleagues hope to develop and validate outcome assessments needed for studying teacher education and professional development. Dr. Brownell has published more than 50 book chapters and papers and has received the University of Florida Research Professor Award.

Karena Cooper-Duffy is an associate professor in and program coordinator for the Special Education Program at Western Carolina University. Her specialty is in the area of severe and profound disabilities. She has worked on three federally funded grants in the area of personnel preparation for teachers of children with low-incidence disabilities. Her research explores personnel preparation strategies for teachers educating children with severe to profound disabilities.

Stanley L. Deno earned his BA degree in biology and began his career as an educator by teaching high school biology. He earned his doctorate in educational psychology from the University of Minnesota with a specialization in the psychology of learning and its applications to instruction. After 4 years of teaching at the University of Delaware, he returned to the University of Minnesota, where he is now a professor in educational psychology/special education. His primary teacher education focus over the past 20 years has been the learning disabilities program, but he continues to teach the foundational courses for all areas of special education licensure. Dr. Deno is, perhaps, best known for his research and development activities related to monitoring student progress in basic skills. This work has resulted in the development of procedures, typically referred to as Curriculum-Based Measurement (CBM), that have been widely disseminated through publication in both technical and professional journals. That work also serves as the basis for what has become known as a problem-solving approach to assessment that has been incorporated into the field of school psychology.

Sharon Field is a research professor and codirector of the Center for Self-Determination and Transition in the College of Education at Wayne State University. Her areas of specialization include self-determination, transition and life skills, and applied positive psychological practices. She has directed several federally funded transition and self-determination projects. Through these projects, Dr. Field and Dr. Alan Hoffman developed a model of self-determination and the Steps to Self-Determination curriculum. In collaboration with Shlomo Sawilowsky, they also created a self-determination assessment battery. Dr. Field has written extensively on self-determination for persons with and without disabilities. Her work has included the development of materials and strategies to promote self-determination at the early childhood, elementary, secondary, and postsecondary levels. She is also the lead author of a set of instructional modules for use in initial preparation and staff development settings that are designed to promote self-determination for teachers. She has direct service experience in schools as a special education teacher, job placement specialist, and administrator.

Russell Gersten is executive director of the Instructional Research Group, a nonprofit educational research institute in Long Beach, California. He is also a professor emeritus in the College of Education at the University of Oregon. Dr. Gersten is a nationally recognized expert in quantitative and qualitative research and evaluation methodologies. He currently is a principal investigator on a large-scale evaluation of reading comprehension instruction. He also plays a leading role in the national Reading First evaluation and directs a large study evaluating professional development using randomized, controlled trials. He has written extensively on translation of research into practice, issues facing English language learners, reading comprehension, and early intervention in mathematics. He was recently given the Distinguished Special Education Researcher Award by the American Educational Research Association.

James M. Kauffman is a professor emeritus of education at the University of Virginia. He is currently director of doctoral study in special education at the University of Virginia and teaches a seminar in special education. Dr. Kauffman received his EdD in special education from the University of Kansas. He is a past president of the Council for Children with Behavioral Disorders (CCBD) and a former teacher in both general elementary and special education for students with emotional and behavioral disorders. He is the author or coauthor of numerous publications in special education, including *Characteristics of Emotional and Behavioral Disorders of Children and Youth*; *Learning Disabilities: Foundations, Characteristics, and Effective Teaching* (coauthored with Hallahan, Lloyd, Weiss, & Martinez); *Special Education: What It Is and Why We Need It* (coauthored with Hallahan); and *Children and Youth With Emotional and Behavioral Disorders: A History of Their Education* (coauthored with Landrum).

Janette K. Klingner is an associate professor at the University of Colorado. She was a bilingual special education teacher for 10 years before earning her PhD in reading and learning disabilities from the University of Miami. Currently, she is a coprincipal investigator for the National Center for Culturally Responsive Educational Systems (NCCRESt), a technical assistance center on the disproportionate representation of culturally and linguistically diverse students in special education, and an investigator for the Center on Personnel Studies in Special Education (COPSSE). She has authored or coauthored 37 journal articles, 7 books, and 11 book chapters. Her research focus includes the disproportionate representation of culturally and linguistically diverse students in special education, reading comprehension strategy instruction for diverse populations, and professional development that leads to the sustained implementation of validated practices. She is coeditor of the *Review of Educational Research* and an associate editor for the *Journal of Learning Disabilities*. In 2004, she served as the chairperson of the Special Education Research special interest group of the American Educational Research Association (AERA). She is also on the executive board of the Council for Exceptional Children's Division for Research. In 2004, she received AERA's Early Career Award.

Paula D. Kohler is a professor in the Department of Educational Studies at Western Michigan University (WMU), where she teaches and conducts research on effective transition education and services. Previously a senior research associate with the Transition Research Institute at the University of Illinois, Dr. Kohler has a background in business administration, educational leadership, career and technical education, and special education. Focused on improving outcomes of youth with disabilities, she has worked to extend transition-related research to practice at the state, regional, and local levels through research, evaluation, policy analysis, and professional development. Her work regarding effective secondary education and transition services includes identification of effective transition programs, transition-related competencies, career and technical education experiences of youth with and without disabilities, work-based education, and other aspects of transition-focused education. Her Taxonomy for Transition Programming is nationally recognized as an effective model for planning, implementing, and evaluating transition-focused education. In 2001, Dr. Kohler received the Oliver P. Kolstoe Award from the Division on Career Development and Transition of the Council for Exceptional Children, and in 2005, the WMU College of Education Trailblazer Award for her contributions through research and scholarship.

Timothy J. Landrum is an associate professor on the general faculty at the University of Virginia. His research and writing have focused on emotional and behavioral disorders, classroom and behavior management, the translation of research into practice, and more recently, large-scale literacy assessment. He is a former teacher of students with emotional or behavioral disorders. Since earning his doctorate in special education from the University of Virginia, Dr. Landrum has been a teacher educator and researcher for the past 15 years.

Sylvia Linan-Thompson is an assistant professor at The University of Texas at Austin. Her research interests include development of reading interventions for struggling readers who are monolingual English speakers, English language learners, and bilingual students acquiring Spanish literacy. She is coprincipal investigator of three longitudinal studies funded by the National Institute of Child Health and Human Development and the Institute of Education Sciences that are examining the oracy and literacy development in English and Spanish of Spanish-speaking children and the efficacy of a three-tiered model of reading intervention in general education classrooms and in bilingual classrooms. She has authored curricular programs, book chapters, journal articles, and a book on reading instruction.

John Wills Lloyd received a PhD from the University of Oregon and is a professor of education at the University of Virginia's Curry School of Education. Dr. Lloyd specializes in learning and behavior problems, reading instruction, and research methods. His studies of the characteristics of students with learning and behavior problems and of procedures for addressing those problems have appeared in special education and behavioral psychology journals. In addition, he has written chapters for edited volumes and books for use by teachers. Dr. Lloyd has also created electronic resources about special education policy, practice, and issues. All things being equal, however, he would rather be cooking.

Patricia A. Lloyd supervises students completing practica and student teaching for the Curry School of Education at the University of Virginia. She received a BA from Northern Illinois University and an MEd from the University of Virginia. She has taught and served as a school administrator since the 1960s, having worked in settings ranging from preschools through group homes and with students ranging from gifted children to adults with multiple disabilities. Although her primary interest is promoting the use of effective instructional practices, she would like to study infrahuman cognition and language.

Samuel L. Odom is the Otting Professor of Special Education at Indiana University. His research interests include prevention and early intervention programs for young children with disabilities and their families, effective practices for children with autism, social development and peer relationships, and quality indicators of research methodology in special education and criteria for evidence-based practice. Dr. Odom's work appears frequently in journal publications and book chapters, and with colleagues, he has edited five books about early intervention and special education. In his current work, he and his colleagues are examining the effectiveness of a preschool curriculum intervention approach to promoting early school success for children living in poverty, children with disabilities, and children who are English language learners.

Paige C. Pullen received her PhD in special education, with a specialization in literacy, from the University of Florida. She is an assistant professor of curriculum, instruction, and special education at the University of Virginia, where she directs the Early Childhood and Developmental Risk Program. In addition to teaching graduate-level courses on reading disabilities and reading instruction, she works with schools in Virginia and in other states to design and implement professional development activities for practicing teachers. She is coauthor of two books, *Phonological Awareness Assessment and Instruction: A Sound Beginning* and *Students With Learning Disabilities* (6th ed.).

Paul T. Sindelar is a professor of special education and associate dean for research at the University of Florida. From 2000 to 2005, with his coauthor, Mary Brownell, he directed the Center on Personnel Studies in Special Education (COPSSE). COPSSE is an OSEP-funded policy center charged with (a) conducting research on teacher supply and demand, professional preparation, and certification and licensure and (b) disseminating findings to inform policy. Before moving to the University of Florida in 1988,

Dr. Sindelar served on the special education faculty at Pennsylvania State and Florida State universities. He earned his PhD from the University of Minnesota in 1977. In his current research, Dr. Sindelar works closely with economists from the university's Bureau of Economic and Business Research. They have undertaken an economic analysis of teacher education program design and, in a separate project, are assessing the cost-effectiveness of teacher preparation alternatives.

Melody Tankersley is a professor of special education at Kent State University. After earning her doctorate degree from the University of Virginia, she was awarded a postdoctoral fellowship at Juniper Gardens Children's Project, a program affiliated with the University of Kansas. Prior to beginning her graduate studies, Tankersley taught students with emotional and behavioral disorders, a population of students who continue to be the focus of her instructional and scholarly endeavors. Tankersley focuses her work on issues related to the prevention of emotional and behavioral disorders, classroom and behavior management, and bringing research to bear upon practice.

Sharon Vaughn is the H.E. Hartfelder/Southland Corp. Regents Chair and director of the Vaughn Gross Center for Reading at The University of Texas at Austin. She has served as editor-in-chief of the *Journal of Learning Disabilities* and is the author of numerous research articles on students with reading and learning disabilities.

Jeanne Wanzek is a doctoral candidate in the Department of Special Education at The University of Texas at Austin and serves as a research associate at the Vaughn Gross Center for Reading and Language Arts. She is involved in research examining interventions for students with reading disabilities and works for school districts and state departments as a consultant translating research into practice. Prior to this work, she was an elementary classroom and special education teacher.

Mark Wolery is a professor of special education at Peabody College, Vanderbilt University. He holds a BA in psychology from Tennessee Temple College, an MEd in special education from Virginia Commonwealth University, and a PhD in early childhood special education and severe disabilities from the University of Washington. He has served as a teacher aide; teacher of elementary-age students with moderate mental retardation; teacher and home visitor for infants, toddlers, and preschoolers children with severe disabilities; teacher supervisor; teacher of children with autism; faculty member in special education; and researcher. His current research focuses on including young children with disabilities in preschool classes, with a special interest focus on including young children with autism in childcare. Specific research interests focus on developing and evaluating instructional strategies, embedding individualized instruction into ongoing activities, and measuring the quality of inclusive childcare.

Naomi Zigmond is a professor of special education at the University of Pittsburgh. She received her PhD from Northwestern University, majoring in language pathology and learning disabilities. Dr. Zigmond has been an active special education researcher and teacher educator for more than a quarter of a century. Two themes run through her work: First is the secondary and postsecondary school experiences of students with mild to moderate disabilities, the impact of graduating or dropping out, and the improvement of high school programs for this very vulnerable population. Second is the organization of special education services for students with learning disabilities in elementary and secondary schools and the impact of program organization—particularly full inclusion—on student achievement. For the past several years, Dr. Zigmond has led a team of researchers and practitioners in the development, implementation, and scoring of the Pennsylvania statewide alternate assessment for students with significant disabilities. She is also codirecting the external evaluation of the Pennsylvania Reading First initiative. Finally, she is actively involved in studying the effectiveness of coteaching as a special education service delivery model.